W9-CUG-450

EDWARD III'S ROUND TABLE AT WINDSOR

EDWARD III'S ROUND TABLE AT WINDSOR

THE HOUSE OF THE ROUND TABLE AND THE WINDSOR FESTIVAL OF 1344

Julian Munby
Richard Barber
Richard Brown

THE BOYDELL PRESS

First published 2007
The Boydell Press, Woodbridge

ISBN 978-1-84383-313-0

This book is volume 68 in the series
Arthurian Studies
ISSN 0261-9814

General Editor: Norris J. Lacy
Previously published volumes in the series
are available from Boydell & Brewer

The Boydell Press is an imprint of Boydell & Brewer Ltd
PO Box 9, Woodbridge, Suffolk IP12 3DF, UK
and of Boydell & Brewer Inc.
668 Mt Hope Avenue, Rochester, NY 14620, USA
website: www.boydellandbrewer.com

A CIP record for this book is available
from the British Library

This publication is printed on acid-free paper

Printed in Great Britain by
The Cromwell Press

Contents

List of illustrations

Black and white plates

Line illustrations

Tables

INTRODUCTION

WINDSOR CASTLE is at once a royal palace and one of the grandest castles in England. Its history is extraordinarily well documented, in royal accounts dating back to medieval times and in massive tomes published at the beginning of the twentieth century. So it is surprising that there are still vital questions which remain unanswered about its past and about vanished buildings on this complex site, so rich in echoes of the ambitions of the kings of England. Opportunities to explore these questions through archaeology are extremely rare, given the nature of the site and the fact that it is one of the most actively used royal palaces today. Such an opportunity arose when the television programme *Time Team* was given permission to dig on three royal sites in August 2006, the year of the Queen's eightieth birthday. The three sites chosen, Buckingham Palace, Windsor Castle and Holyrood House had very different profiles, Buckingham Palace being a purely domestic building acquired by the royal family as recently as 1761, while Holyrood House was originally an Augustinian abbey.

Windsor had been a royal residence since the twelfth century, and the two areas chosen for investigation were the possible site in the Lower Ward of the great hall built by Henry III, and the Upper Ward, whose early history was largely a matter of conjecture, given that the buildings which surround it had been thoroughly remodelled for Edward III by William of Wykeham in the 1360s. Wykeham went on to make his fortune and to found Winchester College and New College, Oxford; but what had been in the Upper Ward before this time? The accounts told us something of the likely structures, parts of which survived beneath the rebuilding, but there was a particular puzzle which had not been resolved. In 1344, Edward III had held a magnificent festival, which had ended with his promise to found an Order of the Round Table. The royal accounts show massive expenditure on the *Domus Rotunde Tabulae*, the 'House of the Round Table', in the months following the festival, and then a tailing-off of activity as other demands on the royal purse took precedence. Something had been built; and something had probably been pulled down by William of Wykeham less than twenty years later. But where had it stood, and was there any physical evidence of its existence? Architectural historians had conjectured that it probably stood in the Upper Ward, and had offered ideas as to its appearance. The mystery was further complicated by the fact that a well-informed chronicler believed that the missing building was two hundred feet in diameter, the largest circular building in western Europe since Roman times.

During the weekend of filming, there was ample opportunity for discussion, and five of us, Julian Munby, myself, Tim Tatton-Brown, as well as David Carpenter and Oliver Creighton who were involved in excavations in the Lower Ward, were able to look in detail at the printed records of the contemporary account rolls for the building of the Round Table. We realised that the finding of the footings of the Round Table in the Upper Ward could be combined to great effect with the surviving official records to offer a detailed reconstruction of the proposed building. Literary and historical sources could provide evidence of the purpose of the building and the ways in which it would have been used. The results of these informal exchanges of ideas were exciting enough for Julian Munby and myself to project a full-scale study of the building and of the Round Table festival of 1344.

This book is the outcome. Working on it has led to further fascinating discoveries. In the realm of architecture, there is the extraordinarily similar castle at Palma in Majorca, whose interior looks like a two-tiered version of the reconstruction hastily produced at Windsor that weekend. Further exploration of the official records has turned up the kitchen accounts for the 1344 festival, which show that it was on the grandest scale. And a tradition, beginning in the early fourteenth century, in the romances about Arthur, that the Round Table was itself housed in a round table, has led to the exploration of the idea of the Arthurian round table with surprising results. We hope that this alliance of archaeology, history, literature and official records, drawing on sources as far afield as Catalonia, Holland and Sicily, has produced a book as exciting to read as it has been to research and write.

Richard Barber

Excavation acknowledgements

A vast number of people were involved in Time Team's Big Royal Dig, when some 450 archaeologists, historians and television production teams were mobilised over three sites for four days. I have attempted to credit those directly involved with the archaeological side of the Windsor Castle Upper Ward Investigations below. My apologies to anyone who has not been included.

My thanks must primarily go to Simon Raikes and Rebecca Woodhead (Time Team Live producer and assistant producer) who initially contracted the archaeologists and then trusted us with the freedom and resources to deliver excavations that were both logistically feasible within the limits of the television production but were also underpinned by robust research aims. GSB Prospection's crucial geophysical survey was supervised by Jon Gator; Chris Gaffney of GSB gave on-site advice and interpretation of the survey results. Dr Michael Turner of English Heritage reviewed all archaeological documentation produced for the investigation. Brian Kerr from English Heritage provided on-site monitoring, invaluable advice and very welcome enthusiasm throughout the project.

The talented and convivial excavation team comprised: Paul Murray, Charlie Newman, Emily Glass, Dave McNichol, Guy Cockin, Robin Bashford, Jane Brant (on-site finds processing) Ian Powlesand (machine excavation) and Fay Simpson (on-site finds specialist). Drawings were produced by the Oxford Archaeology graphics office – mostly by Georgina Slater. Finds and environmental reports were produced by Jon Cotter, Jane Timby, Ian Scott, Rebecca Devenay, Lena Strid, Leigh Allen, Laurence Keen OBE, Philip Powell and Seren Griffiths.

No excavation would have been possible if it were not for the staff and members of the Royal Household who allowed us into what is not simply a monument and castle but also a home, and who were throughout the project extremely friendly, supportive and hospitable.

Richard Brown

Acknowledgements

Many people have contributed to this book since the original discussions at Windsor Castle, in a wide variety of ways. Several sections of the text have come from other hands. We are grateful to Tim Tatton-Brown, who should really be the fourth name on the title-page, for his essays on Windsor before 1344 and on the stones used for the Round Table building, as well as much useful advice on the shaping of the book. Paul Dryburgh transcribed the latter part of the building accounts which are such vital evidence for our case, and also the kitchen accounts, both of which appear in appendix C. Professor David Johnson and Professor Geert Claassens provided the text and translation of Lodewijk van Velthem's description of an Arthurian feast in appendix D, and Nigel Bryant has done likewise for the important passage from *Perceforest* in chapter 8. Professor Nancy Freeman Regalado has given permission for the use of her translation of the entry of the Knight with the Lion at the festival at Le Hem in 1278 in appendix D. Professor Michael Reeve kindly translated the passage from Boccaccio's *De casibus virorum illustrium* in chapter 6. Mark Ormrod read the text at very short notice, with the result that a number of useful improvements were made. Professor Clifford Rogers provided the transcript of the unpublished St Omer continuation of the *Grandes Chroniques*, which he has kindly allowed us to use in chapter 3. Other scholars have responded to detailed enquiries: in particular, Dr Antheun Janse provided a copy of a chapter from his book *Ridderschap in Holland* at very short notice when no copy could be found in British university libraries.

Thanks are also due to Brian Kerr of English Heritage who has made available Stephen Priestley's remarkable series of transcripts of materials on Windsor Castle in the PRO, and to Rebecca Woodhead, who carried out some of the initial research for this book.

Fionnuala Jervis has kept the various contributors in line, and has as always clarified muddled thinking and badly expressed ideas, to the great benefit of the book.

Prologue

Excavating the Round Table, August 2006: a 'Dig Diary'

RICHARD BROWN

*L*IKE THE MAJORITY *of archaeologists I had never had the good fortune to be asked to suggest a research investigation and offered the finances and logistical support to carry it out. I certainly had not imagined that any such offer (if it ever came) would involve a site of such status as Windsor Castle. However this is what Simon Raikes, the Series Producer for Time Team Live, proposed when he contacted me in March 2006. The project was to be an investigation of three Royal residences as a contribution to the celebrations for Her Majesty the Queen's 80th birthday. Tim Tatton-Brown was already involved in his capacity as archaeological advisor to the College of St George and had suggested an investigation to define the location of the thirteenth century Great Hall in the Lower Ward. Simon thought that in terms of the ambitions of the Time Team's television programme'– over a weekend of excavation – a second investigation at Windsor could be carried out. I was perhaps the obvious choice to do this as I had, the year before, been seconded to Time Team for three months as the Archaeological Co-ordinator for their 'Big Roman Dig' and my employers, Oxford Archaeology, are the term commission holders for archaeological works at the Royal Household and Historic Palaces.*

Initially my thoughts focused on the Home Park of Windsor Castle, where the possible remains of a medieval deer-keeper's lodge and in-filled earth-works made for a re-enactment of the battle of Maastricht seemed to offer interesting investigations. However it does not take a very long look at the history of Windsor Castle before one is drawn to the enigma of the Round Table building. That such an apparently substantial and documented building can be so completely 'lost' seemed extraordinary. It was a fortunate coincidence that led me to try to convince Simon that this was the right excavation to do. Firstly I came across an aerial photograph of Windsor Castle from 1964 – a remarkably dry year, that produced pronounced grass parch marks – apparently showing a large round circle in the centre of the Upper Ward Quadrangle, and secondly, on the same day, Julian Munby dropped by my office to discuss a project we were both involved in. Unknown to me, Julian had for years been suggesting to anyone who would listen that an excavation in the Upper Ward to find the Round Table building would be a rather good thing. The aerial photograph of the parch mark turned out to be a complete red herring (as explained below) but Julian's assertion cannot now be faulted.

Windsor Castle is the oldest and largest inhabited castle in the world; it is also a Scheduled Monument and Royal residence. Rightfully, its guardians, The Royal Household and English Heritage, take their roles as its protectors very seriously. Several months of negotiations and the production of project designs and research documents, followed by the issue of licences and consents, went into organising the three day excavation.

The first step towards any excavation is to define the current state of knowledge of the site. A catalogue of all archaeological works that had been carried out at Windsor Castle was made, all site and monument records and national monument records were searched and all secondary sources were reviewed.[1] Although there is an abundance of documentary sources relating to Windsor Castle and much archaeological monitoring has been carried out at the Castle – indeed some significant excavations have been carried out in the Round Tower and State Apartments – nothing was known about the survival of archaeological remains in the Upper Ward Quadrangle.

Because of the scheduled status of Windsor Castle, trench locations have to be agreed well in advance of excavation. They require clear and precisely stated reasons for their location and the results they hope to achieve in order for consent to be granted. In order to help with this a preliminary geophysical survey of the Upper Ward was carried out. The results are shown on Plate XII. Amongst the potential archaeological anomalies recorded there is one dramatic curve (marked L on the map) in the south-east corner of the Upper Ward which immediately catches the eye; and even more strikingly, its approximate extrapolated diameter is 198 feet, corresponding with the diameter of the Round Table reported by a chronicler in the late fourteenth century. It is this feature that is to be the centrepiece of our investigation.

Thursday

It is Thursday 24th August 2006, and I arrive at Windsor Castle in the late afternoon in a transit van creaking with equipment. Time Team's first live broadcast is due to be on the following night. After the necessary security checks I am directed straight to the Upper Ward, which is eerily quiet given the thronging crowds of visitors moving around the rest of the castle. The Quadrangle of the Upper Ward is overlooked by the Round Tower, the Queen's Gallery, the State and Royal apartments. The buildings are largely either constructed or faced in the nineteenth century and 'decorated' with the faux machicolations that were favoured during that period as an attempt to regain some perceived lost medieval character. Although it is a warm summer's day, the imposing buildings, the quiet and the absolutely static bearskin-hatted soldier in a sentry box outside the King's Entrance combine to create an air of solemnity. This is happily broken by the arrival of two armed policemen who stay for a chat and help me put up a couple of tents for finds processing and excavation equipment and records.

By the time everything is stored in the Upper Ward, the castle has closed to the public for the day. The Time Team crew and cable riggers have been at Windsor since Tuesday and a 'production village', including outside broadcast, generator and canteen trucks,

---

[1] See chapter 4 for the archaeological background of the Upper Ward Quadrangle investigation area.

1. Brendan Hughes (Time Team Director), Richard Barber, Richard Brown and Julian Munby as the building is revealed

2. The Upper Ward team

has been set up on the North Terrace. I pass this on the way to the Vicars' Hall in the Lower Ward which is the Time Team incident room and where a briefing is scheduled for 7 p.m.

The Vicars' Hall is an atmospheric oak-beamed and panelled room nestling against the north-west corner of the castle curtain wall. It was built in 1415 and is traditionally thought to be where Shakespeare's *The Merry Wives of Windsor* was first performed before Elizabeth I in 1597. Sixty or so archaeologists, historians and production crew crowd into the hall where Simon and members of the Royal Household welcome us to Windsor. The full crew (of about a hundred people) aren't all here yet, but it does make me do some calculations in my mind about the size of Time Team's hotel bill for the project.

Charlie, who is on the Windsor excavation team, has come to Windsor direct from excavating at Çatal Hüyük so after the briefing we wander across the road to the pub to catch up. We are soon joined by Time Team regulars Matt Williams and Chris Gaffney, who have roped in Brian Kerr from English Heritage and Fay Simpson, the finds liaison officer. Matt, Chris and I worked together last year on a particularly gruelling site, so we reminisce into the evening, forget to eat and only just make it back into the castle before the 12 p.m. curfew hour. All the historians and archaeologists are staying in St George's House which is a seventeenth century mansion next to St George's Chapel. The production team are staying in the Christopher Wren hotel in Windsor town where they will generally stay up every night to the late hours re-writing scripts, videotape insert cues and running schedules.

Friday

First thing on Friday morning I search out Ivan Parr in the incident room. Ivan has been doing work on historic mapping for Tim Tatton-Brown on the Lower Ward. With just a little persuasion Ivan drops a scanned image of a sixteenth-century plan onto a present day base map. The plan shows the location of a fountainhead built in 1555-58 in the Upper Ward. Ivan compares the two and it becomes obvious that a geophysical anomaly over which I had located a trench, because it might possibly be the fountainhead, is now definitely not. In fact the fountainhead has probably been largely removed by a modern cistern. I drop off all the digital images of Windsor I have with Maya, who is the 2D graphics artist, and then set off to find the surveyors.

Walking through the Lower Ward I come across Simon and Rebecca. Rebecca is riding a bicycle from the Upper Ward to the Lower Ward, over and over again, while Simon is timing her and making notes on a clipboard. Later this will be turned into a television piece where presenter Alice Roberts gives a 'live' tour of the castle. I tell Simon about the fountain and explain that this means one out of the four trenches we had agreed is no longer worthwhile. Simon says that the Upper Ward part of the television programme will now concentrate only on the Round Table and nothing else. This is slightly worrying since from the start of the project I had always thought that, even if we did not find the Round Table building, there was a good likelihood of finding some evidence of past *activities in the courtyard, and in fact from a purely archaeological perspective any information at all about the nature of the Upper Ward is extremely useful. However, this now means that if the Round Table building is not found then I have persuaded Time Team to finance a preliminary geophysical survey and carried out months of negotiations for something that gives them no programme content.*

Back in the Upper Ward I meet Robert and Sarka, the surveyors. I give them the trench co-ordinates and they set out the locations using GPS – just to be sure, we check them with 30m tapes. Julian arrives in his usual jovial mood and helps to lay out the excavation equipment, while I put out boarding and terrain sheeting around the trench locations to protect the lawn from the mechanical excavator and the spoil that will be dug out.

Later Chris, Alice and Julian are rehearsing a scene where they discuss the results of the geophysical survey. Someone in the mixing truck watching the camera feeds spots the prepared trenches and thinks that they look untidy, so I spend two hours packing away the boards and sheeting that I have put out. This clearly tickles Chris's sense of humour, but he makes up for his amusement by pitching in to help.

I wait around for the rest of the day for an opportunity between rehearsals to water the turf so that it is in the best possible condition to re-lay after the excavation, but am saved this task by a long downpour of rain.

The live broadcast goes out at 7 p.m. but there is no digging at Windsor today, just an introduction. After dinner in the canteen truck I drop by the video editing suite in St George's House and watch the broadcast programme there with Brendan Hughes, the video director. There are some really interesting pre-shoots of Julian explaining the documentary evidence for the Round Table building, Oliver Creighton and Alice looking at bits of the castle belonging to Edward III's building campaigns and a piece on the origin of the Order of the Garter.

Saturday

On Saturday morning all the archaeological excavators arrive; the Upper Ward team is more or less made up of old friends from Oxford Archaeology. Some of the team have been working for me on an excavation within a hot, noisy and dusty construction site in Southampton, so it's nice to have a a few days in such a congenial location together. We are keen to get going but there is a lot of hanging around waiting for cameras, cables and microphones to be sorted, as Time Team wants to shoot the turf coming off and the start of the dig. As well as the Time Team crew, there is a More 4 team who will be broadcasting live for six hours each day; throughout the weekend they will interview people at a moment's notice. The first sign of this is when Tom Ranson, the More 4 researcher, borrows all the excavation staff in order to film advert links (although all the team seem to enjoy this). Around 11 a.m. we finally start taking the turf off. The first trench is Trench 3 (this can be confusing as the trenches were named some months ago in the site project designs but the production crew understandably like to re-name the first trench opened Trench 1 and so on). The mechanical excavator is a tracked 5 ton, 360° back-actor fitted with a toothless ditching bucket. Because of the prestigious nature of the site the machine has been supplied brand new and still has bubble wrap on the seat and controls. It is driven by Ian Powlesand, another Time Team regular, who is an archaeologist as well as an expert qualified plant operator.

I direct the machine excavation which almost immediately reveals a layer of dumped building material and architectural fragments. This clearly dates to a building campaign carried out by Jeffry Wyatville in the nineteenth century, as it contains pieces of blue Staffordshire transfer ware, some fragments of the flint galetting present in the mortar bonding of the existing façade of the Upper Ward, as well as London stock bricks that, as Brian points out, are only used by Wyatville at the castle. As the rubble is removed a hard compacted chalk is revealed. I assume this to be a working surface or compound floor for Wyatville's works (this assumption is wrong and it later turns out to be an external working surface for the construction of the Round Table building – meaning that Wyatville's nineteenth-century works have cut down through the Quadrangle and sit on the fourteenth century archaeological remains). The trouble with the small five ton excavator is that its arm reach is limited and once you have excavated and moved the machine back you cannot return to the trench and do more machine excavation without making an awful mess. So I signal Ian to gently remove the chalk surface with the machine bucket. This reveals a silty layer with chalk-filled pits cut into it. Regardless of date, this is clearly an archaeological horizon that cannot be machine excavated, since this would destroy the pits before we can understand what they are. So I then direct the excavator to move back. The trench is now at the depth that the linear anomaly (which we are hoping is the Round Table wall) was recorded on the radar survey time slices. Sure enough, the next machine stroke reveals a cut line across the trench. Carrying on the machine excavation at this level, a broad stone and sand filled feature is revealed. The size and shape of the feature along with the character of its fill means that it can only be the line of a wall that has had all the major stonework removed, leaving just the chippings and infill material. Very soon excavation produces a piece of a Surrey white ware jug and some medieval sandy ware that suggest a date of 1225 -1400 for the fill of the feature. This is now undoubtedly the line of the wall of the Round Table building. The evidence of the geophysical survey which shows a large arcing line, the pottery dating retrieved from the feature, and the evidence that it was a wall line show that it cannot be anything else. A building that has been buried, lost and nearly forgotten has been rediscovered after nearly seven hundred years!

We spend the rest of the day cleaning and recording the trench as well as finishing excavating the Round Table wall line. As with all excavations recording is time-consuming and involves producing written key-worded (for database entry) and free-text descriptions, measured drawings in plan and section, as well as black and white, colour and digital photographs of all the deposits encountered. Every record and find item is then issued a unique identifying number so they can all be cross-referenced.

Julian and Chris do a piece to camera on the discovery of the wall line, and Fay confirms the pottery date. Chris is particularly pleased because the trench coincided exactly with his company's geophysical survey results.

Sunday

Sunday morning finds us cracking on with the remaining two trenches. Trench 3 has revealed the Round Table outer wall line but it would be ideal to find something of the floors and internal features of the building. The machine excavation of Trench 2 doesn't at first look promising. The two geophysical anomalies targeted here are structures but they are nineteenth century brick conduits. Likewise a large anomaly in Trench 1 is very quickly identifiable as the flagstone base of the original location of the brass Charles II equestrian statue placed in the Upper Ward in the seventeenth century (now sited below the Round Tower at the western end of the Upper Ward).

The Upper Ward is very hectic today; Julian gives several tours to groups of schoolchildren and Royal Household staff, some of whom are lending a hand by washing the finds. We are also joined by Time Team competition winners Anne and Chris who take it in turns helping out in the Upper and Lower Wards. A rehearsal for a televised piece on falconry is abandoned when the falcon flies off and fails to come back again. Damian Goodburn, a specialist in ancient woodworking techniques, arrives to do a camera piece with Julian and Alice on how it is possible in practice for the Round Table building to have been roofed with timber despite its great diameter.

In Trench 2 Paul and Guy have now realised that a sequence of chalky layers in between the two brick conduits are in fact deposits laid for levelling of the ground prior to the floor laying of the Round Table building. This means the level of the floor surface has been lost in this trench, cut through by Wyatville's reduction of the Quadrangle. But we retrieve some more information from the sequence with pottery dating to 1225-1400 from the chalky layers and to 1150-1225 from the silts below the Round Table building deposits.

To the west of Trench 1 there is a patch of very compact chalk that is likely to have been either the floor of the Round Table building or the base immediately below any more formal surface. It is not initially easy in the south of the trench to distinguish the difference between the rubble foundation surrounding the statue base and the chalk floor surface of the Round Table building. Chalk, being the local stone, is used as building material for all periods of the castle. Emily is cleaning the trench to define these levels when she finds a fourteenth century decorated Penn tile which is mortared to the ground. This coincides with Time Team's rehearsals for the live programme and Emily is instantly miked for sound so that the moment of discovery of what appears to be the Round Table building floor can be filmed. This seems like a suitable end to the day's digging and after Maya has arrived to take digital images for a graphic reconstruction of the floor, it's off to the canteen truck.

Monday

In the cold light of the morning the tile in Trench 1 looks much more as if it is sitting on the rubble around the statue base rather than the Round Table building surface. So I spend a couple of hours chiselling away at the almost concreted chalk around it until I can clearly see that it is sitting over a brick drain incorporated in the statue base foundation. Although this now means the tile cannot be seen as evidence of what floor surface the Round Table building would have had, it poses a question we cannot resolve: how does a fourteenth century tile end up being mortared onto a seventeenth century foundation? In the west of the trench Charlie excavates a section through the Round Table building layers down to the underlying silts. This provides more dating evidence for the sequence as well as lots of unglazed medieval roof tiles.

In Trench 2, Paul and Guy excavate all the way through the archaeological sequence to the natural bedrock. A thick silt overlying this is collected in soil sample buckets, which when later sieved in the environmental department at Oxford Archaeology is found to contain Roman building material and prehistoric pottery. Julian, Brian Kerr and I spend some time going over architectural fragments from the Wyatville rubble layer, deciding which bits would be best kept in order to characterise the layer. The pieces we don't keep are later reburied in the trenches. Some of the pieces are obviously nineteenth-century building offcuts, and some is material that is from medieval (and later) buildings demolished at the same time.

During the day Julian, Brian and I discuss the possibility of doing additional trenching to find some of the inner structure of the Round Table building. This could sensibly look for something like an inner supporting wall, roof column foundation, or postholes showing the roofing was timber-built. However, anything like this is liable to lie somewhere between Trenches 3 and 2 and would involve a large trench joining the two. Both Brian (who has spent much of his time at Windsor digging in the trenches with us) and I are not sure this can be done properly in what remains of the last day. Although for Time Team a last-minute trench and possible discoveries make good TV, Simon doesn't attempt to influence this decision. Happily, an additional trench in the Lower Ward that confirms the location of the Great Hall provides a perfect conclusion to the excavations at Windsor Castle.

The excavation is brought to a formal end with a filmed live group scene in the Upper Ward where Julian and Richard Barber summarise the evidence for the discovery of the Round Table building.

A celebration end-of-site drink is had in the Windsor Arms across the road from the castle. The television programme (I have only seen the first broadcast) has apparently been a success and the discovery of the Round Table building has appeared in all the national press and many international publications. For the first time the production crew are able to relax and Simon is already thinking about possible themes for next year's live special. I chat to Steve, the 3D graphic artist, who is immensely relieved having promised (and delivered) a complete rendered virtual reconstruction of the Round Table building for the last programme while not being at all certain it could be done in time. Later, as I leave the pub, Oliver Creighton is showing an astonishing aptitude for accents by giving Alice, Ian, Matt and Jane a blow-by-blow re-enactment of the four day broadcast in the voices of all the different Time Team presenters.

The excavations in the Upper Ward cannot claim to have definitively explained the built character of the Round Table building. The excavation cannot tell us much about the architectural complexity of the structure, how it was floored, roofed and the *purposes for which it was intended. This must remain a matter of documentary analysis, hypothesis and debate.*

However, a record of the extent and depth of the survival of archaeological remains in the Upper Ward Quadrangle, the discovery of the location of a lost royal monument and its transformation from almost myth to fact, seem to me a reasonably successful weekend.

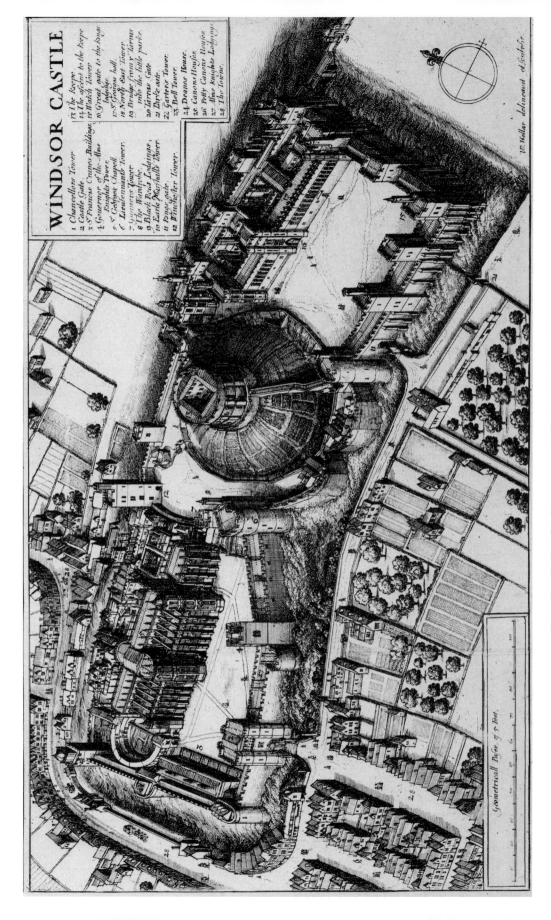

WINDSOR CASTLE

1 Chancellors Tower
2 Castle Gate
3 S.r Francies Cranes Buildings
4 Governor of the Alms
Knights
5 S.t Georges hall
6 Gethrast Chappell
7 Gunners Tower
8 The Wardrybe
9 Black Rods Lodgeings
10 Earle Marshalls Tower
11 Kings gate
12 Winchester Tower
13 The Keepe
14 The ascent to the keepe
15 Watch Tower
16 Great gate to the kings
lodginge
17 North East Tower
18 Bridge from y.e terras
into the little parke
20 Terras Gate
21 Thyte gate
22 Garters Tower
23 Bell Tower
24 Deanes House
25 Canons House
26 Petty Canons Houses
27 Alms Knights Lodgings
28 The Towne

W. Hollar delineauit et sculpsit

Geometricall Paces of 5 Feet.

3 Wenceslas Hollar's bird's-eye view of Windsor Castle c. 1658

I

DISCOVERING THE ROUND TABLE

Windsor Castle before 1344

The early topographical development of Windsor

TIM TATTON-BROWN

Introduction

SIR WILLIAM ST JOHN HOPE'S great pair of tomes, *Windsor Castle: an Architectural History,* was published almost a century ago, and remains to this day the most comprehensive study of any English castle ever undertaken.[1] This fine work about England's largest castle is, however, in need of considerable revision.[2] Its earliest chapters, in particular, need reassessment in the light of much recent work elsewhere, and it is surprising that this has not yet been done.[3] Windsor Castle has been a royal residence for almost exactly 900 years, as we shall see, and because of this continuing use, and because of the presence of the College of St George in the Lower Ward for the last six and a half centuries,[4] it has not been easy to undertake much new architectural and archaeological research within its precincts. There was, however, one major opportunity, after the disastrous fire of November 20 1992, and we await, with eager anticipation, English Heritage's full publication of the post-fire investigations.[5] A few other investigations have also been undertaken, for example in the Round Tower during underpinning work,[6] but most of the archaeological work has been on a very small scale. In the last two decades, much of the investigative work has been in the Lower Ward, in the area of the castle that is still owned by the Dean and Canons of St George's Chapel.[7]

---

[1] W.H. St John Hope, *Windsor Castle, an Architectural History* (1913).

[2] See, for example, *History of the King's Works*, II, 864, where among other things, it is pointed out that regnal and exchequer years are muddled up in the late twelfth and early thirteenth century.

[3] Only R.A. Brown in *History of the King's Works*, II, 864-88 has done some reassessment, but in most areas they follow Hope. D.F. Renn, *Norman Castles in Britain*, 2nd edn, London 1973, 348 summarizes Hope very briefly.

[4] With the founding of the Order of the Garter in 1348, the remains of the royal residence in the north-eastern part of the Lower Ward was handed over to the new college.

[5] For interim reports, see S. Brindle and B. Kerr, *Windsor Revealed: new light on the history of the castle* London 1997, and S. Brindle, 'Windsor Castle: the 1992 Fire, the Restoration, Archaeology and History', in L. Keen and E. Scarff (eds.), *Windsor, Medieval Archaeology, Art and Architecture of the Thames Valley* (British Archaeological Association Conference Transactions, XXV, 2002, 110-124.

[6] Very briefly mentioned in Brindle and Kerr, *Windsor Revealed*, 32-3 and 39.

[7] For a brief report on the important discoveries in 1965 in the Lower Ward, see P.E. Curnow, 'Royal lodgings of the thirteenth century in the lower ward of Windsor Castle: some recent archaeological discoveries,' *Friends of St George's Chapel Annual Report*, 1965, 218-220.

Apart from the post-1992 fire investigations, archaeological and architectural work in the Upper Ward is now very difficult to undertake, and this is not just because it is still a royal palace in use. At the very end of the eighteenth century, after a period of benign neglect, the castle was reoccupied by George III.[8] Under his son, George IV, massive rebuilding and remodelling of all the buildings in the Upper Ward was carried out from 1824-30, and very large sections of Edward III's great palace, and his massive curtain wall, were destroyed during Sir Jeffry Wyatville's hugely expensive rebuilding programme.[9] The Round Tower was also mutilated in 1830-31, when it was given a new upper storey. Despite this, much still remains, including Edward III's unique timber-framed residence within the Round Tower, which was built in 1354-56.[10] To understand visually Edward III's magnificently rebuilt Upper Ward, with its massive towered curtain wall and huge palace of 1357-68, one now needs to look at the fine bird's-eye views by Norden (1607) (Plate I)[11] and Hollar (*c.* 1658) (Figure 3)[12] and the Sandbys' many beautiful eighteenth century drawings and watercolours.[13] Edward III's palace was one of the finest and largest medieval palaces in Europe. It was built after his great victories at Crécy and Poitiers,[14] and eclipsed the king of France's and the pope's rival establishments at Vincennes near Paris and Avignon. With the addition of Edward IV's wonderful new St George's Chapel in the Lower Ward in the late fifteenth century, Windsor Castle became perhaps the most splendid medieval royal residence in Europe. In 1344, however, the royal residences in the Lower and Upper Wards were still relatively modest, and, as we shall see, old and in need of repair.

Old Windsor

Two miles due south-east of Windsor Castle, and close to the river Thames, is the parish church of St Peter and St Andrew, Old Windsor. This modest early thirteenth century structure (heavily restored by Scott in 1863-4)[15] is all that remains, above ground, of a major medieval settlement that was both an urban centre and an important royal residence. The place-name is first recorded as *Windlesora*, which may have been taken from its position on the bank (*ora*) of the winding River

---

[8] Many parts of the medieval castle were superbly depicted by the Sandby brothers in the later eighteenth century, before the destructive rebuildings of the earlier nineteenth century. See J. Roberts, *Views of Windsor*, watercolours by Thomas and Paul Sandby, London & New York 1995.

[9] J.M. Crook and M.H. Port, *The History of the King's Works* VI, London 1973, 373-393.

[10] For a recent very brief discussion of this, see J. Munby, 'Carpentry works for Edward III at Windsor Castle' in Saul, *St George's Chapel*, 233-4.

[11] British Library, Harleian MS 3749, f.3. and conveniently reproduced on the cover of C. Richmond and E. Scarff (eds.) *St George's Chapel, Windsor in the late Middle Ages*, Windsor 2001.

[12] Made for E. Ashmole's, *The Institution, Laws and Ceremonies of the Most Noble Order of the Garter*, London 1672.

[13] See Roberts, *Views of Windsor*.

[14] C. Wilson, 'The Royal Lodgings of Edward III at Windsor Castle: form, function, representation' in L. Keen and E. Scarff, *Windsor*, 15-94.

[15] N. Pevsner, *The Buildings of England:Berkshire*, Harmondsworth 1966, 189.

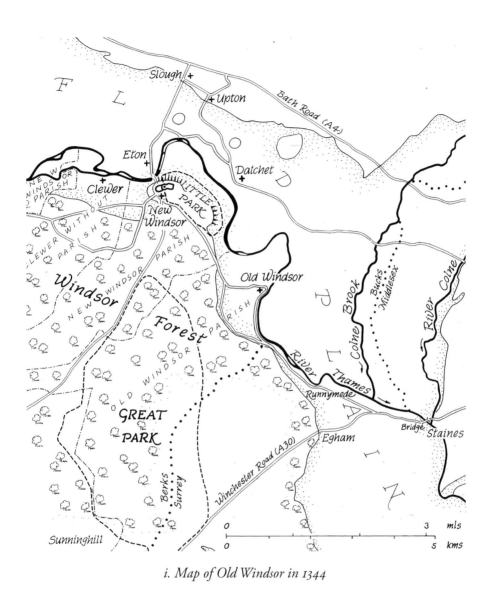

i. Map of Old Windsor in 1344

Thames.[16] Just to the south-west of the church, in a field called 'Kingsbury', excavations were undertaken between 1953 and 1958, by Dr Brian Hope-Taylor, which
uncovered a very important sequence of Anglo-Saxon occupation levels, and water-

---

[16] Though slightly oddly, more recent interpretations of the place-name suggests it means 'a bank with a
windlass'. See E. Ekwall, *English Place-names*, fourth edn, Oxford 1960, 523, and M. Gelling, *Place Names
of Berkshire*, Cambridge 1973-76, III, 841-4.

mills fed by an artificial channel. Sadly, these archaeological excavations have never been published, but very brief interim reports tell us that the settlement seems to have started in the seventh century, been destroyed in the late ninth century (presumably by the Vikings), but then rebuilt (with a new water-mill) in the later tenth century.[17] It then continued until some time after the Norman Conquest, when it was largely abandoned, with just the small settlement of 'Old' Windsor remaining.[18] The present parish church with its small early thirteenth century nave and chancel, was clearly only built for a village population.[19]

The documentary evidence for Old Windsor only starts with King Edward the Confessor,[20] but it is clear that at the end of his reign (between 1061-5) it was the site of a major royal residence beside the Thames.[21] The estate was apparently granted to the king's own abbey of St Peter, at Westminster, in 1065, but the extant charters recording this seem to have been forged in the early twelfth century.[22] After the Conquest in 1066, it returned to the king,[23] and William the Conqueror (and his sons, William II and Henry I) continued to use Old Windsor as a major residence. Many important crown-wearing festivals (at Easter, Whitsun and Christmas) were held here between 1070 and 1107,[24] and the town was still a major settlement. Domesday Book tells us that Old Windsor was the third most important urban centre in Berkshire, after Wallingford and Reading, and it records a royal demesne manor of 20 hides with 95 *hagae* (i.e. urban house plots) in the borough.[25] Trade by water, down the Thames, to London must have been important, because the hinterland behind the town was almost entirely forested with the area lying on heavy London Clay.[26] The reason for the king's residence at Windsor was, by contrast, this very forest with its hunting, and most of east Berkshire, which lay on the heavy London Clay and the poor sandy soils of the Bagshot Beds, remained as a royal hunting forest throughout the Middle Ages. It is also worth noting

[17] B. Hope-Taylor, 'Excavations at Kingsbury, Old Windsor,' *Berkshire Archaeological Journal*, 1954-5, 147, and *Medieval Archaeology* II, 1958, 183-5. See also M. Bond, *The Story of Windsor*, Newbury 1984, 13.

[18] For a more recent reassessment of Old Windsor, see G.G. Astill, *Historic Towns in Berkshire: an archaeological appraisal,* Reading 1978, 69-74.

[19] Jean Rocque's *Actual Survey of Berkshire,* London 1752, shows Old Windsor before all the nineteenth and twentieth century developments, with the main population around Old Windsor Green, half a mile to the west of the church, on the western edge of the flood-plain terrace.

[20] Manuscript E of the Anglo-Saxon Chronicle (the Peterborough Chronicle) records that Aethersige was consecrated abbot (of St Augustine's, Canterbury) at Windsor on St Augustine's day (May 26th) 1061. See G.N. Garmonsway (trans.) *The Anglo-Saxon Chronicle*, 2nd edn, London 1954, 190.

[21] The *villa regalis* is mentioned in the charters, and Henry of Huntingdon tells us that the fight between Tostig and his brother Harold in 1064 took place in front of King Edward in the *aula regia apud Windleshores*. See Henry, Archdeacon of Huntingdon, *Historia Anglorum*, ed. and tr. D. Greenway, Oxford 1996.

[22] The charters of 1065 and 1066 were probably forged at Westminster Abbey by Osbert de Clare in the early twelfth century. See P.H. Sawyer, *Anglo-Saxon Charters*, London 1968, nos. 1040, 1043 and 1141.

[23] *Domesday Book, Surrey,* f.32, under the manor of Battersea, says that 'king William gave this manor (Battersea) to St Peter's (Westminster Abbey) in exchange for Windsor. This seems to have been before 1068, see St John Hope, *Windsor Castle*, I, 3, note 7.

[24] M. Biddle, 'Seasonal festivals and residence: Winchester, Westminster, and Gloucester in the tenth to twelfth centuries,' *Anglo-Norman Studies*, 8, 1985, 64-7.

[25] *Domesday Book, Berkshire*, f. 56v.

[26] British Geological Survey map, Windsor sheet 269, 1981.

that Windsor was never on the main roads out of London. These roads avoided the heavy clay, with the road from London to the south-west (now the A30) crossing the Thames at Staines bridge and then climbing the hill to Egham and Bagshot.[27] The land route to Old Windsor left this road just after Staines bridge, and then ran along a causeway over Runnymede in Surrey, on the south-west side of the Thames. The road crossed the boundary between Berkshire and Surrey (also the boundary between the dioceses of Salisbury and Winchester) just before reaching Old Windsor.

The main road out of London to the west, the 'Bath road' (now the A4) ran north of the Thames, through Slough to Maidenhead bridge.[28] One could leave this road at Upton (near Slough) to go the two miles south-west to Eton before crossing the bridge over the Thames to New Windsor, only after the bridge had been constructed here in the later twelfth century.[29] There is no evidence of, nor likely to have been, any form of ford between Eton and New Windsor, but an early ferry may well have existed here, as well as at Datchet, just to the east.

Stretching south-west from the Old Windsor settlement for over six miles, along the Berkshire-Surrey border, is the ancient parish of Old Windsor. Most of the central area of this parish contains the medieval 'Great Park' of Windsor,[30] and it is interesting to note that the Great Park was part of Old Windsor, rather than New Windsor.[31] Windsor Great Park was cut out of Windsor Forest, one of the five great royal forests in England named in Domesday Book, and this 1086 survey[32] also mentions other woodland that had been 'put in the king's preserve [*missa est in defensa*]', which is probably the first reference to the Great Park itself.[33] Domesday Book also mentions Walter FitzOther, who was both Warden of Windsor Forest and Governor of the New Castle, and as such was the most important royal official in the area. When William the Conqueror reacquired the manor of Old Windsor from Westminster Abbey he said, in the charter, that the place 'seemed suitable and convenient for a royal retirement on account of the river and its nearness to the forest for hunting and many other things'.[34] As Richard Fitz Neal says in his 'Dialogue of the Exchequer' the forest was 'the sanctuary and special delight of

---

[27] It skirts the southern edge of the later medieval Great Park.

[28] The route is shown clearly on Rocque's *Actual Survey of Berkshire.* Its earliest depiction is on the fourteenth century Gough map.

[29] This route is clearly shown on the earliest detailed map of the area, the plan of the honour of Windsor in *c.* 1580 in the Burghley-Saxton Atlas (BL Royal MS 18. C. III fos. 32-2).

[30] The first accurate record of the extent of the Great Park is John Norden's survey of 1607. See J. Roberts, *Royal Landscape, the gardens and parks of Windsor,* New Haven & London 1997, 246-7. The Great Park probably reached this size in 1359, when the northern area, the manor of Wychemere was added to the park by Edward III. See Roberts, *Royal Landscape,* 250.

[31] The main park in New Windsor was Moat Park. This was in private ownership and not annexed to the Great Park until the late seventeenth century. Roberts, *Royal Landscape,* 276.

[32] *Domesday Book, Berkshire,* f. 56v.

[33] The Great Park was enlarged in stages from the late eleventh century until the late fourteenth century. Further areas were added in the post-medieval period, including a large area to the south, in Surrey, in order to create the dam and lake of Virginia Water. For this the main road (the A30) was moved south-eastwards. See Roberts, *Royal Landscape, passim.*

[34] St John Hope, *Windsor Castle,* I, 3, note 8 quoting a lost charter, recorded in W. Camden, *Britannia,* London 1586, 143. See B. Harvey, *Westminster Abbey and its estates in the Middle Ages,* Oxford 1977, 27, 338.

kings, where, laying aside their cares, they withdraw to refresh themselves with a little hunting'.[35]

The first castle

Windsor Castle lies on the top of the remains of a chalk dome (geologically an isolated inlier[36]) which rises to about a hundred feet above the surrounding Thames floodplain. To the north is a steep chalk cliff which has been created by the down-cutting of the river Thames, and this cliff may have given the settlement below it on the north-west its name, Clewer. In Domesday Book it is called *Clivore*,[37] which perhaps derives from the settlement on the bank (*ora*) by the cliff. The Domesday entry for Clewer tells us that the manor was held from the king by Ralph Fitz Seifrid and that it was assessed at 5 hides, but now it is 4½ hides, 'and the castle (*castellum*) of Windsor is on the half-hide.'[38] This fits very well with the later evidence of the parish maps which show the two parishes of Clewer and New Windsor interlocked with a detached portion of New Windsor (Dedworth) lying to the north-west of Clewer. Clewer parish was also later divided into two areas 'within' and 'without' the new borough of New Windsor, and the north-east corner of the parish came right up to the Windsor bridge over the Thames, and to the north-west corner of the castle.[39]

As was long ago suggested by St John Hope, a motte and bailey castle was almost certainly first built on the hill above Clewer in the decade after the Conquest. However, he went on to suggest that most of the castle, as we now know it, i.e. with a great motte and two baileys, was built by William the Conqueror.[40] His suggestion has been followed by most later writers,[41] but this seems to me to be most unlikely. Castle studies of the last half century have agreed that the first 'castles of the Conquest' were earthworks of a 'clearly-defined type' with the dominant feature a 'great flat-topped mound' or 'motte', encircled by a ditch, and with a kidney-shaped enclosure or 'bailey' on one side.[42] This is exactly what we have at Windsor with a large motte (now dominated by the Round Tower) and to the west a bailey that is later called the Middle Ward. Strangely this 'inner bailey' is largely ignored by St John Hope and later writers, who just discuss the 'conqueror's motte and two large baileys', the later Upper and Lower Wards.[43] I would suggest that only the motte and Middle Ward were built by the Conqueror in the 1070s,

[35] Quoted in A.L. Poole, *From Domesday Book to Magna Carta, 1087-1216*, 2nd edn, Oxford 1955, 29.

[36] See B.G.S. Windsor sheet 269 and section.

[37] Ekwall, *Place Names*, 111.

[38] *Domesday Book, Berkshire* f. 62v.

[39] The parish boundary is just outside the Curfew tower (earlier called the Clewer tower). This area just above the bridge is later called Underore.

[40] St John Hope, *Windsor Castle*, I, 10-12.

[41] For example, D.F. Renn, *Norman Castles*, 348.

[42] *History of the King's Works*, I, 23. See also D.J. Cathcart-King, *The Castle in England and Wales, an interpretative history*, London 1988, 62.

[43] *History of the King's Works*, I, 864. See also R.A. Brown, *English Castles*, 2nd edn, London 1976, 84.

and that the earliest Windsor Castle was just a small 'motte and bailey' castle with timber palisades. As we have seen, the new castle was not on any main road, but it was strategically placed overlooking the Thames, above the settlement of Clewer. It was also fairly close to the king's residence at Old Windsor, and to his hunting and sport in Windsor Forest. This situation seems to have continued under William Rufus, and in the early part of the reign of Henry I, and the attendance of the king is recorded at crown-wearing festivals at Old Windsor in 1070, 1072, 1097, 1105 and 1107.[44] Only after this, does a new royal residence come to be built at the castle, and the residence at Old Windsor is abandoned. With the removal of the king's residence to the castle, the urban centre at Old Windsor seems also to have moved to a new urban site, New Windsor, in the early twelfth century.[45] Old Windsor, as it was now called, decayed and by the early thirteenth century, when a new small parish church was built, it was just a small village.

The first royal residence in the castle

Henry of Huntingdon tells us that in 1110, king Henry I held his Whitsuntide Court for the first time at 'New Windsor, which he himself had built.'[46] St John Hope found this statement 'hard to interpret', but by coincidence just at the time his monumental architectural history of Windsor Castle was going to press in 1913, Hope had also recently completed his excavation of the Norman Castle in the 'Inner Bailey' at Old Sarum.[47]

This uncovered a magnificent twelfth century residence that was built for bishop Roger of Salisbury (1107-30), after he had asked for, and been given, custody of the castle by Henry I. Bishop Roger was 'second only to the king' (viceroy) in England for most of Henry's reign, and also erected splendid residences at his other castles, Sherborne, Devizes and probably Malmesbury.[48] The main character of these residences is that they were magnificently built on two levels around a large inner courtyard, and this is almost certainly what was first erected for King Henry on the north side of the Upper Ward at Windsor. Bishop Roger was known as a great builder, who particularly liked architectural display (he also hugely enlarged the cathedral at Old Sarum),[49] and he may well have helped to build the king's new house at Windsor. Unfortunately no documentary evidence for this survives but on January 24 1121, when Henry married his second queen, Adeliza of Louvain, in the chapel of this residence, we are told that bishop Roger wanted himself to conduct

[44] Biddle, 'Seasonal festivals'.
[45] Astill, *Historic Towns*, 59-67.
[46] St John Hope, *Windsor Castle*, I, 12. A similar statement is found in the 'E' version of the Anglo-Saxon Chronicle, tr. Garmonsway, 242.
[47] See the interim report in *Proceedings of the Society of Antiquaries* XXIV, 1912, 52-65. See also *History of the King's Works*, I, 824-5.
[48] E. J. Kealey, *Roger of Salisbury, viceroy of England*, Berkeley, Los Angeles & London, 1972.
[49] William of Malmesbury, *Gesta Regum*, ed. W. Stubbs, RS 90, London 1887-9, 484, 547, and 558.

the wedding, rather than the archbishop of Canterbury, 'because the castle itself stands in his diocese'.[50] He lost this dispute but there is little doubt that Roger's diocese was a key area for the king, and a few months after the wedding the bishop helped Henry I to found the new abbey at Reading, not far to the west of Windsor and also in Salisbury diocese.[51] This abbey was to be Henry's place of burial.

By 1130 there was a keeper (paid 2d a day) of the king's house in Windsor Castle,[52] and at this date the residence must have been complete, and almost certainly surrounded by a rampart and ditch (on the east and south) delineating a new eastern or upper bailey (now the Upper Ward). It seems to me unlikely that this eastern (upper) bailey was created before Henry I's reign, though most historians have followed St John Hope in assuming that it had been created by William the Conqueror. More uncertain is whether any form of stone curtain wall, including one on top of the motte, and along the top of the cliff on the north side of the Upper Ward, was constructed during Henry I's reign. It is very likely, however, that the earliest parts of the stone curtain wall (with large open-gorged towers) that now survive around the Upper Ward were built for Henry II. The Pipe Rolls record many payments from 1171-74 for 'the work of the wall about the castle', as well as for work on the king's houses.[53]

Henry I must also have been responsible for the laying out of the borough of 'New' Windsor, just below the castle on the west At its centre was a new parish church, surrounded by a large triangular market place.[54] A principal street ran south-east from the market place back to Old Windsor, and then on to Staines bridge and the main road to London. Another street led down the hill to the Thames on the north, but no bridge across the river is documented until 1191, when William Longchamp, Richard I's justiciar, is said to have fled from Windsor over 'the bridge below the castle'.[55] The first bridge is likely to have been built well before this, perhaps even in Henry I's time. It is also possible that Henry I created the earliest deer park, later the 'Little Park', on the chalk slope to the south-east of his new residence and eastern bailey.[56]

The castle in the later twelfth century

Little is recorded about Windsor Castle during Stephen's chaotic reign, or at the start of Henry II's reign, but in the early 1160s some small scale repairs are recorded

[50] Kealey *Roger of Salisbury*, 129-130.

[51] Kealey *Roger of Salisbury*, 67-72.

[52] Pipe Roll 31 Henry I, 127.

[53] St John Hope, *Windsor Castle*, I, 16.

[54] Astill, *Historic Towns*, 59-64 examines the new town in more detail. The churchyard and filled-in middle rows now occupy much of the market area.

[55] Gerald of Wales, *Speculum Ecclesie*, ed. J.S. Brewer, Rolls Series 21, London 1873, iv. 403.

[56] Deerparks around his castles at Sherborne and Devizes were also created by bishop Roger. The 'Little Park' at Windsor is not more fully documented until it was enlarged in the later fourteenth cent., see Roberts, *Royal Landscape*, 137.

in the Pipe Rolls. Then from 1165 large amounts of Totternhoe stone were brought from the Eglemont quarries (near Dunstable), and major building work was put in hand on 'the King's houses of Windsor'.[57] The first phase was nearing completion in 1167, when much lead for high quality roofs was brought in, and doors and windows were being painted. From *c.*1171-4, as we have seen, the 'wall about the castle' was being built, and this was followed, in the later 1170s and early 1180s, by more work on the king's houses and the general 'work of the castle'. By the time of Henry II's last visit to Windsor in 1185 most of the work was probably complete. From the evidence of the surviving fabric, one can suggest that Henry II had rebuilt Henry I's courtyard residence in the Upper Ward, and had surrounded the whole Ward (bailey) with a new towered curtain wall, which also ran up the south-east side of the motte to the roughly circular wall of the shell keep on top of it. This first shell keep must also have been built in Henry II's time, and though its heightening and mutilation in 1830-31 have made it much more difficult to study, some excavations in 1989-92 did reveal new details of it.[58]

As well as this, Henry II started to build in the area outside (west of) the Middle Ward, and almost certainly for the first time to initiate the creation of the Lower Ward. The only real evidence for this, at present, is the eastern part of the north curtain wall (on the cliff top), that runs westwards from the probably twelfth century Winchester tower in the north-west corner of the Middle Ward. Along this north curtain some new open-gorged towers were built, which culminated on the west in the great hall and chamber block of a second royal residence. The excavations carried out in this area in August 2006 helped to elucidate the earliest structures, and we can be fairly certain that a great hall was built against the north curtain wall, which was about 100 feet long and 28 feet wide internally. To the west of it, and at right angles to the curtain, was a large 'double' chamber block. Most of the surviving features in the chamber block (including the roof trusses) date from the thirteenth century refurbishment, but small fragments of the walls have small blockwork in them that must date to the twelfth century.[59] The new great hall was probably, for the first time, a 'public' ground floor hall with direct access to the town, unlike that in the Upper Ward where the hall was perhaps already a small 'private' first floor hall within the royal residence. In the later twelfth century the defences of the Lower Ward were almost certainly incomplete, and there was perhaps only a simple rampart and ditch separating it from the market place to the south. This no doubt would have caused problems for prince John in 1193, when he seized the castle (along with Wallingford Castle), and fortified it against his mother, queen Eleanor and Walter of Coutances (justiciar and archbishop of Rouen), after his brother, king Richard I, had been taken prisoner in Austria.[60] A siege followed but in November 1193, John gave up and returned the castles to his mother. Of particular interest is the Pipe Roll for 1194 which records 'the repair of

---

[57] St John Hope, *Windsor Castle*, I, 15-16. For Totternhoe stone, see below, p.53.
[58] Brindle and Kerr, *Windsor Revealed*, 32-33.
[59] Interim report in preparation by Cambrian Archaeological Projects.
[60] St John Hope, *Windsor Castle*, I, 23-4.

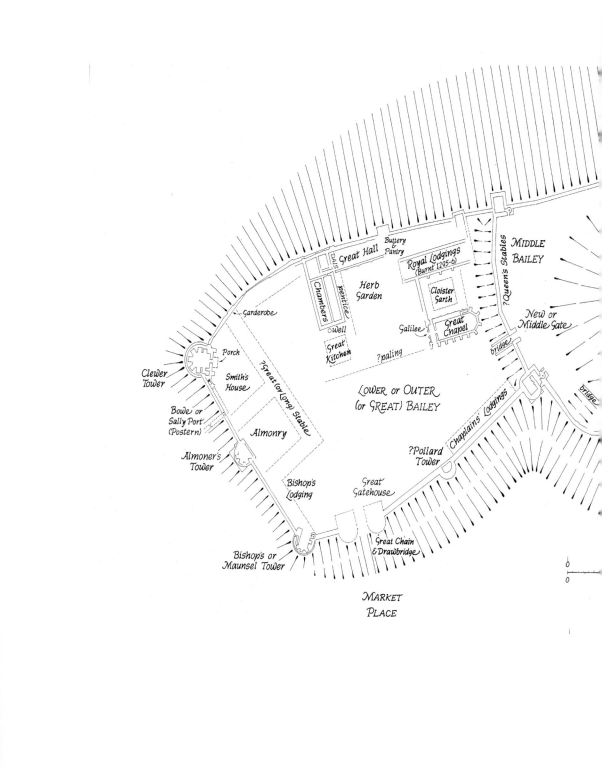

Great Hall

Buttery & Pantry

Royal Lodgings
(Burnt 1295-6)

MIDDLE
BAILEY

Herb
Garden

Chambers

penticc

DAIS

Cloister
Garth

?Queen's Stables

Garderobe

Well

Galilee

Great
Chapel

New or
Middle Gate

Clewer
Tower

Porch

Great
Kitchen

?paling

Smith's
House

LOWER or OUTER
(or GREAT) BAILEY

Bowe or
Sally Port
(Postern)

Almonry

?great (or Long) Stable

?Pollard
Tower

Chaplains' Lodgings

bridge

bridge

Almoner's
Tower

Bishop's
Lodging

Great
Gatehouse

Bishop's or
Maunsel Tower

Great Chain
& Drawbridge

MARKET
PLACE

0

0

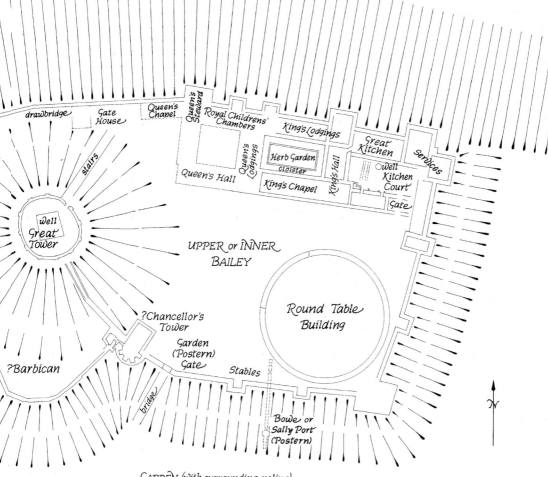

drawbridge Gate House Queen's Chapel Queen's Steward Royal Childrens' Chambers King's Lodgings Great Kitchen Services

stairs

Well Great Tower

Queen's Hall Queen's Lodgings Herb Garden cloister King's Chapel King's Hall Well Kitchen Court Gate

UPPER or INNER BAILEY

Round Table Building

?Chancellor's Tower

Garden (Postern) Gate

?Barbican

Stables

bridge

Bowe or Sally Port (Postern)

GARDEN (with surrounding paling)
(& 80ft. long stable)

N

1100   300   Ft
        100 M

Windsor Castle 1344

After Tim Tatton-Brown

A0407

the gate, and the bridge, and the *camera* and of other of the King's houses which were broken and burnt outside the King's castle of Windsor, through the war.'[61] The gate and bridge may be those of the Middle Ward, and the chamber (*camera*) 'outside' the castle must refer to the chamber block in the Lower Ward. Over the next three years other pipe rolls record 'the making of buttresses (*columpna*) not yet finished for supporting the motte of the castle of Windsor, and for repairing the King's cloister in the same place, and for levelling the ditch, which was between the motte and the King's house', and also for repairs to the 'king's hall at Windsor'.[62] This is the first reference to the hall, and must refer to the great hall in the Lower Ward. The buttress supporting the motte must have been on the south, where there is clear evidence for rebuilding after a collapse. The south side of the motte was obviously a weak spot, which was finally given better protection in the thirteenth century when two large curving walls were built, flanked by large semi-circular towers.[63]

After John became king in 1199, quite a large amount of unspecified works was carried out at the castle. These were probably mainly to the 'king's houses' rather than to the fortifications, and it was from here that John set out to meet the barons on 'neutral' territory (Runnymede) on June 15, 1215. A year later the castle was once again under siege, from June 24 to mid-September 1216. John's constable, Engelard of Cigogné, and sixty knights managed to hold off the attacking army, and its 'engines of war' under the Count of Nevers.[64] The siege was raised only about a month before the king's death, but we have almost no record of the damage done during it.

Rebuilding the castle for Henry III

Small-scale repair work at Windsor Castle started in 1220, but it was not until 1223 that major rebuilding was put in hand. Then for the next seven years very large-scale works were carried out. Unfortunately the details of this work are not often given, but most of the really expensive work in this period must have been to the new defences. By far the most important of these was the building of the large new western defences of the Lower Ward. The accounts for 1230 mention 'the work of a wall with three towers', and the taking down and covering up of the trebuchet.[65] These show clearly that the new defences of the castle (as also of those at Dover Castle), were to be exceptionally strong. The 'three towers' of the accounts were the towers now known as the Clewer, or Curfew tower (on the north-west), the Garter tower and the Salisbury tower. The latter two were not fully completed, but the

[61] Pipe Roll 6 Richard I, 256.
[62] Pipe Rolls 7 Richard I, 250 and 9 Richard I, 185
[63] Brindle and Kerr, *Windsor Revealed*, 33.
[64] W.L. Warren, *King John* (2nd edn, Harmondsworth 1978), 252-3; St John Hope, *Windsor Castle*, I, 26-7; and *History of the King's Works*, I, 865.
[65] St John Hope, *Windsor Castle*, I, 33.

Clewer tower was very elaborately built with a massive rib-vaulted basement, and a long sally-port leading out from it to a postern beyond the western ditch.[66] The upper part of this tower now holds the huge later fifteenth century timber belfry for St George's Chapel, but it may have originally housed the trebuchet mentioned above. As well as the western towers, a new curtain wall was built on the south side of the Lower Ward with semi-circular towers in the centre,[67] and at its east end.[68] There was also probably a new principal gatehouse, but this was replaced in the sixteenth century by the Henry VIII gate (built 1514-17). Around these new defences on the west and south very large ditches were constructed, though these have been progressively infilled and levelled in the post-medieval period.

As well as the work on the defences of the Lower Ward, the great hall here was repaired and rebuilt in 1223-24, and then in 1228 given a new temporary kitchen. Perhaps more important was the documented 'mending of the houses, which are on the motte of our castle of Windsor', which were then covered with 30 carrats of new lead.[69] This refers to the 'Great Tower' on the motte (now the Round Tower), which was completely rebuilt, and the accounts suggest that it had its own hall, kitchen and chapel under its new lead roof. To protect the motte and great tower on the south, two long curving walls were built, which met at a right angle in the centre, and were flanked on the west and east by the Henry III tower and the 'Edward III' tower respectively. Sadly the long curving walls were completely destroyed in the early nineteenth century, but their thirteenth century form, and the unrestored flanking towers are very well depicted in several eighteenth century water-colours by the Sandbys.[70] Well after the main works were completed, the making of a 'barbican' in 1249-50 is documented.[71] This is thought to have been outside the principal gate, but it could refer to the defences on the south side of the great tower on the motte.

Henry III came of age in 1227, and in 1236 married the twelve year old Eleanor of Provence. As a result, the royal domestic buildings in the castle were rebuilt and enlarged because Windsor by now was one of the principal royal residences in the kingdom. Very large sums were spent,[72] and the main residential complex in the Upper Ward was progressively rebuilt for the new queen and her children. Very little of this Upper Ward has survived because of the many later rebuildings.[73] In the Lower Ward, there are surviving fragments of the south wall of a new set of royal lodgings that were ordered to be built in January 1240, along with a new chapel to the south '70 feet long and 28 feet wide'. This highly decorated chapel, which

---

[66] The two steeply descending large vaulted passages at right angles to each other, are a little known feature that still survive in the defences, just to the south of Clewer tower.

[67] Now behind the military knights lodgings.

[68] The now much rebuilt so-called 'Henry the Third' tower.

[69] St John Hope, *Windsor Castle*, I, 60-1.

[70] Roberts, *Views of Windsor*, 88-93.

[71] St John Hope, *Windsor Castle*, 38.

[72] *History of the King's Works*, I, 866-7 suggests that well over £10,000 was spent between 1236 and 1256.

[73] Some traces of them were, however, uncovered after the fire in 1992. See Brindle and Kerr, *Windsor Revealed*, 34-5.

became the first St George's Chapel in 1348,[74] was separated from the lodgings on the north by a grass plot (*pratellum*). Remarkably the monumental west doorway of the chapel still survives, with its magnificent wooden doors covered in decorative ironwork, and flanked by Purbeck marble columns. This superb new chapel reflects King Henry's piety, and it has been suggested that its designer was the royal master mason Henry 'of Reims', who was to start the colossal rebuilding of Westminster Abbey in 1245.[75] When this chapel was finally completed in 1248-49, it became the most important, and like the nearby great hall, the most 'public' chapel in the castle. The great hall itself, which had been repaired in 1223-24, was given a new 'great kitchen' in 1233-34, and in 1240-41 a new pentice (covered walkway) was made between the kitchen and the hall.[76] At this time, the great hall was frequently used as a place for feeding the poor of the surrounding area,[77] and it is clear that it too had been rebuilt and embellished after 1236. We hear of a stone lion being erected on the gable top of the hall, and in 1250 it was ordered 'to make a royal seat in the middle of the table in the hall of the castle of Windsor and paint on it an image of the king holding a sceptre in his hand.'[78] From the excavations of August 2006, we know that this great hall lay east-west along the north curtain wall of the Lower Ward. Adjoining its west end was the twelfth century chamber block, and inside this building we still have a unique scissor-braced roof. There is also a thirteenth century fireplace and cylindrical chimney, and remains of elaborate thirteenth century windows and wall-paintings.[79] This surviving fragment of just one of the chambers made for Henry III in Windsor Castle gives us a fleeting glimpse into the many buildings that were constructed for him and Queen Eleanor in the castle between the 1230s and about 1261.[80]

By the time of the difficult years at the end of the long reign of Henry III, Windsor Castle was both a very strongly fortified castle and a very large royal palace. As we have seen the private part the palace containing the lodgings of king and queen and their children lay in the Upper Ward. It was built along the north side around a series of internal courts. The Lower Ward, by contrast contained the more monumental buildings; the great hall and the Chapel of St Edward, as well as the great kitchen and almonry that provided the food for Henry III's large banquets and frequent charitable giving. When Henry III died at Westminster on November 16, 1272, his eldest son Edward I was away in Sicily, on a crusade, and during the whole of his reign he spent little time at Windsor. There is, however, one

---

[74] It is now the Albert Memorial Chapel.

[75] *History of the King's Works*, I, 869.

[76] St John Hope, *Windsor Castle*, I, 53.

[77] *Ibid*, 54, where the almonry to the west of the hall is documented. See also S. Dixon-Smith, 'The image and reality of alms-giving in the great halls of Henry III', *Journal of the British Archaeological Association* 142, 1999, 79-96.

[78] *Ibid*, 52.

[79] See Curnow 'Royal Lodgings'.

[80] The last documented major works were in the Upper Ward in 1257-9, when the queen's chambers were once again rebuilt on quite a large scale (using Purbeck marble shafts among other things). St John Hope, *Windsor Castle*, I, 66-9.

record of a major fire in the royal lodgings in the north-east corner of the Lower Ward, and we read of the 'oriel before the burnt great chamber leading towards the steps of the great chapel'.[81] St John Hope suggested that these burnt lodgings were left unrepaired until they were handed over to the new canons of the Order of the Garter some fifty years later. This is, however, by no means certain, though the *camera combusta* is mentioned in the survey of 1327 (see below).[82]

The castle in the early fourteenth century

Edward III was born at Windsor, almost certainly in the lodgings in the Upper Ward, on November 13, 1312, at a time when his father, Edward II was using the castle fairly frequently. Edward II's favourite, Piers Gaveston, had been murdered a few months before this and England was in turmoil, so the castle was a secure place for the sixteen year old queen Isabella 'the Fair' to have her first child. Three days later, on Thursday November 16, Edward was baptised in the chapel in the Lower Ward by the papal legate, cardinal Nouvel.[83] Part of the thirteenth century Purbeck marble font in which this event took place still survives. By the time of Edward II's murder only fourteen years after this, little new work had been done on the castle for well over half a century, and its state is carefully described in a survey carried out, at the beginning of the new reign in September 1327.[84] In the early years of the reign, various minor repairs must have been carried out, but still no major new works had been undertaken when the large hordes came to the castle in January 1344 for the feast and tournament arranged by King Edward III. It is perhaps worth completing this chapter by attempting a brief description of the castle at the time.

Just as today, the participants would have arrived at the great gate on the south-west side of the Lower Ward (called the lower bailey at this time). After passing over the drawbridge and through the gateway, they would have seen on their left the great stables and the almonry of the castle. Behind them were two semi-circular towers, still incomplete. Beyond this, however, would have been the very large Clewer (or Curfew) Tower, which still dominates the north-west corner of the castle, and in front of it were no doubt a series of service buildings like the granary, brewhouse and bakehouse, also partly integrated with the almonry buildings. To the east of them was the great kitchen, with the dressing house beside it, and a covered passageway leading to the great hall beyond. This large hall, perhaps about 100 feet long, ran east-west alongside the curtain wall, with its buttery and pantry at the east end,[85] and the high table on a dais at the western end. This was where

---

[81] St John Hope, *Windsor Castle*, I, 86-7.

[82] *History of the King's Works*, I, 870.

[83] For a recent review of these events, see I. Mortimer, *The Perfect King: the life of Edward III, father of the English Nation*, London 2006, 19-20.

[84] St John Hope, *Windsor Castle*, I, 107-9.

[85] These are mentioned specifically in an inquisition of 13 Jan. 1331, *Calendar of Miscellaneous Inquisitions II, Edward II – 22 Edward III*, London 1916, no. 1220.

the ladies had their feast presided over by two queens, in January 1344.[86] West of the great hall was the larger chamber block with a cylindrical chimney protruding from its roof.[87] In front of the great hall was the herb garden with benches in it,[88] and beyond to the right were the 'burnt lodging' and other buildings of the royal lodgings in the north-east corner of the lower bailey. Between them and the magnificent Chapel of St Edward was a cloister (rebuilt in the 1350s, and now the Dean's Cloister). The southern part of the lower bailey, as today, was largely open ground, and it was perhaps here that a great tent was erected in 1344 for the men's feast presided over by the king. Along the southern curtain wall of the lower bailey were the lodgings of the four chaplains and the two clerks of the chapels in the castle, recently supplemented by new lodgings (built in 1337) for the chaplains of the chapel in the park.[89]

After passing through the lower bailey, the visitor would go over another drawbridge, and through the middle bailey gateway. In front of him was the mound, and on its summit, the great tower, which survived little changed until its large scale heightening in 1830. Shortly after 1344, the first clock in the castle was to be installed here.[90] The visitor would pass around the mound to the left (north), and on his left, he would probably have seen the queen's stables, with behind it another large tower (now called the Winchester Tower). To the north-east of the mound he would have passed over another drawbridge, before going through yet another large, but decayed, gateway (rebuilt by Edward III later in his reign, and now called, rather oddly, the Norman Gateway) into the upper bailey. Here he would have seen in front of him a whole series of buildings that made up the queen's lodgings, with behind them, the king's lodgings with halls, kitchens, chapels and many other chambers. All of these were also to be massively rebuilt, later in the reign, with a magnificent new façade on the south side. The royal lodgings all abutted onto the towers of the north curtain wall, but to the east and south, the towers of the curtain wall were much less encumbered with buildings, and it was here in the great courtyard to the south of the royal lodgings that the jousts were to be held. Soon afterwards, as we shall see, the Round Table building was to be erected in the south-east corner of this bailey.

---

[86] Adam Murimuth, *Chronicon*, ed. E.M. Thompson, Rolls Series 93, London 1889, 155-6.
[87] This still survives in part.
[88] First mentioned in 1310: St John Hope, *Windsor Castle*, I, 92.
[89] St John Hope, *Windsor Castle*, I, 109.
[90] R. A. Brown, 'King Edward's clocks', *Antiquaries Journal*, 39, 1959, 283-6.

The early years of Edward III

Richard Barber

WHEN EDWARD III came to the throne in 1327, the monarchy was weak and unpopular. Edward was only fourteen, and was under the tutelage of his mother, Isabella of France, and her paramour Roger Mortimer, earl of March. His father, Edward II, had squandered the goodwill of the magnates who had been loyal supporters of Edward I for most of his reign, both by his lack of skill as a commander and his failure to support the chivalric values which they regarded as proper to a king. His tactless promotion of favourites was highly unpopular, and led to his deposition in January 1327. Edward II was imprisoned in Berkeley Castle in Gloucestershire, and died eight months later in circumstances which can best be described as mysterious: reports that he was murdered were widespread, and Edward III seems to have believed that this was the case, but he may also have considered it possible that he might have escaped from captivity. His father's deposition had been the work of Isabella and Mortimer, and Edward now found himself equally at their mercy. In the autumn of 1330, he staged a dramatic coup d'état at Nottingham castle, seizing Mortimer in Isabella's chamber with the help of a carefully chosen group of nobles and courtiers. Mortimer was beheaded, and Isabella was kept in confinement for the rest of her life, though restrictions on her movements were gradually eased.

This coup showed Edward as an adroit leader of men, as it seems to have been largely of his own devising; and the group of nobles who carried it out with him formed a kind of inner circle at court for the next decade. He was also astute enough to avoid favouring a single member of that inner circle, which included many of his most able contemporaries among the nobility. Over the course of the next seven years, he reinforced their positions in society by patronage, but his grants were generally carefully and discreetly done, compared with the excessive wealth showered by his father on his favourites. Edward was aware that in making his grants, he was either disappointing another possible claimant, or raising the prospect of a challenge to the grant in future years. Transfer of estates was not a simple matter in a feudal society, where property rights were very different. Land usually changed hands only by inheritance or through marriage; sale was almost unknown. So changes of dynastic ownership were rare, and many of the grants came from the royal estates.

When in February 1337 Edward created earldoms for six of the comrades who had helped him to carry out the coup, he was careful to justify his action as being for the good of the nation as a whole:

> Among the signs of royalty we considered it to be the most important that, through a suitable distribution of ranks, dignities and offices, the king is sustained by the wise counsels and protected by the many powers of formidable men. Yet because the hereditary ranks in our kingdom . . . through a failure of issue and various other events have returned into the hand of the king, this realm has experienced for a long time a substantial loss in the names, honours and ranks of dignity.[1]

Not everyone agreed that the nation benefited: the Northumbrian chronicler Sir Thomas Gray looked back on these grants as the cause of the king's heavy taxation in later years: 'So generously did the king distribute his estates to these earls and to his other favourites, that he scarcely retained for himself any of the lands pertaining to his crown, and was obliged to live off windfalls and subsidies at great cost to people.'[2] But there were few such dissenting voices, and in fact many of the grants were made from estates forfeited to the crown by nobles condemned as a result of the disturbances of 1326-30, notably the lands of the Despensers and Mortimers. And no-one could deny the earls' exceptional service to the king at the most critical juncture of his reign; if this was favouritism, it was in return for favours received. Furthermore, by increasing the number of great lords, Edward was avoiding the situation that had prevailed in his father's reign where one or two families wielded exceptional influence. And he was careful not to grant the lands in perpetuity, but either for a term of years or under conditions which meant that there was the possibility of reversion – a reversion which he might want to grant to the original family if they were restored to favour, as happened with Roger Mortimer's son.

There was a further motive in the creation of new earls in 1337: there was a war in the offing, and the earls were the traditional leaders of the army. The long-standing tension between England and France had come to a head over Edward's alliance with Robert of Artois, whom Philip VI regarded as a traitor, even though he was his brother-in-law. Edward owed Philip feudal allegiance for the duchy of Aquitaine, which had belonged to the English crown since Henry II married Eleanor of Aquitaine in 1154: the problem of a sovereign being the vassal of another sovereign in respect of some of his lands had never been satisfactorily resolved, and Philip used Robert of Artois as an excuse to declare that Edward had forfeited his lands by harbouring a traitor. This tangled situation was further complicated by the fact that Edward himself had a claim to the French throne through his mother

---

[1] *Reports from the Lords Committees touching the Dignity of a Peer of the Realm*, London 1819, V 28-32.
[2] Sir Thomas Gray, *Scalacronica*, ed. & tr. Andy King, Publications of the Surtees Society 209, Woodbridge & Rochester NY, 2005, 123.

Isabella, as he was the closest surviving relative of Charles IV. Philip denied this claim on the unproven grounds that the French throne could not be inherited through the female line.

War of some kind was therefore regarded as inevitable. Over the past two centuries, the pattern of Anglo-French relations had been that after a brief spell of open warfare, the two sides would come to a new compromise. The English had generally come off worse, because the resources to fight a war across the Channel were difficult to muster, and the vast domains bequeathed by Henry II had gradually been eroded by the French: Normandy, homeland of the English dynasty, was now the fiefdom of the eldest son of the king of France.

Edward's remarks about the diminishing numbers of great lords when he justified his creation of the new earls were entirely true, because three of the existing earls died in the years 1337-38, and either had no successors or heirs who were not fit for military service.[3] This left just five active earls, rather than the dozen or more who might usually be expected to lead the king's armies, and by creating the additional earls, he was doing no more than making good the losses. These men would serve with substantial retinues: the nine earls who took part in the Brittany campaigns in 1342-43 raised about 900 men-at-arms between them, against about 1100 from all other sources.[4] Six earls are named as the guarantors of the Round Table in accounts of the festival at which it was created: three of them are among the new earls of 1337. The others are Thomas Beauchamp, earl of Warwick, an experienced commander; the wealthy earl of Arundel; and the young earl of Pembroke.

Edward saw the interest of king and magnates as essentially one and the same when he created the new earls. The highly structured state created by the Normans in the eleventh century had been modified gradually over the succeeding three hundred years, but it was still recognisably a unified system, in which the barons had a crucial role. The 'magnates' were a relatively small group,[5] ranging from figures such as Richard, earl of Arundel, capable of lending huge sums to his fellow lords, to knights banneret who had made their way up the social ladder in the king's service, and who owed their status to grants made by their master. Like the king, the greatest of them lived off their estates, and maintained splendid households; and their power, if united against the king, could be fatal to royal ambitions, as Henry III and Edward II had discovered to their cost. In peace, they looked to the king to govern justly and maintain a suitably magnificent court; in war, they wanted a leader who would bring military success and the enrichment that went with the spoils of war. As K. B. McFarlane puts it,

---

[3] Edward of Woodstock, the king's eldest son, aged seven, succeeded John earl of Cornwall. The new earl of Hereford seems to have been an invalid and the earl of Norfolk had no heir.
[4] Andrew Ayton, 'Edward III and the English Aristocracy at the beginning of the Hundred Years' War' in Matthew Strickland, *Armies, Chivalry and Warfare in Medieval Britain and France*, Harlaxton Medieval Studies VII, Stamford 1998, 193.
[5] Jonathan Sumption, *The Hundred Years War: Trial by Battle*, London 1990, i.51, estimates the magnate families at '150 to 200'.

. . . the real politics of the reign were not confined to the short but frequent parliaments; they were inherent rather in Edward's daily personal relations with his magnates. The king's service was profitable; men went to court and to the royal camp, not to express unacceptable views, but for what they could get. Under a ruler who knew his job they were amply rewarded.[6]

Among the magnates there were smaller groups, the knights of the royal household who were most closely associated with the king and were under his personal command, and the earls and barons who frequented the court in various official and unofficial roles. The knights of the household were hugely important in Edward's wars: even a sceptical estimate puts them at only half of the men-at-arms who sailed for Flanders in 1338. Edward was free to choose his followers more widely, and the result was a very varied group, including minor nobility from old families, newcomers to England – often from his father-in-law's county of Hainault (in what is now Belgium) – and professional soldiers of obscure origin who had won their place by their military skills. This harked back to his grandfather's days, when the household knights played a similar role in Edward I's Scottish campaigns, and it was a commonplace that warfare should be waged by a group of men close to the king, an idea that had its origins in the war-bands of Celtic and Germanic tribal society. A 'household knight' was retained by the king, and would receive robes at the new year. The list of the distribution robes, given the often erratic payment of fees to royal retainers, is perhaps the best way of identifying the household. They in turn would recruit men to serve in the royal army, so that sixty such knights on the campaign in Flanders in 1338 had almost eight hundred men-at-arms in their own retinues.[7] In peacetime, the household knights were as prominent in royal tournaments as the great magnates.

Other magnates, such as the marcher lords of the north, rarely came to court, and lived largely in their own country, preoccupied with their own interests. However, if the king's rule started to falter, they were often the first to show signs of rebellion, being independent-minded and wary of the central powers. A successful king had therefore to balance the aspirations of these different groups against his own ambitions; Edward I had done so with great skill, appearing at various times as a chivalric hero and as a great lawgiver, the Justinian of his age. Edward II's failure was a stark warning to his son.

The early part of Edward's personal reign had started as auspiciously in the field as his father's military career had been ill-starred. The longstanding wars against Scotland had resulted in serious English defeats, and while Mortimer was in power,

---

[6] K. B. McFarlane, *The Nobility of Later Medieval England*, Oxford 1973, 120.
[7] Ayton, 'Edward III and the English Aristocracy', 184.

there had been a disastrous campaign in 1327, and a peace treaty in 1328 which was widely regarded as shameful. War broke out again in 1332, and at Dupplin Moor the English, led by Edward Balliol, the claimant to the Scottish throne whom the English supported, were victorious against a large but disorganised Scottish army. The king himself was not present, but he came to besiege Berwick, the key fortress on the border, in the following year; and when a Scottish army came to try to break the siege, he defeated it at Halidon Hill. Although this enabled Balliol to re-establish his rule in Scotland, his opponents scattered throughout the country and continued a kind of guerrilla warfare. The next year, Edward came to Roxburgh to fight a winter campaign: one chronicler recorded that

> Other than the youths of the realm and the magnates, he had few people with him. No one bore the hardships and the harshness [of the winter] or labored more willingly than he; and all the time he greatly comforted his army by words, gifts and deeds, saying that they would all drink from the same cup. And thus he inspired their resolve.[8]

However, for all his qualities as a leader, he was unable to hold Scotland, despite raising one of the largest armies that he ever commanded in the following year. The opposition was too widespread and the tactics of guerrilla warfare were impossible to contain; and the alliance in 1334 between Philip VI of France and David Bruce, the claimant to the throne favoured by the Scots, meant that there was now a possibility of a French invasion of the north. What had begun as a success had become a liability; but Edward's answer was to take the war to Philip, with whom he already had a quarrel over the confiscation of the English lands in Aquitaine some fifteen years earlier, and whose strategy in allying himself with the Scots was partly due to this long-standing antagonism.

England alone could not take on the armies of the vastly wealthier kingdom of France. So in 1337-38 Edward set about constructing a grand alliance based on Flanders, where Philip had been trying to establish his rights over the Flemish towns and where there was considerable hostility to the French. His diplomacy was largely successful, and during the next three years, he established a substantial power-base in north-western Europe: the count of Flanders, an ally of Philip, was forced out, and Edward was given authority over Germany and the Low Countries as the deputy of the German emperor. However, in order to achieve the military alliance, he was forced to adopt a policy of promising huge sums to his allies for the costs of bringing their troops to join his army. This in turn meant that he had to show quick results in order to balance his books.

The grand alliance proved to be a paper tiger. His allies were more than happy to take his money, but much less happy about actually providing the resources for the kind of campaign that Edward had in mind. Other than the financial rewards,

---

[8] *Historia Roffensis*, quoted in Clifford Rogers, *The Wars of Edward III*, Woodbridge & Rochester, NY, 1999, 44.

the rulers whom Edward had signed up – the lords of the various counties and duchies in the Low Countries and the German emperor, Louis IV – had little real interest in taking the war into France. The towns of the Netherlands were chiefly concerned to keep Philip out of their affairs, while Edward needed a considerable military victory if he was to enforce the restitution of the duchy of Aquitaine. Moreover, the allies knew that Edward was thinking of making public his claim to the French throne, at which point the rights of the French king would pass to him, and they would merely have exchanged the threat which Philip posed for a vastly more powerful ruler of France. This hesitation, combined with poor logistics and the seeming inability of the allies to co-ordinate their efforts, led to three years of fruitless manoeuvring along France's north-eastern border. Only the naval victory at Sluys in 1340, when the French fleet and a large army were more or less annihilated, relieved a picture of military failure.

Military failure meant that the costs of maintaining the alliance could not be defrayed by the spoils of war, and what had been intended as a swift campaign dragged on with no end in sight. Edward had to finance this war out of taxation: and the result was one of the heaviest periods of taxation ever seen in England. In the spring of 1340 he had to return home to use such persuasion as he could muster on an increasingly recalcitrant country, and to explain that he had now declared his hand and had publicly laid claim to the French throne by assuming the title 'King of England and France'. Matters came to a head in the autumn of 1340, when the new taxation he had been granted by parliament in the spring yielded only 15% of what had been expected. His closest advisers in England were now thoroughly opposed to the war, and in December Edward sailed back to London. His response to the situation was to attempt to repeat the coup with which his personal rule had begun in 1330: he dismissed the leaders of the council and imprisoned some of the administration, but the results were not what he had hoped. Archbishop Stratford, who had been chancellor since 1330, withdrew to Canterbury, but waged a propaganda war against the king, and refused to answer for his actions except before parliament. When parliament met in April 1341, Edward tried to exclude him, but the other lords forced him to admit the archbishop and to come to terms with him. It was a tremendous blow for a king who had hoped to avoid the troubles of his father's reign; echoes of the fall of Edward II were particularly strong, since Stratford had been a leader of the opposition in the 1320s. The king had to agree to legislation which gave parliament a large role in selecting the royal officials, and to an audit of his finances; and the lords insisted that none of them should be imprisoned without a trial before his peers in parliament.

By the autumn this had all been reversed. On October 1, Edward boldly annulled the legislation, on the grounds that he had been coerced into signing it. Behind this lay a swift personal campaign by Edward to regain the allegiance of the great magnates who had ranged themselves against him. It says much for his personality that he was able to do this, in the face of the record of military failure over the previous three years. An element in this, which has not previously been noted, seems to have been a series of tournaments held during the year: the records

Table 1. Known tournaments of Edward III [9]

1328 (May)	London (entry of queen Philippa)	William of Hainault present with large numbers of knights and spectators
1328 (June)	Hereford (Mortimer family marriage)	Queen Isabella
1329 (March)	Guildford (Shrovetide)	
1329 (June)	Amiens (Edward's homage to Philip)	With French court
1329 (October)	Dunstable	Queen Philippa, many lords
[1330]		
1331 (May)	Dartford (Edward's return from France)	
1331 (June)	Stepney (1st birthday of prince Edward)	Queen Philippa; team of 12-16 kts against all comers; possibly countess of Hainault
1332 (July)	Woodstock (churching of queen Philippa)	Household kts
[1333]		
1334 (Jan. ?)	Dunstable	Many nobles, household kts. 135 participants
1334 (May)	Burstwick	
1334 (July)	Nottingham	
1333/4	Place unknown	[Recorded in Exchequer accounts]
[1335] [1336] [1337]		
1338 (Dec. ?)	Antwerp (churching of queen Philippa)	
1339 (November)	Brussels	Hainault kts
1340 (April)	Windsor (Easter)	
1340 (Oct. ?)	Ghent (truce of Esplechin)	
1341 (February)	Norwich (Shrovetide)	
1341 (February)	Langley (Knighting ceremony)	
1341 (June)	Langley (churching of queen Philippa)	
1342 (February)	Dunstable (Shrovetide, Anglo-Scots truce)	Queen Philippa, leading magnates, nobles, 236 kts; no foreigners
1342 (April)	Northampton	Queen Philippa, many nobles
1342 (May)	Eltham (visit of William IV of Hainault)	Queen Philippa, Hainault kts
1343 (June)	Smithfield (midsummer)	13 kts against all comers
1343 (summer)	A number of tournaments	Majority not attended by Edward
1344 (January)	Windsor (Round Table)	20 kts against all comers; leading magnates, southern nobles, Londoners in attendance
[1345] [1346] [1347]		
1348 (mid February)	Reading	
1348 (late February)	Bury St Edmunds	Small tournament
1348 (4-12 May?)	Lichfield	
1348 (20 May?)	Eltham	Household kts.
1348 (June)	Windsor (churching of queen Philippa)	
1348 (14 July)	Canterbury	Great magnates, household knights
1349 (April)	Windsor (St George's Day, Garter assembly)	
1351	Bristol	
1353 (Christmas)	Eltham	Edward the Black Prince and others*
1355 (February)	Woodstock (churching of queen Philippa)	Edward probably present*
1357 (May)	Smithfield	Edward, John of France, David of Scotland present*
1358 (April)	Windsor (St George's Day, Garter assembly)	Duke of Lancaster, many foreign nobles*
1359 (May-June)	Smithfield	Edward and four eldest sons with 19 others dressed as mayor and aldermen
1361 (April)	Windsor (St George's Day, Garter assembly)	
1363 (November)	Smithfield	Kings of France, Cyprus and Scotland
1375	Smithfield	Alice Perrers as Lady of the Sun
		* Edward III apparently does not participate

9 Based on Vale, *Edward III and Chivalry*, 172-4 and Ormrod, in Saul, *St George's Chapel, Windsor*, 19, for 1348 material.

are almost certainly incomplete, but three tournaments are known to have taken place, which points to a resumption of chivalric activity on a scale not seen since 1331, just after he first came to power. The crucial factor in Edward's reversal of Stratford's coup was his success in rallying the great lords behind him; and this harmony between the king and his magnates was to last until the very end of his reign. It was probably helped by the prospect of a new and more promising strategy in France. Instead of a full-scale invasion of France, Edward now saw an opportunity to achieve his ends by stirring up trouble between Philip VI and his vassals. In 1340 Edward had publicly laid claim to the French throne, and he could now argue that vassals of the French crown should obey him rather than Philip.

The first opportunity to use this strategy came in Brittany in 1341, and although the next two years brought very mixed success, the effect on French politics was considerable. Philip's relations with his great lords were much less congenial than Edward's; and he reacted violently, executing one of the leaders of the Breton revolt when he came to Paris believing himself to be protected by a truce. By 1343, Edward could see the prospect of being able to renew the French war with the aid of disaffected French lords rather than expensive, non-committal foreign allies. In the meanwhile, the splendid series of tournaments continued, playing on the enthusiasm of the English nobility for chivalric sports to strengthen their ties with the king.

We know relatively little about the tournaments at Norwich and Langley in 1341, but there was a major festival at Dunstable in February 1342, to mark the betrothal of Lionel of Antwerp, Edward's third son (at the tender age of three), followed two months later by an event at Northampton on a smaller scale, marred only by the death of John of Beaumont, brother-in-law of the earl of Derby. A month later, on 9 May, the visit to England of Edward's brother-in-law, William IV, count of Hainault, was marked by a tournament at Eltham Palace near London. Although William IV was wounded, this did not deter his chivalric enthusiasm, and the connection with Hainault seems to have been an influential one in chivalric terms. William's father had jousted at the tournament held for Philippa's wedding to Edward III in 1328, and the Hainault knights were also present at a tournament held by Edward III in Brussels in 1339. Sir Walter Manny, a Hainault lord who came to England in Philippa's entourage figures largely in the pages of Jean Froissart, whose chronicles take chivalry and deeds of arms as their central theme. Froissart himself, also from Hainault, was in England in Philippa's entourage in the 1360s.

William IV seems to have been obsessed by chivalry in 1343-5. In 1343, he went to Prussia, to crusade with the Teutonic Knights against the heathen, and was still there in early 1344 when the Windsor festival was held.[10] He returned to Holland on April 8, and almost immediately set in hand preparations for a lavish chivalric festival at the Hague. This was held, like the Windsor feast, from Sunday to Thursday, and was on a considerable scale; the count's officers referred to it as

---

[10] Werner Paravicini, *Die Preussenreisen des Europäischen Adels* (Sigmaringen 1989) I, 57 for William IV's Prussian journeys.

the 'great feast' in their accounts.[11] The count rode straight from the Hague on the Thursday to another tournament. Tournaments, combined with another journey to Prussia, seem to have occupied most of his time in the years 1344-5.[12] In the spring and summer of 1344, he took part in 'festivals' involving jousting on seven occasions, beginning with the events at the Hague and Beauvais. In June he fought at Brussels; in July he was at Bergen, Laon and Gertuidenberg; and in September he was at Metz. The following year there were two tournaments in April, at Nijvel and Mechelen, and in August he returned to the favourite tourneying site of Haarlem. His death the following month brought to an end a chivalric career which surpassed in enthusiasm even Edward's most spectacular efforts.

Edward himself, enthusiast for chivalry though he was, did not carry his passion to the extremes of his brother-in-law. His enjoyment of jousting was subordinated to much more ambitious schemes. It is the mixture of high politics and personal relationships that makes the event with which Edward brought his series of tournaments to a climax, the Round Table festival of January 1344, such a fascinating moment in his career.

[11] H. G. Hamaker, ed. *De rekeningen der grafelijkheid van Holland onder het Henegouwsche Huis*, Werken uitgegeven door het Historisch Genootschap gevestigd te Utrecht, n.s. 24, 1876, II, 85-88, 207, 333, 335, 338.
[12] Smit, III, 129 for his armourer's journeys with horses for tournaments; several tournaments did not take place, and the count failed to appear on other occasions. Another scholar says that the count 'participated in at least ten tournaments in 1344 and 1345' (Antheun Janse, 'Tourneyers and Spectators' in *The Court as Stage*, ed. Steven Gunn and Antheun Janse, Woodbridge and Rochester, NY, 2006, 44).

The Round Table feast of 1344

Richard Barber

There came to the king the young sons of certain barons, saying, more out of lightheartedness than earnestness, 'Lord king, to spread your fame through tournaments and hastiludes, order a round table in the fashion of king Arthur's court, and the glory of it shall be recorded for all times.'

Bohemian Chronicle[1]

WE ARE FORTUNATE in having what may be a first hand account of the festival at Windsor in January 1344. Edward deliberately invited not only knights, but also wealthy citizens from London. It is Adam of Murimuth, a canon of St Paul's, who describes the occasion for us; he was probably either one of the London contingent, or heard about it from a friend who had been there. What he has to say is this:

> In this year the lord king ordered a most noble tournament or joust to be held in his birthplace, that is at Windsor Castle, on January 19, which he caused to be announced a suitable time in advance both abroad and in England. He sent invitations to all the ladies of the southern part of England and to the wives of the citizens of London. When the earls, barons, knights and a great number of ladies had gathered on the Sunday, January 19, the king gave a solemn feast, and the great hall of the castle was filled by the ladies, with just two knights among them, the only ones to have come from France to the occasion. At this gathering there were two queens, nine countesses, the wives of the barons, knights and citizens, whom they could not easily count, and to whom the king himself personally allocated their seats according to their rank. The prince of Wales, duke of Cornwall, earls, barons and knights ate with all the other people in tents and other places, where food and all other necessities had been prepared; everything was on a generous scale and served unstintingly. In the evening dancing and various entertainments were laid on in a magnificent fashion. For the three

---

[1] *Die Königsaaler Geschichtsquellen*, ed. Johann Loserth, in *Fontes rerum Austriacarum, Scriptores* VIII, Vienna 1875, cap.7.

days following, the king with nineteen other knights held jousts against all comers; and the king himself, not because of his kingly rank but because of his great exertions and the good fortune that he had during the three days, was held to be the best of the defenders. Of the challengers, Sir Miles Stapleton on the first day, Sir Philip Despenser on the second, and Sir John Blount on the third, were awarded the prize. On the following Thursday, after the squires had jousted, the king gave a great feast at which he announced the foundation of his Round Table, and took the oaths of certain lords, barons and knights who wished to be members of it. He fixed the day for the holding of the Round Table as the Whitsun following, and dismissed the company thanking them for all they had done. He afterwards commanded that a most noble building should be built, in which to hold the Round Table on the day assigned, and instructed masons, carpenters and other workmen to carry out the work, providing both wood and stone, and not sparing either labour or expense. This work was later stopped for various reasons.

Another version of Murimuth's chronicle, either a second version by Murimuth himself, or possibly by another hand using Murimuth as a basis, adds considerable detail about the elaborate founding ceremony for the Round Table:

This feast lasted from Sunday to Wednesday. That night, after the end of the jousts, the king had it proclaimed that no lord or lady should presume to depart, but should stay until morning, to learn the king's pleasure. When the morning of Thursday came, at about nine o'clock the king caused himself to be solemnly arrayed in his most royal and festive attire; his outer mantle was of very precious velvet and the royal crown was placed upon his head. The queen was likewise dressed in most noble fashion.The earls and barons, and the rest of the lords and ladies, prepared themselves in appropriate fashion to go with the king to the chapel in the castle of Windsor and hear mass, as he commanded them to do. When mass had been celebrated, the king left the chapel; Henry, earl of Derby, as steward of England, and William, earl of Salisbury, as marshal of England, went before him, each carrying the staff of his office in his hand, and the king himself holding the royal sceptre in his hand. There followed him the young queen, and the queen-mother, the prince of Wales, the earls, barons, knights and nobles, with the ladies and all the people flocking to see such an extraordinary spectacle, to the place appointed for the assembly. There the king and all the others at the same time stood up. The king was presented with the Bible, and laying his hand on the Gospels, swore a solemn oath that he himself at a certain time, provided that he had the necessary means, would begin a Round Table, in the same manner and condition as Arthur, formerly king of England, established it, namely to the number of 300 knights, and would cherish it and maintain it according to his power, always adding to the number of knights. The earls of Derby, Salisbury, Warwick, Arundel, Pembroke, and Suffolk, the other barons and very many praiseworthy knights of probity and renown likewise made an oath to observe, sustain, and promote the Round Table with all its appendages. When this was done, trumpets and drums sounded together, and the guests hastened to a feast, where richness of fare, variety of dishes, and overflowing abundance of drinks were all to be found, to their unutterable delight and inestimable comfort. No murmurs spoilt their enjoyment and no cares troubled their cheerfulness. The occasion finished in the same manner that it had begun. When, on this fifth day, the royal feast was ended, everyone returned to their own affairs. [2]

The spectacular nature of the occasion was duly relayed to Edward's arch-enemy, Philip of France, and a continuation of the official chronicle of the French court gives us the reaction to it. This may have been written by a herald, possibly from St Omer, and ends in 1348, so it is almost contemporary with the event:

Once the King of England had arrived in his country, as stated above, he proclaimed a very big joust at one of his castles called Windsor. Knights came there from all countries in order to gain renown. There he had planned to re-establish the Round Table and the adventures of chivalry, which had not been seen since the days of King Arthur. Yet in his heart he was thinking something quite different, which he did not show on the outside, for all this time he was readying a great fleet, and a establishing a large garrison in one of his ports, called Portsmouth. In the midst of these actions, news came to him that Charles, duke of Brittany, had invaded the land of Brittany; and therefore the aforementioned feast was put off, and he once again sent the Earl of Northampton to Brittany to aid the countess of Montfort. [3]

For the French, this chivalric gathering was simply a smokescreen for Edward's active preparation for the renewal of war, though in fact it was not until March that any active steps were taken towards a new campaign.

Most of the other chroniclers who report the event do so much more briefly, and give us only a few additional details. The English version of the *Brut* chronicle,

---

[2] Murimuth's chronicle exists in three versions: for full texts and translations, see Appendix C.
[3] BN MS Fr. 693, f.254; see Appendix C for text. I am grateful to Professor Clifford Rogers for providing both text and translation.

which like Murimuth had London connections, claims that 'of divers lands beyond the sea, were many strangers'. Edward's letter of protection issued before the feasts and addressed to his officials throughout the kingdom make no mention of overseas participants, referring only to knights and others 'of whatever region or place', but it does seem from the evidence of the *Brut* and St Omer chronicles that there was a large contingent of visitors from the Continent. Thomas Walsingham, writing at St Albans forty years later, a monastery which kept a kind of official royal chronicle in the thirteenth and fourteenth centuries, does not actually mention either the feast or the institution of the knightly order. He writes:

> *A Round Table begun in both kingdoms*
>
> *The Round Table in England*   In the year of grace 1344, which is the eighteenth year of Edward's reign, king Edward summoned many workers to Windsor Castle and began to build a house which was called 'The Round Table'. Its size from the centre to the circumference, the radius, was 100 feet, and its diameter was therefore two hundred feet. The weekly expenses were at first a hundred pounds, but afterwards because of news which the king received from France, this was cut back to nine pounds because he needed a great deal of money for other business.
>
> *The Round Table in France*   At the same time, Philip of Valois, king of France, spurred on by what the king of England had done, began to build a round table in his own country, in order to attract the knights of Germany and Italy, in case they set out for the table of the king of England.

Relatively few other chroniclers mention the event; only those close to the court would have regarded it as special, more than just another lavish court spectacle. Sir Thomas Gray, whose *Scalacronica* presents a knight's view of history rather than the more usual monastic or civic versions, described the feast, but the original is lost, and we only have a brief sixteenth century summary of this part of his text. Jean Froissart, the chronicler of chivalry par excellence, was writing long after the event, like Walsingham, and succeeds in confusing the Round Table feast and the foundation of the Order of the Garter four years later, possibly because he was relying on what he was told by knights from the English court, whose accounts may have been contradictory or may have confused him. He writes as follows:

> At that time, king Edward of England wished and decided to restore and rebuild the great castle of Windsor, which king Arthur founded and built in times gone by, and where the Round Table was first begun and established. And the king made an order of knights consisting of himself and his children and the most valiant men of the land. They

were to be forty in all and were called the *Knights of the Blue Garter*, and their feast each year was to be on St George's day. And to begin that festival, the English king assembled the earls, barons and knights from the whole country, and told them his intention and his great desire to establish the feast, to which they cheerfully agreed. And forty knights were elected there, known and reputed to be the most valiant of all. And they swore an oath of mutual allegiance with the king to hold the feast and to follow the ordinances that had been agreed. And the king founded the chapel of saint George in the castle of Windsor and established and put there canons to serve God, and gave them rents, and provided for them well. And so that the feast should be known in all parts, the English king sent his heralds to publish and announce it in France, Sicily, Burgundy, Flanders, Brabant, Germany and everywhere as far as Lombardy. And he gave fifteen days of safe conduct after the festival to all knights and squires who wished to come. And this festival was to be a joust of 40 knights as defenders with forty squires and it was to be on the next saint George's day, in the year 1344, in the castle of Windsor. And the queen of England was to be there accompanied by three hundred ladies and damsels as her attendants, all noble and gentle women and dressed in similar clothes.

Froissart tells a good story, but it is clear that he has little to contribute to our knowledge of what actually happened in January 1344. His statement that heralds were sent far and wide across Europe seems to agree with Walsingham's information that Philip of Valois established a rival table to lure away Italian and German knights from Edward's feast, the *Brut* chronicler's comment that many strangers came to Windsor, and the St Omer chronicle's account. This great chivalric feast was evidently an international affair.

A much more valuable source of information is the royal accounts. There is relatively little in the records about the preparation for this great gathering, but two telling details do emerge from the archives. Edward had pawned his great crown, second crown and queen Philippa's crown in 1339 when he was desperate for money to pay his allies in Flanders. Such transactions were not uncommon, as jewellery was a form of ready cash or security, but to pawn the great crown as well as two others indicates the seriousness of his situation. In 1343 negotiations had begun for its redemption from the archbishop of Treves and the duke of Guelders, although the principal finance had actually been provided by Vivelin Rufus, a Jew from Strasbourg. It seems to have cost around £8000 to redeem them all.[4] At the end of 1343 the great crown was still in pawn, but by January 16 of the new year, Edward

---

4 Stella Newton, *Fashion in the Age of the Black Prince*, Woodbridge & Totowa, NJ, 1980, 18-20. The pawning seems to have been symbolic rather than related to the value of the crown. A list of crowns and circlets in BL, Additional MS 60584, f.58v., shows the maximum value of any one of the crowns in Edward's possession in 1336 to have been £75.

had his second crown back, just in time to wear it at the festivities at Windsor, and he paid the negotiators handsomely for their efforts.

It also seems that the preparations for the festival were made in a hurry, as if the decision to hold the festival had been made on the spur of the moment. Major tournaments usually involved lavish expenditure on costumes designed for the occasion, as well as gifts of robes. However, special costumes are not mentioned in the accounts, and any gifts of robes were probably included in the traditional Christmas hand-out of robes to courtiers a week or two earlier. We do learn that Edward wore two very expensive suits of red velvet, an exotic import, one long and one short, and consisting of six garments in all. An ermine cloak, for which 369 skins were used, and a smaller mantle of 68 skins, may also have been made for the occasion. At the same time as the suits, 118 tunics for the king's squires, men-at-arms and minstrels were made. The accountants note that seven furriers worked 'at great speed' for three days to complete these.

Despite the haste, these sound like clothes designed to present an image of majesty rather than the theatrical splendours of earlier tournament clothes, embroidered with mottoes and elaborate pictorial designs. Edward was no longer playing the knight errant – he had once fought incognito in an earlier tournament under the command of one of his own knights – but was staking his claim to be regarded as a chivalric monarch on a par with Arthur himself.

The Round Table Building

THE WINDSOR BUILDING ACCOUNTS

Julian Munby

The Building Campaign

Without the building accounts it is doubtful that the story of the Round Table would have gained much credence; it would have remained one of those chronicler's tall stories that can be dismissed by sober historians by pointing out inconsistencies in the records. With the survival of one of the principal accounts, and also its enrolment on the Pipe Rolls, the story has been harder to ignore. We are nonetheless required to explain what exactly we can learn from the accounts in terms of what was built, and how much was achieved before work stopped.

The most important factor in using the accounts is to realize what they can and can't tell us. They were never intended to chronicle the development of the building works, or describe how and where materials and men were employed; they simply provided what we would now call a paper trail of how money had been spent.[1] Not all the records survive, and not all the records can easily be identified. At all stages of work, orders were issued for work and for payments, and a prolonged search through various classes of record (e.g. Issue Rolls of the Exchequer) could doubtless reveal more details of some aspects of the campaign. The records actually kept on site probably included daybooks (like a school register) showing who had been employed and at what rate of pay – such as exist for the building works at Eton College a century later.[2] These and other working accounts were then summarised into rolls of 'particulars' by the clerk of works, and these accounts were returned by him to the Exchequer. The arrangement of the accounts is usually to record income from receipts of cash, then expenditure (in this case week by week), and lastly remaining stock and materials.

---

[1] *History of the King's Works*, I, 51 ff, 188. St John Hope in general printed the enrolled accounts for Windsor and only provided quotations from the particulars. A complete set of particulars for Portchester Castle in the 1390s has been printed in Barry Cunliffe and Julian Munby, *Excavations at Portchester Castle IV: Medieval, the Inner Bailey*, Society of Antiquaries. Research Report xliii, London 1985.

[2] D. Knoop and G.P. Jones, 'The Building of Eton College 1442-1460', *Transactions of the Quattuor Coronati Lodge*, XLVI, 1933, 70-114.

Accounts were often prepared in duplicate, and so it is that we have a surviving counter-roll or duplicate prepared by John Walerand,[3] but only a partial transcript of the main account of Alan of Kilham.[4] Once in the Exchequer, the particulars were then enrolled onto the Great Roll of the Pipe (so called after its method of storage) in a summary form. By this date 'Foreign' accounts (those other than the Sheriffs' accounts) including works accounts were added in a separate section at the back of the Pipe Roll for each year. Valuable as these enrolments are, in the absence of other information, they are clearly less important where the particulars survive (they have here been transcribed to demonstrate the manner in which they were abbreviated[5]).

Organisation and personnel
The Clerk of Works was Alan of Kilham, one of the clerks of the Wardrobe, and the comptroller (i.e. the one who prepared the counter-roll) was Brother John Walerand.[6] The date of their appointment is not known, but they were ordered to account to the Exchequer by a privy seal writ of 12 November 1344.[7]

The craftsmen were led by two figures of national renown. In charge of the masons, and very likely the building's designer, was Master William Ramsey, the king's master mason, builder of St Paul's Chapter House and a leading proponent of the new 'Perpendicular' style.[8] Directing the carpenters was Master William Hurley, the king's chief carpenter, designer of that great feat of engineering, the Ely Octagon.[9] Ramsey was in attendance during most weeks of the operations, and Hurley more intermittently.

Preliminaries
In a fascinating preliminary to the main works, two related activities were undertaken: the first was the strengthening of the castle bridges in late January 1344,[10] and the other was the removal of a stable which seems to have been in the Upper Ward and may well have occupied the intended site of the House of the Round Table.[11]

Skilled workers had to be assembled for the project, and the usual letters patent were issued to the chief carpenter and mason in February 1344 to allow them to gather carpenters and masons to come and work on the castle.[12] Carpenters were to be sought in 'cities, boroughs and other places', but the masons were specifically to be found in Kent, Norfolk and Suffolk, Bedfordshire and Northamptonshire. The

---

[3] Appendix C, doc. 4.
[4] Appendix C, doc. 5. A partial transcript of the lost roll is preserved in the Phillipps papers in the Royal Library.
[5] Appendix C, doc. 3. A draft version has also survived (PRO E101/492/25).
[6] Kilham: T.F. Tout, *Chapters in the Administrative History of Mediaeval England*, Manchester 1928, iv, 110; Walerand may have been from the same family as Robert Walerand, one of the attorneys who acted for Edward I in his absence when he succeeded to the throne in 1272.
[7] Appendix C, doc. 3.
[8] J. Harvey, *English Mediaeval Architects. A Biographical Dictionary Down to 1550*, rev. edn, Gloucester 1984, 242.
[9] Harvey, *English Mediaeval Architects*, 154.
[10] Appendix C, doc. 1.
[11] St John Hope, *Windsor Castle*, I, 122.
[12] Appendix C, docs. 2A (carpenters) and 2B (masons).

Table 2: Windsor Building Accounts for 1344

Week	1	2	3	4	5	6	7	8
	Feb		March				April	
Masons Cutting	15	58	106	128	137	127	1	1
Masons Laying	-	18	64	73	73	41	-	-
Bisham Quarry	-	-	10	12	9	9	-	-
Carpenters	4	8	15	15	14	14	1	1
Smiths	-	3	3	5	5	5	-	-
Labour	17	211	401	193	180	180	12	10
Quarrymen	-	72	121	130	71	63	-	-
Total men	*36*	*370*	*720*	*556*	*489*	*439*	*14*	*12*
Cart days	-	-	-	-	-	-	-	4
Cost	£4 6/8	£22 16/1	£45 4/10	£37 12/5	£34 17/10	£26 5/8	36/8	20/8

Week	9	10	11	12	13	14	15	16	17	18	19
			May					June			
Master (7s)	1	1	1	1	1	1	1	1	1	1	1
4s	1	-	-	-	-	-	-	-	-	-	-
3s	2	2	1	1	1	1	-	1	1	1	1
2s 4d	4	4	4	4	4	4	-	3	4	4	4
2s 3d	2	2	2	2	2	2	-	2	2	2	2
2s	2	2	2	2	2	2	-	2	2	2	2
21d		2	2	2	2	2	-	2	2	2	2
15d	-	-	-	-	-	-	-	-	-	-	-
1s	17	17	-	-	-	-	-	-	-	-	-
11d	-	-	-	-	14	17	-	17	17	17	17
10d	-	-	15	15	-	-	-	-	-	-	-
Total	*29*	*30*	*27*	*27*	*26*	*29*	*-*	*28*	*29*	*29*	*29*
Cart days	18	8	10	10	12	5	-	10½	-	-	9
Cost	56/10	55/11½	53/10	52/4	55/10	51/1	21/7	80/-	45/6	46/11	49/9

Table 2: Windsor Building Accounts for 1344

Week	20	21	22	23	24	25	26	27	28	29	30
	July					Aug				Sept	
Master (7s)	1	1	1	1	2	2	2	2	2	2	2
4s	-	-	-	-	-	-	-	-	-	-	-
3s	1	-	1	1	2	2	2	2	2	2	2
2s 4d	3	3	3	3	3	3	3	3	3	3	3
2s 3d	-	-	-	-	-	-	-	-	-	-	-
2s	2	2	2	2	2	2	2	2	2	2	2
21d	-	-	-	-	-	-	-	-	-	-	-
15d	2	2	2	2	2	2	2	2	2	2	2
1s	4	4	-	-	-	-	-	-	-	-	-
11d	-	-	4	4	4	4	4	4	4	4	4
10d	-	-	-	-	-	-	-	-	-	-	-
Total	*13*	*12*	*13*	*13*	*15*	*15*	*15*	*15*	*15*	*15*	*15*
Cart days	-	-	-	-	-	-	-	-	-	-	-
Cost	27/6	27/6	27/6	28/1	37/2	38/2	37/2	41/2	37/2	37/2	37/2

Week	31	32	33	34	35	36	37	38	39	40	41
			Oct					Nov			
Master (7s)	2	2	2	2	2	2	2	2	2	2	2
Messenger	-	-	-	-	-	-	1	-	-	-	-
Carpenters	-	-	-	-	3	3	3	-	-	-	-
Sawyers	-	-	-	-	-	-	2	2	2	2	-
Roofers	-	-	-	-	-	-	3	3	3	3	3
4s	-	-	-	-	-	-	-	-	-	-	-
3s	2	2	2	2	2	2	-	1	1	1	1
2s 4d	3	3	3	3	3	3	-	-	-	-	-
2s 3d	-	-	-	-	-	-	-	-	-	-	-
2s	2	2	2	2	2	2	-	-	-	-	-
20d	-	-	-	-	-	-	-	3	3	3	-
15d	2	2	2	2	2	2	2	-	-	-	-
1s	-	-	-	-	-	-	-	2	2	2	2
11d	4	4	-	4	4	4	4	-	4	4	4
10d	-	-	-	-	-	-	-	-	-	-	-
9d	-	-	4	-	-	-	-	4	-	-	-
Total	*15*	*15*	*15*	*15*	*18*	*18*	*17*	*17*	*17*	*17*	*12*
Cart days	-	-	-	-	-	-	1	4	3	3	5
Cost	37/2	38/8	36/6	39/11	43/2	43/2	41/8	36/7	37/1	27/1	29/9

craftsmen were to be 'chosen', but carriage (presumably horses and carts) were to be 'taken'[13] by William of Langley in Oxfordshire, Berkshire and Middlesex, while the cargo vessels (shouts) on the Thames were to be 'arrested' by John Knight between London and Windsor.[14] A week later further orders were issued for John Walerand to take any shouts required on the Thames between Gravesend and Henley, William Ramsey was empowered to acquire stone for the works (though not to divert any from churches and abbeys), and the mason Hugh of Kympton was specifically given powers to bring stone from Bedfordshire and Hertfordshire.[15]

Labour

The weekly accounts are mainly concerned with the numbers of workers and their rates of pay (*Table 2, above*). The totals show that the overall number of men involved increased from 36 to 370 in one week in February, with a high point of 720 men employed in the first week of March, and above 400 for the rest of that month. This dropped to 12 men in Easter week, then around 30 through May and June (with a week off at Whitsun in Week 15), around 14 for July through to September, and 16 or 17 men in October and November. The number of different craftsmen is fully recorded for only the first eight weeks of the main account,[16] but thereafter the different trades are not distinguished, only their rates of pay. However, from the information given about wage rates in those first weeks, it can be seen that the workers remaining on the site thereafter must at least have included laying masons and labourers.[17] The masons alone hugely outnumbered the carpenters in the first six weeks of the contract. After that the better paid (at 2s to 3s a week, most likely masons) totalled up to ten in May to June, falling to seven in July to September and five in October, while the lower paid labourers (at 1s or 11d a week) totalled some 15 to 17 in May to June, but down to only four in July to November. It is not possible to guess the number of carpenters, though it is perhaps significant that William Hurley was present on site each week from late July to the end of the contract (weeks 24 – 41).

Expenditure

The overall costs are given on the Pipe Roll, showing that over half was spent on wages, a quarter on materials and the remainder on transport. The Pipe Roll figures are not exactly the same as the totals given on the counter-roll, but have been calculated differently (e.g. the counter-roll has included some transport costs in weekly totals). The overall percentages are reliable and can be compared with the

---

[13] Appendix C, doc. 2C.

[14] Appendix C, doc. 2D. William de Langley was (i) clerk of the household 1324, (Vale, *Edward III*, 49); (ii) receiver of Chamber under Edward II, PRO E361/9, Tout, *Chapters* ii, 344; (iii) sheriff of Kent in 20 Edward III [PRO E358/2 & E358/4]; and (iv) at Dover in 1354, *History of the King's Works*, II 639]; Knight has not been traced.

[15] Appendix C, docs. 2E-G. For Kympton, see Harvey, *English Mediaeval Architects*, 169. For the stone (from Totternhoe), see further below.

[16] Appendix C, docs. 4.1 to 4.8.

[17] That is, mason (cutters) were paid 4s, 3s, 2/6 and below; mason (layers) 2/3, 2/2 and 20d; carpenters, 3s, 2s, 21d.; and labourers 12d or 11d.

Table 3 Total expenditure (Pipe Rolls Totals)

	Account figures	Totals	%
Materials	£108 17s ¼d		
Tiles	£7 6s 8d	£125 5s 1 ¾ d	25%
Tools etc.	£9 1s 5½d		
Carriage	£82 1s 6d	£82 1s 6d	16%
Wages	£254 3s 3½d	£300 11s 3d	59%
Wages	£46 8s		

1390s building campaign at Portchester Castle, where, in a contract three times larger, the materials formed 32% of the cost, transport 13% and wages 55%.[18]

Tools and machinery

The purchase of 'necessaries' is always the most revealing part of the accounts for explaining the building operations.[19] Tools such as mattocks and axes were bought, and equipment like sieves and barrows (made of both planks and hurdles). Iron fittings for wheels and machines were included, while grindstones and 6 sheafs of steel were brought for keeping the masons' tools sharp, and a wooden chimney was built for the smiths' forge. The lime kilns required a certain amount of gear, and the masons had buckets, water carriers and ladles for their work, and also some special fixings for stones of pitch, resin and wax. There were two special items, five fir-poles for measuring the 'hall', and a counting cloth – a chequer board for the accountants to cast their accounts. The Pipe Roll account ends with a list of remaining stock of tools, including 67 barrows.[20]

Lime and Sand

It was customary with large building projects to mix up the mortar close at hand, and work in the lime kiln ('lime pit') and sand pit features throughout the accounts, first as an (unspecified) number of labourers working there, and then in fuel and equipment for making mortar. This included troughs for mixing mortar and bowls and tubs for water, iron rakes and forks used at the lime pits, and provision of hurdles (normally used as planks). A dozen men kept watch by night at the kilns for five weeks, and the storehouse had hooks and hasps, presumably for the doors.[21] A source for the lime may have been 'the quarrie' in the Little Park just east of the castle (see below).

The kilns consumed a large amount of fuel, requiring purchase of ready-prepared bundles of fire wood. Four labourers spent eleven days making 'talwood' [bundles of firewood] and faggots 'for the lime pits',[22] while ready-made purchases from six different individuals included over 4,000 of 'talwood', and a thousand faggots (the comparison in price showing that the faggots were two-thirds the size of

---

[18] J. Munby, 'Documentary sources for building works', in Cunliffe and Munby, *Portchester Castle* IV, 162.
[19] Appendix C, doc. 4.47.
[20] Appendix C, doc. 3.
[21] Appendix C, doc. 4.47.
[22] Appendix C, doc. 4.44.

talwood).[23] In one of the few references to carting wood or timber '1250 of talwood' was brought from Hartley Park to Windsor.[24]

Other craftsmen

Up to five blacksmiths were working in the first few weeks, and doubtless continued thereafter; there are specific references to making or mending tools in July-October,[25] and we have noted above the provision of steel and a chimney for the forge. There is a single reference to a plumber and his mate in the first fortnight of March,[26] but no clue as to what he was fixing. The roofers working in November consisted of the tiler and a team of up to ten men.

Timber felling and transport

The main weekly accounts record that up to fifteen carpenters worked in February and March, though as discussed above the numbers thereafter are very uncertain. It is not even certain where they were working, though from one reference to a carpenter 'within the castle'[27] one might deduce that others were elsewhere, and were felling and converting timber in woods. A separate timber account specifically deals with carpenters working at Bletchingley and Reigate in Surrey in February and March, and at *Holshet* (?Holdshott, Hants) in March and April.[28] There is mostly no indication of the number of trees, though a dozen trees were lopped in the 'Forest of Worth' (Sussex) and at Ruislip (Middlesex),[29] possibly just for fuel wood. A second entry for work at Reigate Park in May to July mentions that it

Table 4 Timber and Wood for the House of the Round Table

Place	Days work	Trees	Carriage
Bletchingley (Surrey)	252 days (Feb – March)		
Reigate (Surrey)	33 days (?Feb/March)		
	91 days (May – July)		
Holshet (Hants?)	242 days (March)		
Worth (Sussex?)	ʹ	12 trees	
Ruislip (Middlesex)	127½ days (March-April)	12 trees	
Easthampstead (Berks)			'timber'
Hartley Park (Bucks)			1250 talwood
[Taplow]		52 oaks	

---

[23] Appendix C, doc. 4.46. For fuel wood see O. Rackham, *Ancient Woodland*, London 1980; and J.A. Galloway, D. Keene and M. Murphy, 'Fuelling the City: Production and Distribution of Firewood and Fuel in London's Region, 1290-1400', *Economic History Review*, NS 49, 3, 1996, 447-472.

[24] Appendix C, doc. 4.47. Hartley Park is most likely Hartley in Cippenham: *VCH Bucks iii*, 1925, 165-84, an ex-royal manor – (cf licence to fell trees in Hartley in 1338).

[25] Appendix C, docs. 4.23, 4.25, 4.32, 4.34.

[26] Appendix C, doc. 4.44.

[27] Appendix C, doc. 4.2.

[28] Appendix C, doc. 4.43. Bletchingley: *VCH Surrey iv*, 1912, 253-65: manor held by Hugh de Audley, Earl of Gloucester. Reigate: *VCH Surrey iii*, 1911, 229-45: manor held by the Countess of Surrey in dower. Holdshot, a manor in Heckfield (Hants) on the Berkshire border, belonged to Merton Priory. *VCH Hants iv*, 1911, 31, 46.

[29] *VCH Middlesex iv*, 1971, 134-7: manor of alien Abbey of Bec, in the king's hands.

was supervised for 21 days by the carpenter William of Winchelsea, who worked at Westminster.[30] Fuel wood purchases have been mentioned above, and the only other entry on the account comes under the heading of 'carriage', and includes an unspecified quantity of timber carried from the royal manor of Easthampsted (Berks),[31] in addition to fuel wood from Hartley Park. It is only from an entirely different source (an exchequer Issue Roll) that we learn that 52 oaks were felled inthe woods of the Prior of Merton (Surrey) near Reading (Berks), presumably in the priory manor of Taplow (Bucks).[32] The Prior was paid for the oaks which had been taken 'for the Round Table at Windsor' and subsequently removed to Westminster for the king's works.

The end use of the timber is problematic. On a more detailed account it might be expected that there would be mention of felling, dressing, sale of bark for tanning, sawing, and carriage of timber. The lack of carriage is telling, and there are relatively few instances of carriage of unspecified materials that could in fact be timber. The other use for the timber, or rather its by-product wood, was to provide fuel, as mentioned above. Some of the timber and labour would have been for scaffolding, which may account for the ten days spent by two sawyers in the castle at the beginning of March.[33] Scaffolds involved poles and hurdles rather than planks; there was also timber centring for vaults and arches, as well as the preparation of doors and window shutters. Two carpenters spent a week working on the well in August,[34] which had a wheel that was repaired,[35] and carpenters were also brought in for the last weeks to assist with roofing the walls (presumably a make-shift roof frame to support the tiles).

The normal building process was for felling, preparation and working of timber in close succession, and then carriage of the pre-fabricated parts to site (as famously happened with Westminster Hall roof in the 1390s, which was first made at Farnham with timber from Alice Holt forest). Unless the intended roof was brought to site in October it may be that the timber elements never got to Windsor, and like the 52 oaks of the Prior of Merton, went on to be used elsewhere.

Was the building complete or usable?

Building work stopped abruptly in November 1344, though not without warning. Tiles had been purchased from Penn (home of the later floor-tile industry), and in November the walls were covered with tiles.[36] This work involved carpenters, so some actual or rudimentary roof must have been constructed. This could simply have covered the 'walls', if they were being roofed against inclement winter weather (just as unfinished walls were often covered with thatch to protect them from

---

30 Appendix C, doc. 4.44. Harvey, *English Mediaeval Architects*, 337.
31 Appendix C, doc. 4.48, *History of the King's Works*, II, 925-7.
32 Appendix C, doc. 6. Taplow:*VCH Berks iii*, 1925, 240-45.
33 Appendix C, doc. 4.44.
34 Appendix C, doc. 4.27.
35 Appendix C, doc. 4.34, 4.47.
36 Appendix C, doc. 4.50.

frost), but the description could equally apply to a vaulted building whose 'walls' were being properly roofed. Just as with the aisle of a cathedral roof a one-bay vault would only require a lean-to roof. From the quantity of tiles purchased (40,000) it can be calculated that an area of 800 square metres could be covered, which would be enough for a lean-to roof of about the size that is envisaged in the reconstruction.[37] Either the work ceased wholly unexpectedly (or was completed), because the quantity of tiles remaining at the end took two men with carts half a day to clear away once a man and a boy had packed them.[38] Since doors had been made for the building, it may actually have been completed as a shell, even if not fully fitted out.

[37] Calculated with a tile 150 x 250mm, with a coverage (=visible overlap) of 200 square cm. With reference to Table 7, p. 125 below, the area of a roof with an outer diameter of 188 ft (57.3 m) and inner diameter of 155 ft (47.24 m) is 8890 square feet, or 826 square metres.
[38] Appendix C, doc. 5.

The Building Stone used for the Round Table

Tim Tatton-Brown

Some insight into the form of the Round Table building can be gained from the accounts of the acquisition of a whole variety of different building stones. Most of the stone was brought to Windsor by the Thames, and on February 24, 1344 we read of a commission 'to arrest on the river Thames between Gravesend and Henley as many cargo vessels ['shouts'] for stone and other necessaries which the King has ordered to be purveyed in divers places along the river for the said works, as shall be required'.[39] This was how the Caen stone, Kentish Ragstone, Reigate stone and Stapleton stone were brought to Windsor from London, and we will look at these materials shortly, and at the bringing of chalk block down river from Bisham.

Totternhoe stone
First, however, we should note that another commission issued on February 24 was for Hugh of Kymton 'to take as required in the counties in Bedford and Hertford sufficient cartage for stone of Eglemound which the King has ordered to be purveyed in those counties for the same works'.[40] This refers to the bringing by ox- or horse-drawn carts overland of Totternhoe stone, the quarries for which lie 28 miles north of Windsor on the edge of Chiltern Hills near Leighton Buzzard.[41] 'Eglemound' (sometimes 'Eglemont' or 'Eglemunt') was probably the name of the motte and bailey castle just above Totternhoe, and it was first being used 'for the work of the King's houses of Windsor' in 1165-70.[42] In the early to mid fourteenth century finely cut Totternhoe stone was chosen for all the main new work at St Albans Abbey like the enlarged Lady Chapel and the middle section of the south side of the nave (which had collapsed in 1323).[43] In the *Gesta Abbatum*, we are told that abbot Michael Mentmore (1335-49) at last 'acquired a large section of the stone quarries at Eglemont',[44] so he may have allowed some of his stone to go to Windsor. By this time the stone must have been coming from the underground quarries (like Reigate – see below), entered by horizontal shafts on the north (scarp) face of the Chilterns. It is worth noting that, in 1358, Edward III's charter to the nearby Dunstable Priory mentions half an acre and half a rod of quarry, 'lying in *le Newequarer de Eglemond in campo del North de Totornho*, of which 1½ rods lay beneath the *forlong* next the quarry of Richard Pour, mason, and one rod lay in

[39] St John Hope, *Windsor Castle*, I, 113 quoting Patent Roll, 18 Edward III, part i m. 34d. Appendix C, doc. 2F.
[40] *Ibid.* Appendix C, doc. 2G.
[41] See *VCH Beds*, I, 1904, 371; III, 1914, 448; E. Roberts, 'Totternhoe stone and flint in Hertfordshire churches', *Mediaeval Archaeology.* 18, 1974, 66-89.
[42] St John Hope, *Windsor Castle*, I, 15 and 20. See also T. Tatton-Brown, 'The Medieval building stones of St Alban's Abbey: a provisional note', in M. Henig and P. Lindley (eds.), *Alban and St Albans, Roman and Medieval Architecture, Art and Archaeology,* Leeds 2002, 118-123.
[43] T. Tatton-Brown, 'The Medieval Building Stones'.
[44] Thomas Walsingham, *Gesta Abbatum Sancti Albani*, ed. H. T. Riley, RS 28, London 1868, II, 361.

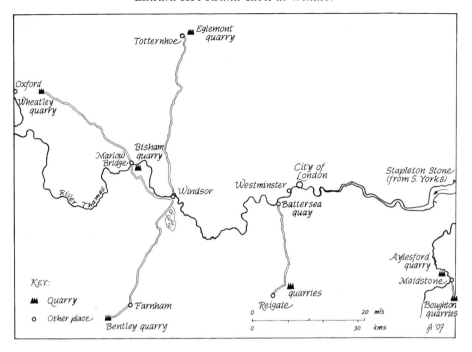

*iii. Map of stone quarries from which stone used for the
House of the Round Table was brought*

Table 5 Stone used for the House of the Round Table

Caen, Normandy	106 gobbetts	
	180 gobbetts	
	100 of measure	
	101 quart' gobbetts*	*or, 100 and one quarter (125)
	150 ft from Kent	
	100 gobbetts	
Caen Marchant	400 small stones	
	50 cune merchant	
	400 1 quart CM	
'Corbels'	27 @ 4d	*Supplied by John Marbler with 150 ft of Caen and the Kent rag*
Kent rag	1800 ft	
Wheatley, Oxon	63 ft of *skues*	
	1000 ft	
Reigate, Surrey	18 stones	
Stapelton, Yorks	67 pieces	
Bentley, Hants??	228 ft	

54

the same field on the hill called *quarehul*.'[45] Much extraction of high quality stone was taking place at Totternhoe immediately after the Black Death, and the records for its use in other royal works give an indication of how it may have been used in the Round Table building. For example 'stone from Eglemont to the value of 10s.' was used for the statue of St Stephen at Westminster in St Stephen's Chapel. It was carved by William Patrington, mason.[46] On August 16, 1355, Thomas of Canterbury, mason, was ordered to buy 20 cartloads of stone of 'Egelmont by Dunstable' for the works of the palace of Westminster, and to 'take carriage for the same'.[47] In 1368-9, at Langley Palace, the bathhouse was paved in Totternhoe stone, and it was used for a fireplace in the King's Chamber.[48]

Of particular interest to Windsor is the record of 100 shillings, paid to Dan. Simon of Swanland on March 3, 1354, 'for a vault of Egremont stones bought in bulk for the treasury [aerary]' at the new college of St George in the Lower Ward. This fine building, above the beautiful 'Porch of Honour' in the Dean's Cloister, still survives, and all the lower internal masonry of the porch is in Reigate stone. For these vault stones, 16s. 6d. was paid for the carriage of the stone from 'Horfelde to Windsor, 12 leagues' (i.e. 36 miles).[49] All of this makes clear that the Totternhoe stone was being used for carved statues, fireplaces, etc., as well as for plain ashlar work, paving and vaulting. One final, and illuminating, record is of the great abbot of St Albans, Thomas de la Mare (1349-96) who 'pulled down the wall of the refectory adjoining the cloister, which was weak and ruinous, and caused it to be supported internally and strengthened with stouter columns cut from large blocks of stone of Egelmounde, as is clear to all who now see it'[50] (but alas, no longer!).

Chalk

Totternhoe stone is a hard form of chalk that occurs in the Lower Chalk stratum, in a bed that is between two and five metres thick.[51] By the fourteenth century, as we have seen, it was highly prized and was considered greatly superior to ordinary chalk. However, it is also clear that much 'ordinary' chalk was also being used in the Round Table building. Windsor Castle is itself famous for being situated on top of an outlier of Upper Chalk that had been cut away on the north of the River Thames, to leave a steep cliff which became the principal northern defence of the castle.[52] Chalk was certainly obtained from quarries in the Little Park (now the Home Park) to the south-east of the castle, and in 1375, when Edward III enclosed 15 acres of land at Uppenore and added them to the park, this was said to include

---

[45] *VCH Beds. iii* (1914), 448.
[46] *History of the King's Works*, I, 521.
[47] *CPR Edward III* (1354-58), 277.
[48] *History of the King's Works*, II, 974.
[49] St John Hope, *Windsor Castle*, I, 150.
[50] *Gesta Abbatum* III, 386, and L. F. Salzman, *Building in England, down to 1540*, Oxford 1952, 399.
[51] M.G. Sumbler, *British Regional Geology: London and the Thames Valley* (fourth edn., Norwich 1996) 83.
[52] Geological Survey of Great Britain, Windsor sheet 269.

'The Quarrie' immediately to the east of the castle.[53] Nevertheless, the accounts for the building of the Round Table tell us that large numbers of men were working in the 'Quarry of Bristlesham'. This was a large quarry, right beside the Thames, which was the nearest alternative source of chalk to Windsor, about 13 miles upstream. Bristlesham is now called Bisham,[54] a village (formerly with a large abbey) half a mile south of Marlow Bridge. The quarry, however, is half a mile east of Marlow bridge on the south side of the river, where there is a sharp bend in the river at the bottom of a steep chalk cliff. A minor road from Marlow Bridge to Cookham runs up the steep hill here, with two 'hairpin' bends, through woodland still called Quarry Wood. One can see traces of the former quarry beside the bend in the Thames where a small stream enters it from the south-west, though modern houses now occupy the area beside the river bank where the shouts would have tied up.

It seems clear from the 1344 accounts that chalk block was being cut and shaped in the quarry in increasing amounts from the second week of work onwards.[55] This chalk block was almost certainly being used for the internal wall faces and core of the masonry walls (i.e. the parts of the wall that would not be exposed to the weather, and would usually be covered by a plaster face and be roofed over). The accounts also list the number of shouts being used to transport the stone from Bustleham to Windsor, at 6s. 8d. each. Many boats are listed as making this journey during the spring, summer and autumn of 1344.[56]

Caen stone

We are also told that 'divers stones both of Caen and Kentish rag and of Whateley' were brought to Windsor for the work. Caen stone was being brought into south-eastern England in very large quantities from soon after the Norman Conquest. It was then used throughout the Middle Ages for many fine buildings, like Canterbury Cathedral,[57] and its use in London was very common by this time. A number of large institutions were stockpiling it to use in their own building work. Hence we find that a large quantity of Caen stone, worth £40, was bought for the Round Table building from the dean of St Pauls, as well as from Richard of Colchester and William of Abbotsbury. Walter Harrard also supplied '106 gobets of Caen stone bought in the same place', worth £3 3s.[58] All this Caen stone must have been in a yard in London, where it could easily have been taken to the Thames for shipment up river in a shout. Gobbetts is a fairly common term for the large rough blocks both of Caen stone, sent from Normandy, and of Kentish rag.

---

[53] Roberts, *Royal Landscape*, 137. The quarry at Windsor is mentioned in 1344 (St John Hope, *Windsor Castle*, 118) but it was probably only being used for lime.

[54] Gelling, *Place-Names of Berkshire*, I, 59-61. Bisham is in Berkshire, while all the land north of the river is in Buckinghamshire.

[55] St John Hope, *Windsor Castle*, I, 114-115.

[56] Appendix C, doc. 4.49.

[57] T. Tatton-Brown, 'La Pierre de Caen en Angleterre' in M. Baylé (ed.) *L'Architecture Normande au Moyen Age*, Caen 1997, 305-14, and Salzman, *Building in England*, 135-7.

[58] Appendix C, doc 4.45.

The accounts also mention quite large quantities of stone (over 900 stones) called 'Cune Marchant' being brought in three ships from 'the parts of Caen'.[59] St John Hope suggested these might be 'stepping quoins', but it is perhaps more likely that they were a form of paving.[60] They could also have been used for large steps.

Kentish rag

This was sent up the Medway to the Thames from the Kentish ragstone quarries around Maidstone.[61] Kentish ragstone, often called the 'hard stone of Kent,' was commonly used at this time, for large plinth blocks and for major quoins, but by the fourteenth century it was also being carved for a whole mass of other uses like window tracery, moulded doorways and windows, and ashlar work.[62] When the nave of Canterbury Cathedral was being rebuilt from 1377 most of the external dressings were made with Caen stone, but the plinth and the external buttresses were largely constructed with long blocks of Kentish ragstone.[63] Other specialist uses for Kentish ragstone were as stringcourses, and for the large corbel blocks that supported fireplaces and internal floor-joists. The 1344 accounts mention '150 feet of quoins from the parts of Kent' and 27 corbels at 4d. each.[64] It seem likely that at the Round Table building in Windsor, Caen stone was also the main external decorative facing material, with Kentish rag being used for plinths, buttresses, corbels and stringcourses. Any spiral staircases are likely to have used large wedge-shaped blocks of Kentish rag for the newel stones, while the plain ashlar work was perhaps of Totternhoe stone, Caen stone and some Reigate stone (see below). A similar combination of materials can be seen in the outer face of the Warden's House (now Deanery) and Knights' Chapter House in the east cloister walk of the Dean's Cloister at Windsor, which was being built in the early 1350s.[65]

Wheatley stone

There is also a passing reference to 'stones of Whately'. This is Wheatley stone from quarries just east of Oxford, a fine shelly limestone that was commonly used in and around Oxford as a 'freestone' until the later fourteenth century. After this Headington stone and Taynton stone were more commonly used.[66] Wheatley stone

---

[59] Appendix C, doc. 4.45.

[60] St John Hope, *Windsor Castle*, I, 116.

[61] Salzman, *Building in England*, 135. He also records, in 1320, the purchase at Westminster of '50 gobettes of Caen stone and also long gobettes of Aylesford stone (i.e. Kentish rag), chosen and worked for the flying buttress (*archibuterasio*) which stands in the Thames'.

[62] B. C. Worssam and T. Tatton-Brown, 'Kentish Rag and other Kent building stones', *Archaeologia Cantiana*, 112, 1993, 93-125.

[63] T. Tatton-Brown, 'The Rebuilding of the nave and western transepts, 1377-1503' in K. Blockley, M. Sparks and T. Tatton-Brown, *Canterbury Cathedral Nave, Archaeology History and Architecture*, Canterbury 1997, 128-146.

[64] Appendix C, doc. 4.45.

[65] T. Tatton-Brown, 'The Deanery, Windsor Castle', *Antiquaries Journal*. 78 (1998), 345-390. See especially 349, fig. 3.

[66] E. M. Jope, 'The archaeology of Wheatley stone' in W.O. Hassall (ed.), *Wheatley Records, 956-1956*, Oxon Record Society, 37, 1956, 17-26.

can best be seen in the early work at Merton College chapel (particularly in the four crossing arches) of the late thirteenth/early fourteenth century and the accounts there show that the stone was being cut and dressed in the Wheatley quarries before cartage to Oxford. At Windsor we read of 63 feet of 'skues de Whatele' and 1000 feet of Wheatley stone at 1¼d. per foot.[67] The Wheatley skews are probably 'skew ashlar' a term commonly used in the fourteenth and fifteenth centuries for ashlar cut at an angle to use, for example, in battered plinths.[68] All this Wheatley stone was taken overland to Windsor in 116 carts 'on 30 turns' at a cost of £8 and 6d.,[69] and it is worth noting that large quantities of Wheatley stone, along with Taynton and Reigate stone, were used in the rebuilding of Edward III's great palace, and other buildings in the Upper Ward of the castle, after the Black Death.

Reigate and Bentley stone
Reigate stone is only briefly mentioned in 1344, William Abbot was paid £1 10s. for 98 'petris de Raygate',[70] but its use at Windsor Castle was very common indeed, from the twelfth to the fourteenth centuries.[71] Much Reigate stone can still be seen in the castle, but this fairly soft glauconitic sandy limestone was only used internally from the fifteenth century. The new St George's Chapel, for example, which was built from 1475 onwards, uses Taynton stone (and some Caen stone) for the external masonry, while inside we find much Reigate stone, along with Taynton and Caen. In the mid-fourteenth century some Reigate stone was still being used externally, but its most common use was for the ashlar and the beautiful carved masonry inside major buildings. The finest surviving use of Reigate stone at Windsor is for the exceptionally fine early Perpendicular vault and the blind tracery in the side walls of the the 'Porch of Honour' built beside the Dean's Cloister in 1353-54, just a decade after the Round Table.[72] It seems likely that in 1344 only a small quantity of Reigate stone was used, but it is not possible to suggest for what purpose.

Reigate stone comes from the Upper Greensand just below the North Downs some 16 or so miles south of London (it was carted over the Downs to the wharves beside the Thames at Battersea and Kingston[73]). Thirty miles west of the Reigate quarries, on the same geological outcrop of Upper Greensand (and at the extreme north-west corner of the Wealden Basin), is the village of Bentley (near Farnham), which also had small areas of stone quarries.[74] The 1344 accounts mention 233 feet of Bentley stone, at 4s. 6d. per hundred, bought from Robert

[67] Appendix C, doc. 4.45.
[68] Salzman, *Building in England*, 104.
[69] Appendix C, doc. 4.48.
[70] Appendix C, doc. 4.45.
[71] See T. Tatton-Brown, 'The quarrying and distribution of Reigate stone in the Middle Ages', *Medieval Archaeology* 45, 2001, 189-201.
[72] J.A.A. Goodall, 'The Aerary Porch and its influence and its influence on Late Medieval English vaulting' in Saul, *St George's Chapel*, 165-202.
[73] T. Tatton-Brown 'The quarrying of Reigate stone', 193-4.
[74] Large quantities of Bentley stone were used for the Bishop of Winchester's castle at Farnham.

le Hore, but once again it is not possible to say what exactly the stone was used for.[75]

Stapleton stone

One other type of stone is mentioned briefly in the 1344 accounts, Stapleton stone. We read that £7 10s. was paid to William of Wighthill 'for 67 pieces from the parts of Stapleton coming to London in a ship, weighing 20 loads, for each by weight 5s.'.[76] Stapleton stone was one of the many types of Magnesian limestone quarried in South Yorkshire, which were not only being used locally (in York and neighbouring areas), but were also taken down the river Ouse to the Humber estuary, and then southwards by sea to London.[77] Stapleton and Huddlestone quarries are well-documented in the fourteenth century, and it is clear that much stone from these quarries was being stockpiled in London during the fourteenth and the fifteenth centuries, for use at Westminster Abbey, the Tower of London, and many lesser buildings. It was also being taken to Canterbury in the early fifteenth century for the rebuilding of the south-west tower of the cathedral,[78] and to Rochester castle in 1367-69.[79] Huddlestone and Stapleton stone were also being used at Windsor Castle and Eton College at this period, as well as at Sheen Palace in Surrey.[80] The Magnesian limestone is a very hard freestone, and it was ideal for use in plinths. It can still be seen in the plinth of the great gatehouse at St Alban's Abbey, with a moulded plinth of Kentish ragstone above it. Magnesian limestone is also used for the basal course (with Totternhoe stone above it) of the fine processional doorway from the south-east corner of the abbey nave into the cloister.[81] Another possibility to be considered is that the number of these stones (67) is close to 64 (i.e. 2 x 32, or 4 x 16), which could possibly relate to the number of large capitals or bosses required for the vault or arcade of the building if reconstructed in the manner proposed here (see pp. 121, 125 below).

Purbeck marble

Sadly there is no trace on the accounts of the use of Purbeck marble, such as would have been used for the table itself, though 'John the marbler' was one of the stone suppliers.[82]

---

[75] Appendix C, doc. 4.45. The Bentley stone is geologically slightly different from Reigate stone; it is more calcareous, harder and known locally as malmstone. The two types could be distinguished if found by excavation.

[76] Appendix C, doc. 4.45.

[77] E. Gee, 'Stone from the medieval limestone quarries of South Yorkshire', in *Collectanea Historica, Essays in memory of Stuart Rigold*, Maidstone 1981, 247-55.

[78] At Canterbury and Westminster Abbey it is also called the 'Northern stone' for obvious reasons. See T. Tatton-Brown, 'Building stone in Canterbury, c.1070-1525' in D. Parsons (ed.) *Stone, quarrying and building in England AD43-1525*, Chichester 1990, 70-82.

[79] Some building accounts for 1367-69 at Rochester castle are transcribed in *Archaeologia. Cantiana*, 2, 1859, 111-132.

[80] Gee 'Stone from the limestone quarries', 251-55.

[81] Tatton-Brown 'The Medieval Building Stones', 121.

[82] John the Marbler may have been the London marble supplier John Ramsey III, who was operating in the 1340s, Blair, 'Purbeck Marble' in J. Blair and N. Ramsay, *English Medieval Industries*, London 1991, 46.

THE ARCHAEOLOGY OF THE UPPER WARD QUADRANGLE AND THE EVIDENCE FOR THE ROUND TABLE BUILDING [83]

Richard Brown

Prior to the investigation in August 2006, the Windsor Castle Upper Ward has only ever been archaeologically examined during the rescue excavations carried out after the fire of 20th November 1992 by English Heritage. Although a drawing supplied by the Royal Household before the Time Team excavation showed multiple services crossing the site and a substantial subway/service corridor cutting north-south through the eastern quarter of the site, none of this modern work had been accompanied by formal archaeological or geotechnical recording. The underlying geology is that of the castle in general, described in Chapter One; 'clay with flints' in pockets over Upper Chalk bedrock underlies the central part of the quadrangle, but there had been little opportunity to study the depth and contours of these natural levels, or of the depth and character of the deposits which overlay it.

The investigation area in the Upper Ward was for practical purposes defined by the limits of the central grassed area, which measures some 92m east-west and 42m north-south. The surface of the grassed area slopes gradually from east to west and from north to south. The location of trenches was also constricted due to the number of service ducts below the turf.

Residual prehistoric and Roman artefacts have been retrieved in excavations and watching briefs across the entire Castle site and these imply early occupation of the bluff. The site's topographical dominance of the surrounding landscape and any possible river crossing at Windsor would certainly be a good location for an Iron Age hillfort or Roman fortification, but no structural evidence of such activity has yet been found. It is not clear whether the substantial twelfth-century curtain wall represents the primary enclosure of the Upper Ward, or whether there was some earlier fortification. Whichever is the case, the area's situation on the chalk bluff adjacent to the Round Tower implies the possibility that archaeological evidence for activities such as temporary occupation structures, industrial processes (lime kilns, saw pits, metal working) and stabling, as well as features related to tournaments and festivities, could exist under the Quadrangle.

The earliest detailed documentary indication of activity in the Upper Ward Quadrangle is the most enigmatic, namely the records concerning the creation of the *domus tabulae rotundae*, or 'House of the Round Table'. W. H. St John Hope dedicates a chapter to the construction of the Round Table in the first volume of his classic work on the castle, in the course of which he details all known accounts of the works. Hope suggested the Upper Ward as the location of the structure, partially on

---

[83] The full technical report on the archaeology of the site can be found in Appendix A, with detailed references to source material.

4. *The Upper Ward during excavations*

the basis of its given dimensions but also in relation to accounts for strengthening of the bridges – in the plural – for transport of construction materials; this can only be explained in the context of the need for access to the Upper Ward. The case for the Upper Ward as the location of the Round Table Building was made in more detail by Julian Munby in his paper on Edward III's carpentry published in 2005.

The next available evidence for potential archaeological remains in the central area of the Upper Ward is given by the Eton view of the Castle, dating from 1445-50. This sketch depicts a circular structure, possibly with a square base, in the centre of the area. This may be a precursor of the fountain head on which work for provision of a 'new' water supply had commenced in 1551. The fountain was fed from a source in Blackmore Park and lead pipes were laid for this purpose; the work had eventually been completed with the installation of an ornate fountain head in 1555. Hope gives a detailed description of the fountain head based on Norden's 1607 birds-eye view of the castle and the plans prepared by the surveyor Henry Hawthorne. The water supply to this fountain head seems to have required much subsequent attention. Rehabilitation of the conduits, cisterns and pipework was carried out in 1609 and 1611. In 1629, commissioners found it beyond repair, and a proposal for its reconstruction was drawn up, but this was cancelled in 1635. After the theft of the lead pipes and fittings from the conduit head in 1649 the water supply was declared useless and orders were given in 1650 for the lead pipe to be dug up and used in maintenance works around the castle. Wenceslas Hollar's bird's-eye view of the castle published in 1672 shows the central part of the Upper Ward to be empty.

A brass equestrian statue of Charles II was commissioned in 1679, and this was positioned in the centre of the Upper Ward the following year. At some point, probably during the eighteenth century, landscaping and a more formal arrangement of pathways within the quadrangle was introduced in order to enhance the setting of the statue. These features do not appear in the 1711 view of Windsor Castle in

Kip's '*The Duke of St Alban's House at Windsor with a view of Windsor Castle from the South*', but W. H. Pyne's 1819 '*View of the Round Tower from the east*' appears to show something of this kind.

The extensive works carried out for George IV and his successors by Sir Jeffry Wyatville between 1824 and his death in 1840 included substantial remodelling of the Upper Ward. Two 'Grand Corridors' were constructed, running adjacent and parallel to the southern and eastern apartments and the State Entrance Tower was built. A list of Wyatville's works completed up to 1830 includes 'lowering the courtyard from three to six feet; removed 13,000 cube yards'. While at first glance this seems to imply severe truncation of the quadrangle, 13,000 cubic yards spread across the area of the Quadrangle (prior to Wyatville) gives an average of 2½ feet across the area. This would mean that if some areas were reduced by six feet other parts may not have been reduced at all. In addition a site visit carried out in the early days of the project showed that the grand corridors are cut to about two metres below ground, and this could account for much of the removed material.

Another possible indicator of the extent of Wyatville's truncation of the Quadrangle is an aerial photograph taken by the Ministry of Defence in 1964. Here the base of the Charles II statue can be seen as a parch mark and the surrounding grassed area shown in Pyne's 1819 view is visible as it is outlined by parch marks presumably caused by the surrounding pathways. This suggested that truncation of the ground levels caused by Wyatville's work was not sufficient to remove the entire depth of either the statue foundations or the paths.

There is anecdotal evidence of a later nineteenth century water tank in the centre of the Upper Ward quadrangle, which appears to have been confirmed by the geophysical survey.

Before the current excavations began, a geophysical survey had been carried out on the area by GSB Prospection Ltd during the early part of June 2006. This was needed to provide information as a background to the proposal for 'intrusive' investigation. A graphic interpretation of the results of this is shown as Plate XII. The geophysical investigations combined gradiometry, resistance and ground penetrating radar surveys across the entire lawned area of the Upper Ward. This successfully mapped a number of modern buried services and defined the extent of a subway/service corridor.

The survey, in particular the ground penetrating radar, identified a number of anomalies of possible archaeological interest. The most promising was a curving response in the south-east corner of the lawn (L on the geophysical survey results). A second curving response at the western edge of the lawn (F on the geophysical survey results) is presumably associated with the Round Tower moat or the ditch around the original motte and shows what may be structural features. There was an unusual response in both the resistance and ground penetrating radar data in the centre of the lawn (H on the geophysical survey results) which may be a former path or roadway as shown in W. H. Pyne's 1819 view, and may possibly be the cause of the parch marks seen on the 1964 aerial photograph. A presumed water tank

(B on the geophysical survey results) was located in the centre of the lawn. Several other anomalies which appeared to indicate archaeological remains (geophysical survey results – G, D, I, J and K) were also recorded.

The archaeological investigation consisted of excavating three trenches, each three metres wide and five metres long, based on plans prepared in advance, in the light of the geophysical survey. After machine excavation of the topsoil, the trenches were dug in accordance with a project design approved by English Heritage.

Trench 1 focused on a geophysical anomaly that was proved to be the original foundations of the equestrian statue of Charles II. Because this occupied a large part of the targeted area, it was only possible to examine the underlying sequence at the west end of the excavation. The lowest layer, a dark silt accumulation, yielded a sherd of pottery dated to the eleventh/twelfth century. Above this, a series of chalky silt levelling deposits were sealed by a compacted chalk surface. Just below this chalk surface, mid-thirteenth/fourteenth century pottery and small fragments of tile (including a plain unglazed peg tile) were found. These ceramic finds support the interpretation which we made on site, that the section represented a floor preparation surface related to Edward III's Round Table building.

The base of the Charles II statue overlaid this floor surface. It consisted of flagstones laid on a compacted rubble surface, incorporating a brick-built drain. A fourteenth century Penn tile (presumably disturbed from elsewhere) had been mortared to the brick drain. The statue of Charles II was moved to the west side of the courtyard near the base of the Round Tower during Wyatville's work in the Upper Ward. When Wyatville reshaped the Quadrangle, a layer of rubble was deposited over the statue base in the process of landscaping the area.

In Trench 2, it was possible to investigate the full archaeological sequence. The lowest layer was the expected natural clay with flints, and above this was a thick dark clay silt accumulation about half a metre deep. A 100 litre bulk sample was retrieved from this silt, and when sieved proved to contain worked flint, burnt flint, bone, abraded prehistoric pottery and pottery dating to the eleventh/twelfth century. The character of the deposit suggested that it had built up via a gradual accumulation derived from organic decay and frequent (but small-scale) midden dumping. The homogeneous nature of the deposit suggested constant re-working of the soil through animal/human trample and weathering. These two layers probably represent the total depth of soil deposition from the end of the last glacial period to the time of the building works in the fourteenth century.

As in Trench 1, the silt accumulation was overlain by a series of silty-chalk levelling deposits which are likely to represent the activities of ground levelling and floor preparation for the internal part of the Round Table building. These were hand excavated and contained mid thirteenth/fourteenth century pottery and medieval tile (as well as some very worn fragments of Roman tiles).

At either end of Trench 2 brick-built conduits had been cut into the chalky levelling layers. These were covered by the same levelling-up rubble from Wyatville's work that was found above the chalk layers in the centre of the trench.

In Trench 3 we were able to record the full archaeological sequence. The dominant feature was a robber trench, where foundations had been dug out. At the base of this, the natural clay with flints was revealed. The upper edges of the robber trench showed weathering to the natural clay, while deeper within the base of the robber trench, patches of chalk bed rock were apparent. Above the clay and chalk layers, there was a dark silt accumulation, similar to those revealed in Trenches 1 and 2. Three shallow sub-circular features were cut into the silt in the central-west part of the trench; these were filled entirely with lime-rich mortar.

Above these features, and above the silt, there was a compacted chalk surface in the western part of the trench. To the east of the trench a sequence of silty chalk levelling layers overlay the silt accumulation. In the centre of the trench, the chalk surface and levelling layers were separated by a substantial (2.5m wide, 1.75m deep) vertical-sided, flat-based robber trench which was orientated north-east to south-west This was filled with loose sands and rubble tip layers. Two sherds of mid-thirteenth/fourteenth-century pottery were retrieved from these fills, and 21 stone fragments were retained for petrological analysis.

The upper level of the robber trench was cut to the north of the trench by a land drain. This in turn was overlain by the nineteenth century levelling rubble deposit found in the other two trenches.

Conclusions

The archaeological investigations have shown that man-made levels about two metres in depth survive in the centre of the Upper Ward Quadrangle. Undisturbed natural clay with flint deposits probably undulates in level across the site and drops off towards the edge of the bluff. A re-worked silt accumulation was apparent in all the trenches. This overlies the natural geology, and contains abraded prehistoric pottery and Roman building material as well as medieval pottery. These results show that further features and structures spanning these dates could also exist within the area of the quadrangle at these levels.

The upper part of the sequence shows the nineteenth-century truncation of the medieval and post medieval levels, followed by rubble and dumping relating to Wyatville's programme of works during 1824-40. This part may be of little intrinsic interest; however, the survival of the seventeenth-century flagstone statue base in Trench 1 shows that isolated earlier structures may exist close to the surface.

The finds retrieved from the investigation were sparse, as would be expected from such a small-scale excavation, and serve mainly to support the chronological interpretation and characterisation of the archaeological deposits.

The large curving robber trench in Trench 3 and the associated evidence for levelling and floor preparation recorded in all the trenches are without doubt the remains of Edward III's Round Table building. This is supported by pottery dates, architectural fragments and the broad arc of the foundation that is visible on the geophysical survey results. Little can be inferred from the depth of the robber trench; it is, as would be expected, cut deep enough to allow foundation of the structure on the natural bedrock. However, the width of the trench (2.5m) does indicate a structure of sufficient size to support a building of some height or more than one storey. The floor preparation layers seen in all trenches imply landscaping to create a level and durable surface for the centre of the building. Since this 'floor platform' is not reflected in the existing surface contours of the courtyard, the gentle slopes that now exist in the Quadrangle are likely to be the result of Wyatville's work. This means the extent of survival of the remains of the Round Table building may vary greatly across the site, with possibly greater survival to the north and east of the investigations.

The investigation has succeeded in defining the location and survival of the archaeology of the Round Table and confirming the integrity of the documentary evidence. There is still much to learn of its architectural form and function but perhaps it is suitable that such a long standing enigma does not relinquish its archaeological secrets too rapidly.

II

THE IDEA OF THE ROUND TABLE

What was a Round Table?

Richard Barber

KING ARTHUR and the Round Table are so inseparably linked in our ideas about the Arthurian legend today that it comes as a surprise to find that the Round Table is not part of the earliest accounts of Arthur. It does not appear in the Welsh stories, and Geoffrey of Monmouth, whose *History of the Kings of Britain* created an international audience for the Arthurian legends, tells us nothing about it. Arthur is a straightforward royal figure, a king who wins an empire for himself. He has close companions, particularly his nephew Gawain, and loyal followers. He restores order to Britain before embarking on his career of conquest in Europe, but there is nothing out of the ordinary about him except the mystery of his death.

The Round Table is first mentioned in about 1155 in a free translation of Geoffrey of Monmouth's work into Norman French, some twenty years after the original had appeared. The poet, Robert Wace, came from the Channel Islands, and wrote the *Roman de Brut* for Henry II's court. Wace tells us how Arthur established a new type of seating arrangement at his court which was intended to avoid the quarrels which arose when there was a clear place of honour, at the king's right hand, and the status of an individual was judged by how closely he was placed to the king. Arthur withdraws from the main table in his own hall, and replaces it by the Round Table:

> Never did one hear of a knight who was in any way considered to be praiseworthy, who would not belong to his household, if it were possible to have him. If he wished to serve for recompense, nonetheless he never left to gain recompense. For the noble barons he had, each of whom felt that he was superior [to the rest] – each one believed himself to be the best, and nobody could tell the worst – King Arthur, of whom the Britons tell many stories, established the Round Table. There sat the vassals, all of them at the head of the table, and all equal. They took their places at the table as equals. None of them could boast that he was seated higher than his peer. All were seated in the place of honour, and none was at the far end. At this table sat Britons, Frenchmen, Normans, men from Anjou, Flanders, Burgundy and Lorraine.[1]

---

[1] Beate Schmolke-Hasselmann, 'The Round Table: Ideal, Fiction, Reality', *Arthurian Literature* II, 1982, 48.

5. Arthur seated as the equal of his knights at the Round Table
mural from Schloss Runkelstein, Italy, c.1400, illustrating the romance of Garel

At the outset, the Round Table was therefore the answer to a political problem, and it reflected the difficulties that Henry II had had at the beginning of his reign. He had inherited a kingdom torn apart by civil war and the rivalry of great lords, and had imposed order on it. But just as Arthur's fame came in the end, not from his place in the supposed history of Britain, but from his image as a paragon of the new ideas of chivalry, so the Round Table too was transformed into a chivalric institution. The new romances written at the end of the twelfth century about Arthur and his knights drew on the idea that knighthood, originally simply a form of reward for military service, had a wider symbolic meaning, a meaning which sprang at once from the church's anxiety to control this potentially lawless class and from the new courtly culture which emerged at this time, with its emphasis on the cult of the lady and the possibility of romantic love.

The Round Table is mentioned by all the early writers of romance; it begins as an incidental part of Arthur's court, as in the writings of Chrétien de Troyes, where Arthur is the central but rather nebulous figure around whom the world of his heroes revolves. Here, as in Wace's *Brut*, the knights of Arthur's court are referred to as 'ces de la Table Reonde' – those of the Round Table – on three occasions, and there is a similar reference in the poems of Marie de France, a contemporary of Chrétien. In these early romances, the Round Table is no more than a synonym for Arthur's court, with no idea of specific membership or specific rules; it is Arthur's court, rather than the Round Table itself, which is home to the best knights in the world.

However, the poets are also interested in the Round Table as an object, and in its symbolic meaning. One of the few recorded physical round tables of the period belonged to Roger II of Sicily; but this was a silver table, engraved with the mapping of the cosmos carried out by the philosopher Edrisi. It was made in 1154. Now one romance, Béroul's *Tristan*, tells us that the Round Table 'turns like the world', which might imply some connection with this cosmic table. A variation on this symbolic table is the description in the Middle English translation of Wace's poem which makes the Round Table both portable and able to seat sixteen hundred knights, in other words a kind of magic object. Layamon, who produced this translation in about 1200, is the first writer to tell us how the table was made. Arthur's wish for equality among his knights is caused by a fracas, which Arthur has to quell by force, at a feast in London. After this, he goes to Cornwall, where a carpenter comes to him and says:

> 'I heard that there was news from overseas that your knights began to fight as they sat down to eat, and many fell on that midwinter's day. Their pride led to murder, because each thought his lineage meant that he deserved the highest place. But I will make you the fairest of tables, which will seat sixteen hundred or more, so that none will have precedence; they will be equal, man to man. And when you travel, you will be able to carry it and set it up wherever you want. You need never fear, to the ends of the world, that any dissatisfied knight will quarrel there, because the greatest will be equal with the least'
>
> So wood was brought, and the table was begun; and in four weeks the work was completed.[2]

Robert de Blois, writing in the mid-thirteenth century describes the Round Table in rather different terms. It is not made of wood, but of precious materials: he gives the same reasons for its creation as Wace, but the table itself is made 'not of pine or *erauble*, but of crystal banded with gold, and was surrounded with all kinds of precious stones, the most sought-after and expensive'.[3]

The concept of the Round Table becomes more elaborate in later versions of the Arthurian romances, beginning with the work of Robert de Boron in about 1200. The Round Table is established by Merlin for Uther Pendragon, though it is not called by its familiar name at this point. Merlin tells Uther that two tables had been established by Christ, that of the Last Supper, and that of the Grail, in memory of the Last Supper. Uther should set up a third table, in honour of the Trinity. He agrees, and Merlin establishes it at Carduel in Wales, selecting fifty knights who are

---

[2] *Laȝamon: Brut*, ed. G.L. Brook and R.F. Leslie, London 1978, EETS OS 277, II, ll.11428-41.
[3] Robert de Blois, *L'Enseignement des Princes*, ll.1180-1236, in John Howard Fox, *Robert de Blois: son oeuvre didactique et narrative*, Paris 1950.

to sit at it. At the end of the inaugural feast, the knights tell the king that they have no wish to leave the table, and say that while 'some of us have never seen each before, yet now we love one another as sons love their fathers': the table has the power of creating this fraternal love.[4] Later, when Arthur comes to the throne, Merlin tells him of the background to what he now calls the Round Table:

> 'Your father was a most worthy man, and in his time the Round Table was established, which was made to symbolise the table at which Our Lord sat on the Thursday when He said that Judas would betray him. It was made, too, as a reference to the table of Joseph of Arimathea, which was established for the Grail, when the good were separated from the wicked.'

Merlin goes on to explain that Arthur will conquer Rome, 'but first you must be sufficiently worthy and valiant to enhance the glory of the Round Table'. He declares that the Table 'will be greatly exalted, and throughout the world people will speak of the fine chivalry which in your time will assemble there'.[5] The Round Table is part, therefore, of the pre-ordained sequence of events which leads from the Crucifixion to the accomplishment of the quest for the Grail, a secular successor to the holiest of all tables, that of the Last Supper. It has become more than a symbol of the equality of knights; it stands for the highest aspirations of chivalry as a secular equivalent to the priesthood, and it is repeatedly said to be the home of the best knights in the world. In the fullest version of the story of Arthur, the so-called *Lancelot-Grail* or Vulgate Cycle, Perceval learns from a holy recluse, his aunt, the story of the three tables, in what amounts to a sermon on the holiness and symbolism of these sacred objects. She ends by telling him:

> After the Table of the Holy Grail there came the Round Table, established according to Merlin's advice, and laden with symbolic meaning. The name Round Table signifies the round shape of the earth and the disposition of the planets and other elements in the firmament where one sees stars and other heavenly bodies. One can thus rightly assert that the Round Table represents the world. You can see that to the extent that knights come to the Round Table from any country where chivalry exists, whether Christian or pagan. If God grants them the privilege of becoming a member of the Round Table, they consider themselves more fortunate than if they controlled the whole world. They abandon their fathers, mothers, wives and children for it. You yourself have seen this happen. Ever since you left your mother and became a member of the Round Table, you have felt no

---

[4] *Merlin and the Grail: the trilogy of Arthurian Romances attributed to Robert de Boron*, tr. Nigel Bryant, Arthurian Studies XLVIII, Woodbridge & Rochester, NY, 2001, 93.

[5] *Merlin*, 112-113.

desire to return but have been overcome instead by the tenderness and fraternity that exists among these companions.[6]

It is in these prose romances, which for the first time tell the whole story of Arthur's reign and integrate the quest for the Holy Grail into that story, that we encounter the Round Table as both an object and a clearly defined institution within Arthur's court. In these lengthy accounts of the deeds of Arthur and his knights, known to scholars as the *Lancelot-Grail*, the Table becomes a society or company with a limited and defined membership and at the same time the physical object where those members assemble. The number of knights is repeatedly given as one hundred and fifty, and they are called members or companions of the Round Table.[7] They are bound to each other by certain conditions; there is evidently an oath which they swear on admission to the company, though the terms of it are never precisely spelled out, and we only gather from passing references what these conditions might be. They are in general not very different from the behaviour expected of any member of the order of knighthood, which the Lady of the Lake explains to Lancelot before he is knighted, such as the obligation to help women in distress. 'For when King Arthur seated you at the Round Table, you swore, in your first oath, that you would never fail to help a young woman who asked for assistance.'[8] Nor should they attack knights who do not wish to fight.[9] There is an underlying ethical attitude which may seem surprising in view of the fierce pride in their status which is a hallmark of the knights – 'they say that the Round Table was founded upon humility and patience.'[10] These obligations and ideas seem incidental beside the much more prominent insistence on the importance of the relations between the members of the Round Table. First and foremost, the companions are bound by oath to help each other. When Gawain is fighting Hector, another knight reproaches him fiercely for attacking a fellow member of the Round Table, and succeeds in stopping the combat: 'As for Sir Hector, your companion, by the oath of the Round Table you are bound to him and to all the others who are companions of the Round Table, so that you can't kill them except in self-defense without becoming the falsest and most foresworn knight of all.'[11]

Indeed, the members of the Round Table are bound to help each other, to the extent of avenging any defeat suffered by another of the companions: 'the custom of the Round Table is such that if I see my companion defeated or killed, I must avenge him before I leave and must kill with my own hands the man who fought him, unless both are companions of the Round Table.'[12] This has become more

---

[6] *Lancelot-Grail: The Quest for the Holy Grail* tr. E. Jane Burns, IV.26.

[7] The only exception is in the Merlin section of the *Lancelot-Grail*, where Merlin chooses fifty knights for Uther Pendragon when he establishes the table (*Lancelot-Grail* I.197); it is not at this point called the 'Round Table'. This passage is based on Robert de Boron's *Merlin*.

[8] *Lancelot-Grail: The Quest for the Holy Grail* IV.36.

[9] *Lancelot-Grail: The Post-Vulgate Quest for the Holy Grail* V.184.

[10] *Lancelot-Grail: The Quest for the Holy Grail* IV.50.

[11] *Lancelot-Grail: The Merlin Continuation* V.58.

[12] *Lancelot-Grail: The Post-Vulgate Quest for the Holy Grail* V.185.

than a mere custom: it appears that there is now an oath which all knights have to swear, though we never learn its exact wording. It certainly involves an oath of brotherhood ('Remember the oath and pledge of the Round Table, in which we are brothers and companions . . .'[13]), and it also includes an oath of obedience to the king. When, in the closing pages of the story, Arthur has at last learned the truth about Lancelot and Guinevere, and is told that Agravain has set a trap for them, he commands a group of knights to seize them: ' . . . do what I've told you, and see that they are captured together, if you can; and I command you to do so by the oath you swore to me when you became knights of the Round Table.'[14] Surprisingly, given that the Round Table is the centrepiece of his court, and he is its lord, the king does not have unrestricted powers as to who should be admitted to the Round Table:

> . . . if King Arthur, who was deeply grieved by this matter [Gaheriet's murder of his mother, Arthur's sister] could have taken from Gaheriet the honor of his Round Table seat, he would gladly have done so, but he could not easily do this, for if he wanted to put another in the seat, he could not do so until his name was [magically] found written on the seat.[15]

Elsewhere, we learn of an older tradition which seems more appropriate to a pagan war band than to a chivalric gathering:

> 'When King Uther Pendragon held his court at high feasts and the knights of the Round Table had taken their places to eat, the clerks – whose duty it was to record their adventures in writing exactly as the worthy men to whom they'd happened recounted them – were all prepared and went among the tables to see whether anyone was seated there who didn't have a wound on his face, because in those days it was the custom that no one could sit down there unless he was wounded.'

However, this has led to the death of four knights, and the custom has been ended.

> 'But they've established another custom that's no less unpleasant than the other,' continued Sir Yvain, 'since no one can take his place at a high feast unless he swears on holy relics that he's defeated a knight by deed of arms within the week.'[16]

And finally, the knights have a role within the royal court and in warfare: they are specifically described in the context of battles as household knights, the knights

---

[13] *Lancelot-Grail: The Post-Vulgate Quest for the Holy Grail* V.210.
[14] *Lancelot-Grail: The Death of Arthur* IV.119.
[15] *Lancelot-Grail: The Merlin Continuation* V.54.
[16] *Lancelot-Grail: Lancelot* III.174.

retained directly in the king's service, and they fight together as a group: 'These knights are all members of my uncle's household and companions of the Round Table …'[17] 'And in the last battalion, where those of the Round Table were …'.[18]

When these romances were written, these ideas were new and without parallel in the real world. Although the military religious orders were well-established, there were no knightly orders which owed allegiance to a secular lord, and what we can see here is the emergence of the idea which was eventually realised in the fourteenth century, with the foundation of institutions such as the Order of the Garter. How does the fictional Round Table link to Edward III's creation of a real Order of the Round Table in 1344? The first question we need to look at is how far Edward III would have known the Arthurian romances. We know a little about the books which Edward possessed, though there is no complete list of what must have been a modest royal library. It probably did not compare with that of Charles V later in the century,[19] but we do have records which show that Edward owned romances from the beginning of his reign. He and his father possessed at least 23 books of romances, as well as 23 'pieces' of romances, some of which were not bound; these were listed in 1341.[20] Only two of the books can be definitely identified as Arthurian. The first is a copy of *Perceval* which was probably a version of Chrétien de Troyes' romance of that name. At the end of his reign, the *Perceval* may still have been in his possession, as a romance of Perceval and Gawain is listed in the books which passed to Richard II at his death. More important for our purposes is a volume called 'a romance of king Arthur' which stands at the head of the list, and which is valued at nearly twice as much as any other book; either it was a very large volume, perhaps a copy of the *Lancelot-Grail*, or a finely illuminated copy. It was clearly an important object, and confirms the likelihood that Edward was familiar with the details of the story of Arthur.[21] It is possible that the book which he purchased from his cousin Isabella de Lancaster in 1335 for the huge sum of £66 13s 4d was also an Arthurian romance; it was bought specifically for his use, and the record of the purchase noted that it 'remains in the chamber of the lord the king'.

Beyond the specific records of book ownership, we can point to a long family tradition of involvement with Arthurian romance, from the first appearance of the stories in the twelfth century. Henry II was said to have been involved in the discovery of Arthur's tomb at Glastonbury in 1189; Richard I gave a sword said to be Excalibur to Tancred of Sicily in 1191.[22] Edward I, according to Rusticiano of Pisa, who wrote an Italian version of the story of Tristan, took a volume of Arthurian romance to Palestine with him when he went on crusade, and it was from this

---

[17] *Lancelot-Grail: Lancelot* III.256.

[18] *Lancelot-Grail: Lancelot* III.312.

[19] Charles V owned at least thirteen volumes of Arthurian romance; see C. Meale, 'Manuscripts, readers and patrons in fifteenth century England: Sir Thomas Malory and Arthurian romance', *Arthurian Literature* IV, 1985, 94.

[20] J.Vale, *Edward III and Chivalry*, appendix 9.

[21] R. F. Green, 'King Richard's Books revisited', *The Library*, 5th Series, 31, 1976, 235-39.

[22] 'Benedict of Peterborough', *Gesta Regis Henrici Secundi Benedicti Abbas*, ed. W. Stubbs, RS 49, London 1867, II, 159.

copy that Rusticiano made his translation.[23] And romances could be heirlooms: Edward II rewarded a minstrel who brought him a book of romance which had belonged to Eleanor of Provence, his grandmother, and had been bequeathed by her to Edward I.[24] Edward I's interest in Arthurian stories is confirmed by a series of Arthurian spectacles held during his reign; we shall return to these when we look at the Round Table as festival. Another source from which Edward may have learned about Arthurian romance was his mother, Isabella of France. He inherited some of her romances, but she also owned 'a large book covered in white leather [vellum] about the deeds of Arthur', 'a similar book about the Holy Grail',[25] and 'a book about Tristam and Isolda'; these together would cover all the major Arthurian stories, particularly as another set of accounts identifies the first book as *Lancelot*, and tells us that the two books were sent to her by her father from Paris.[26] In this case, we can say that Isabella almost certainly owned a copy of the *Lancelot-Grail*, though after her death this went not to Edward, but to his sister Joan, queen of Scotland. Edward need not have owned or even read the romances of Arthur to have learned about the Round Table and its reputation. There is still much debate as to how common what we would call 'reading' today was in the middle ages. Reading silently to oneself in private may have been the least common way in which manuscripts were used. There is a famous miniature of Chaucer reading his poetry to the court of Richard II, and a century earlier Alfonso X of Spain had prescribed that books of knightly deeds should be read aloud at meals at his court, to encourage the practice of arms and chivalry.[27] We should not take it for granted that Edward was familiar with all the details of the history of Arthur and his knights, but the combined evidence makes it reasonably certain that he was keenly aware of the literary background of the Round Table.

---

[23] E. Löseth, *Le Roman en prose de Tristan*, Bibliothèque de l'École pratique des Hautes Études 82, Paris 1890 (rp Geneva 1974) 424.

[24] H. Johnstone, *Edward of Caernarvon*, Manchester 1946, 18.

[25] The clerk has entered it as *de sanguine regalis*, probably because it was titled in some way as *sangreal*, which he misread as *sang real*. A similar reading is found in John Lydgate's *The Fall of Princes*, l. 2788 (ed. H. Bergen, EETS ES 123, Oxford 1924, 901.

[26] PRO E101/393/4 f.8; BL Cotton Galba E XIV.

[27] *Las Siete Partidas*, tr. S. Parsons Scott, ed. R. I. Burns, SJ, Philadelphia 2001, vol.2, 428-9.

Why did Edward III hold the Round Table?
The political background

Richard Barber

EXACTLY A YEAR before the Round Table festival, a truce had been agreed with France. It was intended to last for three years, but neither side seems to have believed this would be the case. Philip did all he could to prise Brittany from the English grasp without actually mounting a campaign. Edward recruited important allies among the French nobility, Olivier de Clisson and Godfrey de Harcourt, and was able to recruit disaffected nobles in Gascony, while his Breton allies continued a guerrilla war against the French. Nor did he intend to take seriously the avowed reason for the truce, which was to enable a peace conference to take place at Avignon. At the end of 1343, although there were no specific plans for a campaign in France, Edward had every reason to prepare the ground for renewed fighting; he refused to take the peace talks seriously, sending junior government clerks to meet the French princes of the realm, while supporting the partisans in Brittany.

It was clear that the task of raising an army would not be easy. He had to persuade parliament to vote yet another tax for the purposes of the war, and he had only Flanders on his side on the Continent, which meant that his army would have to be raised almost entirely from within England. The Breton situation was too confused to expect any substantial force from his supporters there, and Gascony needed all the troops he could spare, whether local or English. A measure of the problems he faced is that in 1345, when the Crécy campaign was being planned, he introduced a special bonus for the English men-at-arms who fought overseas, while on the other hand he introduced a new method of assessing the military liabilities of landowners by relating it to their income. All this implies deep concern about the levels of recruiting.

The festivities at Windsor in January 1344 were all part of this recruiting drive. Since his early successes in Scotland, he had only the naval victory at Sluys to his credit; on the debit side were the later stalemate in Scotland and the failure of the great alliance in Flanders. To launch yet another campaign, he had to present a bold and brave face to his subjects, to impress on them that he was indeed capable of leading them to victory. This is where the pomp and ceremony of the festival of 1344 comes in, with its appeal to the chivalric and romantic view of warfare, and its invocation of the greatest conqueror that Britain had ever known: Arthur was not necessarily seen as a fictional character, for he figured in many of the accepted popular histories of the island. If Edward conquered France, he would be emulating Arthur's moment of triumph. And membership of the proposed Round Table would bring with it high military and chivalric prestige if the king succeeded.

Edward III, like his grandfather, used tournaments to mark the end of military campaigns. When he had fought, with little success, in Flanders in 1338-40, the last event of his stay was a tournament at Ghent, though the terms of the truce signed at Esplechin were hardly a cause for celebration. Similarly, at the end of 1333, he had held jousts at Smithfield, the traditional site of tournaments in London, to underline his recent military successes in Scotland. Even political victories, such as the suppression of the earl of Kent's rebellion and the fall from power of his mother and her favourite Roger Mortimer, both in 1330, were marked by tournaments. The object of such occasions was to impress the onlookers, particularly the great nobles, with a display of royal power, and thus to enhance the king's reputation. This tradition of royal tournaments, which had begun under Edward I but had more or less vanished under Edward II, gave the Round Table festival its chivalric framework.

When Edward made his plans for his new order, the romances which would have been familiar to his contemporaries contained no specific statutes for Arthur's Round Table, but the texts imply that an oath of loyalty to the king was required of knights before they could take their seats. Later versions of the Arthurian romances, which may have been modelled on the enterprise of 1344, change the nature of what is depicted until then as a fellowship based entirely on knightly deeds. When Boccaccio wrote his *De casibus virorum illustrium* in the 1360s, he described the Round Table as having 'laws and ordinances'. He sets out briefly the laws, which are broadly based on the chivalric principles outlined by earlier writers on knighthood, but which he distils into a specific code:

> The especial law for all was not to lay down their arms; to seek marvellous adventures; to defend the rights of the weak if so required with all their strength. They should do no violence and should not suffer it to be done to others, and should fight for the safety of their friends. They should risk their lives for their country. They should seek nothing for themselves save honour. They should not on any account break faith. They should be very diligent in honouring religion. They should give hospitality freely to all. They should relate all that they had done, whether to their honour or shame, to those who were charged with keeping the history of the Round Table.[1]

According to Boccaccio, the institution of these laws was the reason why the name of the Round Table was still revered in his own time. Its reputation in Italy

---

[1] Translated from Boccaccio, *De casibus virorum illustrium*, quoted in Lydgate, *Fall of Princes*, IV, 327.

was such that in the early thirteenth century there were a number of 'fellowships of the round table' (*de tabula rotunda societas*), and even St Francis in the mid thirteenth century refers to his friars as 'his brothers of the round table'.[2] The fellowships were not chivalric, but consisted of a group of citizens bound by an oath, usually with some charitable or social purpose; in Tuscany such societies were widespread, to the extent that 'in some cities you wil not find a youth who does not belong to such a society'.[3]

Boccaccio's fame as a writer ensured that his works were translated into French and English in the following decades, and John Lydgate gives an extended version of the 'laws' (based on the French translation) calling them 'statutes' and talking of the order's 'register'. The loose association of the Round Table has become a formal knightly order of the kind that flourished in the later fourteenth century, but its regulations, apart from the requirement that knights should risk their lives for their country, belong to the world of chivalry rather than the much more practical rules of the real-life orders.

Interestingly, Sir Thomas Malory, writing in the troubled times of the Wars of the Roses, changed the nature of the Round Table once more, from this very chivalric group into the means by which Arthur re-established his authority in his kingdom in the early years of his reign. In return for the lands and wealth which the king gives the knights, they swear an oath each year at the great feast of the order at Whitsun:

> never to commit outrages or murder, always to flee from treason, and to give mercy to those who ask for it, on pain of forfeiting the good opinion and lordship of king Arthur for evermore; and always to help ladies and damsels, gentlewomen and widows, and to strengthen their rights and never to rape them on pain of death. And none should take up arms in a wrongful cause, whether for love or for worldly reward.[4]

The order now has a straightforward feudal bargain at its heart: in return for the king's gifts, the knights are to enforce law and order. The oath of loyalty to the king found in the romances of the thirteenth century and which would have been the current view of the Round Table in 1344 has disappeared in favour of a more pragmatic view.

The idea that recruitment may have been the driving force behind the proposed Order of the Round Table and the Windsor festival is confirmed by activity on the other side of the Channel. Early in 1344, John, heir to the French throne, wrote to the pope asking for permission to establish a new collegiate church, served by twelve

---

[2]   Quoted in D. Delcorno Branca, *Boccaccio e le storie di re Artù*, Bologna 1991, 98.
[3]   Quoted in Delcorno Branca, *Boccaccio e le storie di re Artù*, 78.
[4]   Modernised and punctuated from Sir Thomas Malory, *Works*, ed. Eugène Vinaver, rev. P. J. C. Field, Oxford 1990, I, 120 See R. L. Kelly, 'Royal Policy and Malory's Round Table', *Arthuriana*, 14, 2004, 43-71.

canons and twelve priests; but in addition there were to be two hundred knights forming a communion or congregation, who were to foregather on St George's day, April 23, and the feast of the Assumption of the Virgin, August 15, 'not for jousts or tournaments or for any other act of arms, but for devotion to the same church'. This may have been a direct response to Edward's announcement of the Order of the Round Table. All we know of its constitution comes from letters written by Clement V on June 5, 1344, which naturally emphasise the religious aspect of the project. As we have seen, Thomas Walsingham, writing in the 1380s, remembered that Philip VI had built a round table in 1344, to compete with Edward. But this may have been a mistaken memory, for John's project, when it came to fruition in 1352, was described by the Flemish chronicler Jean le Bel as 'a fine company, great and noble, of the Round Table, which existed in the days of king Arthur'.[5] This order, whose insignia was a star, was to be an order of five hundred knights, based like Edward's order in a royal residence, the manor house at St Ouen, on the edge of Paris, which had a fine hall suitable for such a gathering. Although we cannot be certain that these three separate organisations – the collegiate church, the 'round table' and the Order of the Star – are one and the same, it seems clear that Philip and John were also playing the chivalric card, if only, as Walsingham says, to attract German and Italian knights who might otherwise have joined Edward's order.

We have therefore one projected and one actual order on both sides of the Channel. Curiously, the religious element in John's project of 1344 reappears in the Order of the Garter in 1348, while the chivalrous gathering proposed by Edward for the order of the Round Table in 1344 is apparently the model for John's Order of the Star in 1352. But the important innovation which all these plans introduce is the idea of chivalry as having a national element. This is true of both the Hungarian Society of Knighthood of St George and of the Order of the Sash in Spain. Whereas the military orders had been international in scope, and had possessed great power and wealth beyond the control of local rulers, just as the Church itself was international, the new secular orders were centred round the king as head of his nation. The mid fourteenth century is a time when nationalism is beginning to be sharply defined: one of the bogeys with which Edward III frightened parliament into granting him funds to wage war was that the French would invade England to 'destroy the English language'. Edward's choice of the Round Table as the basis of his new order emphasised this nationalism, because Arthur was a national hero.

By the time the campaign of 1346-47 had ended Edward himself was a national hero, winner of a famous victory over the French army at Crécy. Most of the knights present at Windsor in 1344 very probably served in this army, but when the king returned, he did not, as might have been expected, use the spoils of war to revive the Round Table. Instead, the building languished in an unfinished state while he pursued a new idea, a much smaller order designed to commemorate his recent

⁵ Jean le Bel, *Chronique*, ed. J. Viard and E. Déprez, Société de l'Histoire de France, Paris 1914, II. 204.

triumph in France. It was to be highly exclusive, consisting of the king, the prince of Wales, and just twenty-four knights. This group represents the English high command in the campaign, with only one or two exceptions, as well as a handful of younger knights associated with the prince of Wales. The statutes of the Order of the Garter are concerned chiefly with the establishment of a college of canons and knights, and with the celebration of religious festivals: the duties of the knights are only lightly sketched. It is a very different creation from the original Round Table, despite Froissart's confusion of the two a decade or so later, and it was only when its great reputation had been established that it was used for recruitment: and then it was recruitment at the highest level, the bestowal of the Garter on foreign princes who were sought as allies.

Of the six earls who guaranteed the order of the Round Table in 1344, four were still alive at the end of 1348. Salisbury had died immediately after the festivities in a tournament accident, and Pembroke died in August 1348; he may already have been ill when the knights of the new order were chosen. Two of the four survivors became founder members of the Order of the Garter. The earls of Derby and Warwick had been the senior commanders in the campaigns of 1346-47; Suffolk, who commanded the rearguard at Crécy, was elected later in 1348 on the death of one of the founding knights. Salisbury's son was also a founding knight. The only omission was therefore Richard earl of Arundel, who never became a knight of the Garter. This is something of a mystery, but the absence of another leading earl, William Clinton, earl of Huntingdon, may help to explain Arundel's failure to gain a place. They were both in charge of home affairs in the great crisis of 1341, and Edward seems to have regarded their failure to support him with the necessary funding at this crucial juncture of his military and diplomatic fortunes in Flanders as a serious blemish on their records.[6] We have no records of the parts played by the other Garter knights in the 1344 ceremonies, though two or three of the prince's companions would probably have been too young to take any important part.

The victory at Crécy and the taking of Calais had transformed Edward's situation with regard to recruitment, because the lure of profits of war was now a real one. Accounts of the taking of Caen in 1346 emphasise the riches that could be won if a town was taken:

> And those who could carry away booty came back with a vast amount of treasure from the houses. . . . The English eagerly returned to the work of despoiling the town, only taking jewels, clothing and precious stones because of the abundance. The English sent their booty to their ships . . . [which] found such a mass of goods sent to them that they could not transport all the spoils from Caen and elsewhere.[7]

Profits of war could also come from the changing nature of the king's armies,

---

[6] Vale, *Edward III and Chivalry*, 89-91.
[7] R. Barber, *Life and Campaigns of the Black Prince*, Woodbridge & Rochester, NY, 1986, 33-34.

which were now on a different financial footing. In the thirteenth century, as the enforcement of feudal duty to serve in an army became increasingly difficult, a system of contracts, called indentures, had grown up, by which each of the great magnates, and beneath them the individual captains, contracted to supply specific numbers of troops in return for financial reward and repayment of expenses. By the 1340s this had been almost standard practice, but as men were still reluctant to come forward, a bonus for actually recruiting the troops, called a *regard*, was paid during the time of their service; this could sometimes be doubled for particularly valuable service. This increased payment indicated the raising of an army had become a matter for the professionals and career soldiers. The structure of the army was now based not only on the contracts with the magnates and captains, but on a chain of indentures which ended with individuals or small groups of men. If the Round Table festivities had been aimed at attracting a wide range of knights who were likely to bring retinues to an army, the Order of the Garter included those likely to provide the largest retinues as well as potential captains who might build up a following. One of the Garter statutes provides that

> if any expedition is made, or any other thing which pertains to the honour of chivalry, the sovereign of the order must graciously give preference to the companions of the order before all others.[8]

In other words, the knights of the Garter were to have the best opportunity to profit from war (as well as being the preferred members of royal tournament teams). Many of them made notable sums from the Poitiers campaign in 1356: the earl of Warwick ransomed the archbishop of Sens for £8,000, and Sir Bartholomew Burghersh sold the count of Ventadour, whom he had captured, to the king for 10,000 marks (£6,667).[9]

The other aspect of warfare reflected in the order of the Garter was the close companionship of men who had fought side by side for as many as fourteen months, from the beginning of the campaign on 11 July 1346 to the end of the siege of Calais in September 1347. This service formed a strong bond, as all but three of the founding knights had probably taken part in the campaign, the exceptions being the leading commanders in Gascony at this period. The hardships and difficulties of the months in camp and the dramatic moment of victory meant that this was a group with a very large degree of common experience.

The House of the Round Table probably survived until 1358-1361, when William of Wykeham remodelled Windsor in a major building campaign. In the meanwhile, the chapel in the lower ward of the castle built by Henry III had become the chapel of the new Order of the Garter. This emphasises another difference between the

---

[8] L. Jefferson, 'MS Arundel 48 and the earliest statutes of the Order of the Garter', *EHR* CIX, 1994, 382-3, ch.30.

[9] W. M. Ormrod, *The Reign of Edward III*, Stroud and Charleston, SC, 2000, 99.

1 View of Windsor Castle by John Norden, 1607, showing Henry VIII's fountainhead in the Upper Ward

II Arthur and his court seated at the Round Table: from a late fourteenth century manuscript written in Italy
(Bibliothèque Nationale, MS Fr. 343, f.3)

*III Edward III and Edward, prince of Wales and Aquitaine: a contemporary portrait
from the charter granting Aquitaine to the prince*
(BL, MS Cotton Nero D. vi, f.31)

IV A tournament, from a manuscript of the romance of Meliadus written in Italy within ten years of the Round Table feast
(BL, Additional MS 12228, f.187v-188)

V Castell de Bellver: aerial view

VI Castell de Bellver: upper gallery showing vaulting

VII *Castell de Bellver: interior courtyard at ground level*

VIII *Castell de Bellver: upper gallery*

IX Castell de Bellver: interior courtyard from above

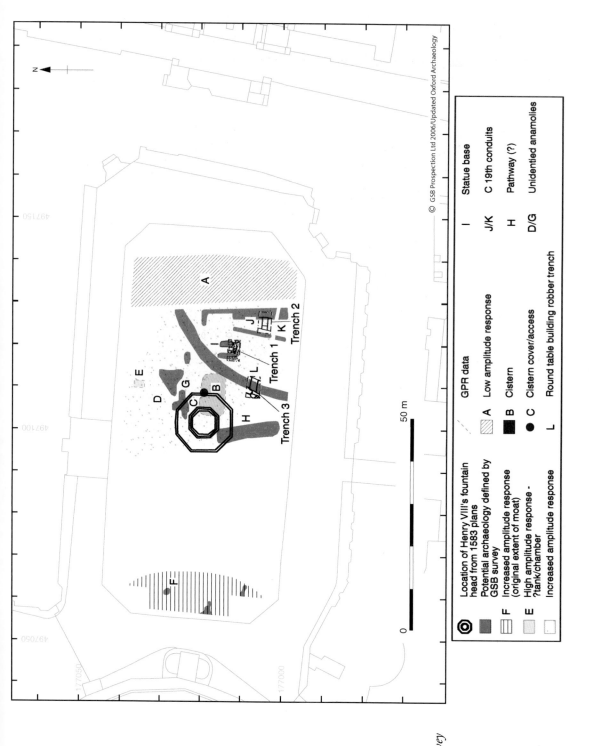

	Location of Henry VIII's fountain head from 1583 plans				Statue base

Potential archaeology defined by GSB survey

GPR data

I Statue base

F Increased amplitude response (original extent of moat)

A Low amplitude response

J/K C 19th conduits

E High amplitude response - ?tank/chamber

A Low amplitude response

H Pathway (?)

Increased amplitude response

B Cistern

C Cistern cover/access

D/G Unidentifed anamolies

L Round table building robber trench

A

E

D

G

C

B

H

I

J

K

L

Trench 3

Trench 1

Trench 2

F

N

497150

497100

497050

177050

177000

0   50 m

X Geophysical Survey

XI Trench 3: The Round Table building wall robbing trench

XII Trench 3: The Round Table building wall robbing trench

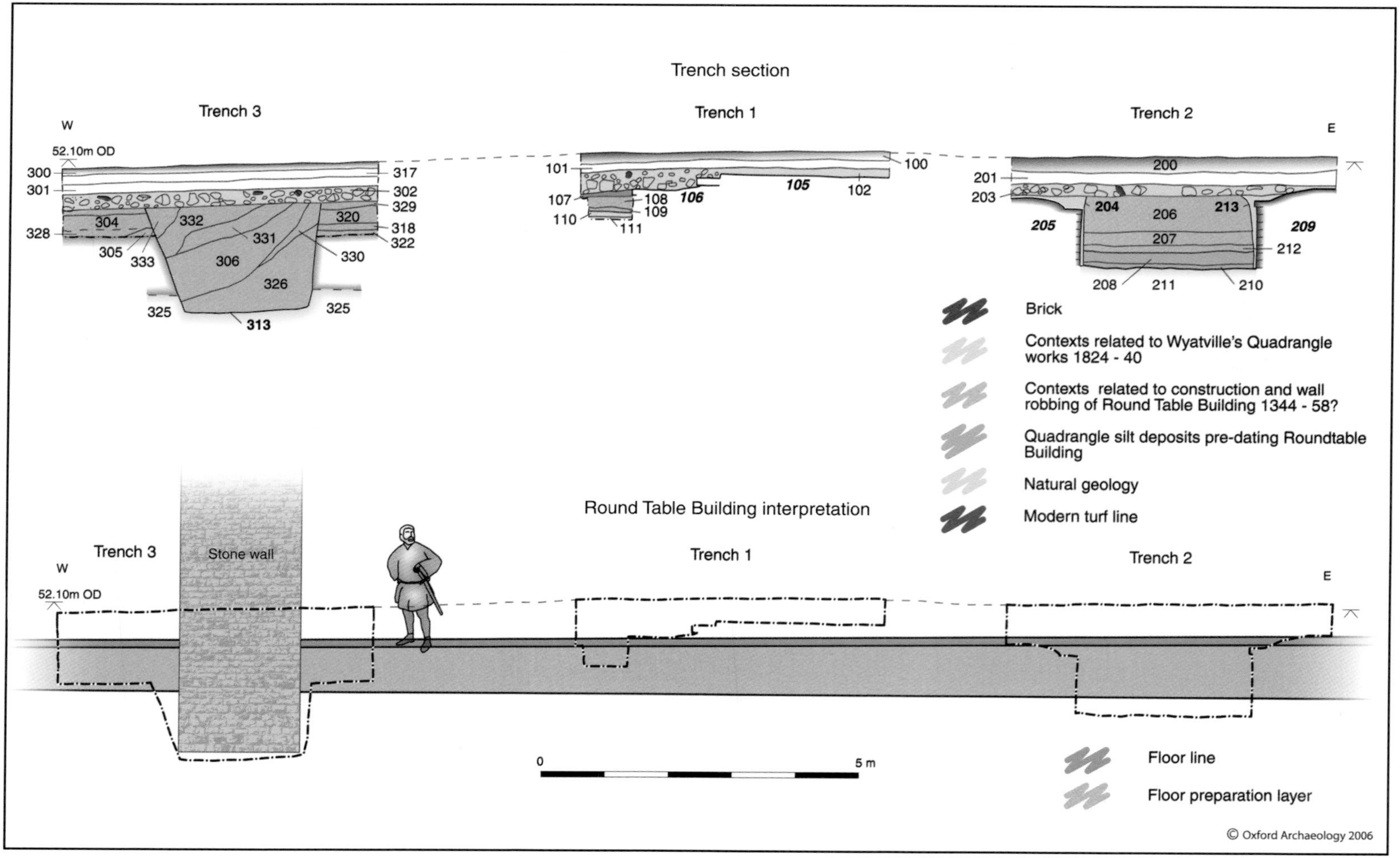

Trench section

Trench 2

E

200

209
212
210
213
206
207
211
208
204
205
201
203

Brick

Contexts related to Wyatville's Quadrangle works 1824 - 40

Contexts related to construction and wall robbing of Round Table Building 1344 - 58?

Quadrangle silt deposits pre-dating Roundtable Building

Natural geology

Modern turf line

Trench 1

100
102
105
106
108
109
111
101
107
110

Round Table Building interpretation

Trench 2

E

Floor line

Floor preparation layer

© Oxford Archaeology 2006

Trench 3

W

52.10m OD

317
302
329
318
322
320
330
325
331
326
306
313
332
333
325
304
305
328
300
301

Trench 1

Trench 3

W

52.10m OD

Stone wall

0   5 m

XIII. Trench sections

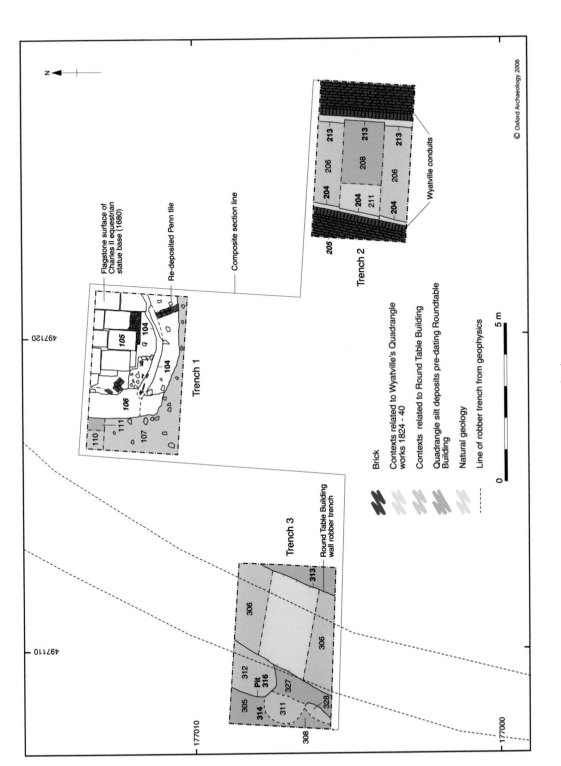

N

Flagstone surface of
Charles II equestrian
statue base (1680)

Re-deposited Penn tile

Composite section line

497120

104

105

104

106

111

110

107

Trench 1

Trench 2

205

204

204

204

206

211

208

213

213

213

206

Wyatville conduits

© Oxford Archaeology 2006

Brick

Contexts related to Wyatville's Quadrangle
works 1824 - 40

Contexts related to Round Table Building

Quadrangle silt deposits pre-dating Roundtable
Building

Natural geology

Line of robber trench from geophysics

0   5 m

Trench 3

Round Table Building
wall robber trench

313

306

306

312

Pit
316

327

328

305

314

311

308

497110

177010

177000

XIV. Trench plans

XV Graphic reconstruction of Round Table building

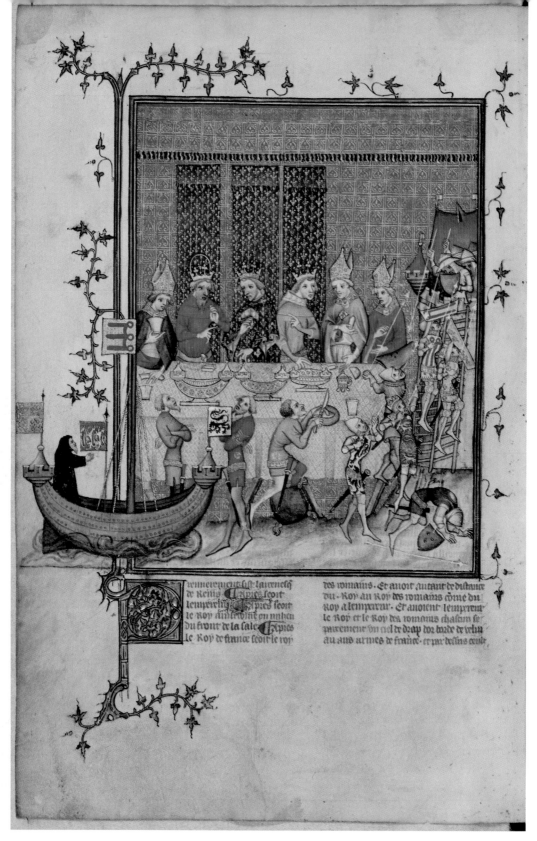

XVI. Feast at St Denis, given by Charles V in 1378; the illumination shows the dramatic interludes of a ship at sea and the taking of Jerusalem which were staged in the hall. From a manuscript of the Grandes Chroniques *finished in 1379*

two orders. That of the Round Table would seem to have been intended as an almost purely secular order; the Garter is at heart a traditional religious confraternity with secular members, and it is easy to forget that the bulk of the early statutes are concerned with the appointment of twenty-six canons and vicars, twenty-six poor knights, and arrangements for the services held in the chapel, as well as the terms of membership of the knights. Indeed, the secular obligations of the knights were minimal: in return for preferential treatment when it came to warfare or tournaments, they were required to be loyal to the king, and not to fight against each other for pay. Even the question of loyalty was not directly stated, but a series of practical injunctions against such matters as travelling abroad without the king's permission amount to the same thing.[10]

If the Order of the Round Table had been carried forward after Edward's return from Calais in 1347, would it have had the same enduring success as the Order of the Garter? Most of the other secular orders founded at this period survived for only a few decades: we have to move forward to 1430, when the Order of the Golden Fleece was established by Philip the Good of Burgundy, to find another order which has survived to the present day. Philip modelled his new order very closely on the Garter, in that it had twenty-four knights in addition to the sovereign, and the same element of religious confraternity. Both orders succeeded for similar reasons. Their founders survived for thirty or more years after the order was created. A suitably magnificent home was provided in a royal palace: Edward followed the rebuilding of the chapel by the creation of St George's Hall in the Upper Ward at Windsor in 1365. The original knights of the order were in both cases famous for their military and chivalric prowess, and the lustre that this brought to the order meant that subsequent membership was a mark of real distinction. The obligations of the knights, in the case of the Garter, were relatively light; those for the Golden Fleece were more restrictive. But the key seems to have been the limitation on numbers, which meant that the order was less likely to include a mass of relatively undistinguished knights. If the Round Table project had gone forward, it would probably have survived for a time and there might have been some spectacular festivals as a result: but there is no evidence that it would have had the focus and dynamism of the Order of the Garter. Indeed, like its fictional forebear, it might well have dissolved into civil war between its members. And in times of financial hardship, it would have been a much greater drain on the royal finances. In the end, both order and building were a dream, ambitious and marvellous in their way, but something which even Edward III could not translate into reality.

[10] D'A. J. D. Boulton, *The Knights of the Crown: The Monarchical Orders of Knighthood in Later Medieval Europe 1325-1520*, rev. ed., Woodbridge & Rochester, NY, 2000, 139-40.

Why did Edward III hold the Round Table?
The chivalric background

Richard Barber

SPECTACULAR FESTIVALS had long been part of the tradition of chivalry. One of the great chivalric virtues was *largesse* or generosity; for an extreme example of the excesses to which this could lead, there is the notoriously extravagant behaviour of the knights who gathered at Beaucaire in 1177, supposedly to celebrate the reconciliation of Henry II with the king of Aragon and the count of Toulouse. Only the count of Toulouse actually turned up, and the lavish show of wealth was intended to enhance his reputation: he gave 100,000 sous to a knight who promptly redistributed it to a hundred other knights. Others followed his lead, with increasing absurdity:

> Bertran Raimbaut had the castle grounds ploughed by twelve pairs of oxen, and then coins up to the value of 30,000 sous sown into it. Guilhem the Fat of Martel, who had 300 knights with him (the court in fact comprised about 10,000 knights) is reported to have cooked all the food from the kitchens with wax and pitchpine torches. At the same time the countess of Urgel sent a crown worth 40,000 sous; they arranged for Guilhem Mita to be called King of all minstrels lest he have any reason for being absent. Raimon of Vernoul burned thirty horses in a fire with everyone watching, because of a boast. [1]

This was conspicuous consumption with a vengeance, but magnificence and display were important on a more serious level. They were among the means by which the kings and great magnates underlined their power, and there was often a strong theatrical element in the way in which magnificence was presented. By the sixteenth century, this evolved into complex pageants and court theatricals, leading eventually to the beginnings of modern opera. But the same theatrical instinct was present in some of the earliest examples of royal display, and it is not surprising to find that it centred on the Arthurian legend, particularly as the normal mode of presenting the romances may have been through dramatic readings rather than the leisurely perusal of a manuscript; it is only a small step from a recital

---

[1] Quoted in R. Harvey, 'Occitan Extravagance and the Court Assembly at Beaucaire in 1174', *Cultura Neolatina*, LXI, 2001, 56.

6. *The Round Table at Winchester*
This table top, now hanging on the wall of Winchester Castle, is currently dated to
c. 1290, and is thus the earliest representation of Arthur's Round Table as an object.
The painting is early sixteenth century.

by a single actor-narrator to a full re-enactment.[2] The concepts of chivalry had evolved alongside the first medieval romances and the early tournaments. One of the chief features of the tournaments was an increasing emphasis on individual prowess. This made the idea of acting out the tales of the knightly heroes of the Round Table a very attractive proposition. We find the earliest example of this at a date almost contemporary with the writing of the central text of the Arthurian romances, the *Lancelot-Grail*, many pages of which record tournaments in minute detail. Chroniclers, alas, gives us far too little detail about real events of this kind, and surviving documents probably tell us about only a very small proportion of the Round Tables and Arthurian festivals that actually took place.[3]

The first record of a re-enactment of the Round Table that survives comes from the kingdom of Cyprus in 1223. The feudal lords of the kingdom of Jerusalem, of which Cyprus was part, were just as enthusiastic for chivalric exploits as their counterparts in western Europe.

> It happened that the lord of Beirut made his two elder sons knights, in Cyprus; one was sir Balian, who was later constable of Cyprus and lord of Beirut; the other was sir Baldwin, who was steward of Cyprus. And this knighting was the greatest festival and the longest of which anyone knows which was held beyond the seas; much was given and spent, and there was much holding of bohorts and imitation of the adventures of Britain and the Round Table and many kinds of games.[4]

Bohorts are a kind of tournament, probably using padded linen armour or *cuir bouilli* rather than full war armour. Most ordinary tournaments were organised simply as sport, with no other purpose in mind, but they were social occasions. This gathering takes the idea of a tournament a step further, and gives it a clear ceremonial purpose in association with an important social ritual, the knighting of a lord's sons.

From 'imitation of the adventures of Britain and the Round Table', a particular kind of tourneying event emerged, which was actually known as 'a round table'. We have no real idea what this implied, as no account of how a round table was organised has survived. But it was a recognised form of tournament, and one which was expected to attract a large number of knights. It is possible that there was some kind of oath of brotherhood sworn for the duration of the event to reduce the danger of personal quarrels getting out of hand. The kings of England, who had kept strict control of the sport of tourneying, effectively operated a licensing system whereby tournaments could only take place at specified sites. But when

---

[2] See E.B. Vitz, *Orality and Performance in Early French Romance,* Woodbridge & Rochester, NY, 1999, 164-204.

[3] See R. S. Loomis, 'Chivalric and Dramatic Imitations of Arthurian Romance' in *Medieval Studies in memory of A. Kingsley Porter,* ed. W. R. W. Koehler, Cambridge, Mass, 1939, rp New York 1969, pp. 81-97.

[4] *Les Gestes des Chiprois,* ed. G. Raynaud, Société de l'Orient Latin, V, Paris 1887, 31.

central authority was weak, as in the years of the minority of Henry III in the early thirteenth century, it was not difficult to organise unlicensed events, and all the king could do was to issue stern warnings against taking part in such occasions; there are examples in 1232 and 1252.[5] It is in one of these writs that we first come across the term 'round table' as a kind of tournament. In 1232, Henry III was concerned that such a gathering might lead to rebellion and disorder while he was absent on the Welsh marches, and sent a writ to his sheriffs couched in threatening terms:

> The king to all his faithful subjects, who have gathered for a round
> table, greetings. When we are on our way to Shropshire to hold
> talks with Llewellyn, prince of Aberffrau and lord of Snowdon, we
> order you, on the faith that you owe to us, to follow us in haste and
> in no way to gather for the aforesaid table or to presume to hold a
> tournament in breach of this our prohibition. Know for certain, that
> if you do this, we shall do grievous harm to your goods and bodies,
> and you and your people will feel this, and furthermore we will not
> permit you to hold tournaments in our land.[6]

Records of round tables are usually incidental to some other topic; in other words, we only learn of them because some other element is present: for example, when pope Gregory IX launched a new crusade in 1234-35, using Dominican friars to preach his message, 'many barons from Flanders took the cross at Hesdin, where they were taking part in a round table'.[7] The success of the preachers and enthusiasm for the crusade was such that later in the year Gregory had to ask the French bishops to prevent the crusaders from setting out before the appointed time.

The best evidence about round tables comes from literary works or from chroniclers with literary aspirations. The autobiography of Ulrich von Lichtenstein, a knight from Styria, is a wonderful mixture of fact and fiction, but there does seem to be some historical value in what he has to say. Although he refers to only two historical events, at the beginning and end of the poem, almost all the characters he mentions can be shown to be actual people. He himself was an important official from a politically influential family. According to his own account, which is not supported by any outside evidence, he undertook two journeys in the course of which he jousted with all comers. One was in honour of his first lady in 1227; the second, in honour of a new lady when the first had rejected him, was his 'Arthur' journey in 1240.

The beginning of this journey is missing in the only copy of the text, but from the outset we are in an Arthurian play.[8] The second knight to challenge him is compared

---

5   *Calendar of Patent Rolls, Henry III*, 1247-1258, London 1908, 157, dated 15 April 1252.
6   T. Rymer, *Foedera*, London 1816, I.i. 205.
7   Alberic des Trois Fontaines, *Chronica* in Monumenta Germaniae Historica: Scriptores XXIII,, Hanover 1872, 937.
8   Ulrich von Liechtenstein, *Frauendienst*, stanzas 1400-1619, tr. (into modern German) V. Spechtler, Klagenfurt 2000, pp. 493-553.

to the hero Feirefiz of Anjou from Wolfram von Eschenbach's *Parzival*, and Ulrich names the next challenger Calogrenant, a character from Chrétien de Troyes' *Yvain*. He is greeted by 'Calogrenant' as 'the noble King Arthur', and he speaks of his enterprise as a 'round table'. When there are no challengers, we are told:

> Then I rode friendless on,
> So that none of them yet
> Came rightly to the round table.
> Anyone who broke three faultless spears
> Against me in the joust, he is a man
> Who may once have been remote from me
> But now his place at the round table takes.[9]

We meet in succession 'Lancelot', 'Yvain' and 'Sagremors', who qualify to join 'Arthur' on his journey, and undertake some of the jousting on his behalf. At Klagenfurt, there are a whole host of challengers, and 'Tristan' is added to the companions. It is here that a messenger comes from Friedrich duke of Austria, welcoming 'Arthur' on his arrival from Paradise to visit his country, and declaring the duke's intention to take part in the round table. The next major encounter was at Neustadt, outside Vienna, where the duke sent his retainers, but did not appear himself; instead, a messenger from Bohemia invited them to joust there. Although Ulrich names and praises the duke's men, none of them is given an Arthurian name. The tent of the round table is pitched and a ring surrounded by banners and spears planted in the ground is set up. Only those armed for the joust are allowed to ride in it, and 'Arthur' selects 'Gawain' (his brother Heinrich), 'Yvain' and 'Lancelot' to defend it against all comers until nightfall.

The next day 'Arthur' himself takes the first encounter. Other Arthurian knights appear, 'Parzival', 'Ither' and 'Erec'; they and 'Sagremors' hold the field all that day – 'there were many jousts here and there in the field, and the cry of "Hurta, hurta" went up'. There were musicians too, playing flutes, trumpets, drums and shawms, even though the noise of the fighting often drowned their efforts. The jousting lasted for five days, until another messenger from the duke came to ask that single combats should now replace the general mêlées, because the duke wished to break three spears with 'Arthur'. The tournament continued for another day, but then, to general consternation, a messenger came from the duke telling the knights to cease on pain of his anger. The duke then summoned Ulrich and forbade him to cross into Bohemia, on the grounds that he might be captured there, and the journey ended with a rather half-hearted tournament at Krumau.

All this is a mixture of literary charade and sporting commentary. Ulrich is writing for the hardened enthusiast, and even he occasionally cuts short a long series of detailed descriptions of the encounters, saying that he has talked enough about jousting. The Arthurian background gives the jousting a suitable context, and

---

[9] *Frauendienst*, stanza 1429.

by invoking the hugely popular romances, the somewhat humdrum and repetitive sport gains a new glamour. But however fictional it is, the concept of the round table becomes a little clearer: in this story, the 'round table' is a select group, chosen by Ulrich as leader of the enterprise, who band together to fight with all comers, and who are in effect the 'holders' or 'those within' of the French tournaments.

Twelve years later, we have a historian's account of a round table, from Matthew Paris, the greatest of the semi-official chroniclers who worked at St Alban's Abbey. The event took place at the abbey of St James at Saffron Walden, and his information probably came from a monk or knight who was present. It is clear that there was an agreement as to the type of weapons to be used, and that any breach of the agreement, particularly where there was a background of enmity between the participants, was regarded as extremely serious. In this case, spears blunted by a crown were to be used, which would have been incapable of penetrating armour; but one of the knights used a war-lance with a sharpened steel tip. Whether this was by accident or deliberate was very much an open question:

> *On a certain tournament which knights call a round table*
> In the same year, some knights wishing to test their skill and courage in military exercises, organised, not a hastilude of the kind commonly called a tournament, but rather that knightly game which is called a round table, to test their strength. A large number of them from both north and south, and also from foreign parts, therefore gathered near the abbey of Walden, on the octave of the birth of the Blessed Virgin. And according to the rules of that martial game, that day and the next, certain English knights jousted energetically and with much delight, so that all the foreigners present looked on with admiration. On the fourth day, two very distinguished knights, Ernaldus de Munteinni and Roger of Leyburne, fully armed and on horseback, mounted on their best war-horses, jousted against each other. Roger struck Ernaldus under the chin, and his lance, the tip of which was not crowned, pierced Ernaldus's throat, cutting the trachea and arteries, because he had no collar and his throat was uncovered. Mortally wounded, he fell to the ground, and Roger was stricken with grief, or so it seemed. He died almost immediately. And because the dead man left no-one in England who could be called his equal or even his second, the assembled knights mourned him very greatly. Thus what began joyfully ended in sorrow and lamentation. His body was honourably buried in the nearby abbey, that of Walden, with many tears shed. No-one mourned the death of the knight more than the agent of his death, the aforesaid Roger, who immediately took the cross for the salvation of his soul. When he declared that he had inflicted the fatal wound on Ernaldus without knowing and against his will, he was not contradicted or accused of his death.

There were among the company of knights many of the nobles of England, including the earl of Gloucester, who had the fragment of lance taken out of the knight's throat, with the broken wooden shaft which remained in the wound.

When it was cut out and the knights looked at it, the point of the lance was very sharp, and as broad as a knife; it should have been blunt, and in the form of a small crown, called a *vomerulus*, or *soket* in French. From this it was supposed that although Roger pretended to be innocent, he was suspected of having acted treasonably and having perpetrated the crime; especially since Ernaldus had broken Roger's leg in another tournament. But God, who sees all things, alone knows the truth.[10]

The idea that such events had a formal organisation is confirmed by the record of an occasion in 1257 when 'a round table *sat* at Warwick about the feast of the Assumption of the Blessed Mary,'[11] rather as a court might sit. Elsewhere, the term seems to be used simply as a synonym for tournaments or jousts, as in the description of the meeting of Jaime I of Aragon and Alfonso X at Valencia, probably in 1272:

> 'no man could describe the decoration of the house and the games and diversions, the round tables and joined platforms for jousts between wild knights, tourneys, knightly exercises'[12]

One of the most detailed records of a chivalric festival is the poem by a *jongleur* called Sarrasin which describes a tournament held at Le Hem in 1278, near Péronne in north-eastern France, the region in which the sport had first developed a century earlier. It was a local affair, organised by two young lords from Artois, Huart de Bazentin and Aubert de Longueval.[13] For the first time there is a detailed account of the 'plot' of the tournament, and of the Arthurian characters who appear in it. The event begins on the eve of Saint Denis, 9 October, when 'Guinevere' arrives at Hem with a large retinue. During supper, the first interlude is acted out: 'Soreda-mors' appears and begs for the queen's help against her rival, who has imprisoned

---

[10] Matthew Paris *Chronica Majora* V, ed. H. R. Luard, RS 57, London 1880, 318-19. The round table was banned by royal order on 6 September 1252; *Calendar of Close Rolls, Henry III, 1251-3*, London 1928, 251.

[11] *Annales de Wigornia* in *Annales Monastici* ed. H.R. Luard, Rolls Series 36, London 1869, IV, 445.

[12] Ramon de Muntaner, *The Chronicle of Muntaner*, tr. Lady Goodenough, Hakluyt Society Second Series XLVII, I 59.

[13] Sarrasin, *Le roman du Hem*, ed. A. Henry, Travaux de la faculté de philosophie et lettres de l'Université de Bruxelles IX, Paris 1938; N. F. Regalado, 'Performing Romance: Arthurian Interludes in Sarrasin's *Le roman du Hem* (1278)', in *Performing Medieval Romance*, ed. E. B. Vitz, N. F. Regalado and M. Lawrence, Woodbridge and Rochester, NY, 2005, 103-119.

her beloved. A hundred knights offer to go, but the queen defers her decision until the next day.

At dawn, 'Kay' appears for the first joust, but meanwhile news comes that four of the queen's ladies have been imprisoned in a local castle, after they were sent to invite ladies of the neighbourhood to come to the tournament. 'The Knight with the Lion' goes in search of them, and rescues them by defeating their captor, the 'Lord of the Wooden Castle'. In the second interlude, the 'Lord of the Wooden Castle' is sent by 'the Knight with the Lion' to surrender to the queen accompanied by six knights, and they ride into the hall to do so. 'Kay' mocks them, but the queen takes them into her service despite this: thirty-eight jousts follow. Later that day, in the third interlude, the four ladies and 'the Knight with the Lion' arrive in the lists, and the jousting continues: the lion, which has accompanied its master, is terrified by the noise.

The next interlude is the arrival of a knight imprisoned in a wicker cage; he is released by four of the queen's maidens and fights in the lists. In the fifth interlude a girl appears with a sword and lance tied round her neck; she is being beaten by a dwarf, and is crying and screaming. She is condemned to this punishment by her lover for saying that the queen's knights are the best in the world. But one of the knights defeats the girl's tormentor, and he has to beg her forgiveness. The girl is offered the choice between entering the queen's service or rejoining her lover, and chooses the latter. The day ends with feasts and dancing. The next day is entirely occupied by fifty-six jousts, at the end of which the 'Knight with the Lion' and the count of Clermont accompany 'Guinevere' back to her court, where a further twenty jousts are held by torchlight.

All the characters are drawn from the Arthurian poems of Chrétien de Troyes; Soredamors is Gawain's sister, and Kay is Arthur's bad-tempered steward. 'The Knight with the Lion' is Yvain, hero of the romance of that name, played by Robert II, count of Artois, nephew of St Louis, who was killed at the battle of Courtrai in 1302. Many of the other knights appear in the records in the king's service or on crusade, so despite the local nature of the event, it was evidently a distinguished gathering. It is possible that a royal ban on tournaments was in force, and that the count of Artois had given permission for the tournament. Although the occasion is never called a 'round table', it is quite evident that it is a successor to Ulrich von Lichtenstein's combination of literature and sport, and the detailed plot shows how jousting and play-acting could be intertwined. The interludes took up a fair amount of time; the last three interludes on the second day only left room for seven jousts after the entry of the 'Knight with the Lion'.

Although we only know the identity of the knight who played ' the Knight with the Lion', it is clear that the Arthurian knights are played by their real-life equivalents; and even the knights who were given no specific parts joined in enthusiastically. When Guinevere appeals for a knight to rescue 'Soredamors' ' lover, a hundred of them come forward. Other parts are character roles: Kay, as the royal steward, not only plays out the crusty and irritable figure of the romances, but also actively supervises the setting up of the lists and the organisation of the banquet; in other words, he carries out the duties of a real steward. The dwarf would have been an honoured member of one of the noble households taking part in the proceedings. The pretence was carried to elaborate lengths: the identity of the 'Knight with the Lion' is the subject of much speculation, and when he loses his helm in a joust, he hides his face, but is forced to admit that he is Robert of Artois. This apparently accidental unveiling of the star actor is underlined by the fact that none of the other players has their identity revealed. Other knights appear as themselves, and this mixture of reality and fiction heightens the illusion. The entry of the 'Knight with the Lion' is carefully choreographed, with singers and musicians as well as the eleven actors, and forms an elaborate set piece at the centre of the proceedings.[14]

Another account of the proceedings at a round table hovers between fact and fiction. The Dutch chronicler Lodewijk van Velthem describes a festival held by Edward I when he marries the daughter of the Spanish king. It is true that Edward married Eleanor of Castile, but this was before he became king, and the historical details are hopelessly astray: all we can say is that this seems to be a plausible account of an event held during Edward's reign, but there is no way of telling when it took place.[15] There is a possibility, but no more than a possibility, that it was in some way connected with the tournament at Winchester in 1290 for which the Round Table was probably made.[16]

The description is full of revealing details, which may shed some light on how these play-acting festivals were organised.[17] A round table 'of knights and squires was prepared such that whoever wished might take up weapons and joust with them'. This 'round table' presumably consisted of the group of defenders, corresponding to the king and nineteen knights who played the same part at Windsor in 1344. It would explain why the Round Table itself, assuming it belongs to this festival, was relatively small. The painting and the Arthurian names are of course sixteenth century, but a group of twenty-four knights would be a suitable figure for the defenders. If this interpretation is correct, it sheds some light on the organisation of round table jousts. Just as Edward III and his defenders at other non-Arthurian jousts might impersonate the pope and cardinals,[18] or the Lord Mayor and aldermen of London,[19] so the defenders at a round table joust impersonated Arthurian knights.

This would naturally lead into a re-enactment of the romances, usually with a topical angle. Velthem specifically says that 'that there was enacted a play of Arthur

---

[14] See appendix C for a translation of the account of the Knight with the Lion's entry.

[15] G. Huet, 'Les traditions arturiennes chez le Chroniqueur Louis de Velthem', *Le Moyen Age*, XXVI, 1913, 173-197, believes that the entire episode is invented by Velthem, who had translated Arthurian romances into Dutch. A later section of the romance describes Edward's campaign in Wales in Arthurian terms; but this could perfectly well derive from an Arthurian re-enactment at the Snowdon festivities of 1284.

[16] Martin Biddle, *King Arthur's Round Table*, Woodbridge & Rochester, NY, 2000, 386.

[17] A full translation of the text is given in Appendix D. The original is in Lodewijk van Velthem, *Voortzetting van den Spiegel Historiael (1248-1316)*, ed. H. Vander Linden, W. de Vreese and P. de Keyser, Commission royale d'histoire 38, Brussels 1906, I, 295-31.

[18] Pope and cardinals: Smithfield 1343, Murimuth, 146, 230-1.

[19] Lord Mayor and Aldermen: 1359, Vale, *Edward III and Chivalry* 67.

the King' and the members of the Round Table were named after the knights in the Arthurian romances.

> There was Lancelot and Gawain
> and Perceval and Agravain,
> and Bors and Gareth
> and Lionel and Mordred,
> and a Kay, too, was created there.[20]

The knight who played Kay had the least welcome part: in the first round of jousting, all his fellow knights defeated their opponents, but – one hopes according to a pre-arranged and staged plan – Kay was set on by twenty young knights and knocked off his horse. At the feast which followed, the king declared that he would like to 'hear some news' before he continued with his meal, a rather prosaic way of evoking Arthur's refusal to begin a feast before some wonder had occurred.

With this the play-acting proper began. First, a squire spattered with blood appeared, and told the king that the Welsh had attacked him; he demanded revenge on his attackers, and Arthur agreed to deal with them as soon as the feast was at an end. The next course was served without incident, but before the third, Arthur again demanded news. This time, a squire rode in, bound hand and foot, and halted in front of Lancelot: when he had been untied, he gave Lancelot a letter from the king of Ireland, in which the king challenged him to single combat on the Welsh coast, calling him a traitor. Lancelot accepted the challenge, and said he would set out once the feast had ended.

Once again, the king demanded news before the next course was served, and the most theatrical of the interludes began, with the appearance of a 'loathly damsel', the traditional hideous messenger who reproves Perceval for failing to achieve the Grail quest in the romances. In a spectacular disguise, with asses' ears, a goitre, long rank hair, and a grotesque nose, she demanded that Perceval should go to Leicester, where the lord of the castle was attacking his neighbours, and deal with him, while Gawain (the other Grail knight in the early romances) was to go to Cornwall and put an end to a civil war there. Her message delivered, the loathly damsel slipped away and vanished. Velthem tells us that it was one of the king's squires in disguise, who quickly stripped off the costume and make-up, which had been made for him on the king's orders, and merged with the crowd. At the end of the festival, the king demands that the knights carry out their vows in real life, which seems to be a purely literary embellishment on Velthem's part; when they have done so, the whole episode concludes with another feast for the knights of the round table.

[20] Velthem, *Spiegel Historiael*, ll. 1188-1192.

If we take Velthem's account in conjunction with the account of the tournament at Le Hem, which was written perhaps twenty years earlier, it is reasonable to see the two poems as confirming that the events they described do correspond in some measure with the real proceedings at round table festivals. Both are literary rather than historical, but they are designed for audiences who would have been familiar with such occasions. The important common factors are the use of Arthurian romances as a storyline, extensive disguising, and the provision of actual scripts rather than simple dressing up as Arthurian knights. The earliest armorials containing the coats of arms of Arthur's knights date from this period, and one of these assigns the arms of the Mautravers family to a non-existent 'Sir Gawain Mautravers'. The suggestion is that this may represent 'some sort of a record of a Round Table at which one of the Maltravers masqueraded as Gawain';[21] as the roll in which it appears dates to 1270-80, it is just possible that this is the Gawain of Velthem's account. At all events, the assignation of shields to the Arthurian heroes – which dates back to the beginnings of heraldry in the twelfth century – made the question of role-playing in jousts and tournaments very much easier, as the shield and the crest were the normal method of identifying knights in their otherwise anonymous armour.

Similar play-acting seems to have been part of the coronation feast of Henry of Champagne, the last king of Jerusalem to rule in Palestine. His reign began with high hopes and great celebrations in 1286, despite the desperate state of his realm:

> In the said year, at the feast of our Lady in August, the said king Henry was crowned king of Jerusalem at Tyre, and he was crowned by brother Bonacours, archbishop of Tyre, and a great feast was held at Tyre; and when the king came to Acre, he held a festival for fifteen days in a place at Acre called the inn of the Hospital of St John, where there was a very large palace. And the festival was the finest that anyone had known for the last hundred years, of pleasures and *bohorts*. And they imitated the Round Table and the queen of Femenie, that is knights dressed as ladies, and jousted together; then they played nuns who were with monks and held a *bohort* among themselves, and they imitated Lancelot and Tristan and Palamedes and many other fine and delightful and pleasant games. And then the king left as bailiff in his place at Acre lord Baldwin of Ibelin, constable of the kingdom of Cyprus, and the king went to Cyprus.[22]

The idea of including a part for Palamedes, the Saracen knight who is in love with Iseult and is Tristan's unsuccessful rival, would of course have been highly appropriate in the Frankish east And the use of the Hospitallers' great establishment

[21] G. J. Brault, *Early Blazon*, 2nd edn, Woodbridge & Rochester, NY, 1997, 43.
[22] *Les Gestes des Chiprois*, in *Recueil des historiens des croisades, Documents latins et francais relatifs à l'Arménie, Documents arméniens*, Paris 1906, II 793.

at Acre, with a magnificent hall, indicates the scale of the occasion: this was probably the largest of the 'round tables' of which we have a record other than the Windsor festival itself. But chivalric festivals were a distraction from the real business of defending the remains of Henry's lands; five years later the Saracens were lords of the whole of the kingdom.

If the idea of holding round tables was widely spread throughout western Christendom, it is only in the late thirteenth century there is evidence of anything that resembles a continuous tradition of such festivals. In England from the 1270s onwards we get some indication that they had become a regular event in chivalric circles. A Round Table at Kenilworth in 1279 was remembered by a local chronicler a century and a half later as the occasion for a love affair between Roger lord Mortimer and Blanche, widow of the king of Navarre, who was married to the earl of Lancaster. She sent him barrels of gold coins, 'like a latterday queen of Pamphylia in love with Hector', and he wore a jewel on his armour in her honour for the rest of his life, a story which probably belongs to the realms of family romance.[23] Roger Mortimer held another Round Table at Warwick in 1279 and again at Kenilworth in 1282 when 'having gathered an innumerable multitude of knights and ladies . . . [he] held a most famous gathering, at the most profuse yet vain expense, which knights are wont to call by the name of round table in the common tongue, dedicated to the exercise of arms. The round table was celebrated on the Thursday of the vigil of St Michael, and after a few days had vanished away like morning dew.'[24] This of course is a monk's view of the vanities of the world, and most of the entries in chronicles about such festivals are brief in the extreme. The Mortimers, a powerful family whose semi-independent lordship lay on the borders of Wales, were particularly enthusiastic about such occasions; but the royal festivals were probably more lavish. It was with a round table at Nefyn in 1284 that Edward I celebrated his victory over the Welsh: 'The English knighthood and many nobles from abroad, about the feast of St Peter ad Vincula, celebrated a round table in dancing and jousting.' Edward had just gained the 'crown which once belonged to king Arthur', surrendered to him by the Welsh along with many other jewels.[25] And twenty years later, on campaign in Scotland, he held a round table at Falkirk, perhaps in part to impress the inhabitants of the land he was trying to conquer with the splendour of his court.

Although we have no direct evidence as to the original context for which the Winchester Round Table was created, it seems very likely that it belongs to the festivities for the betrothal of Edward I's daughters.[26] The royal family gathered at Winchester in April 1290, and a tournament was held there on April 20, somewhere just outside the town. It was not on the grandest scale, although a very large payment was made to Edward's nephew, John of Brittany, for the expenses he

[23] Foundation history of the priory of Wigmore in W. Dugdale, *Monasticon Anglicanum*, ed. J. Caley, H. Ellis and B. Bandinel, London 1830, VI, 350-1.
[24] *Annales Monastici*, III, 281, IV, 26, 477.
[25] *Flores historiarum*, ed. H. R. Luard, RS 95, London 1890, III, 62.
[26] Biddle, *King Arthur's Round Table*, 361 ff.

incurred in taking part. And there is no need to hunt for literary examples in which the original Arthurian Round Table is limited to this small number: the 'canonical' number is one hundred and fifty, as we have seen. The Winchester table fits the model suggested by Ulrich much more closely and would work well in the context of a tournament 'round table', but not as a recreation of the Arthurian court as described in the romances. It was made for a relatively modest occasion, and this is perhaps why the tournament of 1290 did not attract the notice of the chroniclers: it is only because of entries in the royal accounts that we know anything about it. But it is the most vivid evidence of the obsession of the English kings with Arthur, which was to resurface with Edward III.

Edward may well have been present at round table feasts organised by his mother's lover, Roger Mortimer, grandson of the Roger Mortimer who organised such events around 1280. One chronicler commemorates what he sees as the frivolity of another member of the Mortimer family in the late 1320s, when Edward was in his teens:

> And about the same time, Sir Geoffrey Mortimer the younger, Mortimer's son, called himself the King of Folly; and he did indeed become the king of folly afterwards , for he was so full of pride and evil ways that he held a round table in Wales for all comers, and imitated the manner and customs of King Arthur's table, but totally failed in his intention, for the noble king Arthur (unlike him) was the most worthy and famous lord in the whole world in his day.[27]

The other country where round tables were well-established was the kingdom of Aragon. One of the earliest examples on record connected with Aragon was held at the feast for the betrothal of Edward I's daughter Eleanor to Alfonso of Aragon at Oloron-Sainte-Marie at the foot of the Pyrenees in May 1287.

> And when the betrothal had been settled the feast began again, much greater than it had been before. And the Lord King of Aragon had a very high stage set up and always threw three daggers so marvellously that the English and the other people admired it much and the ladies likewise were full of admiration. And afterwards they had jousts and martial exercises and then round tables. And so likewise you might have seen knights and ladies dance and sometimes the two Kings with the Queens and with countesses and other great ladies; and the Infante and the *richs homens* on both sides danced. What shall I tell you? The feast lasted full a month, and one day the Lord King dined with the King of England and on the next day the King of England dined with the Lord King of Aragon.[28]

---

[27] *The Brut* ed. F. W. D. Brie, EETS OS 131, London 1906, i. 262.
[28] Ramon de Muntaner, *Chronicle*, II, 404.

This account is by Ramon de Muntaner, a distinguished soldier himself; his phrasing implies that the 'round tables' meant for him a separate kind of sport within the framework of the feast, rather than a feast which embraced a variety of activities. This is confirmed by a papal bull in 1314, issued by Clement V in anticipation of a new crusade, in which he expresses his anxiety that knights and horses should not be lost in the pursuit of mere sport. He therefore bans tournaments and jousts throughout most of Europe, and adds:

> Because in participating in the . . . jousts which are called round
> tables in certain countries in the common tongue, the same sins and
> dangers are present as in the aforesaid tournaments, they are subject
> to the same ban.[29]

Ramon de Muntaner confirms this classification of round tables as a kind of joust by his other descriptions of festivals which include round tables, rather than being called round tables as an overall title: two examples are in Barcelona in 1290 and Calatayud in 1291.

> And the Lord King remained at Barcelona with all the court, and
> if ever you saw games and diversions, then might you do so, round
> tables as well as dagger throwing, martial exercises and jousts and
> dancing of knights and citizens and townsmen and members of every
> guild of the city, exerting themselves in all games and diversions.[30]

At Calatayud, Roger de Luria, the highly successful admiral of the Aragonese fleet, set out to display both his own martial prowess and the wealth he had gained from his campaigns. However, the hazards of the lists put a premature end to the round table itself:

> It is the truth that when the Kings were at Calatayud, as you have heard
> already, the Catalans were asking everyone : 'Which is the admiral of
> the King of Aragon to whom God has shown so much favour?' And
> he was pointed out to them with a hundred or two hundred knights
> following him, as two or three men might follow another man; and
> they never tired of gazing. And the admiral, in honour of the King
> and Queen of Castile, had a round table cried at Calatayud, and set
> up a platform for jousts and had a wooden castle made at the top of
> the lists, from which he would issue at the approach of a knight. And
> on the first day of the round table he, all alone, wished to hold the
> castle against any man who wished to break a lance. . .
> All that plain of Calatayud, where the round table was held, was so
> full of people that they could not all stay there ; so that, if it had not

---

[29] D. Wilkins, *Conciliae Magnae Britanniae et Hiberniae 1268-1349*, London 1737, II 437-8.
[30] Ramon de Muntaner, *Chronicle*, II, 419.

been that it was winter, men could not have tarried there, but at that season there was little rain. And when the kings and all the people were there, there came a knight challenger, very beautifully arrayed and with a fine countenance, ready for a joust. And as soon as they of the wooden castle saw him, they sounded a trumpet and, at once, the admiral issued out of the castle, likewise finely and nobly arrayed, and he looked a very handsome knight. And if anyone asks me: who was the knight challenger ? I say it was En Berenguer A. de Anguera, of the city of Murcia, who was very brave and bold and one of the handsomest knights of Spain, and he was of the company of the King of Castile, and tall and stately and well-made. And this I can tell you likewise of the admiral, who was one of the best riders and handsomest knights of the world.

What shall I tell you ? The umpires brought two very large staves to the said En Berenguer A. de Anguera and he took the one he liked, and the other they gave to the admiral. And then the umpires placed themselves in the middle of the *sheet*, and gave the signal to each to advance and they prepared to advance towards each other; and he who saw these two knights advance, may well say that they were knights of great valour, for never could knights advance better according to what was suitable to each, nor in a more manly fashion. And En Berenguer A. de Anguera hit the admiral so great a blow on the front quarter of the shield that the stave came to pieces, and the admiral so hit him on the visor that the helmet flew off his head to a distance greater than the length of two lance staves, and the lance broke into more than a hundred pieces. And as the visor was hit the helmet came down so hard on the face of the said En Berenguer A. de Anguera that it crushed his nose, so that it has never been straight since, and the blood was flowing down the middle of his face and between his eyebrows so that every one thought he was killed. However he was so good a knight that, though he received so great a blow, he was nothing daunted. Both kings, who loved him much, ran to him, fearing he was killed when they saw him all covered with blood and his nose all cut and crushed. And they asked him how he felt, and he said that he felt well, that he was not hurt ; and they picked up his helmet. But they commanded the round table should be stopped, for they did not wish more to be done, for fear a quarrel should ensue. [31]

That there was still a large element of danger in the lists was demonstrated when John duke of Brabant, whose betrothal to Edward I's daughter Margaret may have been the occasion for which the Winchester round table was made, was killed at Bar in 1294:

---

[31] Ramon de Muntaner, *Chronicle*, II, 432-4.

This year the duke of Brabant, a man from a great family, held a
Round Table in his lands, at which English and French knights, as
well as those from other nations. And the duke himself was killed
in the first encounter, run through with a lance by a certain French
knight, and died the same day.[32]

We have already mentioned the enthusiasm of Edward III's brother-in-law,
William IV of Hainault, for chivalric activities, and Flanders, the Low Countries
and north-eastern France remained one of the most active centres of the sport.
The Flemish towns held civic jousts, and in 1331 the jousters at Tournai took as the
theme the Arthurian hero Galehault, inventing a list of thirty-one kings whom he
had conquered, who also participated in the jousts. The following year there was
a round table at Paris; this was an unusual event, because the French kings were
generally very suspicious of tournaments, which they saw as an opportunity for
dissatisfied nobles to gather and plot against them.

At the beginning of William IV's career, there had been a round table at Haarlem
on the occasion when he was created titular count of Zeeland on 28 September
1333. He was the official sponsor of the event, at which his father William III gave a
supper for the knights of the round table and their ladies, on the evening before the
ceremony.[33] But in 1344, just after his return from Prussia and three months after
his brother-in-law's festival, William IV held a great round table at The Hague.
This is the great feast already mentioned;[34] we know it was a round table, because
it is specifically described as such in the accounts, which are our only source of
knowledge of this event; we have no record of the proceedings. The financial
details are not entirely helpful, as they are simply a list of payments to various
people, with little to tell us what they were for; and it seems that the officials were
somewhat overwhelmed by the occasion, for there are three subsequent payments
for lists of items which had been overlooked at the time. The total expenditure
came to £791 11s 8½d, a very substantial sum, though not on the scale of Edward's
outlay at Windsor.[35] In the 1340s, Alfonso XI of Castile was always involved in
'tournaments and round tables and jousting'; but it is interesting that, apart from
isolated examples in the Low Countries, there are no records of round table festivals
after 1344.

[32] *Annales Monastici,* III, 388-9.
[33] Antheun Janse, *Ridderschap in Holland,* Hilversum 2001, 339.
[34] See pp. 36-7 above.
[35] The Dutch pound was 20 shillings of silver, weighting 30 grams in all; H. J. Smit, ed., *De rekeningen der graven en gravinnen uit het Henegouwsche Huis,* Werken uitgegeven door het Historisch Genootschap gevestigd te Utrecht, third series, 69, 1939, III, 208.

8

Imaginary buildings

Richard Barber

WE HAVE LOOKED at the literary background for Edward's Round Table, and the practical politics that lay behind his project. But there is also another possible dimension: just as the idea of the Round Table itself came from fiction, so the design of the building which was to house it may also have its origins in contemporary literature, the romance of *Perceforest*. It is a vast work, which few scholars have read from end to end, running to almost as great a length as the whole story of Arthur and his knights in the *Lancelot-Grail*. It tells how Alexander the Great came to Britain, which he gave to his companion Brutus (hence the name of the island). The plot describes his adventures in the island, which was in the power of an evil enchanter and his kin, and how twelve knights led the way in overcoming the enchantments that had been cast on the island.

Perceforest is the completion of two earlier romances written for the counts of Hainault, and we have already explored the common chivalric enthusiasms of Edward and Philippa's family. However, the connection between *Perceforest* and the English court, and its relation to the proposed House of the Round Table, is not easy to establish. We have no contemporary copy of the text, the earliest being a hundred years later, and no precise date for its composition, but its most recent editor dates it to the period 1337-44. It was certainly completed after the death of Philippa's father, William III of Hainault, in 1337, because there is a eulogy of him which is in the past tense.[1] One possible indication that it was well known at Edward's court is the tournament at Dunstable in 1334, when Edward fought using the arms of 'Lyonel'. Now Lionel is a minor figure in the standard Arthurian romances such as the *Lancelot-Grail*, but he plays a very large role in *Perceforest*, and this would be a more plausible explanation for Edward's adoption of this character.[2]

One passage in particular stands out as exceptional; it is a detailed description of a building, which is very unusual in medieval romance, and the picture which is drawn is remarkably similar to what we know of Edward's Round Table project. The setting of *Perceforest* is the pagan kingdoms of Britain before Arthur's time and before the coming of Christianity, when the inhabitants worshipped the Sovereign God. It is, in Hollywood terms, a prequel to the stories of Arthur, and foreshadows

[1] *Perceforest: quatrième partie*, ed. G. Roussineau, Geneva 1987, I. ix-xiv.
[2] Vale, *Edward III and Chivalry*, 68-9.

the events of the Arthurian romances. After the death of Brutus, the first king of Britain, Perceforest becomes king. His court is a glittering showcase of chivalry, but he falls ill, and as a result becomes lethargic and uninterested in deeds of arms. In due course Perceforest recovers, and just after this, he finds that his palace has been magically transformed, and that a magnificent hall has appeared, which is to be called the 'Franc Palais', or 'Noble Palace'. The beginning of the adventure is signalled by the doors and windows being shut fast and a great light appearing in the hall, just as in the description of the appearance of the Grail at Arthur's court in *The Quest of the Holy Grail*.[3] The theme of the knight whose pride leads him to sit at the table despite dire warnings that he is not worthy to do so, and who is killed by mysterious means as a result, also has parallels in the death of Moise in the earlier Grail stories.[4]

> While they were seated at the tables [in the garden], celebrating as no-one in the world had ever done for the return of the king and for the health which God by His grace had restored to him, they heard the windows of the great hall slam shut all together with such a crash that it was astounding to hear. When the king and everyone heard the noise they wondered what it could mean. But no sooner had they looked up than all the windows began to open again, whereupon they beheld a light shining in the hall as bright as if a hundred torches had been blazing. The king asked where such a light could be coming from, and why the windows had thus closed and reopened, and a knight who was the castellan, the castle's governor, said:
>
> 'In faith, my lord, I don't know: I've never seen such a thing.'
>
> 'Castellan,' said the king, 'go and see who the people are who've brought such a light to the place.'
>
> So the castellan went to the great hall, but when he came to the door he turned straight back to the king and said:
>
> 'My lord, I've been to the hall and can report a great mystery: the doors are locked fast against me, and I can hear a terrible noise of hammering inside, as if it were full of smiths!'
>
> And as the castellan said this, the king listened and heard the hammering and was amazed – as was everyone present, for no-one could explain it. While they were all busy exchanging opinions, they saw a group of twelve maidens pass by, each carrying a shield hung from her neck covered with a green cloth. And truly, they walked right past the tables without saying a word to any knight or lady.
>
> When the king saw the maidens passing, shields at their necks, addressing no-one, he wondered what it could mean, and he ordered the castellan to follow them and see where they would go. He set off

3   *Merlin*, 37-9.
4   *Lancelot-Grail: Quest for the Holy Grail*, IV, 7.

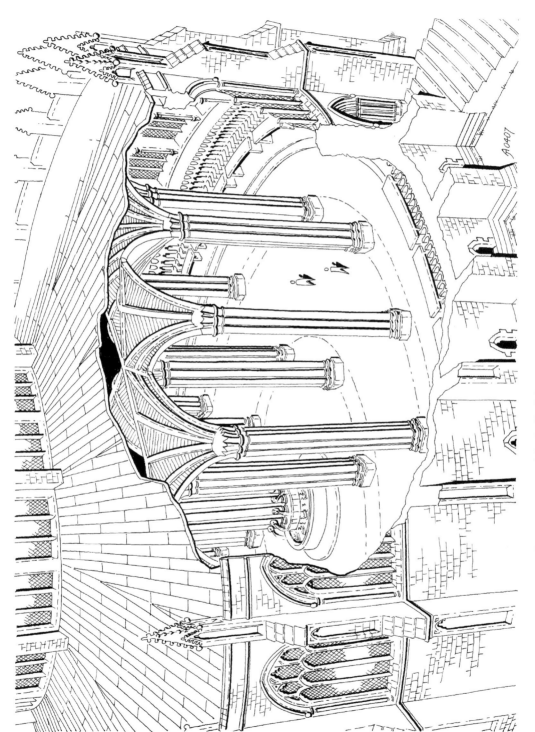

v. *Reconstruction of the hall of the Franc Palais as described in Perceforest*

after them and followed them until he saw them enter the great hall, whereupon the doors closed fast behind them. Then he returned to the king and reported what he had seen, and the king replied:

'There's a meaning to this. God grant that it be to our honour and to the kingdom's!'

Hardly had these words left the king's lips when he looked towards the castle and saw the twelve maidens mounted on their palfreys and returning the same way they had come. And when they began to pass before the tables the king commanded the castellan to go and ask whose household they were from. The castellan did as he was bidden, and then returned to the king and said:

'My lord, I've been to the maidens and asked them where they were from, and they told me it would soon be revealed and that I shouldn't worry about it for now!'

When the king heard this he decided to forget the matter, for he did not want to spoil the feast: he could see that everyone was so keen to celebrate that he would have hated to dampen their spirits. They were served so splendidly that all were more than satisfied, and when the feasting was finally done they rose from the tables and all the knights and ladies began to dance. Meanwhile the king drew aside and summoned some of his knights and told them he was mystified as to what had happened in his hall.

[. . .]

Then torches were lit and they set out towards the hall. But when they came to the doorway at the foot of the stairs, the king stepped forward and found the two doors shut tight; then he looked up and saw written on the arch above, in great and elegant letters of gold, the following:

> 'Let all men know that from this day
> This is the door to the *Franc Palais*⁵
> Where honour on the worthy shall be bestowed
> And the worthless shall dishonour know.'

When the king had read these letters he showed them to the ladies and knights in his company. They were astonished: several knew for certain that before sunset no inscription had been there, which made the king wonder who could possibly have written the letters so quickly, and he said to Sarra, who was standing beside him:

'Truly, damsel, I think this has been done by magic. I beg you, for love's sake, tell me if you know how this has happened.'

'In faith, my lord,' the lady replied, 'I don't know who has done this: it's nothing to do with the maidens of the forests. But I do believe this will be for the greater glory of all chivalry, for the cowards and

---

⁵ 'noble hall'.

sluggards will strive to better themselves, and the worthy will find reward and recognition.'

'Damsel,' said the king, 'I hope it proves to be as you say. Come, we must go inside: I long to know if there's some new wonder there.'

Then the king stepped forward and told the castellan to let them in, which he did, commanding a boy to open the doors. As soon as they were open, the king and all his company entered; and once the torches had been placed in the middle they could see the whole hall clearly. Now, so that you may better understand what we shall tell you in due course, you need to know what the great hall was like. Know, then, that it was on the first floor of a round tower of an amazing size: the diameter of the hall was more than two hundred feet. In the centre stood an enormous pillar that supported the vaulted ceiling; inside this pillar was a pipe running from a beautiful spring, and around it were twelve taps supplying water whenever it was needed.

Right around the hall curved a marble table, most beautifully made, standing quite high off the ground on pillars; and it ran so close to the windows that anyone sitting at the table would be resting his back against the tower wall. The two ends of the table finished in front of the hall's main door, and such was its circumference that it could seat fully three hundred knights abreast You cannot believe how beautiful this table was to behold, and it was smoother than any ivory. It was impossible to move it, but a good many more tables were set up in the hall on trestles, so that twelve hundred knights could dine there without impeding the servants. But now we'll return to our story, for you'll hear how the hall was arranged later in the book.

When the company entered the great hall, the king, who was at the front with Louvezerp and le Boceu, came up to the marble table, which was blacker than jet or ink; and he saw that above it were finely made iron hooks, fixed in the wall in careful order all around the hall, numbering in total three hundred or more. The king, Louvezerp, le Boceu de Suave and several other noble knights and ladies and maidens and girls were astonished by this; then the king looked ahead and at the far end of the great hall, on twelve of the hooks, he saw twelve shields hanging.

'My lords,' he said, 'there's another surprise at the end of the hall: there are twelve shields hanging on the hooks. Let's go and see what this is about.'

So they set off towards them, and as soon as they reached the shields the queen said: 'In faith, my lord, these are the shields of the twelve knights who fulfilled the twelve vows of the hermit at the great tournament between Scydrac and Tantalon at your brother King Gadifer's coronation.'

[. . .]

'Truly, my lord,' said the castellan, 'I think these are the twelve shields carried by the twelve maidens who passed our tables without speaking, for I saw them enter the hall and close the doors behind them.'

'I think you're right, castellan,' said the king.

While the king was talking to the castellan, the queen looked at the marble table and saw that there were white letters written upon it. She called to the king and said:

'My lord, behold another wonder! There are white letters written on the table. Come and see what they say.'

The king looked down and saw the letters written on the marble, saying:

> Pay good heed to this warning:
> No man should sit at this table
> Unless his shield be hung on the hook above –
> If not, I cannot protect him
> From the gravest harm.
> I have no wish to see him in trouble
>   And do not advise him to sit in any other seat.
> I want him to take these words to heart.
>   Let him go and sit at the tables below,
>   For there he will be safe.

The king was amazed by the remarkable words he had read, and said: 'Sirs, it seems to me it would be unwise for any knight to sit at the marble table unless his shield is hung above him. If it's not, he should go and sit at the ordinary tables elsewhere in the hall.'

'My lord,' the knights replied, 'that seems indeed to be the intention of the one who arranged all this, and it's a mystery to us all.'

The knights who sit at the round table in this hall are chosen mysteriously when their shields appear on the hooks around the wall, and one knight who attempts to sit at the table and to hang up his shield himself is killed by a thunderbolt. The king addresses the knights after this dramatic death and explains the principles behind the Order of the Noble Palace:

> 'Sirs,' said the king, 'we should consider and learn from the example of this knight who has been put to death for his sin. For I understand that the dead knight was the boldest and most valiant knight in his land and, if judged by his great prowess, he was worthy to have a seat at the table of the Franc Palais and a hook to hang his shield, for otherwise, it appears, no knight can sit there without coming to grief. But I'm reminded of the words of a hermit who warned me once that, even if I had all the possessions and wealth of King Alexander, all the

wisdom of King Solomon and all the chivalry of the valiant Hector of Troy, pride alone, if it reigned in me, would nullify all.

'Sirs,' the king continued, 'this dead knight had wealth and wisdom and chivalry. But pride reigned in him, that's clear beyond doubt; it was the great pride in him that drove him to covetousness and vanity: wicked covetousness when he senselessly yearned to have the first seat at the table, and vanity when he sat in a place destined for a finer knight than he. And because of this covetousness and great vanity born of his pride, the Sovereign God did not wish him to have a seat, either high or low. So by this example, sir knights, you can see that, no matter how wealthy, wise or strong a knight may be, if he's stained with vices – especially pride, which leads a man to fall into all the others – he is not worthy to be called a knight or to sit at the table of the noble Franc Palais.'

[. . .]

'And because I wish it to be revealed without dispute which knights shall be worthy to sit at the table of the Franc Palais, I command all who wish to compete in the tournament and attain this high honour to have one of their shields brought here to the hall, as I shall bring my own, and then the hall shall be locked; for such is my faith in the power of the Sovereign God that I believe that, at the dinner after the tournament, those who are worthy will find their shields hung on the hooks, and thereby know where they are to sit.

'And I command that the head of the knight who was killed here for his sin shall be hung on a chain from the ceiling of the hall, as a reminder and a sign that henceforth no man should be so presumptuous as to sit at the table unless he sees his shield hung above his seat. Go now, sirs, and make your preparations. And order your lives: be like the maid and worthy of the name of knight, so that you may sit at the noble table of the Franc Palais for the rest of your life, and end it at the table of the Sovereign God in his holy Paradise. Amen.'

The parallels with the Round Table are very striking. Perceforest founds a new order, which consists of three hundred knights or more. Edward establishes an order 'to the number of 300 knights, and would cherish it and maintain it according to his power, always adding to the number of knights.' In both cases, the halls are two hundred feet in diameter. And the Order of the Franc Palais and the proposed Order of the Round Table are both based on the Round Table as found in the Arthurian romances.

They also share one key discrepancy with their Arthurian model. Throughout the *Lancelot-Grail*, the number of knights is consistently given as 150 knights. Other romances do give widely varying figures, but never three hundred. Now *Perceforest* is portraying a period supposedly near to that of classical Rome; Brutus was regarded in the romances as the contemporary of Aeneas, ancestor of the Roman people. The origin of knighthood was traced by learned writers to the *equites* of Rome, supposedly founded by Romulus, the founder of Rome. These were the cavalry of the infant Roman state, consisting of a hundred horsemen from each of the original Roman tribes, and therefore numbering 300 in all.[6] I would suggest that this classical model was deliberately applied by the author of *Perceforest* to the fictional order he creates; it makes sense in the context in which he was writing. There is no obvious reason why Edward should depart from the traditional Arthurian number of 150, unless he was using *Perceforest* as the template for his new order.

This is not a conclusive argument, and what is important about *Perceforest* for our purposes is the detail which it offers. It solves the problem of how a circular hall might contain three hundred knights: they sit with their backs to the outer wall, with a circular marble table in front of them, running round the hall. This table is not solid, but forms a circle within the outer circle, leaving a space in the centre. *Perceforest* differs from the Windsor building in an important respect, in that the hall is on the first floor of a great keep – an enormous structure, which would be about twice the diameter of the largest surviving circular keep. However, the central pillar with a fountain could have had a parallel at Windsor. The pillar could have been a separate feature, and not part of the building's structure; the technical problems of vaulting a space two hundred feet wide would not matter to a writer of romance, and it is possible to envisage a classical column rather than a supporting central pillar. If this is so, there could have been a similar structure at Windsor; fountains often figure in the accounts of royal pageantry from the late fourteenth century onwards, such as the royal entries into London.[7]

To support the argument that the House of the Round Table could have been modelled on a literary precedent, we need to look briefly at other imaginary buildings in the romances, and at other cases where there seems to be a literary or cultural programme behind the architecture. Three other instances come to mind, two of them Arthurian, and one from *The Canterbury Tales*. In an Italian version of the Arthurian romances, *La Tavola Ritonda*, there is a highly coloured description of the Round Table and its setting which, as in *Perceforest,* describes the building which contains the Table as being circular.

> You should know that in King Artù's court there were principally four kinds of seats. The first was a single one, the Seggio Periglioso: no one sat in it, because Merlino had prophesied that whoever sat there would dissolve and be corrupted in every limb unless he were the virgin knight who by the power of his virginity would achieve the adventure of the Sangradale. (This was going to be Sir Galasso, the son of sir Lancilotto, who was born and brought up in a great convent of women.)

---

[6] Livy, *History of Rome*, ed. & tr. B. O. Foster, London 1919, I, 13, 15.

[7] One difficulty with this suggestion is that when the 'conduit' or fountain in the Upper Bailey was created in 1551, it required a separate, new water supply. However, a fountain which only ran when festivals were held in the house of the Round Table would have merely needed a temporary arrangement.

The second kind of seat was the Seggio Reale, where King Artù sat. The third was the Seggio Avventuroso, and in these sat the knights of adventure, those who never came to the table at great festivals without wonderful news, and who never refused a battle.

The fourth kind were seats of less prowess, and in them sat the knights who because of some accident could not take part in adventures. These four kinds of seats were in the great hall of the palace, which was all painted and decorated with ladies and maidens and other noble figures. In the middle of this hall was a thick column of jasper, made in three sections, and in the bottom of the third were thirty taps of gold and silver from which there continually ran rose water in which to wash their faces. At each tap hung a towel of clean white silk. In the middle part of the column were set beautiful mirrors to look in, and on the top part were carved these words: 'To all the knights errant who desire the honor of chivalry. I reveal unto you that love is the condition and the way which leads all to prowess and courtesy, and love is the resting place for all fatigue. As you desire honor and a name for prowess, serve love loyally and well, and hold love in your heart.'

And all the knights errant should know these words well, those who came every morning to the column to wash and look at their faces, and to read what was written there. By such customs was the Tavola Ritonda known.

Around the seat where the king ate with many barons there was this custom: one who brought good news drank from a golden cup, but if the news were otherwise he drank out of silver. And the palace and the hall and the walls were all round, so that as they sat at the table, all the men could see the faces of all the others. When they were here within, they were a circle, that is to say, one thing, and all were at one post and faithful to one sign. They were at the post of obedience and bore one symbol, the sign of love. All of them were knights in love, who lived and were named for prowess throughout the world.

From every country they came here, each one seeking to prove himself through deeds of arms. They proved themselves many times over until they were found so excellent that they could be received as knights errant. If they were not good enough, they set out on their own adventures as foreign knights, since they could not yet be called knights errant.[8]

The arrangement of the hall is very much as in *Perceforest*, and this romance may be the source from which *Perceforest* got the idea, because it probably pre-dates *Perceforest* by twenty years or more. It also introduces the idea that Merlin actually founded a separate round table for king Uther, which is called 'the Old Table'

---

[8] *La tavola ritonda*, ed. M.-J. Heijkant, Milan 1997, 267-9; quoted from A. Shaver, *Tristan and the Round Table, A Translation of La Tavola Ritonda*, Binghamton, NY, 1983, 148-9.

(*Vecchia Tavola*), rather as the table which is magically created for Perceforest is a predecessor of Arthur's round table.

In terms of architectural descriptions of imaginary buildings, the most extraordinary example is the vision of the temple of the Grail in Albrecht von Scharfenberg's romance known as *The Later Titurel*, a rather laboured completion of an unfinished poem on the early history of the Grail by the much greater poet, Wolfram von Eschenbach. Like Wolfram, Albrecht delights in brilliant images: lists of precious stones and descriptions of paintings and elaborate musical automata are all part of his account of the building, an account so detailed that it has given rise to voluminous papers attempting to reconstruct its appearance or to identify it with existing buildings. This is part of Albrecht's lengthy description; a nineteenth-century reconstruction and plan are shown overleaf. The building is once again circular, on a vast scale:

> Wherever the choir turned outwards there was the altar, so that the priest could turn his face correctly to the Orient when he desired to increase the bliss of Christians and God's praise in the Mass.
>
> The greatest of the choirs pointed to the Orient. Two entire galleries were given to this direction, for it was dedicated to the Holy Ghost in all elegance of ornamentation, enriched at special expense, since he was the patron of the whole temple.
>
> The one next to it was dedicated to the Virgin, who is the mother of that child who has both Heaven and Earth in His power and their population. John was the name of the lord of the third choir. The rest of the twelve disciples were housed close by.
>
> The inside of the temple had such rich craftsmanship, built in beauty for the love of God and the Grail, everywhere equally so, save that the choirs lacked such ornament as was bestowed upon the rest of the temple. The whole work was completed in thirty years.
>
> There was only one single sanctified altar there, the choirs around it were empty. Such a wonder of wealth was invested in it. In front of the belfry stood rich ciboria with images of the saints. Each carving told its own story there.
>
> High above one of the gates, elegantly facing the Occident, was an organ, a construction with a clear, sweet note, a great pleasure to hear; it accompanied the office on feast days, as is still the case all over Christendom:
>
> A tree of red gold, equipped with all desirable foliage, twigs and branches, with birds perched everywhere of those kinds whose sweet voices are praised. Wind went in from a bellows, so that every bird sang in its fashion, one high, the other low, depending on the manipulation of the key. Laboriously the sound was conducted back down into the tree. Whichever bird he wished to press into action, the master was well acquainted with the key according to which the birds sang.

vi. Elevation of the Grail Temple from Jüngerer Titurel
as reconstructed by Sulpice Boisserée in 1835

Four angels were perched on the ends of the branches in immaculate pose, each holding a horn of gold in his hand; these they blew with a great din, whilst with their free hand they beckoned as if to say 'Rise up, all ye dead!' . . .

Two most exquisite doors led into each choir there. Between them stood an altar, over which hung chancels, vaulted, supported by two spindle columns, each forming a circle of some six feet, with the area between them filled with special ornament.

The doors in front of all the choirs had railings of rich gold, so that people could see and hear better from all directions. The walls by the doors also all had rich railings, closed with clasps, and everything was studded with precious stones.[9]

---

[9] Albrecht von Scharfenberg, *Jüngerer Titurel*, ed. W. Wolf, Deutsche Texte des Mittelalters XLV, Berlin 1955, I, 96, stanzas 370-385, 391-397; translation by C. Edwards, *Arthurian Literature*, XX, 2003, 95-96.

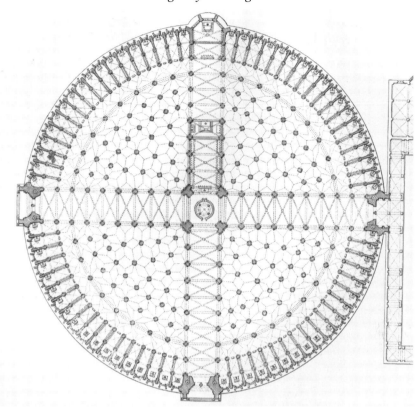

vii. Plan of the Grail Temple from Jüngerer Titurel
as reconstructed by Sulpice Boisserée in 1835

For our purpose, this text shows that medieval writers were capable of imagining elaborate and detailed building plans, and that *Perceforest* is not an isolated example. More specifically, the Grail temple is definitely not modelled on an existing building, and indeed the overall plan is not clear, and apparently impractical – just as the two hundred foot stone vault in *Perceforest* seems impractical. The surviving texts are not clear, and we cannot be sure whether Albrecht intended the temple to have twenty-two or seventy-two choirs or surrounding chapels.[10] Albrecht himself says later in the poem:

> I have constructed the temple elegantly for the instruction of noble Christian people, that they may desire to look with loyalty to God, guided by the temple's design.[11]

Even if Albrecht's building is symbolic, he imagines it in terms of a real structure, though without regard to practicalities. The hall of the Franc Palais in *Perceforest*

[10] *Jüngerer Titurel,* I, 86, stanza 341 and note: *Arthurian Literature,* XX, 91.
[11] *Jüngerer Titurel,* I, 138., stanza 516.

is only lightly symbolic and therefore described in less detail, but in both cases a spectacular architectural space has been created in the author's imagination.

Our next example brings us back to the world of fourteenth-century England, and to the court culture of the period. It is from Chaucer's *Knight's Tale*, which is set in ancient Greece. Like *Perceforest*, the assumption is that even in classical times a chivalric culture prevailed, and the story revolves round the love of two friends for the same woman. They quarrel, and arrange to fight a duel; Theseus, duke of Athens, creates a monumental circular amphitheatre for their encounter. Ignoring the fact that its dimensions are impossibly large – over fifteen hundred feet across and a mile in circumference – the arrangement of the spectators' galleries around it corresponds quite closely to drawings of the stands at tournaments.

> I judge it would be held for negligence
> If I forgot to tell of the dispense
> Of money by the Duke who set about
> To make the lists a royal show throughout.
> A theatre more noble in its plan
> I dare well say was never seen by man.
> It had a circuit of a mile about,
> Well walled with stone; there was a ditch without.
> Shaped like a circle there it stood complete
> In tier on tier, the height of sixty feet,
> So that a man set in a given row
> Did not obstruct his neighbour from below.
> Eastward there stood a gate of marble white
> And westward such another rose to sight;
> Briefly, there never was upon the face
> Of earth so much within so small a space.
> No craftsmen in the land that had the trick
> Of pure geometry, arithmetic,
> Portraiture, carving and erecting stages
> But Theseus found him and supplied his wages
> To build this theatre and carve devices.[12]

What Chaucer depicts is a straightforward Roman amphitheatre, which he embellishes by the addition of three temples dedicated to Venus, Mars and Diana, which are rich with carvings and statues, and with elaborate paintings on the interior walls. These are the excuse for a long discourse on the legends and symbols associated with each deity. Similarly, the House of the Round Table may have been intended to have an impressive gateway, perhaps with statues of Arthur and his principal knights in niches around it.

---

[12] Geoffrey Chaucer, *The Canterbury Tales*, tr. N. Coghill, London 1977, 74.

What takes place within this vast arena is not a joust between the two knights, but a full-scale tournament of a hundred on each side. When such tournaments were fought in open country, they ranged over many miles, and the famous fifteenth-century tournament book of René d'Anjou shows the assembled riders spurring their horses out of the wooden barriers enclosing the lists as soon as the signal to start the tournament is given. This would explain the huge scale of the imagined building. A circular form is more appropriate to a mêlée of this kind, rather than to jousts, which were run with a barrier down the middle and consisted of two knights charging each other in a straight line. Rectangular stands were the norm for watching this kind of encounter. Full-scale mêlée tournaments were rare by Chaucer's time, and he is describing something that few people would actually have seen.

The Canterbury Tales were written towards the end of the fourteenth century, mostly in the last decade; but Chaucer had known Edward and his court when he was a young man. He had served Edward's daughter-in-law, the wife of Lionel duke of Clarence, and had been on the campaign of 1359, in the course of which he was captured and ransomed. The Order of the Garter was only a decade old when he is first recorded as a member of the duchess of Clarence's household, and although the chivalric activities of the court were less prominent than in the early years of Edward's reign, many of those around him would have taken part in the king's great tournaments. *The Knight's Tale* is one of the closest reflections in literature of the splendour of Edward's chivalric pageants.

Lastly, we have to remember that castles were not simply defensive and warlike. The castle has an important role as palace and as a political symbol which aimed to enhance the ruler's prestige and to impress all those who saw them. At Syracuse, Castel Maniace has a well-defined defensive purpose, guarding one of the finest harbours in the Mediterranean. Its main hall, however, is on the grandest of scales, and is a possible analogue for Edward III's projected Round Table building.[13] It is now thought that Frederick II, who commissioned it, may have had a literary text in mind when he created it. This was the poem in praise of his father, Henry VI, emperor of Germany, by Peter of Eboli, *Liber ad honorem Augusti*, in which the imperial chancellor is shown receiving the homage of the Arabs and the Indians in a building with twenty-four bays, near a fountain called Arethusa.[14] This fountain is to be found at Syracuse, but in Peter of Eboli's day nothing like the palace he depicts existed in the city. Frederick II may have picked up this literary idea of a great hall, which is labelled in the miniature '*teatrum imperialis palacii*', the 'theatre of the imperial palace', and transformed it into the reality of the hall at Castel Maniace, with precisely the same number of bays.

Castles with an imperial echo were to be found in England under Henry II: the keep at Dover, with bands of different coloured masonry, echoed that of the

---

[13] See p. 119 below.
[14] Petrus de Ebulo, *Liber ad honorem Augusti sive de Rebus Siculis*, ed. T. Kölzer and M. Stähli, Sigmaringen 1994, 231.

imperial Roman forts, such as Colchester, which the Normans had converted into castles, and Orford castle has architectural details which suggest that it is intended to echo classical and imperial themes. In 1240-41, Henry III built a water-gate at the Tower of London faced with polychrome stonework.[15] And at the height of his Welsh conquests, Edward I built an imperial castle at Caernarfon, near the site of the Roman fort of Segontium. It stands on the mouth of the river Seiont, whose name is a reminder of the Roman past. Edward's new castle was also to have Roman and Byzantine echoes: perhaps inspired by the discovery of what was believed to be the body of Magnus Maximus, the father of the emperor Constantine, in the town in 1283, he and his architects may have consciously echoed the sixth-century town walls of Constantinople, with their patterned masonry of bands of different-coloured stone and their polygonal towers, in the walls of the new castle, and the visual similarities are striking. They were also perhaps influenced by a description of a great Welsh city in the twelfth-century Welsh romance 'The Dream of Macsen Wledig' (i.e. Magnus Maximus):

> He saw how he came to an island, the fairest in the whole world, and after he had traversed the island from sea to answering sea, even to the uttermost bound of the island, he could see valleys and steeps and towering rocks, and a harsh rugged terrain whose like he had never seen. And from there he saw in the sea, facing that rugged land, an island. And between him and that island he saw a country whose plain was the length of its sea, its mountain the length of its woodland. And from that mountain he saw a river flow through the land, making towards the sea. And at the river mouth he could see a great castle, the fairest that mortal had ever seen, and the gate of the castle he saw open, and he came to the castle. Inside the castle he saw a fair hall. The roof of the hall he thought to be all of gold; the side of the hall he thought to be of glittering stones, each as costly as its neighbour; the hall doors he thought to be all gold. Golden couches he saw in the hall, and tables of silver.[16]

The castle is later named as Aber Seint, and a great fortress is built there for Macsen, with earth brought especially from Rome. So the design of Caernarfon could be a conscious attempt to recreate Magnus Maximus's fortress, appealing to the Welsh traditions in the same way as the fact that Edward's first son was to be born in Wales and become the first of the English princes of Wales.

Architecture was just one of the weapons through which a king could invoke the past to enhance his present prestige. On the same campaign which saw the beginning of Caernarfon castle, we have already seen how Edward was presented

---

[15] See A. Wheatley, *The Idea of the Castle*, Woodbridge & Rochester, NY, 2004, ch.4; Tower of London watergate pp. 136-7.

[16] *The Mabinogion*, translated by G. Jones and T. Jones, London & New York 1974, 80.

with the crown which once belonged to 'the famous Arthur, king of the Britains',[17] and he had held a round table at Nefyn in Snowdonia. It was the culmination of his long-standing Arthurian enthusiasms, just as the House of the Round Table and the feast at which it was founded was to be the culmination of Edward III's chivalric enthusiasm for Arthur: and in both case the tangible symbol of this enthusiasm found expression in architecture.

[17] *Annales Monastici*, IV, 489.

Quinborow Castle in Ey[?]Mano

7. *Wenceslas Hollar's drawing of Queenborough Castle before its destruction, 1656*

III

RECONSTRUCTING THE ROUND TABLE

A0407

vii. Reconstruction of timber Round Table building

Reconstructing the Round Table
Windsor and beyond

Julian Munby

I   THE WINDSOR ROUND TABLE

The tantalizing glimpse of the House of the Round Table revealed by excavation has shown that it was indeed a building of around 200ft [61 m] in diameter, with a substantial outer wall of stone, but an interior of which we know very little. Both the stone purchases and the amount of masons' activity in the building accounts indicate extensive masonry features, while the general lack of recorded activity by carpenters suggests that timber did not play a huge part in the building, at least as far as it had progressed by November 1344. Therefore the immediate questions to be answered are whether the building was intended to be roofed or remain open, and whether it was to be completed in stone or timber. Later one might ask what other buildings might have influenced its design, and whether it had any architectural precursors or indeed successors.

A fully-roofed building
There can be little doubt that the House of the Round Table could have been fully roofed, though it would have taken a large number of columns to provide the necessary support for a stone vault or timber roof. There were precedents for many-columned interiors in Islamic architecture (e.g. in Moorish examples in Spain) that may have derived from Byzantine examples (such as the subterranean cisterns in Constantinople). Stone columns in a rectilinear layout would support a vault with arcades crossing at right angles, like that at Castel Maniace in Syracuse, square in plan (with a diagonal of about 210 feet) and vaulted with 16 columns (about as many as would be needed on a circular plan) with a generous bay spacing of over 25 ft.[1] The height and span of the vaults would of course vary the number of columns required. Just to take two thirteenth-century English examples, the choir of the Temple Church in London has aisles 16ft wide and the centre span of 26ft supporting a stone vault, while the Lincoln Cathedral Chapter House has a span of

---

[1]   H. Götze, *Castel del Monte*, Munich and New York 1998, 33ff.

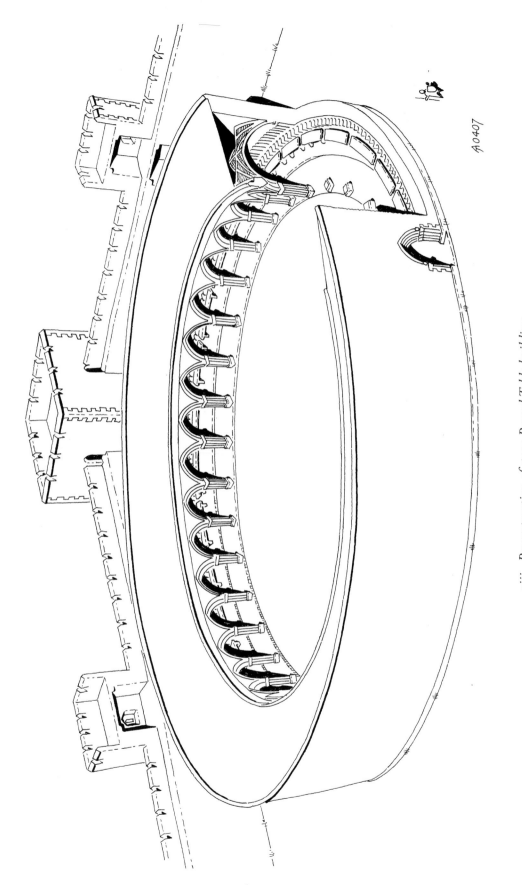

viii. *Reconstruction of stone Round Table building*

around 28ft between the walls and the central column that carries the stone vault.[2] While a rectilinear layout could have been followed at Windsor, a circular arrangement is perhaps more likely. On this model the House of the Round Table (with an internal diameter of say 190 ft) could have been roofed with a vault supported by 20 to 56 columns arranged in two, three or four concentric arcades around a central pier, depending on the following bay sizes:-

Table 6   House of the Round Table: parameters for vault spans

Diameter	Aisle span	No. of arcades	No of piers	In each arcade
190 feet	32 feet (6 x 32 = 192)	Two arcades	20 piers	8 + 12
190 feet	24 feet (8 x 24 = 192)	Three arcades	48 piers	8 + 16 + 24
190 feet	19 feet (10 x 19 = 190)	Four arcades	56 piers	8 + 12 + 16 + 20

But despite the literary model of a dark hall with a central pier described in the last chapter, this elaborate forest of stone piers is perhaps the least likely solution, although it cannot be said that the evidence of the building accounts is against it. It is perhaps worthy of comment that the building shows no sign of buttresses, and seems to have relied on the breadth of the outer wall to carry the required forces. That may mean a timber roof, and it would not be hard to imagine a similar array of timber posts, perhaps carrying a flat or sloping roof, with long beams and scarfed lengths joining together shorter pieces. Here, however, the building accounts are suspiciously silent about the preparation of any significant quantity of timber, and if such a roof were envisaged the timber would have been being prepared in 1344. The last alternative is for a partial roofing, with the centre tented over like a circus big top. This is possible, and tents were regularly in use for military purposes as well as in the travels of the peripatetic court, and it would still have required an array of timber posts.[3]

A partially roofed building (in timber)

Even despite the vagaries of the English weather, a partially-roofed building seems the most attractive and practicable, and a not improbable solution (we shall consider later a fair-weather parallel on the island of Majorca). This could be in stone or timber. A few years ago, when the prospect of ever investigating the site of the Round Table seemed unlikely, I suggested as a reconstruction the most simple solution, which was to build a timber lean-to building against the outer wall, and a sketch of this scheme was published.[4] This notion arose from examination of the Canons' Cloister at Windsor which was built by Edward III in the 1350s, an

---

[2]   These and other following measurements are solely intended to be indicative of scale, and are based on plans rather than precise values obtained in the buildings. (N.B. for metric conversion, 1 foot = .3048 metre).

[3]   For further information, see 'History of Tents' website of Stephen Francis Wyley: *http://www.geocities. com/historyoftents/*.

[4]   J. Munby, 'Carpentry Works for Edward III at Windsor Castle', in Saul, *St George's Chapel*, 225-37, fig. 35.

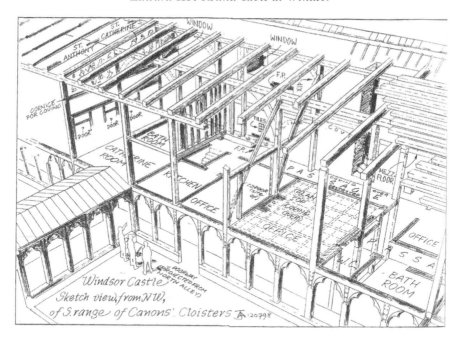

ix. Construction of the Canons' Cloister at Windsor

unremarkable building in some ways, but certainly a very unusual survival of a set of timber-framed lodgings in a castle. The two-storey lodgings are built around the cloister, between the castle curtain wall on the north and the wall of the Dean's Cloister to the south, so the timber frame is constructed with a high stone wall at the rear. They are of somewhat unusual character, being of two storeys with a lean-to roof and having a covered walkway set within the building at ground floor level rather than outside. There is also no overhanging jetty at first floor level, and so the storey posts rise to the roof.

The framing of the Canons' Cloister is rather basic in character, and lacking any great refinement, but deserves to be described. Three storey posts of descending height, at the rear, centre and front, form the basic frame. The rear posts are (or were) arch-braced at the top to a wallplate along the front of the stone wall, the central posts are braced to the purlin running along the centre of the roof, but no bracing has been identified on the front posts. Two large tension braces have been exposed in one dividing wall, running forward and down from one post to another and trenched across a mid-rail. On the ground floor the central posts are braced to the floor joists in the dividing wall, and to transverse joists. These transverse joists run along the building and give support to the common floor joists, which pass over the passage wall and lodge on the front wallplates. The floor joists are substantial and closely spaced (a foot apart), but no indication of any unusual jointing has been observed. The roof is of unusually simple construction, and consists of common rafters laid on the slope from the rear wallplate, over the central purlin and down

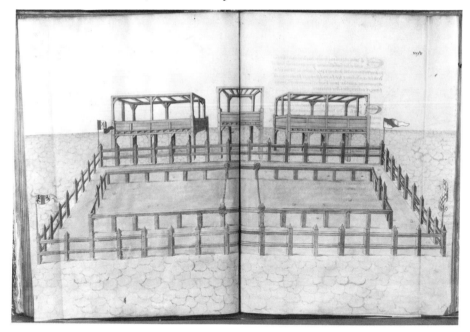

8. *Stands and barriers for a mêlée tournament, from Rene d'Anjou,* Livre des tournois

to the front wallplate; this was then boarded transversely for a lead covering. There is no visible trace of the original fenestration, though there are original openings looking out onto the garth, which are unglazed, trefoil-headed, openings (three in each bay).

The plain and utilitarian design of the Canons' Cloister may tell us no more than the usual manner of building timber-framed lodgings in stone castles. However, it also has affinities with another type of utilitarian structure, the 'grandstand' constructed for the lists. A series of mid-fifteenth century illustrations from René d'Anjou's treatise on tournaments (c.1455-60) is helpful in this respect, in separately depicting the spectators' stands both occupied and empty of all people and decoration. (Figure 8)[5] The timber framing is plain and utilitarian, with a principal level above a low base, and a lean-to roof. The similarities with the Windsor cloister are striking, but need mean no more than that common form was being followed. Thus if we seek to reconstruct the House of the Round Table with a framed building around an open central space, then this would be the simplest and most appropriate way of doing it. It could either work as a grandstand with a principal level at first floor, or have had a more substantial table on the ground floor.

This reconstruction would fit with the walls (as seen on Figure vii) lacking any buttresses, since such a frame might have been thought to present less outward

---

[5] R. Barber and J. Barker, *Tournaments. Jousts, Chivalry and Pageants in the Middle Ages,* Woodbridge and New York 1989, 178-183, and endpapers.

thrust, but there is still the problem of the lack of substantial amounts of timber in the building accounts. Timber was normally acquired, selected, felled and prepared shortly in advance of being brought to site, and it might have been expected that more carpenters and sawyers would have been employed in the course of 1344 had such timber structure been intended.

A partially roofed building (in stone)

A circular building constructed in stone around a central open space would be likely to resemble a cloister in some way, with a pitched or lean-to roof over an arcade. At its most elaborate this could have had a series of rooms on the outside, an inner passage or cloister, and a central court, but at its simplest it could have been a stone arcade, perhaps fronting onto a stone-vaulted roof. This could have provided an imposing interior space, and have given the clearest view of activities in the centre of the courtyard. Built on the scale of a cathedral cloister, the width of the vault could have been around 15 – 16ft, allowing 32 bays of arcading each about 15ft wide (see Table 7).[6] On a much larger scale a more generous vault spanning around 26½ ft would allow 16 bays of arcading each 26½ ft wide. The bay divisions could have been formed with transverse arches spanning between the outer wall and inner arcade, but if the vault was continuous then these arches would simply have been vault ribs. The outer wall could have taken the thrust of the vault without external buttresses, and it is notable that few free-standing cathedral cloisters have external buttresses (though they usually have internal ones). The reconstruction drawing (Figure viii) is based on 32 bays.

If the House of the Round Table was constructed as a large vaulted cloister, this would go some way to explaining the somewhat elaborate arrangements for covering of the 'the walls' at the end of the building campaign, and the relative unimportance of carpentry in the structure. It would also have provided an open but partially weather-proof setting for feasts and observable activities in the central space. There is a detailed description of a purpose-built 'cloister' being used for a royal banquet, at the Château de Saumur (Dépt. Maine-et-Loire) in 1241. Jean Joinville's *Life of St Louis* specifically compares this to a Cistercian cloister, and although some of the architectural implications are uncertain, it is clear that both the covered wings and open centre were used. Not only was this (lost) feature at Saumur built by Henry II, but it is a lone literary representative of what seems to have been a not uncommon feature of English palaces, as Ashbee has shown,[7] alongside the more usual 'pentices' or roofed passsages joining buildings.

---

[6] For examples of cloister vault design, etc., see M. Henig and J. McNeill (eds), *The Medieval Cloister in England and Wales*, = *Journal of the British Archaeological Association*, 159, 2006.

[7] Jeremy Ashbee, 'Cloisters in English Palaces in the Twelfth and Thirteenth Centuries', in *The Medieval Cloister in England and Wales*, 71-90.

Table 7 House of the Round Table: Parameters for Spacing of Arcades with different Vault spans

Diameter	Circumference	Vault Bay	Arcade Bay	Arcades no.
188	590½	-	-	-
157	493	15½	15½	32
157	493	15½	31	16
156	490	16	15¼	32
156	490	16	30½	16
155	487	16½	15¼	32
155	487	16½	30½	16
135	414	26½	13¼	32
135	414	26½	26½	16

Overall diameter of 200 feet reduced by 2 x 6 foot walls = 188 feet (circumference 590.6 feet)
Overall diameter of 188 feet reduced by 2 x 15½ foot vaults = 157 feet (circumference 493 feet)
Overall diameter of 188 feet reduced by 2 x 16 foot vaults = 156 feet (circumference 490 feet)
Overall diameter of 188 feet reduced by 2 x 16½ foot vaults = 155 feet (circumference 487 feet)
Overall diameter of 188 feet reduced by 2 x 26½ foot vaults = 135 feet (circumference 414 feet)

The Round Table

As should now be apparent, it is not essential that the *Domus Rotunde Tabulae* should actually have contained a table, but it is not unlikely that one was intended to be present. Again we turn to the imaginary Round Table of *Perceforest*:

> Right around the hall curved a marble table, most beautifully made, standing quite high off the ground on pillars; and it ran so close to the windows that anyone sitting at the table would be resting his back against the tower wall.[8]

Such a table was not wholly a thing of fantasy, for there was one in the King's great hall at Westminster. It was there before the major rebuilding of Richard II in the 1390s, for it existed in Edward I's reign, and was repaired for Edward II's coronation in 1307. Dugdale described it as the 'long marble table' where the Chancellor sat on a marble chair in the centre (in the Court of Chancery), and this was of course the seat used by the king at the Coronation Feast.[9] The marble supplied in 1307 came from the marble merchant Adam of Corfe, and was thus of Purbeck marble from the nearby quarries in Dorset, no doubt provided in long slabs of the kind regularly used for setting monumental brasses.[10] No representation of the table is known, but parts of the supporting 'legs' have been found in excavations at Westminster

---

[8] See p.104 above.
[9] *History of the King's Works*, I, 544.
[10] *Ibid.*; Blair, 'Purbeck Marble'.

Hall, in Purbeck marble 38ins high and a yard deep (970 x 920mm), in the form of a chamfered arch between upright pilasters.[11] Had the House of the Round Table been completed, it would doubtless have been furnished with a table of similar composition.

[11] A part formerly displayed in the Westminster Jewel Tower was found in 1960, and other parts were found recently during the refurbishment of the Hall by the Museum of London, reported in *British Archaeology*, 89, July/August 2006.

9. *Castel del Monte from the air*

II WINDSOR AND BEYOND
CENTRAL PLANNING IN MEDIEVAL EUROPE

It was not only in literature and imagination that extraordinary buildings could be found; they could also be visited by the inquisitive tourist (whether merchant, diplomat, pilgrim or crusader), who could find large round buildings scattered about Europe and the near east. For carpenters, masons or military engineers the sight of a complex structure would be sufficient to bring away some notion of how it might be replicated, while the description of an intelligent observer would not be without some value. The pedigree of the round (or 'centrally-planned') building is long, and its offspring have included some of the finest buildings of the Renaissance and later. But it is to Rome that we must look for the most obvious sources that stand at the head of the tradition. From Nero's Domus Aurea in Rome, with its domed dining room and central oculus open to the sky we are led on to Hadrian's Pantheon with its vast concrete dome that has amazed visitors to Rome ever since it was built. From Baiae near Naples to Diocletian's Palace at Split (Spoleto) the circular domed space could be found in public and religious buildings.[12] Thus

---

[12] J.B. Ward-Perkins, *Roman Imperial Architecture*, London 1992; Goetze, *Castel del Monte,* 135 illus.

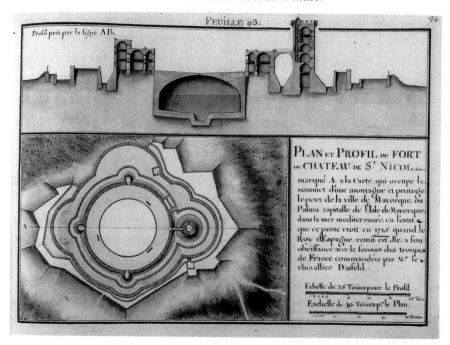

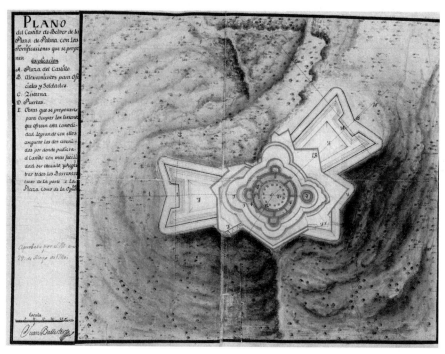

10. Plan and section of Castell de Bellver in 1715 (Vincennes, Atlas de Masse, f.93) and 1740 (Centro Geografico del Ejercito, Bal. No. 54)

it was not surprising that the form should have been adopted in early Christian architecture, most notably by Constantine in building the church on the site of the tomb of Christ in Jerusalem: the Church of the Holy Sepulchre, dedicated in 335 AD. Although damaged and rebuilt on various occasions, the form of the great rotunda enclosing the aedicule containing the tomb has survived, and was always a major destination for pilgrims and crusaders.[13] As rebuilt in the twelfth century, the rotunda had an arcade and two tiers of matching openings above, with a giant order of pilasters rising to the base of the dome, and an aisle or ambulatory around the outside.[14]

From the Holy Sepulchre extended a whole series of early Christian centrally-planned buildings, including the sixth century San Vitale in Ravenna (with a central octagon and encircling ambulatory) and the greatest of all churches, that of Haghia Sophia in Constantinople (with a vast dome on a square base). Charlemagne's imperial palace chapel at Aix la Chapelle (Aachen) was built in 792-805 and probably owes as much to Ravenna as to any direct link with the Holy Sepulchre.[15] However, the fame of the church was aided by pilgrim's accounts, the most famous being Adomnán's *De Locis Sanctis*, written on Iona but based on first-hand evidence of a visitor to Jerusalem, who drew plans of the main holy places including the Holy Sepulchre.[16] This work was important and influential, though the text and its integral plans were better known through Bede's epitome of Adomnán, which had a much wider circulation.[17] So plans of the church of the Holy Sepulchre were available in some monastic libraries to corroborate the reports of visitors. For the crusaders, the protection of the sacred places in Jerusalem was their very raison d'être, and they could not fail to have knowledge of the church.

The most direct descendants from the Holy Sepulchre were, unsurprisingly, the churches of the Knights Templar, which were often (but not invariably) modelled on the Holy Sepulchre. In England there was the Temple Church in London, and a number of parish churches (Cambridge, Chichester, Little Maplestead, Northampton) dedicated to the Holy Sepulchre, even if not necessarily of Templar affiliation. The great Templar church at Tomar in Portugal survived the infamous purge of the order by their refoundation as a new Order of Christ. These churches have a round body with a circular arcade separating a lower aisle or ambulatory from a taller nave in the centre (with clerestory windows above), and then a separate chancel as an apsidal or rectangular addition. None (except Tomar) is of great size.

Perhaps the most interesting offshoot of this form in religious buildings was the Islamic use of the plan in varieties of greater or lesser geometrical complexity, and starting with the Dome of the Rock constructed on the Temple site in Jerusalem

[13] M. Biddle, *The Tomb of Christ*, Stroud 1999.

[14] R. Willis, *The Architectural History of the Church of the Holy Sepulchre at Jerusalem*, London 1849.

[15] Götze, *Castel del Monte*, 136 (Ravenna), 207-8 (Aachen).

[16] D. Meehan (ed.) Adamnan's *De Locis Sanctis* (Scriptores Latini Hiberniae III, 1958); M. Gorman, 'Adomnán's De Locis Sanctis: The Diagrams and the Sources', *Revue Bénédictine* 116.i, 2006, 1-41.

[17] T. O'Loughlin, 'The Diffusion of Adomnán's *De Locis Sanctis* in the Medieval Period', *Eriú*, LI (2000), 93-106.

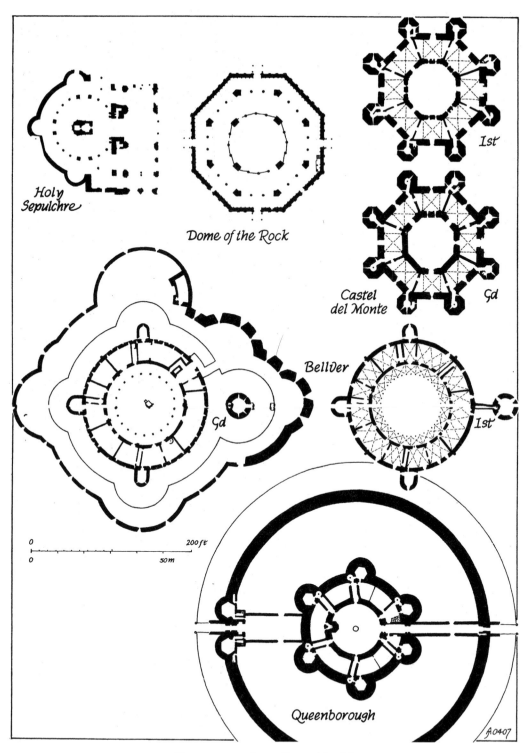

Holy Sepulchre

Dome of the Rock

Castel del Monte

1st

Gd

Bellver

Gd

1st

0   200ft
0   50m

Queenborough

A0407

x. Comparative plans of round buildings

between 685 and 691.[18] This mosque was expressly based on the Church of the Holy Sepulchre (and indeed planned to rival and exceed it in magnificence), and then itself became an exemplar for countless other mosques.[19] It was, however, octagonal in plan, thus departing from the circular plan of the Holy Sepulchre, even if it matched it closely in the dimensions of the dome.

When the Hohenstaufen Emperor Frederick II (1194-1250) came to build his extraordinary octagonal castle in Apulia in the early thirteenth century (1230-40), the Castel del Monte, it was supposedly inspired by his visit to the Dome of the Rock, and its complex geometry certainly has Islamic affinities.[20] However, the extraordinary interest of the building lies as much in its blending of northern Gothic with southern Classical features and eastern Islamic patterns. Neither is it the only remarkable building in his kingdom, where a dazzling array of geometric forms were used for castles and other structures built in his reign.[21] As a fortress and centre of rule for the Kingdom of Sicily, the Castel del Monte was a wholly secular building, and its extraordinary affinities were intellectual rather than spiritual. Its octagonal plan with a central courtyard provides eight trapezoidal chambers of equal dimensions, with vaulted roofs; around it were eight octagonal towers.[22] It was hugely impressive, and not small, though it would have fitted comfortably into the courtyard of the Round Table building (see Table 8 below).

While Frederick himself was regarded as the *stupor mundi*, the renown of his extraordinary buildings cannot be known, but it may be that reports of the Castel del Monte promoted the idea of a circular castle to king Jaime II of Majorca (1276-1311) when he came to build his Castell de Bellver on the prominent hillside outside Palma as a summer retreat. Built around 1300-1310 (its building accounts survive in the Royal Archives), this is a quite remarkable building that has been unjustly neglected in castle studies.[23] The castle is surrounded by a deep ditch, and consists of a circular bailey with a separate donjon or Tour d'Hommage joined by a bridge (as at Aigues-Mortes, see below). The curtain wall has three towers and three turrets,

---

[18] Götze, *Del Monte*, 137.

[19] K. A. C. Creswell, *The origin of the plan of the Dome of the Rock*, British School of Archaeology in Jerusalem, Supplementary papers 2 (1924).

[20] These are extensively discussed by Götze, *Castel del Monte*, but not the date; the castle was 'completed by 1240' according to the World Heritage Site Inscription.

[21] Götze, *Castel del Monte*, intro chapters.

[22] Plans: Götze, *Castel del Monte*, 89 (vaults), 171 (dimensions).

[23] The standard account is by M. Durliat in his *L'Art dans le Royaume de Majorque. Les débuts de l'art Gothique en Roussillon, en Cerdagne at aux Baleares*, Toulouse 1962, 234-47, with a plan and section; he also printed the (Catalan) building accounts: 'Le Château de Bellver à Majorque', *Études Roussillonnaises* V, 1956, 197-212. Illustrated guidebooks by Gaspar Sabatier, *El Castell de Bellver*, Palma 1990, and J.A. Aguiló i Ribas, A. Llabrés i Bernat, and G. Valero I Martí, *Guia de Bellver*, Palma 1995, are of value, the latter especially for its description of the surrounding area of *garrigue* vegetation. The proceedings of an anniversary conference contains useful material: [Ajuntament de Palma], *Bellver 1300-2000 700 anys del castell*, Palma 2001, including papers by Jaume Sastre Moll on the building campaign, Sebastiana Sabater Rebassa on the painted decoration of the castle, Miquel Ferrer Florez on prisoners and Elvira Gonzalez Gozalo on their graffiti. Historic plans of the castle are reproduced in Juan Tous Meliá, *Palma a Través de la Cartografía (1596-1902)*, Palma, 2002, and the first-floor plan reproduced here is from L. Salvador, *Die Stadt Palma*, Leipzig, 1882, 292.

and a ring of buildings round the interior, with a central courtyard built over a large underground cistern. The apartments are joined and accessed by an internal cloister on two levels, so the courtyard is entirely surrounded by a two-tier open gallery. On the courtyard level there are round arches and a wooden ceiling, and on the first floor there are larger arched openings of two lights with simple tracery, while the gallery walk (like the rooms) is fully vaulted. While the ground floor had a series of minor apartments and service rooms (granary, wine store and forge are listed in an inventory of 1345),[24] the first floor had a generous disposition of public rooms and apartments: kitchen, hall(?), suites of chambers, and chapel. The first floor itself is of timber, but these apartments are vaulted throughout, with a total of 27 bays of vaulting, while the internal gallery has 21 bays of vaulting (one for each double opening). (See Plates V-X).

The castle could thus function as a palace, and was indeed occupied as early as 1314 by King Sanche; when the kingdom of Majorca was annexed by Aragon the castle became a place of imprisonment for the Majorcan royal family in 1349. It was for long after a state prison, though the castle was once more inhabited by the King John I of Aragon in 1394. The castle and its surrounding woodland was granted to the Carthusians at Valdemossa in 1403 and was held by them until 1835. The most famous prisoner was Gaspar Melchior de Jovellanos in 1801-8 who occupied his time writing aboute the history of Majorca, and wrote delightful accounts of the history and natural history of the castle and its environs.[25] Possible visits to Majorca by English diplomats of Edward III are discussed in the appendix to this chapter on p. 135.

Bellver has two possible successors, of which one, the Château de Montaner in southern France, has a direct filiation since it was built by a member of the Majorcan court circle. While its polygonal walls almost could refer to the Castel del Monte, it needs no other source than Bellver.[26] The second and more intriguing successor would seem to be the enigmatic lost castle of Queenborough on the Isle of Sheppey in Kent.[27] Built in 1360 for Edward III, and favoured by him as a place to visit, the appearance of the castle (which is known only from a sixteenth-century plan and a drawing by Wenceslas Hollar) is remarkably close to Bellver in several ways. Although Queenborough has usually been treated as an exceptional one-off design, without precedent, and somehow anticipating the artillery castles built by Henry VIII, consideration must now be given to the possibility that it was planned

---

[24] Antonio Mut Calafell, 'Inventarios de los castillos de Alaró, Bellver …', *Bolletí de la Societat Arquelogica Lul-liana* XLI (839), 1985, 57-78.

[25] G.M. de Jovellanos (1744-1811), *Memorias historicas sobre el Castillo de Bellver en la isla de Mallorca, etc*, Palma 1813, and other parts of the work published posthumously; the 'Memoria del Castillo de Bellver, Descripción Histórico-Artística' has often been reprinted in collected works, such as *Obras en Prosa*, ed. José Caso Gonzales, Madrid 1969, which explains the complex publishing history of the various parts (*ibid.*, 51-8).

[26] Pierre Tucoo-Chala, avec Roger Barbe et Philippe Araguas, *Le Château de Montaner*, Supplement to *Revue de Pau et Bearn* Pau 1984.

[27] *History of the King's Works*, II,793-804, fig. 63, pl. 47B. The site of the castle was investigated by Time Team (broadcast 12 March 2006), and the castle walls located.

with direct knowledge of Bellver.[28] Perhaps the most striking element is the profile, seen in Hollar's picturesque view, with a ring of modest-size towers rising above the curtain (Figure 7, p.116 above), and where Bellver had a lobed outer rampart, at Queenborough there was an outer bailey of circular plan, some 330ft (100.58m) in diameter, or 395ft (120.4m) including the moat. There was no donjon, but the larger gatehouse tower may have included larger apartments, in addition to those spaced around the wall, with access to the turrets.

Table 8   House of the Round Table and Circular Buildings

[In metres]	External Diameter (outer)	External Diameter (inner)	Internal Diameter (central area)	Towers
Church of the Holy Sepulchre	36.5	33.2	20.9	3
Dome of the Rock	54	-	20.37	0
Castel del Monte	40.50	35.38	17.85	8
Castell de Bellver	48	44.5	30 / 23	3 + 1
Château de Montaner	?54	?25	?25	1
Restormel Castle	38		20	0
House of the Round Table	60.96 (200 ft)	57.30 (188 ft)	47.25 (155 ft)	0
Queenborough Castle	42	34	18	6

It may be objected that there was no shortage of home-grown precedents for circular buildings to draw on.[29] William Marshal's circular keep or donjon at Pembroke Castle (1190-1200) is an interesting example with a domed stone vault, while the fine detached donjon at Flint built in 1277-86 has a striking plan arrangement, offset at one corner of the castle, and one might be forgiven for suggesting that its builder had been to Aigues-Mortes, built on France's narrow Mediterranean shore, where the donjon (the Tour de Constance, completed in 1248) is offset at the corner of the town walls in exactly the same way.[30] Since Aigues-Mortes bordered one of the mainland portions of the kingdom of Majorca, at Montpellier, it is not surprising that the semi-detached donjon was also replicated at Bellver. However, these donjons were on a much smaller scale (both under 20m in diameter), and the more obvious sources are the small number of so-called 'shell keeps', to be found at various castles in England and Wales, including of course

[28] John Newman, *Buildings of England: North East and East Kent*, Harmondsworth 1969, 404 observed the relation to Bellver and Castel del Monte.
[29] I am very grateful to John Goodall for his observations on this point.
[30] Pembroke: Flint: *History of the King's Works*, I, 308-18; E Hubbard, *Buildings of Wales: Clwyd*, Harmondsworth 1986, 348; M. Bellet, *The City of Aigues-Mortes*, Paris, 2001.

Windsor.[31] These did not necessarily have buildings within them, or buildings attached to the outer wall: at Launceston (Cornwall) a circular donjon was built inside a surrounding wall, possibly by Richard Earl of Cornwall (1227-72). A later example was built at Restormel in Cornwall by Earl Richard (if not by his son Edmund). Richard, as King of the Romans and prospective Emperor, should also be remembered as builder of the ultimate Arthurian fantasy castle at Tintagel, but at Restormel he infilled the older stone keep on the ringwork with a very regular array of rooms round a central courtyard that, like Windsor in the 1350s, had space for a hall, chamber and kitchen and guest apartments, and at a scale comparable with Bellver and Queenborough (see Table 8).[32] In the early fourteenth century Totnes Castle (Devon) had a stone wall built round the top of the motte, but no principal structure within it.[33]

Innovation was not solely the province of the stone mason, and the early fourteenth century was par excellence the age of Gothic carpentry, combining exciting special forms with daring attempts at creative engineering. William Hurley, the master carpenter of the House of the Round Table was after all the man responsible for rebuilding the Ely Octagon with its amazing cantilevered timber lantern built over a huge octagonal span of 70ft (21.3m).[34] His association with the House of the Round Table is intriguing for a building that seems to have had so few timber components, and it is not impossible that he had a hand in its design.

In seeking affinities for the House of the Round Table we should perhaps not make too much of all the possible associations, or suggest that there was some compulsive *leitmotif* in king Edward's initiation of the Round Table building in the 1340s, his creation of a circular home in the great Round Tower at Windsor in the 1350s, and his fondness for Queenborough Castle in the 1360s. Rather, what the sequence of buildings does show is that there were any number of precedents for round buildings in early fourteenth century Europe, and that a building like Bellver shows how an arcaded courtyard with an open centre could be planned. But whether Bellver, as a likely source for Queenborough, could in some way have inspired the Round Table cannot be determined, any more than we can know whether the builder of Bellver had in his hand a plan of the Holy Sepulchre, or indeed the initiator of the Round Table had it in his mind. But we can with confidence say that the House of the Round Table, if a unique attempt to build a fantastic Arthurian building, was not entirely without architectural precedent.

[31] D.J. Cathcart King, *The Castle in England and Wales*, 64-6; English Heritage 'monument description': http://www.eng-h.gov.uk/mpp/mcd/sub/shell12.htm.

[32] C.A. Ralegh Radford, *Restormel Castle*, London 1980.

[33] Derek Renn, *Three Shell Keeps*, London 1969.

[34] Cecil Hewett, *English Cathedral and Monastic Carpentry*, Chichester 1985, 114-22.

Appendix: Anglo-Majorcan relations, 1340-1344   RICHARD BARBER

In 1340, when Edward had just proclaimed himself king of France, ambassadors arrived from Jaime III, king of Majorca, to seek a marriage alliance with the English royal house. Edward, who 'had a genius for turning other men's quarrels to his own account and recruiting traitors and malcontents to his cause'[35] saw an opportunity to stir up trouble in the south of France, for the kingdom of Majorca included territories in the south of France under French overlordship. In other words, the relationship between Philip VI and Jaime III was identical to that with Edward in Aquitaine, in that all three were sovereigns in their own right, but Jaime III and Edward held fiefs from the French king. They had a common interest in weakening Philip's power over their French fiefs, though Edward's position was more difficult in that the French had seized Aquitaine in 1324 and he ruled only a portion of the lands for which he had done homage.

Negotiations for the alliance involved meetings first in Ghent and later in Bordeaux. It seems that the proposal had come from Jaime III, and that Edward was initially sceptical about the possibilities. He wrote to Jaime on November 18 1340 from Ghent, regretting that the Majorcan ambassadors who had recently visited him did not have the necessary authority to conclude a marriage treaty between Jaime's eldest son and one of his daughters; and he promised, after consulting with his council, to send plenipotentiary ambassadors to Majorca to settle the terms.[36] In February 1341, Raymond Corneill, who had experience of diplomacy in Spain, was sent to the kings of Aragon and Majorca to negotiate an alliance against Philip VI, which was presumably to include the marriage; but his mission was inconclusive. What the English do not seem to have known is that Pedro of Aragon was playing a double game, with the object of reuniting the kingdom of Majorca with Aragon. The kingdoms had only been separated under the will of Jaime I of Aragon , who died in 1276, and the kings of Aragon had made repeated attempts to reverse this. At the same time two envoys were sent to the king of Majorca to negotiate in secret an alliance, since that negotiated at Ghent had not come into force.[37]

Jaime, before the ambassadors arrived, had overplayed his hand. He did so in a somewhat extraordinary way. He went to Montpellier, which was the chief city of his French domains, and issued a charter founding a church at Perpignan, using the formulas appropriate to a sovereign prince. He then proclaimed jousts at Montpellier for February, in defiance of a ban on tournaments issued by Philip VI and reinforced by Philip's steward in the area. Jaime responded by tearing down the French standards from houses in Montpellier, and held the jousts almost immediately. When he rode into the lists, he was accompanied by a local nobleman

---

[35] Sumption, *The Hundred Years War*, I.293.

[36] F. Bock, *Das deutsch-englische Bündnis von 1335-1342 i. Quellen*, Quellen und Erörterungen zur bayerischen Geschichte NS XII, Munich 1956 561, no. 148; printed in Pierre Chaplais, *English Diplomatic Practice in the Middle Ages* (Hambledon and London, 2003), 119, and 172. For an earlier secret mission to Castile, Aragon, Majorca and Portugal by John Darcy and William Trussel in 1331, see *ibid.*, 168 and 171, and *Foedera* 790.

[37] Bock, *Das deutsch-englische Bündnis*, 563, nos. 149-150.

and six of the latter's knights, whose horses had the arms of England on their caparisons. When this squadron entered the lists, they used the English warcry, 'Guyenne, Guyenne', this being one of the names for Aquitaine. The jousters set up 'tables', possibly the 'round tables' to be found at other Catalan tournaments, as part of the organisation of the event. Two more days of jousting followed before a truce was negotiated between Jaime III and the French royal steward.[38]

Jaime's unusual but rather clumsy defiance of Philip was the catalyst for his downfall; Peter of Aragon and Philip manoeuvred him into a position where they could legitimately claim that he had broken feudal law, and Peter was able to seize Majorca in 1343.

How far these dealings implied that English diplomats or knights might have visited Palma during these years is hard to gauge, because Jaime III spent a good deal of time in his French dominions, which were much more accessible. There were also links with the merchants of Palma, at that period a wealthy city and an important trading centre; but contacts with Majorca and Aragon were far less frequent than those with Castile, where Edward's agents had been buying the much-prized Castilian horses since the beginning of his reign. So despite Jaime III's rebellious display of chivalry in the English colours at Montpellier, we cannot show that there was any direct knowledge of Palma or of Bellver.

[38] C de Vic and J. Vaissete, *Histoire générale de Languedoc*, 2nd edn., Toulouse 1885, IX, 529-31.

The Order of the Round Table

Richard Barber

W E HAVE JUST ONE document which gives us some idea of what was in Edward's mind when he proposed to found the Order of the Round Table, and to build a suitable home or *domus* for his new creation. It is of course the account of the festival of January 1344 given by Adam Murimuth, and we need to look again very carefully at what he says about Edward's agenda for the new order, ignoring all the splendour surrounding the occasion and concentrating on what the king had in mind for the future.

> This feast lasted from Sunday to Wednesday. That night, after the end of the jousts, the king had it proclaimed that no lord or lady should presume to depart, but should stay until morning, to learn the king's pleasure. When the morning of Thursday came, at about nine o'clock the king caused himself to be solemnly arrayed in his most royal and festive attire; his outer mantle was of very precious velvet and the royal crown was placed upon his head. The queen was likewise dressed in most noble fashion.The earls and barons, and the rest of the lords and ladies, prepared themselves in appropriate fashion to go with the king to the chapel in the castle of Windsor and hear mass, as he commanded them to do. When mass had been celebrated, the king left the chapel; Henry, earl of Derby, as steward of England, and William, earl of Salisbury, as marshal of England, went before him, each carrying the staff of his office in his hand, and the king himself holding the royal sceptre in his hand. There followed him the young queen, and the queen-mother, the prince of Wales, the earls, barons, knights and nobles, with the ladies and all the people flocking to see such an extraordinary spectacle, to the place appointed for the assembly. There the king and all the others at the same time stood up. The king was presented with the Bible, and laying his hand on the Gospels, swore a solemn oath that he himself at a certain time, provided that he had the necessary means, would begin a Round Table, in the same manner and condition as Arthur, formerly king of England, established it, namely to the number of 300 knights, and would cherish it and maintain it according to his power, always adding to the number of knights. The earls of Derby,

Salisbury, Warwick, Arundel, Pembroke, and Suffolk, the other barons and very many praiseworthy knights of probity and renown likewise made an oath to observe, sustain, and promote the Round Table with all its appendages.[1]

First of all, the founding of the Round Table is not part of the festival itself, but a separate occasion after the jousts and feasting had concluded. The ceremony takes place with all the formal pomp that can be mustered, and Edward wears his crown, a symbolic act which normally happened only on certain specified occasions. He also carries the royal sceptre, which would indeed have been a highly unusual act even at a major court feast, and the chief royal officers of the court, the steward and marshal, also carry their ceremonial staffs. The assembly takes place, not in the chapel as might be expected, but in what appears to have been an outdoor environment; Murimuth would have specified a place such as the great hall if it had been indoors. The staging of the occasion, as we have seen from the accounts, was carefully choreographed. The king had one of his most splendid sets of robes made for the occasion, an item which stands out even among the vast sums recorded in his accounts with his tailor. The crown, even though it was only his second best crown, was also highly symbolic, since it had been in pawn for the previous four years, together with the great crown. Although a treasury list of 1337 shows that Edward possessed a number of 'crowns' most of these are really coronets, and only three crowns are valued at £40 or above.[2] This may well have been the first time since 1337 that Edward appeared in full state regalia; it is likely that he did so when his eldest son was created duke of Cornwall, and six of his closest associates were raised to the rank of earl. If so, it implies that the founding of the Round Table was intended, not as a simple adjunct to a joust, but as a moment of great political significance. Alternatively, could it be that Edward is play-acting, and the ceremony is a theatrical re-enactment of Arthur's foundation of the Round Table with Edward taking the part of Arthur? We need to look at the other details which the chronicles provide.

Perhaps the most curious of this is the opening of the solemn oath sworn by the king. Instead of declaring outright his intention to found the Round Table, Edward prefaces his words with 'provided that he had the means'. In 1344 these words would have had a very specific resonance. The greatest crisis of Edward's reign had been three years earlier, when his extravagant plans for buying himself an alliance of German princes for his campaign against France had led him to near-bankruptcy and to a rift with the council charged with ruling England in his absence. The royal finances were only just on the mend, as witness the recent redemption of the crown, and this was an undertaking that was likely to cost a great deal. Already the expenditure on feasting alone for this week amounted to £1954 18s 3¼d.[3] To

---

[1] Murimuth, *Continuatio Chronicarum*, 232.

[2] The great crown may not have been one of these; however, it is clear that the two crowns pawned in Germany were symbolic security, as the loans raised far exceeded their actual worth as jewellery.

[3] See summary accounts of the kitchen, item 7 in Appendix C, pp.238-40 below.

put this in perspective, without attempting a false analogy with modern currency, it was approximately three months of normal kitchen expenditure for the king's household, and although the feast in 1337 when the duke and earls were created cost £439 2s 8¼d, there were no other festivities at that time. In comparison with the costs of mounting a military campaign, the kitchen expenditure for the Windsor festival would have paid the wages for Edward's army on the Crécy campaign two years later for seventeen days. Obviously the inaugural occasion was a special one, but to provide for an assembly of 300 knights on a regular annual basis was not going to be cheap if it was to be done in high chivalric style.

This number is the next detail which the writer gives us. The way in which he explains the membership of the Round Table is not entirely clear: I read it to mean that the total number of knights was to be 300, but that it would begin with a smaller number, and that Edward undertook to continually recruit knights until it reached that number. Otherwise, the membership would effectively have no limit, and the evidence from the size of the construction relates very well to the restricted number of 300. A ceremonial order of this size had no precedent. The Hungarian Society of Knighthood of St George twenty years earlier was restricted to 50 knights. The Castilian Order of the Sash had no formal limit, but the records supply a total of 63 names for the first decade. So both the size of the order, the scale of the building and the scale of expenditure on the inauguration coincide: this was to be something quite exceptional. As a one-off event, it was manageable, but with the costs of providing the *domus* and with annual gatherings, even Edward seems to have realised that this was going to stretch his resources.

Edward's reservations at the inauguration were of course to be proved correct; once there was a real prospect of renewal of open war with France, his means were insufficient to support the building expenses, which amounted to £509 12s 11¾d by the time work stopped. Most of this was spent between February and April 1344. This is a monthly rate of expenditure as high as that on the whole of the work done when Windsor Castle was remodelled by William of Wykeham in 1356-61.[4] Wykeham's work was funded by the profits of the war with France; in 1344, there were no profits as yet, and a huge debit in prospect for the costs of the new campaign.

Given the lavish scale of the inaugural feast, what did Edward III have in mind when he proposed to found the Order of the Round Table? Such an institution had very few precedents in real life, and the idea of creating a real Round Table in the form of a knightly order was a very novel one. In the twelfth century, the church had harnessed the enthusiasm for knighthood in the service of the crusades, and the great military orders had been the result. The Templars, Hospitallers and Teutonic Knights were bound by formal rules which owed much to the monastic orders which had helped to create them, and their model was very much based on the rules of monastic life. These orders had been in existence before the idea

---

[4] The total expenditure listed by St John Hope, I, 178-219, totals £6868 8s 4d for 60 months, giving an average of £114 14s 8d per month.

of Arthur's round table was invented, and the concept of an order of knighthood which owed its allegiance to the king rather than to the world of religion had no counterpart in real life until the existence of the religious knightly orders began to be questioned. With the loss of Palestine at the end of the thirteenth century, the Templars and Hospitallers were deprived of their main reason for existence, the defence of the kingdom of Jerusalem and the pilgrims who made their way to the Holy City. They were rich and powerful organisations, and it was not long before the wealth of the Templars led Philip VI of France to plot their dissolution.

The complex story of the trial of the Templars is outside our present subject; but much of the property belonging to the Templars passed, at least temporarily, into the control of the kings of Europe. In Spain, where the wars against the Muslim rulers of the south formed a second crusading front, the kings were anxious to maintain the armed support which the Templars had supplied; and there was already a tradition of royal involvement with the foundation of military orders, beginning with the Order of Santiago in 1170. So instead of simply letting the Hospitallers take over, as happened elsewhere in Europe, they set about establishing replacement orders. The first of these was the Order of Christ in Portugal, set up in 1317 by king Dinis, and approved by the pope; similarly, in Aragon, king Robert set up the Order of Montesa two years later, and papal bulls were issued in March 1320. The exact power wielded by the kings over the two orders is not defined in their statutes, but there is clear evidence in their subsequent history that the orders soon became a kind of hybrid between religious and secular orders of knighthood, with a large element of royal influence which had been totally lacking in the days of the Templars. Furthermore, these were no longer international orders, but had a specifically national base. Alfonso XI of Castile was slower off the mark, and after long negotiations over the fate of the Templar lands and castles, he asked for the establishment of a new order in 1331 to take over these estates, only to be told that it was too late to do this.[5]

A further factor in changing attitudes towards the orders of knighthood may have been the increasingly secular power wielded by the Teutonic Knights as rulers of Prussia; Prussia itself had been 'pacified' by 1272, and it was only in 1302 that new crusades against its pagan neighbours were announced. These expeditions, unlike the huge armies which were raised for the crusades in the East, were small scale, and often a number of individual knights would travel to Prussia, where the year's campaigns would then be organised by the Teutonic Knights, beginning with largely secular ceremonials and even tournaments. This was chivalry in the service of the state, in a way that had never been seen in Palestine.

So the idea that knighthood as an order was a matter for the Church – which had after all first promoted this as a way of harnessing the dangerous power and energy of the new knightly class – began to fade in the first decades of the fourteenth

---

[5] Sebastiano Pauli, *Codice diplomatico del sacro militare ordine gerosolimitano oggi di Malta*, Lucca 1738, II 80.

century. This may explain why from 1325 onwards a succession of kings chose to establish secular orders of knighthood; the changing nature of kingship and the emergence of the nation-states of later medieval Europe were also important factors. The first was 'the Fraternal Society of Knighthood of St George', which appears in Hungary, under the auspices of Károly I. This was to consist of a group of knights loyal to the king, and was limited to fifty knights only when the order first met in 1326. The model for Károly's society was closer to that of the confraternities or guilds which were a feature of the everyday life of medieval Europe. These groups, often drawn from a single trade, functioned as a kind of mutual support besides regulating the business with which they were connected; they might undertake to look after members who fell sick and to say masses for departed brethren, as well as ensuring that there were no internal quarrels. The guilds are chiefly associated with the growth of the cities from the twelfth century onwards, but among the Anglo-Saxon records we find a guild of thegns operating in tenth century Cambridge, linked by their status in society as much as by any skills as fighting men that they may have possessed.

However, we have no records of chivalric associations of this kind until well after the time of Edward III's proposed Order of the Round Table. In a sense, Károly I's foundation relates mainly to the political situation in Hungary at the time; he had urgent need of a loyal following in order to break the power of the great magnates who were hostile to a king who had invaded the country in order to claim his inheritance. By formalising the allegiance of a group of knights to himself, he was trying to ensure that he could rely on their support and suppress any quarrels between them. Furthermore, it was a means of rewarding the new barons whom he had created and setting up a new court culture as a symbol of his power, in contrast to the anarchy in which the great magnates had prospered. But what he created was not a fully-fledged 'order' of knighthood of the type that became familiar in the later middle ages. Throughout the statutes it is called a 'fraternal society', as if the term 'order' was reserved for the military orders of knighthood; and the king is not at the head of the order, which is under the control of two 'judges' elected by the knights, of whom one is to be a layman and the other a cleric. The king, however, is clearly the driving force behind the Society of Knighthood of St George, and the statutes give him power over the election of members and the addition of new statutes, as well as declaring that he can make use of the society for the defence of his person and kingdom.[6]

The inspiration for this foundation is unlikely to have come from the religious orders or from the guilds, but may reflect the temporary associations which knights seem to have formed in order to hold tournaments. The earliest documented example of such an association is in Ulrich von Lichtenstein's account of his chivalric career, discussed earlier.[7] Records of such societies, ephemeral and without any legal standing, are few and far between. There may have been a tourneying

[6] Boulton, *Knights of the Crown*, 33.
[7] See pp. 87-89 above.

society of this kind set up by the count of Holland in the 1290s,[8] and there is firm evidence of such an organisation headed by Henry earl of Derby in Lincolnshire in 1344, for which letters patent were issued on February 10 licensing 'a certain number of knights chosen for the purpose' to joust annually at Lincoln under the earl's captaincy. Many of the early knightly orders seem to have had clauses in their statutes relating to the holding of tournaments by their members. The statutes of Károly I's Society of St George probably refer to this, albeit indirectly, when the members are required to 'follow the king in an outstanding way in every recreational activity and knightly game'.

Three other orders founded within fifteen years of the Society of St George are fraternal orders, but do not seem to have included tournaments in their activities. The Order of St Catherine, created by Humbert II in the Dauphiné in the third decade of the fourteenth century, was an association of knights and little more, but two German institutions seem to have a fairly strong religious element. The first, the Company of the Cloister of Ettal, founded about 1330, was modelled on the Spanish military orders and had a mixture of lay knights and monks, and allowed the lay knights to be married. They lived in the strategically placed monastery of Ettal which commanded the Brenner pass between Italy and Bavaria, rather as the knights of the Spanish Order of Santiago manned the great border fortresses on the frontier with the Arab kingdoms. It was short lived, but the cousin of its founder created another order, this time in Vienna in about 1337, which was also fraternal in nature. However, it was not an enclosed order like that at Ettal, and it seems to have had a literary background, because the knights were known as the 'Company of the Templars'. The German word for 'Templar' which is used is not that for the Knights Templar (*Tempelherren*), but the word used by Wolfram von Eschenbach in his masterpiece *Parzival* about the guardians of the Grail Temple (*Templeisen*), and this indicates a very clear Arthurian connection.

These orders are little more than shadows on the face of history compared with the first secular association to be called an 'Order', the Order of the Sash in Castile. We know a good deal about this order, as we have the original statutes, lists of members and accounts of their activities in contemporary chronicles. There are even Castilian gold coins of the period with the order's insignia. It was founded in 1330 by Alfonso XI of Castile, and in the chronicle of his reign for that year we read:

> The king being at Vittoria, because in times past the men of his kingdoms of Castile and Leon had always practised chivalry, and he had been told that they did not do so in his day, in order that they might be more eager to practise it, he commanded that some knights and squires of his household should wear a sash on their clothes, and he, the king, would do likewise. And being at Vittoria he sent orders to those knights and squires whom he had chosen for the purpose

---

8   Maurice Keen, *Chivalry*, New Haven and London 1984, 181.

to wear clothes with, on them, the sash which he had given them.
And he also put on clothes with a sash: the first clothes made for the
purpose were white, and the sash dark. And from then on he gave
each of these knights similar clothing with sashes each year. And the
sash was as broad as a man's hand, and was worn over cloaks and
other garments from the left shoulder to the waist [i.e. diagonally]:
and they were called the Knights of the Sash [*de la Banda*] and had
statutes among themselves on many good matters, all of which were
knightly deeds. And when a knight was given the sash, he was made
to swear and promise to keep all the things that were written in that
book of statutes. And the king did this so that men, wishing to have
that sash would have reason to do knightly deeds. And it happened
afterwards that if a knight or squire did some feat of arms against the
king's enemies, or tried to perform such a feat, the king gave him a
sash and did him high honour, so that all the others wished to do
good knightly deeds to gain that honour and the goodwill of the king,
like those who already had it.[9]

The Knights of the Sash reappear on two further occasions in the *Chronicle*:
before Alfonso's coronation at Burgos in 1332, when jousts were held at which
the knights held the lists against all comers, and again in 1333 at Valladolid in a
tournament at which they fought together against the challengers, the king doing
great deeds on their side.

The only supporting documents are sixteenth-century copies of the statutes. The
language and style point to a direct copy of an almost contemporary manuscript,
and the prologue claims that the rules which follow were laid down by Alfonso
XI at the foundation of the order in the year of his coronation, which does not
agree with the *Chronicle*, though the discrepancy is only a minor one. The statutes
proper begin with the reasons for founding the order: 'because chivalry should be
greatly honoured and advanced, and because that thing in all the world which most
appertains to a knight is truth and loyalty, and which is most rewarded by God, for
that reason [the king] ordered this book to be made of the order of the Sash, which
is founded on two principles: chivalry and loyalty'.[10] There follow the twenty-two
headings of the rules, as follows:

> How the Knights of the Sash should try to hear Mass each morning
> What the Knights of the Sash should have in the way of arms and
> equipment
> How the Knights of the Sash should avoid playing dice, especially on
> campaigns

---

9   Translated from Cayetano Rossell (ed.), *Cronicas de los Reyes de Castilla*, Biblioteca de autores españoles
    66, Madrid 1953, I, 231-2.
10 L. Tadeo Villanueva, 'Memorial sobre la orden de Caballeria de la Banda de Castilla', *Boletin de la real
    academia de la historia*, LXXIII, 1918, 436-65, 552-74.

The speech and clothing to be adopted by the Knights of the Sash
How the Knights of the Sash should behave when eating and drinking
How a knight should be invested with the sash
How a Knight of the Sash should act if another knight wishes to challenge him for the sash
How a knight should act if challenged for the sash outside the Royal court
The penalty for striking or drawing a sword against another Knight of the Sash
How a Knight of the Sash who has a grievance against the king should proceed
What the Knights of the Sash should do if any knight repudiates his homage to the king or to the king's son
How a Knight of the Sash should proceed if another knight of the order is found guilty of a capital crime
The Knights of the Sash to form one squadron in the royal army on campaign
Chapters of the Order to be held at least three times a year
How the Knights of the Sash are to behave in jousts
What should be done if two Knights of the Sash quarrel
Procedure at a knight's marriage
Procedure at a knight's death
Procedure at a tournament
How the Knights of the Sash are to observe everything in this book
The organisation of tournaments
The organisation of jousts.[11]

It is clear from this outline that jousts played as large a part in the order's affairs as did the conduct of war. But this element is probably accounted for by Alfonso's personal prowess as a jouster, if we may believe the *Chronicle* on that score. More important are the provisions for loyalty to the king and avoidance of quarrels, as well as those for behaviour. All these statutes seem to aim at a distinctive corps d'élite, set apart both by their way of life as the most polished of courtiers and by their special oaths of loyalty, as well as their function as the royal bodyguard in war. This is borne out by the terms of the oath administered to the knights when they joined the order. The king and at least six knights were to be present

> and the knight to whom the sash is to be given shall come fully armed: and they shall ask him whether he wishes to take the sash and be a member of the Knights of the Sash. And if he says yes, they shall say: 'You have to swear two oaths. The first is that you will serve the king

11 Villanueva, 'Memorial sobre la orden', 554.

all your life or will always be a vassal of the king or of one of his sons: but if it befalls that you leave the king's service or that of his sons, you shall return the sash to the king ... And the second oath that you have to swear is that you will love the Knights of the Sash as your brothers, and that you will never challenge a knight of the Sash unless it is to help your father or brother. And if two Knights of the Sash quarrel or fight, you shall do everything to part them, and if you cannot part them, you shall not help either of them.'[12]

Alfonso had particular reason to value loyalty to his person and peace among his knights. He had come to the throne before he was two, and a troubled regency of thirteen years had followed. Continual revolts and intrigues had seriously weakened the kingdom, and much territory was lost to the Moors. Though Alfonso's first campaigns in 1327 and 1330 regained some of this, his domestic troubles continued. He had one of the former regents assassinated in 1326: but another former regent was still rebellious in 1332, and became a vassal of the king of Aragon at about this time. Nor were matters improved by Alfonso's rejection of his Portuguese queen in favour of his mistress Leonor de Guzman, whose bastard son brought about civil war after his father's death. Furthermore, Alfonso's relations with the military orders of Santiago, Alcantara and Calatrava were poor, though they had not yet deteriorated to the nadir of the 1340s when Alcantara was in open revolt. So the Order of the Sash may have been an attempt to bind the nobles to personal loyalty to himself, improve the royal army for campaigns against the Moors, and provide an alternative to the existing military orders. The later history of the Order of the Sash did not bear out these hopes. It scarcely appears in the history of Alfonso's own reign, but experienced a brief revival under Pedro the Cruel, when buildings in Seville were decorated with the arms of the knights. It is mentioned in the *Victorial* of Don Perez Niño, the 'unconquered knight', early in the fifteenth century, and in 1457 a visiting German nobleman recorded that he was given the order of 'la banda de Kastylla' as a personal honour from the king. It was revived in the sixteenth century but even then only survived for a few years. If it arose out of a period of political turbulence, it needed a degree of political stability to survive: and Castile at this period could not offer that stability.

The Order of the Sash is the first order to set out statutes which cover knightly behaviour in the outside world as well as the organisation of the body to which the knight is to belong. This idea of classifying the particular attributes and duties of a knight is to be found in two earlier and very influential Spanish works, the *Siete Partidas* of Alfonso X and the *Llibre de l'ordre de cavalleria* by the Catalan writer Ramon Llull, which William Caxton put into English as *The Boke of the Ordre of Chivalrye*. Alfonso X's *Siete Partidas* is an extraordinary work; it is part law code (and as such still forms part of the law of Louisiana, once a Spanish colony) and part a manual on the structure of the medieval state. Alfonso's second *partida*

---

[12] G. Daumet, 'L'ordre castillan de l'écharpe', *Bulletin hispanique*, XXV, 1923, 12-13.

contains a section on knighthood which is not unlike the statutes of the new order in the way it prescribes how knights should behave. Even if Alfonso is talking about knighthood in general, it is clear that this work, and the subsequent adaptation of the *Siete Partidas* by Llull, are at the root of Alfonso XI's order.

Edward's idea of an Order of the Round Table is therefore part of a general movement towards the secularisation of knightly orders, and to their use in the context of royal power. This is underlined by the proposal for a knightly order, from John, duke of Normandy and heir to the French throne, within a few months of the Round Table festivities. This was approved by pope Clement VI in six bulls dated June 5, 1344. However, the disaster at Crécy two years later delayed the execution of the scheme, and it was not until 1352, soon after John became king, that the Order of the Star was actually inaugurated.

We have no real evidence of what Edward had in mind in terms of the detailed statutes of the order, but there are strong common factors in the other fraternities and orders, and it is reasonable to assume that he would have included these elements, tempered by his desire to refound the Arthurian round table, which would have required certain specific features not found elsewhere. Just as we can attempt to reconstruct the proposed 'House of the Round Table' from the evidence of the royal accounts, it is reasonable to attempt a reconstruction of the concept of the order from the evidence of its contemporaries. The evidence of the building itself provides some clues. The orders of the period can be divided into associations with a primarily religious purpose, as in a charitable guild; and into orders whose primary purpose is to strengthen the king's military resources. The first group are the German orders, and the Order of the Star as originally conceived. The second group are the Society of St George in Hungary, the Order of the Sash and the projected Order of the Round Table. The first group are religious to the extent that they specifically or implicitly exclude jousting on the grounds that it breaches the edicts of the church against such sports. The second group, however, have a strong religious element despite their acceptance of jousting; it is an element in their prime purpose, the nurturing of knightly skills that can be used in warfare, and the establishment of a secular brotherhood whose loyalty and companionship are extremely valuable in a military campaign.

Edward promises to 'begin a Round Table, in the same manner and condition as Arthur, formerly king of England, established it'. The barons, in response to his promise to establish, 'cherish and maintain it', swear to 'observe, sustain and promote' the new institution. This implies that there were to be rules, ordinances or statutes which had to be 'observed'; but do we have any idea what these might have been? We have already looked at the question of the 'statutes of the Round Table', which are distinctly elusive. It is worth making one brief speculation: Boccaccio, writing just two decades later, could conceivably have picked up a draft of the proposed statutes made for the Order of the Round Table, as we have no evidence that this set of rules comes from an earlier Arthurian source. Are these rules what we might expect Edward to have put in place, and if not, what would be the most likely form of rule?

Because the idea of secular orders of knighthood was a novelty in 1344, we have little against which to test the statutes given in Boccaccio. However, the most obvious feature of the secular orders, common to both the Hungarian Society of St George and the Castilian Order of the Sash, as well as to their numerous successors, is the oath of loyalty to the sovereign. Boccaccio knows nothing of this, merely offering a general condition that the knights should lay down their lives for their country. On the other hand, loyalty to the king is clearly specified in the *Lancelot-Grail*, of which Edward's mother almost certainly owned a copy. At the critical moment in the last romance in the cycle, when Arthur at last realises that Lancelot and Guenevere have committed adultery, he orders his knights to seize them, saying 'I command you to do so by the oath you swore to me when you became knights of the Round Table'. The implication of personal loyalty to the king is clear.[13] In the other comprehensive version of the Arthurian stories which was widely circulated, the *Prose Tristan*, the terms of the oath are quoted, but they are different: the new knight swears to increase the honour of the Round Table and never to fight against its members unless by way of 'game or festival'.[14] The other 'statutes' that we can pick up from the romances are on the lines of what Boccaccio proposes, such as the upholding of justice and the defence of the weak, but these are general principles of chivalry, set out in such popular poems as *The Order of Chivalry*.[15]

Perhaps we should try another approach to the concept of the Round Table in the romances. For Arthur, it combines the idea of high honour with the practicalities of the royal household. The story of Arthur contains not only the chivalric stories of love and tournaments, but also accounts of military campaigns, notably his conquest of France, and his war in France against Lancelot. In these campaigns, the Round Table takes on a different aspect, and becomes the equivalent of the group of knights at the English royal court known as the household knights. In 1338 Edward's household knights numbered 62, and contributed with their followers something like 60% of the army.[16] It is conceivable that the Round Table was to be an extension of the institution of household knights, giving the king even larger resources of manpower under his own direct control. The pomp and ceremony attached to it would then have been largely aimed at recruiting additional knights; if the core was to be the existing knights of the household, Edward's remarks about continually adding to the number make sense. At one point in the romances, the idea of a series of tables within the court is put forward; knights begin at the novices' table, proceed to that of the castle watch, and finally, if they are found worthy, proceed to the Round Table itself. And John Lydgate, writing eighty years later about the institution of the Round Table, adds as part of it a 'martial academy'

---

[13] There would have been a very personal resonance for Edward in this, for he had seized his mother and Roger Mortimer in similar circumstances, with a small band of knights, in 1330.

[14] E. Löseth, *Le Roman en Prose de Tristan*, Bibliothèque de l'École pratique des Hautes Études 82, Paris 1890, rptd Geneva 1974, 149.

[15] *L'ordene de chevalerie* in Raoul de Houdenc, *Le roman des eles*, ed. Keith Busby, Amsterdam and Philadelphia 1983.

[16] Andrew Ayton, 'Edward III and the English Aristocracy', 184.

where young knights could learn to bear arms, and avoid 'the idleness of youth'. We also find both in the romances and in Lydgate the idea that the deeds of arms of the knights of the Round Table should be recorded by clerks: it was actually part of the statutes of the Order of the Golden Fleece by the time Lydgate wrote.

If this view is possible, the Round Table becomes both a training ground and a serious military grouping. Such an organisation might justify the creation of a *domus*, but what we know of the building indicates that unlike the *domus* of the Order of the Star or the lodgings built for the Order of the Garter, this was not intended as the headquarters of a permanently staffed organisation, but as a place for feasting and chivalric ceremony. A large enclosed space open to the sky – if that was indeed what the *domus* was to have been – would have its uses as a training ground, but few advantages over the usual jousting areas annexed to castles. We know that the Upper Ward was used for jousting, as there is a reference in the accounts to the special chamber provided for the king when he armed himself for jousts there.[17] Even with the Round Table building occupying a large part of the corner of the Upper Ward, the space outside would still have been larger and better able to accommodate the lists. However, it is worth pointing out that the area required for lists for trial by combat was specified by Thomas, duke of Gloucester in the fifteenth century as '60 pace long and 40 pace broad, . . . and that the listes be strongly barred about'. A pace is about three feet, perhaps slightly less, so this area would fit within the Round Table building, even allowing for seats, table and arcade around the outside. The problem is that trial by combat was usually on foot, and this specification would not therefore allow for jousting. And the shape of the building would be wrong for a jousting arena, even though an Elizabethan writer, Sir John Ferne, in *The Blazon of Gentrie*, talks of lists as 'a place circular and rounde, compassed in with lowe rayles or pales of wood, painted with red'.[18] There are no surviving documents which give the measurements for a fourteenth-century jousting arena, and the style of fighting at tournaments was in the process of changing from the old-fashioned mêlée involving a large number of knights, to the joust in which one knight challenged a single opponent. When Chaucer describes Palamon's contest with Arcite for the hand of Emily in *The Knight's Tale*, he does not depict a duel, but a combat between a hundred knights on each side: Palamon is defeated because a group of Arcite's supporters capture him and he is therefore forced to withdraw from the fighting. Fifty years later, we would expect such a quarrel to be settled by a challenge in the lists, and the merits of the two knights would be decided by their jousting performance.

This may lead to an explanation of the function of the Round Table building. We only have literary descriptions of the detail of the fighting in such events, which naturally tends to concentrate on the heroes of the romances and their superhuman deeds. We do know, however, that spears were used in the mêlée in the fourteenth

---

[17] St John Hope, *Windsor Castle*, I, 111.
[18] *Antiquarian Repertory*, ed. F. Grose, London 1807, I.324.

century, and this implies a much larger space for fighting than that required for the later form of the mêlée, which was fought with swords. In the magnificent treatise on tournaments by René d'Anjou, king of Naples, in the mid-fifteenth century, he illustrates the start of a mêlée. The opening ceremony takes place within a set of barriers, where the two sides are ranged against each other, with banners displayed. At a signal from the heralds, the fighting starts, but because it is fought with swords only, the combatants remain within the barriers. Illustrations of German civic tournaments show that fighting with lances could take up the whole of a town square, which would likewise be surrounded by barriers. Given the disposition of the House of the Round Table in the Upper Ward, we could envisage the knights assembling within the open space at the centre of the building for the opening ceremony. At the signal from the heralds, the great doors would be opened, and the fighting would continue in the larger space of the Upper Ward. This can only be – as with so much of our reconstruction – a hypothesis, but it fits well with what we know of the organisation of the events known as 'Round Tables'.

For all discussions of the fourteenth century concept of the Arthurian Round Table lead us back to the series of festivals called round tables which are documented from 1232 onwards, when Henry III refers in an official document to knights assembling *ad rotundam tabulam*, 'for a round table'. The celebrations at the knighting of John of Ibelin in 1223 would probably have been called a round table, and the chronicler describes the content of future round tables very succinctly: 'they enacted the adventures of Britain and the Round Table'. We have already reviewed the detailed evidence for such events, and what emerges from it is a pattern of increasingly elaborate scenarios based loosely on the characters of Arthur's court rather than on the actual events of the romances. Both at Le Hem in 1278 and in Velthem's account of an undated round table of Edward I, the emphasis is on role-playing. The characters are limited to the central figures of Arthur's court; at least, there is no mention of minor roles: we have evidence for knights playing Lancelot, Tristan, Palamedes, Yvain, Gawain, Kay, Perceval, Agravain, Gareth, Bors, Lionel and even Arthur's treacherous nephew Mordred. Ladies played Guinevere and Soredamors. There appear to have been scripts written for the occasion, with a reasonable amount of detail in them, and evidence from the century following the Windsor festival of 1344 shows an increasing literary element in later tournaments, often departing entirely from an Arthurian framework.

If play-acting seems an unexpected activity for a fourteenth-century royal court, we have only to turn to a contemporary historian's description of the elaborate theatrical staging at a French royal feast in Paris in 1378.[19] The theme was probably inspired by Charles V's interest in leading a new crusade, and centred on the story of Godfrey of Bouillon and the conquest of Jerusalem in 1099. The first scene represented a ship carrying Godfrey to Palestine, which was moved by men inside

---

[19] Laura Hibbard Loomis, 'Secular Dramatics in the Royal Palace, Paris, 1378, 1389, and Chaucer's "Tregetoures"', *Speculum*, 33, 1958, 242-255.

it in such a way that 'it seemed like a ship floating on the water'; this was followed by a representation of Jerusalem itself, including the lifelike touch of 'a Saracen making the call to prayers, in the Arabic tongue'. One copy of the chronicle has an almost contemporary, possibly eyewitness, illustration of the occasion (Plate XVI). Chaucer describes such an occasion in *The Franklin's Tale*, apparently the work of specialists in this kind of entertainment, whom he calls 'tregetours'.

These chivalric charades took place within the framework of a great feast In the romances, Arthur traditionally refused to dine on high days and holidays until some adventure had taken place, such as the arrival of a mysterious messenger asking for help or offering a challenge. Imitating this in real life – as van Veltham depicts the process – gave the perfect cue for an Arthurian interlude to become part of the occasion. This line of thought leads us to the opening of the greatest of all English Arthurian poems, *Sir Gawain and the Green Knight*:

> This king lay at Camelot one Christmastide
> With many mighty lords, manly liegemen,
> Members rightly reckoned of the Round Table,
> In splendid celebration, seemly and carefree.
> There tussling in tournament time and again
> Jousted in jollity these gentle knights,
> Then in court carnival sang catches and danced;
> For fifteen days the feasting there was full in like measure
> With all the meat and merry-making men could devise,
> Gladly ringing glee, glorious to hear,
> A noble din by day, dancing at night![20]

The poet goes on to describe the richness of the setting, the chivalric courtesy of knights and ladies, and the character of Arthur himself, who announced

> that he never would eat
> On such a fair feast-day till informed in full
> Of some unusual adventure, as yet untold,
> Of some momentous marvel that he might believe,
> About ancestors, or arms or other high theme;
> Or till a stranger should seek out a strong knight of his,
> To join with him in jousting, in jeopardy to lay
> Life against life [21]

The stranger who arrives to lay life against life is hardly what Arthur expects: a knight green from head to foot, bearing a great axe and a holly branch, a warrior as courteous as any of his knights but carrying the symbols of an earlier age. The

---

[20] *Sir Gawain and the Green Knight*, tr. Brian Stone, Harmondsworth 1974, 22.
[21] *Sir Gawain and the Green Knight*, 24.

Green Knight offers not a joust, but a bargain: one of Arthur's knights is to behead him, and must seek him out in a year's time to stand a return blow. All that he proposes, says the Green Knight, is an entertainment:

> So I crave in this court a Christmas game,
> For it is Yuletide and New Year, and young men abound here.[22]

It is not difficult to imagine this scene being acted out at Edward's court; the poem is generally dated to after 1360, and its authorship and origins have been much debated. But its cultural context is firmly within the milieu of Edwardian chivalry, and the unique manuscript ends with a version of the Garter motto, *Hony soyt qui mal pence*.

The Round Table project looks backwards to a golden age of chivalry, and romanticises the present by attempting to revive the ancient glories of Arthur's court. It is however typical of the time: Jean Froissart, whose imaginative version of the Hundred Years' War still colours our vision of the harsh warfare of the times, makes ordinary knights and mercenary captains into men governed by chivalric ideals. Chaucer gives an admiring portrait of the Knight in *The Canterbury Tales*, in awe of his chivalric record. The patronage of chivalry by the courts of Europe, which had made it a kind of *lingua franca* of the knightly class, reached its apogee in the late fourteenth and early fifteenth century; but it was patronage with a purpose. Frederick II and his contemporaries had built great castles to impress their subjects with their power, castles which were not always strategically necessary but were highly visible, as at Enna in Sicily and Castel del Monte in Apulia. Now monarchs turned to chivalric festivals for the same purpose. It is the beginning of a tradition which leads to the great pageants of the Renaissance and to the court entertainments of the Italian princes, the age when 'the art of festival was harnessed to the emergent modern state as an instrument of rule'.[23] I would argue that this process first emerges much earlier than has usually been acknowledged, particularly as we find one of the first examples of a 'royal entry' with a symbolic programme in London in 1357, when the Black Prince brings king John of France to the city as a captive after Poitiers. Edward III's agenda at Windsor has moved beyond the conspicuous consumption enjoined by the chivalric virtue of *largesse* to a novel use of chivalry. Note that the ceremony of inauguration of the Round Table is carefully orchestrated, and that Murimuth records that all the people flocked to see the spectacle. This is chivalry as public relations, an extension of Edward I's use of the round table at Snowdon in 1284 to make a specific political point.

The Round Table failed, however. It was too ambitious, too extravagant; and one of its purposes, to recruit knights for Edward's wars in France, ceased to have the same urgency once warfare was seen as a highly profitable occupation after the campaign of 1346. There was no intrinsic obstacle to its revival in 1347; the half-

---

[22] *Sir Gawain and the Green Knight*, 31.
[23] Roy Strong, *Art and Power*, Woodbridge & Rochester, NY, 1984, 19.

finished buildings were still in place. But its time was past. Edward no longer had to establish himself as the leader of the chivalric world, having won a great reputation with the victory at Crécy and the taking of Calais. Instead of inducements to win over new supporters, he could reward those who had helped him to achieve these triumphs. The Order of the Garter succeeded because from the outset its context was a newly self-confident court and nation, and many of its members were already famous for their deeds. So instead of the House of the Round Table, it was the Garter lodgings and St George's Chapel which became the focus of English chivalry; and the Order of the Garter proved as durable as the Order of the Round Table had been ephemeral.

APPENDICES

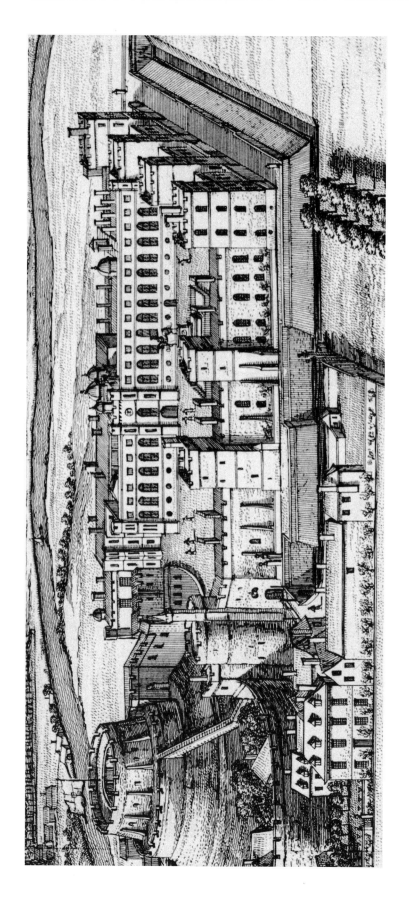

11 *Extract from* Windsor Castle from the South *by John Kyp and Leonard Knyff, 1711, showing the original location of the equestrian statue of Charles II in the Upper Ward*

APPENDIX A

Archaeological Report on the 2006 Excavation

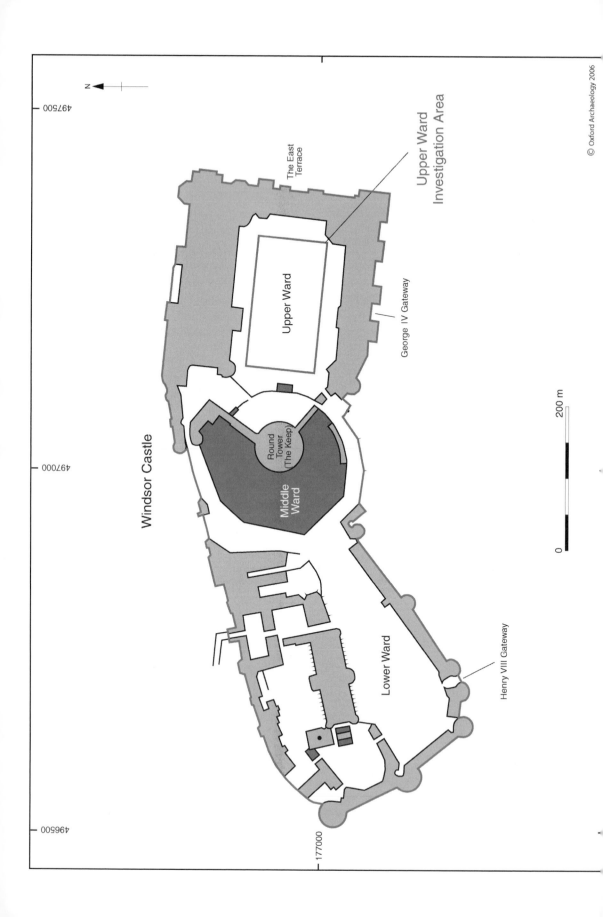

Windsor Castle

Upper Ward Investigation Area

The East Terrace

Upper Ward

George IV Gateway

Round Tower (The Keep)

Middle Ward

Lower Ward

Henry VIII Gateway

497500

497000

496500

177000

0   200 m

© Oxford Archaeology 2006

N

Summary

From 26th-29th August 2006, Oxford Archaeology (OA) carried out archaeological investigations on behalf of Wildfire TV/Time Team/Channel 4 in the Upper Ward at Windsor Castle. These investigations formed part of series of live television programmes focusing on the archaeology and history of Buckingham Palace, Windsor Castle and Holyrood House in Edinburgh, a project developed in conjunction with Channel 4 as a contribution to Her Majesty the Queen's 80th birthday celebrations.

Three trenches were excavated in the Upper Ward. These trenches clarified the previously uninvestigated nature, date and extent of survival of archaeological deposits within the Upper Ward Quadrangle. Evidence was revealed for Edward III's Round Table building and the original location of the Charles II equestrian statue base. In addition mapping rectification carried out during the work indicated the probable previous location (and likely historic destruction/removal) of Henry VIII's fountainhead.

All geophysical work was carried out by GSB Prospection Ltd supervised by John Gator. All excavation work was carried out by Oxford Archaeology supervised by Richard Brown. The Project Design was formulated and documented[1] by Richard Brown in consultation with English Heritage, The Royal Household and Wildfire TV.

Governmental Designations, licences and consents

Windsor Castle is within the non-civil parish of Windsor and Maidenhead in the historic County of Berkshire. The castle (as defined by the existing curtain walls and the eastern limit of the Upper Ward State Apartments) is a Scheduled Monument (ref. WN 80). The Castle (including the grassed slopes external to the curtain wall) and surrounding Home Park is within a Registered Park and Garden (ref. 4189).

The investigation was carried out under a Section 42 licence for geophysical survey (ref. CB63/E; AA056157) and Scheduled Monument Consent for excavation (ref. HSD 9/2/8308). The Section 42 licence was issued by Dr Michael Turner, Inspector of Ancient Monuments and Historic Buildings, Government Historic Estates Unit. Scheduled Monument Consent was granted by the Department for Culture Media and Sport on the authorisation of the Secretary of State under advice from Dr Turner. This publication forms part of the discharge of Monument Consent conditions, along with deposition with the Archaeological Data Service (ADS) of an AutoCAD® plan drawing of the excavations, online entry of the investigation results at ads.ahds.ac.uk/project/oasis and deposition of the excavation archive with the Curator of Windsor Castle.

---

[1] Oxford Archaeology/Cambrian Archaeology 2006, *Windsor Castle – Upper Ward and College of St George, Project Design for an Archaeological Investigation V.1-3.0(1)* unpublished client document
Oxford Archaeology/Cambrian Archaeology 2006, *Windsor Castle – Upper Ward and College of St George, Updated Project Design for an Archaeological Investigation V.4-5.0(1)* unpublished client document
Oxford Archaeology 2006, *Archaeological Investigations – Upper Ward, Windsor Castle, Post-Excavation Assessment and Publication Proposal V.1.1*, unpublished client document

The geology, geography and topography of the Upper Ward
Windsor Castle is located[2] on top of an isolated chalk dome which has been cut away on the north to form a steep cliff, by the Thames. At its highest the dome rises to approximately 52 m above Ordnance Datum. To the west the site is bounded by Thames Street, the northern extension of Windsor High Street. To the north, east and south the greater part of the Castle limits are surrounded by the more rural setting of the Home Park. The site is on an outcrop of Upper Chalk in places covered with 'clay with flints' and surrounded by Terrace gravels.[3] The scheduled monument is c 5.3 ha in area.

The investigation area in the Upper Ward is defined by the limits of the central grassed area within the Upper Ward quadrangle. This area measures c 92 m east-west and 42m north-south (3864m²). The surface of the grassed area slopes from the east to west and from the north to the south. The north east corner of the grassed area is at 52.80 m OD, the south east corner is at 52.42 m OD, the north west corner is at 51.68 m OD, the south west corner is at 50.76m OD.

A drawing supplied by the Royal Household[4] shows multiple services crossing the site and a substantial subway/service corridor cutting north-south through the eastern quarter of the site. For security purposes the service information has been removed from the illustrations.

Prior to excavation there was a poor understanding of the depth and topographical contours of the 'clay with flints' and chalk bedrock underlying the central part of the quadrangle or of the depth, character and date of overlying deposits.

The archaeological and historical background of the Upper Ward Quadrangle
Whilst new evidence on the development of the Upper Ward gained through the rescue excavations carried out in 1992 by English Heritage and Central Archaeology Service[5] has greatly contributed to the authoritative works carried out by W. H. St John Hope[6] the character of deposits underlying the central part of the Upper Ward remained poorly understood. Although the area has been much impacted in modern times by service and utility works no formal archaeological or geotechnical recording had been carried out in this area.

POTENTIAL PRE-CASTLE ARCHAEOLOGICAL REMAINS
Residual prehistoric and Roman artefacts have been retrieved in excavations across the site,[7] which may imply early occupation of the bluff. This would be entirely plausible given the sites topographical dominance of the surrounding landscape.

---

[2] NGR SU 969 770 – 496985/177029 centred.
[3] Geological Survey of Great Britain, Sheet number 269.
[4] Plowman Craven & Associates, Drg No. WC-08-SS-QEX.
[5] Published in Brindle and Kerr, *Windsor revealed : new light on the history of the Castle.*
[6] St John Hope, *Windsor Castle.*
[7] My thanks to Brian Kerr for supplying unpublished finds lists from Castle Hill excavations in 1989-90, the Round Tower and 1992 rescue excavations.

MEDIEVAL

Regardless of whether the substantial twelfth century curtain wall is the primary enclosure of the Upper Ward, the area's situation on the chalk bluff adjacent to the Round Tower implies the possibility that archaeological evidence for activities such as temporary occupation structures, industrial processes (lime kilns, saw pits, metal working) and stabling as well as tournament/festivity related features could exist in the investigation area. Any such remains could potentially date from the origin of the Castle to the post-medieval period.

The preliminary geophysical survey (Plate XII) identified what appears to be the full extent of the Round Tower moat to the west of the quadrangle. Although the moat and its primary fills are presumably contemporary with the construction of the Round Tower Mound, the upper fills (and likely the bulk of its infill) were deposited in the nineteenth century during Wyatville's remodelling of the Upper Ward.

The earliest specific documentary indication of activity in the Upper Ward central area is the most enigmatic and contentious – the Round Table or Round Table building. Hope dedicates a chapter to the construction of the Round Table in Volume I of his work and details all known accounts of the works. Hope suggested the Upper Ward as the location of the structure, partially on the basis of its given dimensions but also in relation to accounts for strengthening of the bridges (plural) for transport of construction materials, which can only be necessitated by the need for access to the Upper Ward. The case for the Upper Ward as the location of the Round Table Building was more recently made by Julian Munby in his paper on Edward III's carpentry[8] given at the 1998 British Archaeological Association conference.

The next available evidence for potential archaeological remains in the central area of the Upper Ward is given by the 1450 Eton view of the Castle. This sketch depicts a circular structure or square based with circular structure on top, to the centre of the area. This is possibly a precursor of the fountainhead on which work for provision of a 'new' water supply from a source in Blackmore park and the laying of lead pipes had commenced in 1551 and eventually been completed with the installation of an ornate fountain head in 1555.[9] Hope gives a detailed description of the fountain head[10] based on Norden's 1607 birds-eye view of the castle and the surveyor Henry Hawthorne's plans.[11]

[8] 'Carpentry Works for Edward III at Windsor Castle', in Saul, *St George's Chapel*, 225-37.

[9] H. M. Colvin, D. R. Ransome, and J. Summerson, *The History of the King's Works, 1485-1660*, London 1975, III.i, 302-333

[10] St John Hope, *Windsor Castle*, I, 258.

[11] Reproductions of Henry Hawthorne's plans for Queen Elizabeth's Gallery are included in the portfolio of plans (Plan VII) accompanying St John Hope, *Windsor Castle*. The original plans were produced prior to the construction of the gallery in 1583. The 'second scheme' design, although never fully realised, does map the base of the fountainhead.

POST-MEDIEVAL

The supply to the fountain head seems to have required much attention, rehabilitation of conduits cisterns and pipework was carried out in 1609 and 1611, in 1635 a proposal for reconstruction of the fountain which the commissioners of 1629 had found beyond repair was cancelled. After the theft of some lead pipes from the conduit head in 1649 the water supply was declared useless and orders were given in 1650 for the lead pipe to be dug up and used in maintenance works around the castle.[12] Wenceslas Hollar's bird's-eye view of the castle published in 1672 shows the central part of the Upper Ward to be empty.

A brass equestrian statue of Charles II commissioned in 1679 was positioned in the centre of the Upper Ward in 1680. Although not indicated by the 1711 view of Windsor Castle in Kyp and Knyff's '*The Duke of St Alban's House at Windsor with a view of Windsor Castle from the South*'. W. H. Pyne's 1819 '*View of the Round Tower from the east*' implies some landscaping and more formal arrangement of pathways within the quadrangle in order to enhance the setting of the statue.

The range of works carried out by Wyatville between 1824 and his death in 1840 included substantial remodelling of the Upper Ward including the construction of two 'Grand Corridors' running adjacent and parallel to the southern and eastern apartments as well as the construction of the State entrance Tower. A list of Wyatville works completed up to 1830[13] includes 'lowering the courtyard from three to six feet; removed 13,000 cube yards'. While at first glance this seems to imply severe truncation of the quadrangle, 13,000 cube yards spread across the area of the Quadrangle (prior to Wyatville) gives an average of 2½ feet across the area. This would mean that if some areas were reduced by 6 ft other parts may not have been reduced at all. In addition a site visit showed that the grand corridors are cut to *c.*2 m below ground which may also account for much of the removed material.

Another possible indicator on the extent of Wyatville's truncation of the Quadrangle is a MOD AP taken in 1964.[14] Here the base of the Charles II statue can be seen as a parch mark and the surrounding grassed area shown in Pyne's 1819 view is visible as it is emphasised by parch marks presumably caused by the surrounding pathways. This suggested that truncation of the ground levels caused by Wyatville's work was not sufficient to remove the entire depth of either the statue foundations or the paths.

Anecdotal evidence of a nineteenth century water tank in the centre of the Upper Ward quadrangle[15] appears to have been confirmed by the geophysical survey (see below).

Summary of the preliminary geophysical survey
A Section 42 licence (ref; CB63/E; AA056157) was issued by English Heritage for preliminary geophysical survey. The survey of the proposed investigation area was

---

[12] Colvin et al., *History of the King's Works, 1485-1660*, III.i, 302-333.
[13] St John Hope, *Windsor Castle*, I, 356-7. Thanks to Brian Kerr for bringing this to my attention.
[14] Shown in Roberts,, *Royal Landscape*, 183.
[15] *pers comm*. Richard Mole – Royal Household.

carried out in order to inform this proposal for 'intrusive' investigation. A graphic interpretation of the results of this is shown on Plate XII. However, full methodology for the survey and analysis of the geophysical data is contained in GSB Report 2006/46.[16]

The geophysical investigations combined gradiometry, resistance and ground penetrating radar surveys across the entire lawned area of the Upper Ward. This successfully mapped a number of modern buried services and defined the extent of a subway/service corridor.

The survey, in particular the GPR, identified a number of anomalies of possible archaeological interest. The most interesting was a curving response in the southeast corner of the lawn (L on the geophysical survey results). A second curving response at the western edge of the lawn ('F' on the geophysical survey results) is presumably associated with the Round Tower moat and shows potential structural features. There was an unusual response in both the resistance and GPR data in the centre of the lawn ('H' on the geophysical survey results) which may be a former path or roadway as shown in W. H. Pyne's 1819 *'View of the Round Tower from the east.'* This implies some arrangement of pathways within the quadrangle that surround the grassed area on which the Charles II equestrian statue is sited. A presumed water 'tank' ('B' on the geophysical survey results) was located in the centre of the lawn. Several other anomalies which appeared to indicate archaeological remains (geophysical survey results – G, D, I, J and K) were also recorded.

The investigation methodology

Three 5 m x 3 m investigation trenches were excavated. These were located by GPS (carried out by Plowman Craven Associates) using OS co-ordinate data supplied by Oxford Archaeology and extracted from the AutoCAD® trench location plan. Trench positions were also verified by hand/tape measurement against scaled trench location plans.

Machine excavation to the top of the archaeological horizon was carried out under archaeological supervision. Archaeological recording was carried out in adherence to a Project Design[17] approved by English Heritage and the Oxford Archaeology field manual.[18]

In addition to the excavations, mapping rectification work was carried out in order to plot the historic location of the 1550s fountain head as shown on Henry Hawthorne's 1583(?) plans onto modern OS mapping.

---

[16] GSB Report 2006/46 along with a survey database form has been submitted to the Archaeometry Branch Archaeological Science, English Heritage in adherence to the terms of the Section 42 Licence.
[17] Oxford Archaeology/Cambrian Archaeology 2006, 'Windsor Castle – Upper Ward and College of St George, Updated Project Design for an Archaeological Investigation V.5.0(1)', unpublished client document.
[18] 'OAU Field Manual', ed. D Wilkinson, 1992.

12. Trench 1, showing the Charles II statue base

Trench results

TRENCH 1

Full excavation of Trench 1 was partially impeded by the presence in the greater part of the trench of the Charles II equestrian statue base. To the west of the feature it was possible to excavate a slot into the underlying sequence without disturbance to the structure.

The revealed sequence was comparable to the sequences revealed in Trenches 2 and 3 (see below). A dark silt accumulation (context 111) was revealed at 51.10 m OD. This was overlain by a series of chalky silt levelling deposits (contexts 110, 109 and 108) which in turn were sealed by compacted chalk surface 107. A sherd of pottery from silt 111 was dated to the 11th-12th century. Layer 108 contained mid thirteenth/fourteenth century pottery and 38 small fragments of tile including a plain unglazed peg tile.

The pottery dating supports the on-site interpretation of a gradually accumulated courtyard soil overlain (truncated?) by construction/levelling deposits, capped by either a floor or floor preparation surface related to Edward III's Round Table building.

The floor/floor preparation layer (107) was overlain by the Charles II statue base (contexts 112, 106, 105, 104 and 103). This structure comprised a flagstone base (105) laid on a compacted rubble surface (106) which incorporated a brick-built drain (structure 104 filled with silt 103). A re-deposited Penn tile was found adhering to

13. The Penn tile found in trench 1

14. Trench 2 showing the Wyatville brick conduits at the ends of the trench and the slot excavated through the Round Table building chalk-laid preparation layers to the centre

the brick drain. The statue was placed in the courtyard in 1680 and moved to the base of the Round Tower during Wyatville's work in the Upper Ward (1824-40).[19] The base was overlain by a landscaping/rubble deposit (context 102) associated with Wyatville's reforming of the Quadrangle.

TRENCH 2

In Trench 2 the full archaeological sequence was investigated revealing the natural clay with flints (context 211) at 50.40 m OD. This was overlain by a *c.* 0.4 m thick dark clay silt accumulation (contexts 210 and 208). A 100 litre bulk sample was retrieved from deposit 208 which contained worked flint, burnt flint, bone, abraded prehistoric pottery and pottery dating to the 11th-12th century. The character of the deposit suggested deposition via a gradual accumulation derived from organic decay, frequent but small-volume dumping and possibly minimal importation. The homogeneous nature of the deposit suggested constant re-working of the soil through animal/human trample and weathering. It is probable that deposits 210 and 208 represent the total sum of soil deposition from the last glacial period to truncation/capping in the mid 14th century.

The silt accumulation was overlain/truncated by a series of silty-chalk levelling deposits (contexts 212, 207 and 206) which are likely to represent the formation (ground levelling and floor preparation) of the internal part of the Round Table building. These were hand excavated and contained mid 13th-14th century pottery and medieval tile (as well as some re-deposited fragments of Roman tegula and imbrex).

At either end of Trench 2 brick-built conduits (structures 209 and 205) were contained in construction cuts into the chalky levelling layers. These were overlain by the landscaping/rubble deposits associated with Wyatville's work (context 203) which directly overlaid the chalk levelling layers in the centre of the trench.

TRENCH 3

In Trench 3 the full archaeological sequence was recorded. This comprised the natural clay with flints (context 325) revealed in the base of a robber trench (see below) at 49.84 m OD. In the sides of the robber trench cut the natural showed weathering on its upper horizon deeper within the base of the cut patches of chalk bed rock were apparent. The natural geology was overlain by a dark silt accumulation (contexts 305=322, 318=309 and 308=319) similar to those revealed in Trenches 1 and 2. The silt was cut to the central-west part of the trench by three shallow sub-circular features (cuts 316, 314, deposit 328) filled entirely with lime rich mortar.

The features were overlain in the western part of the trench by a compacted chalk surface (context 304). To the east of the trench a sequence of silty chalk levelling layers (contexts 329 and 320) overlay the silt accumulation.

The chalk surface and levelling layers were separated in the centre of the trench by a substantial (2.5 m wide, 1.75 m deep) vertical sided, flat based cut (context 313)

---

[19] St John Hope, *Windsor Castle*, I, 362.

which was orientated north east – south west. This was filled with loose sands and rubble tip layers (contexts 326, 306, 331, 332 and 333). Two sherds of mid 13th-14th century pottery were retrieved from these fills, and 21 stone fragments were retained for petrological analysis. The upper fill of the robber trench was cut to the north of the trench by a land drain. This in turn was overlain by a landscaping/rubble deposit (context 302) related to Wyatville's work in the courtyard.

Conclusions and Discussion

The investigations have shown that *c.* 2m depth of archaeological strata survives in the Upper Ward Quadrangle. Undisturbed, geological, clay with flint deposits were recorded at 50.40 m OD in Trench 2, it is likely that this horizon undulates across the site and drops off towards the edge of the bluff. A re-worked silt accumulation apparent in all the trenches overlies the natural geology, this deposit contained abraded prehistoric pottery and Roman building material as well as medieval pottery and suggests that discrete features and structures spanning these dates could also exist within the area of the quadrangle at these levels.

The large curving robber trench in Trench 3 and its associated floor preparation and makeup levels recorded in all the trenches can only be the remains of Edward III's Round Table building. This is supported by pottery dates, architectural fragments and the geophysical survey results. Little can be inferred from the depth of the robber trench which sensibly is cut deep enough to allow foundation of the structure on the geological bedrock. The width of the trench (2.5 m) however does indicate a structure of sufficient size to support a building of some height or more than one-storey.

The rectification of Henry Hawthorne's plans (see above) showing the location of the 1550s fountainhead suggest that this structure is likely to have been substantially removed (to the east) by the insertion of a modern cistern, no trace of structural remains of the western part of the fountainhead was apparent in the geophysical survey results.

The upper part of the sequence evidences truncation of the earlier levels, followed by rubble and dumping relating to Wyatville's programme of works during 1824-40. These may be of little intrinsic interest; however the presence of the 17th century flagstone statue base in Trench 1 shows that isolated earlier structures may exist close to the surface.

The finds retrieved from the investigation were sparse, as would be expected from such a small-scale excavation and serve mainly to support the chronological interpretation and characterisation of the archaeological deposits.

The Finds

Pottery JOHN COTTER (MEDIEVAL & POST MEDIEVAL) AND JANE TIMBY (PREHISTORIC)

The medieval pottery retrieved from the excavations is generally in a fairly scrappy fragmentary condition with very few diagnostic pieces (rims, bases etc) present, although most of the sherds are fairly fresh and unworn. The nineteenth-century sherds, however, are fairly large and fresh.

Apart from the sieved pottery (see below) the excavated assemblage falls into two distinct groups. The first is modern or nineteenth-century material, and the second is medieval (here eleventh to fourteenth century). There are no intervening groups of late medieval or earlier post-medieval pottery.

Nineteenth-century pottery comprises one third of the assemblage (13 sherds). This mostly comprises mass-produced Staffordshire-type white earthenwares (tablewares), modern English stonewares and flowerpots. This material comes from three contexts. Apart, perhaps, from a fragment of a probable stoneware water filter (102) – suggesting a concern with the provision of clean drinking water – the assemblage is unremarkable.

The remaining two-thirds of the assemblage (26 sherds) is of medieval date. Because of the limited number of diagnostic pieces present, and because some of the pottery industries represented here were long-lived, only fairly broad date ranges for individual contexts can be suggested. Pottery types present are summarised below. Most of the medieval contexts have been dated to the thirteenth to fourteenth century largely due to the presence of glazed jug sherds from identifiable pottery traditions. As well as tablewares represented by jugs (and possibly tripod pitchers?), kitchenwares are also present in the form of jar/cooking pots with sagging bases, several of which show sooting from use as cooking vessels.

The commonest medieval pottery type or fabric represented is a brown sandy ware present in the form of glazed jugs – some showing incised horizontal groove decoration or simple linear decoration using white slip paint – and in the form of unglazed jars/cooking pots. This probably comes from the Ashampstead kilns near Newbury (Berks.). The glazed jugs are compatible with a thirteenth-fourteenth century date. A groove-decorated jar/cooking pot from context 208, however, could be of twelfth to early thirteenth-century date, partly due to its association with sherds of early medieval shelly ware. Other thirteenth-fourteenth century glazed jug industries are represented by a single sherd each of Surrey whiteware (possibly Kingston-type ware?), Brill/Boarstall ware from west Buckinghamshire, and London-type ware. Windsor is located at a point where the known distribution of these wares overlaps. The Surrey whiteware sherd (context 306) is from the base of a green glazed jug which is quite probably a conical jug; these can be as early as the mid-thirteenth century but were predominantly late fourteenth-century in date.

Other medieval kitchenware/coarseware industries represented include a few sherds in an early medieval-type fabric with abundant coarse fossil shell temper (eleventh to early thirteenth century?), and two types of reduced (grey) sandy ware fabrics with sparse to moderate finer shell temper (late twelfth to fourteenth century?). These shelly and shelly-sandy fabrics have similarities with types of shelly wares and grey wares produced in north-west Kent and which are commonly found in London. Pottery of similar character, however, may have been produced in neighbouring Surrey and perhaps further afield in areas where fossil shell-rich clays were exploitable (possibly the Woolwich Beds?).

LATER PREHISTORIC POTTERY

Eighteen sherds of pottery weighing 78g in weight were recovered from context 208. The sherds are heavily worn and abraded with slightly patinated surfaces. The pieces all appear to be bodysherds, with one thicker-walled piece possibly from a base. There are no distinctive defining features or surviving evidence of any surface treatment. Wall thickness generally falls into the 6-9mm range with one sherd at 12mm. Two fabrics can be distinguished:

F1: A moderately hard, sandy paste with a sparse scatter of ill-sorted, fine calcined flint fragments, some protruding from the surfaces. Inclusions are up to 3mm across but mainly finer. In fresh fracture occasional colourless, rounded, grains of quartz, iron oxides and organic impurities in the clay can be discerned at ×20 magnification. Sixteen of the sherds fall into this category.

G1: A slightly softer fabric with a soapy feel. In fresh fracture sparse fine grog and rare sub-angular to rounded quartz grains and iron oxides are visible at ×20 magnification. Two sherds.

CHRONOLOGY AND AFFINITIES OF THE ASSEMBLAGE

The character of the material, despite the absence of any featured pieces, would suggest it is most likely of later Bronze Age date. Sandier fabrics with the finer flint have been observed elsewhere in the locality as increasing at the expense of the coarser flint-gritted fabrics typical of the of the mid-later Bronze Age moving from the later Bronze Age into the early Iron Age, notably at Runnymede Bridge and Petter's Sports Field, Egham.[20] Both fabrics fall within the range described from other sites in the locality for sites dating this period.[21]

Later Bronze Age sites are well documented in the middle Thames Valley and a number of sequences have been studied in the Reading area, Reading Business Park,[22] Aldermaston Wharf and Knights Farm[23] and to the southeast of Windsor at Egham and Runnymede Bridge.

[20] D. Longley, *Runnymede Bridge 1976: excavation in the site of a late Bronze Age settlement,* Surrey Archaeol Res Vol 6, Guildford 1980, 65; M. O'Connell, 'Petters Sports Field, Egham. Excavation of a late Bronze Age/ early Iron Age site', Surrey Archaeol Res , 10, Guildford 1986, 72.

[21] C.f. E. Morris, 'Later prehistoric pottery', in A. Brossler, R. Early and C. Allen, *Green Park (Reading Business Park). Phase 2 Excavations 1995 – Neolithic and Bronze Age sites,* Thames Valley landscapes monograph 19, Oxford, 2004, 61-2.

[22] M. Hall, 'The prehistoric pottery', in J. Moore and D. Jennings, *Reading Business Park: a Bronze Age landscape,* Thames Valley landscapes: the Kennet Valley, monograph 1, Oxford 1992, 63-82.

[23] R. Bradley, S. Lobb, R. Richards, and M. Robinson, 'Two late Bronze Age settlements on the Kennet gravels: excavations at Aldermaston Wharf and Knight's Farm, Burghfield, Berkshire', *Proceedings of the Prehistoric Society* 46, 1980, 217-95.

Pottery identification table

Context	Context Spot-date	Sherds	Weight (gms)	Comments
102	c1850-1900	8	289	3x modern Eng stoneware incl moulded decorated rim or base frag from sanitary item – prob a water filter. 1x frag Bristol-type glaze brown-topped ginger beer bottle etc. 1x blacking bottle rim. 3x Staffs blue transfer printed dish – incl 1 poss Pearlware c1820-30s. 1x flowerpot base. 1x unident soft brown sandy ?pottery or mortar etc w ext ridging or impressions?
103	c1850-1900	1	15	Mod Eng stoneware blacking bottle rim JOINS 102
108	c1225-1400	2	18	1x prob Brill/Boarstall ware jug neck w speckled green glz. 1x prob Ashampstead-type brown sandy jug sh with broad vertical band of white slip under clear glz – poss L12/13C?
111	11-12C?	1	17	Cook pot rim – everted thickened & flattened/ext bevelled early med type. Grey-br surfs w dark grey/black core. Abund coarse prob fossil shell temper – mostly clam-like bivalves. Fairly sand free. Poss local or London/NW Kent-type EMSH (Vince & Jenner 1991)
200	c1825-1900	3	127	2x Staffs blue transfer print 'willow pattern' dish. 1x plain white Staffs complete small ointment/salve pot (ht 30mm, max diam 59mm) with ext recess for lid. '1/2' impressed mark under
206	c1175-1400	3	28	Bodysherd jug London-type ware (LOND) 13-14C type or-br fine sandy fabric with smeared white slip allover ext under patchy clear glaze with few copper-green flecks. 2x sandy unglazed? Ashampstead-type or more local? (same vess?)
207	c1225-1400	12	162	6x sandy brown? Ashampstead-type prob all jug sherds incl 3 fully glazed ext (clear; greenish-brown; patchy copper-flecked) incl jug shoulder bs w spaced incised horiz grooves (as sample in OA reference coll). Incl 1 coarser/grittier & incl 2 sagging base sherds. 1 harder-fired oxidised finer? Ashamstead or roof tile? 4x wheel-thrown med hard grey sandy wares with sparse-mod fine shell incl sagging base (prob cpots as sooted), 1 similar WT but oxidised & with slightly more & coarser shell; all v similar to NW Kent greyware M38A & related shelly-sandy EM36 but prob more local source. Poss related London SSW (12-13C) shelly-sandy ware? Overall dating could be 13C?
208	c1150-1225?	6	84	2x early med sand-free shelly ware incl sag cook pot base (sooted). 4 sherds (1 vess) in dense sandy brown ware with iron-stained rounded quartz (up to 1mm), reduced int. Poss handmade but with crude ext horiz grooved dec or rilling – poss done with stick or tool? Fabric similar to Ashampstead but looks earlier, also similar to Limpsfield type (E. Surrey) coarsewares (1150+). Trace of soot on un-grooved near-basal sherd (sag base of this vess present in additional sieved sample <1>)
300	c1825-1900	1	2	Staffs blue transfer. Prob teacup bs
306	c1240-1400	2	37	Base prob Surrey whiteware jug (Kingston-type ware?). Flat plain base (knife-trimmed under) with inward-leaning wall – poss from a conical-shaped jug? Specks of copper-green glaze along angle. 1x body sherd prob WT med sandy ware with sparse-mod fine shell
TOTAL		39	779	

The Ceramic Building Material

LEIGH ALLEN/JOHN COTTER

Context	Frag count	Tile type	Comments
200	1	Brick	very abraded fragment
203	1	Brick	Complete Georgian stock brick 227 x 100 x 65mm (with shallow frog)
300	2	Brick	Two very abraded brick fragments
102	1	Floor tile (decorated)	See report below
106	1	Floor tile (decorated)	See report below
207	1	Imbrex (Roman)	Abraded imbrex fragment
208	1	Peg tile	Plain, unglazed with a circular nail hole
108	1	Peg tile	Plain unglazed with a circular nail hole
103	1	Peg tile	Plain, unglazed
306	2	Peg tile	Plain, unglazed
300	2	Peg tiles	Plain, unglazed with a circular nail hole through each fragment
206	3	Peg tiles	Plain, unglazed with a circular nail hole through each fragment
207	2	Peg tiles	Plain, unglazed with a circular nail hole through each fragment
103	3	Ridge tile	Plain, unglazed
206	32	Roof tile	Plain, unglazed
206	1	Roof tile	with light brown splatter glaze
207	7	Roof tile	Plain, unglazed
108	36	Roof tile	Plain, unglazed
108	1	Roof tile	with light green splatter glaze
102	3	Roof tile	Plain, unglazed
103	1	Roof tile	Plain, unglazed
306	5	Roof tile	Plain, unglazed
308	3	Roof tile	Plain, unglazed
326	5	Roof tile	Plain, unglazed
302	1	Roof tile	Plain, unglazed
302	1	Roof tile	Brown and light green splatter glaze
300	1	Roof tile	Plain, unglazed
206	1	Tegula (Roman)	Tegula flange fragment

The Penn Floor-Tiles

LAURENCE KEEN OBE

Two floor-tiles were recovered from the excavations. The more complete, from context 106 is 110mm square, 20mm thick, with a slight chamfer and a plain back. The fabric is well mixed and the firing has resulted in a reduced core. The other, from context 102, is less complete and has the same fabric but is slightly thicker. Both are decorated in white slip which has been applied into the lightly stamped designs. The second tile is much more worn than the first, so the design is much more indistinct.

Both tiles belong to the well known floor-tile products from Penn, Buckinghamshire, the most extensive, successful and well-organised commercial tile workshop in medieval Britain. It is not surprising that these examples should have been found at Windsor, for the Royal accounts show that tens of thousands of floor-tiles were purchased between 1351 and 1365. The most important surviving pavement is that of the Aerary in St George's College, which can be dated to 1355.[24]

Neither tile was *in situ* so the tiles cannot be considered part of the floor of the Round Table. Although such would not be impossible, Dr Steven Brindle has kindly informed the writer that the accounts do not contain any references to floor-tiles being purchased in 1344.[25]

Tile 1 appears to be similar to a tile from London in the British Museum.[26] Tile 2 (Figure 13), a circle enclosing an eight-foil motif, is paralleled at St Alban's Abbey and in the parish churches at Wheathampstead and Aldbury, Hertfordshire.

A distinctive feature of the floor-tiles from Penn is that the majority have designs confined to a single tile. This meant that the tiles could be laid easily in panels of the same design with minimum complexity, but nevertheless, producing a satisfactory overall effect.

The Metalwork
IAN SCOTT

There are only 20 metal objects or fragments from the Windsor Castle trenches. Fourteen objects come from the metal detector survey of the turf/topsoil layers (Trench 1, context 100, 10 objects; Trench 2, context 200, 3 objects; and Trench 3, context 300, 1 object).

Thirteen objects were recovered from Trench 1; ten from the turf/topsoil layer (100) and the remaining three objects from a context associated with Wyatville's landscaping (102). None of the objects needs be earlier in date than the nineteenth century.

Five objects came from Trench 2, three from topsoil (200), one from the imported loam layer (201) under the topsoil layer, and the final object a fragment of nail stem from a layer possibly dating to the fourteenth century (sampled deposit 208). The nail fragment is handmade and could be medieval in date. None of the other finds needs date earlier than the nineteenth or twentieth centuries.

Only two objects were recovered from Trench 3. One – a fitting made of wire – was from topsoil (300). The other object was a fragment of leaded copper alloy casting, and came from one of the fills (306) of the robber trench of the Round Table building wall. Unfortunately the function of the fragment cannot be identified, and is not datable.

---

[24] L. Keen, 'Windsor Castle and the Penn Tile Industry', in L. Keen and E. Scarff (ed.), *Windsor: Medieval Archaeology, Art and Architecture of the Thames Valley*, British Archaeological Association Conference Transactions, XXV, 2002, 219-37.

[25] S. Brindle and S. Priestly, 'Edward III's Building Campaigns at Windsor and the Employment of Masons, 1346-1377' in Saul, *St George's Chapel*, 203-23.

[26] E.S. Eames, *Catalogue of Medieval Lead-glazed Earthenware Tiles in the Department of Medieval and Later Antiquities British Museum*, London 1980.

Metalwork

Comments	Length	Breadth	Context	SF No	Count	Fragts	Metal
Wire nails with flat circular heads. Modern			100		4	4	fe
Handle escutcheon or plate. For small handle. Slightly dished. Modern.	60mm	38mm	100		1	1	fe
Possible flat circular button, gilded, with floral motif engraved in centre. Scar on back for attachment of loop.		28mm	100	101	1	1	ca
Melted lead waste			100		1	1	pb
Plate fragment with one edge folded at a right angle. Light, possibly aluminium. Modern			100		1	1	aluminium
Melted waste, light, probably aluminium			100		2	2	aluminium
L-shaped clamp with traces of mortar on surfaces	190mm	130mm	102		1	1	fe
L-shaped holdfast with tapering stem and flat head	165mm		102		1	1	fe
Tapering spike or nail stem	95mm		102		1	1	fe
Probable heel iron fragment	66mm		200		1	1	fe
File, modern half round.	250mm		200		1	1	fe
Length of thin pipe, rolled with butt joint. Light alloy, possibly aluminium	137mm		200		1	1	uncertain
Melted lead waste			201	100	1	1	pb
Nail stem fragment			208		1	1	fe
Fitting of thick wire with a head or fixing point at each end. Modern?	57mm		300		1	1	fe
Fragment from a cast circular object (c. 45mm diam). Made from a leaded copper alloy. It had a squared edge. One face is flat, but slightly concave the other has a stepped profile. Possibly had a central hole.	30mm		306		1	1	ca
Total					20	20	

Glass

RICHARD BROWN

A single glass marble and a sherd of clear glass were retrieved from context 102. Two sherds of glass were retrieved from context 300. Both contexts are nineteenth century or later.

The Clay Pipes

JOHN COTTER

A total of 5 pieces of clay pipe weighing 13g was recovered from 3 contexts. All the pieces are from pipe stems which are of limited dating value. Two of the pieces are of nineteenth-century date, one is possibly late eighteenth- or early nineteenth-century, one is probably eighteenth-century and one is seventeenth-century. The latter two however are fairly worn and are residual in a nineteenth-century context (200).

Context	Spot-date	Stem	Bowl	Mouth	Total sherds	Total Weight (gms)	Comments
100	19C	1	0	0	1	2	Stem bore c1.5mm
102	19C	2	0	0	2	3	Stem bores c1.5mm & 2mm, latter poss L18-E19C?
200	18C	2	0	0	2	8	Both fairly worn & thick stemmed. Stem bores 2mm (18C) & 2.5mm (17C)
TOTAL		5	0	0	5	13	

Stone

PHILIP POWELL AND JULIAN MUNBY

Twenty-one fragments of stone were retrieved from the Round Table building robber trench in Trench 3 (deposit 306). These included:

7 pieces of chalk – Presumably dug on-site from the underlying geology, or brought from Bisham (see chapter 4)

5 pieces of Upper Greensand (Lower Cretaceous) – Places around Reigate, for example Merstham, are a likely source. The building accounts mention 'Raygate'.

2 pieces of Caen stone – This may correspond to the 'petris de caine' in the building accounts.

6 pieces of coarse-grained, pellet limestone, the same buff colour as Caen. This may be a variety of Caen.

The accounts mention stone from Wheatley and also Kentish Rag, but no specimens of either were retrieved.

The material retrieved from the Wyatville deposits (see table below) includes offcuts/debris from Wyatville's programme of works, and from the demolition of earlier structures. Flint galetting , which consists of decorative bonding inclusions and can be seen in the present building faces of the Upper Ward, was also noted from the excavation but not retained. The range of materials present clearly characterises deposits 102, 203 and 302 as a single layer and confirms the on-site interpretation that these belong to the 1824-40 phase of construction.

Architectural and stone fragments from Wyatville deposits

Context	Comments
102	Baluster fragment. Similar to ones to be seen in the windows of the Upper Ward in St John Hope, *Windsor Castle*, plate XLIV, The Upper Ward 'before' Wyatville's works. Likely to date to Late seventeenth century/Charles II programme of work under comptroller Hugh May
102	Column fragment 1450mm dia, oolitic limestone, traces of paint and white wash show that the piece has been in place for some time and is demolition material rather than building surplus.
102	Tooled ashlar slab, oolitic limestone
203	Ashlar block with vertical tooling. Probable Wyatville offcut
203	Yorkstone? Floor fragment
203	Dressed ashlar oolitic limestone fragment
203	Tooled Reigate ashlar block
203	Tooled ashlar block with window glazing groove
203	Tooled ashlar block with window glazing groove
203	Fragment of marble paving
203	2 x column fragment 1450mm dia , oolitic limestone, traces of paint and white wash
203	2 x tooled Reigate ashlar block
203	Slate floor paver
302	Porphyry/Marble decorative floor piece

Flint

REBECCA DEVANEY

A total of four flint flakes and 66 fragments (770g) of burnt unworked flint were recovered from context 208 during the excavations. The flint cannot be reliably dated on typological or technological grounds.

Context	Flint category	Total	Broken	Weight gms	Comments	Cortication	Post Depositional Damage
208	Burnt unworked	2		37			
326	Natural /discarded	1					
208	Natural/ discarded	1					
208	Flake	1			Hinge termination, dorsal flake scars, irregular, but genuine flake removal	Uncorticated	Moderate
208	Flake	1	1		Proximal & distal breaks, side trimming, gravel flint	Uncorticated	Moderate
208	Burnt unworked	63		732	<1> >10mm		
208	Natural/ discarded	58			<1> >10mm		
208	Burnt unworked	1	1		<1> >10mm		
208	Flake	1			<1> >10mm. Hard hammer struck, secondary removal	Uncorticated	Moderate
208	Flake	1			<1> >10mm. Possibly naturally struck	Uncorticated	Slight

The Animal Bones

LENA STRID

QUANTITY OF MATERIAL AND RECORDING METHODOLOGY

The animal bone assemblage consisted of 132 re-fitted fragments. A record of the assessed assemblage can be found with the site archive. The contexts were either associated with the building of the House of the Round Table in the mid fourteenth century, or from pre-mid-fourteenth century silt deposits (see table below). The animal bone was recovered through hand collection during excavation and from wet sieved bulk samples (processed using 500µm residue mesh and 250µm flot mesh). 43% of the assessed bones derive from hand-retrieved contexts, and 57% from sieved contexts. All sieved contexts were dated to pre-fourteenth century.

The bones were identified to species using a comparative reference collection, as well as osteological books and articles. Sheep and goat were not identified to species at this stage, but rather classified as 'sheep/goat'. Ribs and vertebrae, with the exception for atlas and axis, were classified by size: 'large mammal' representing cattle, horse and deer, 'medium mammal' representing sheep/goat, pig and large dog, and 'small mammal' representing small dog, cat and hare.

The condition of the bone was graded using criteria stipulated by Lyman (1996).[27] Grade 0 being very well preserved bone and grade 5 indicating that the bone had suffered such structural and attritional damage as to make it unrecognisable.

For ageing, mandibles with two or more recordable teeth (Grant 1982),[28] cattle horncores (Armitage 1982)[29] and fused and unfused epiphyses (Habermehl 1975)[30] were noted. Sex estimation was carried out on cattle metapodials and pelves, sheep pelves, and pig canine teeth, using data from Boessneck et al (1964),[31] Prummel and Frisch (1986),[32] Schmid (1972)[33] and Vretemark (1997).[34] Measurable bones were noted according to von den Driesch (1976).[35]

THE ASSEMBLAGE

The assessed assemblage consisted of 118 fragments, of which 33 (28%) could be determined to species. The species present included cattle, sheep/goat, pig, roe deer

---

[27] R.L. Lyman, *Vertebrate taphonomy*, Cambridge 1996

[28] A. Grant, 'The use of toothwear as a guide to the age of domestic ungulates', in *Ageing and sexing animal bones from archaeological sites,* eds B. Wilson, C. Grigson and S. Payne, BAR British Series 109, Oxford 1982, 91-108.

[29] P. Armitage, 'A system for ageing and sexing the horncores of cattle from British post-medieval sites (with special reference to unimproved British longhorn cattle)', in Wilson, *Ageing and sexing animal bones,* 37-54.

[30] K.-H. Habermehl, *Die Altersbestimmung bei Haus- und Labortieren.* 2nd edn. Berlin, Hamburg 1975.

[31] J. Boessneck, H.-H. Müller, and M. Teichert, M. 'Osteologische Unterscheidungsmerkmale zwischen Schaf (Ovis aries Linné) und Ziege (Capra hircus Linné)', *Kühn-Archiv*, 78. 1964.

[32] W. Prummel, and H.-J. Frisch, 'A guide for the distinction of species, sex and body side in bones of sheep and goat', *Journal of Archaeological Science*, 13, 1986, 567-577.

[33] E. Schmid, *Atlas of animal bones. For prehistorians, archaeologists and quaternary geologists.* Amsterdam, London, New York 1972.

[34] M. Vretemark, Från ben till boskap. Kosthåll och djurhållning med utgångspunkt i medeltida benmaterial från Skara, Skrifter från Länsmuseet Skara, 1987.

[35] A. von den Driesch, A. *A guide to the measurement of animal bones from archaeological sites.* Harvard 1976.

and hare. Some indeterminable bird bones were also found. The presence of dog is evidenced by gnaw marks on a sheep/goat tibia.

Most bones were in a good condition. Traces of burning were absent. One bone from mid-fourteenth-century deposits displayed gnaw marks from a carnivore, likely dog.

The assemblage seems to consist almost exclusively of domestic species. The predominance of cattle, sheep/goat and pig is to be considered normal, regardless of time period. The presence of roe deer in the mid -fourteenth-century assemblage indicates the eating of venison at court.

Age estimation could be carried out on nine bones and one jaw. The majority of the sheep/goats were found to be sub-adult/adult, whereas the majority of the pigs were juvenile/sub-adult. (see table 5 and 6). A pig maxillary canine was found to derive from a male. No other bones could be sexed.

Butchering marks and pathologies were absent.

Identified bones/species

Species	Pre mid fourteenth C.	Mid fourteenth C.	nineteenth C.
Cattle		4	
Sheep/goat	2	3	
Pig	5	3	
Roe deer		1	
Hare		1	
Indeterminate bird	2		
Fish			
Medium mammal	12	6	
Large mammal	3	7	1
Indeterminate	54	14	
Total fragment count	78	39	1
Total weight (g)	153	390	8

Preservation level for bones

	Cattle			Sheep/goat			Pig		
	UF	IF	F	UF	IF	F	UF	IF	F
Early fusion								1	
Mid fusion						1			
Late fusion	1	1			1	1			

Mandibles and bones in the assemblage providing data for ageing, sexing and measuring data.

	Cattle			Sheep/goat			Pig		
	UF	IF	F	UF	IF	F	UF	IF	F
Early fusion						1	1		
Mid fusion									
Late fusion							1		

Epiphyseal fusion of cattle, sheep/goat and pig in the pre mid fourteenth century. assemblage.
UF = unfused, IF = in fusion, F = fused

	N	0	1	2	3	4	5
Pre mid fourteenth C.	78		94.9%	5.1%			
Mid fourteenth C.	39	2.6%	64.1%	33.3%			
nineteenth C.	1		100.0%				

Epiphyseal fusion of cattle, sheep/goat and pig in the mid fourteenth C. assemblage.
UF = unfused, IF = in fusion, F = fused.

	Pre mid fourteenth century	Mid fourteenth century
Ageable mandibles	0	1
Ageable bones	3	6
Sexable bones	1	0

Environmental and Economic Assessment Data

Seren Griffiths

One bulk sample of 100 litres from context 208 was examined. The context was a deposit of around 500mm thick of what was considered during excavation to be a gradually accumulated silty soil. Artefacts recovered from the layer included material culture ranging from later prehistory to the thirteenth century. The deposit was cut at each end of the trench by nineteenth century drains. The deposit is interpreted as including material from organic decay and small-scale domestic dumping events mixed by animal and human trampling. Re-deposited material may also originate from landscaping associated with construction of the curtain walls.

The sample was processed by flotation using a modified Siraf-type machine, the flot being collected onto a 250 micron mesh. The remaining material was then wet sieved through a sieve column for the recovery of small bones and artefacts. The residue was washed onto 500 micron mesh and retained. The flot and residue were air-dried and the flot scanned under a binocular microscope. The residues were sorted for bones and artefacts down to 2mm and the remaining material retained.

Ecofactual remains

The sample produced a flot of *c.* 100ml. The majority of the flot comprised wood *Quercus* (oak) sp. charcoal. No cereal grains or other economic plant remains were present. Charred weed seeds from the *Rumex* sp. (nettle) were common. A range of molluscs were present including *Trichia hispida*, *Vertigo* sp., and potentially modern *Cochlicopa* sp. Small bones were present in the flot including a large *Conger conger* (Conger eel*)* vertebra, and a Pleuronectiformes (small flat fish) vertebra.

Environmentally recovered finds

Pot, burnt flint and an iron object were recovered from the sample. These are included in the finds compendiums above.

Discussion

A range of ecofactual material is present in the sample, probably resulting from domestic refuse dumps. Nettle seeds may represent a hiatus in deposition, allowing colonisation by this ruderal weed. The taphonomy of the deposit is complex and mixing, at least some of which appears to have occurred post-depositionally, means that the sample is of negligible use for reconstructing ancient environments and economies.

There is limited archaeobotanical evidence for diet or environment; a single type of wood charcoal was identified, but the fragments are generally infused with sediment, making speciation difficult. The potential 'old wood' effect of the *Quercus* spp. charcoal makes it unsuitable for radiocarbon dating. The nature of the assemblage means that the weed seeds are unlikely to represent the ancient environment of the site. Molluscs and bone are clearly preserved in the calcareous soils at the site, but again the mixed nature of this deposit precludes further interpretation.

Sample No	Context No	Flot vol (ml)	Type of context	Charcoal	Weeds	Molluscs	Environmentally recovered finds and residues
1	208	100	Mixed silt and domestic dump deposit. Material culture from later pre-history to 13th	++++ (mostly Quercus spp.)	+++	Trichia hispida ++, Cochlicopa sp ++, Vertigo sp ++, others ++	P++, BF ++, Fe+

Key: +=present (up to 5 items), ++=frequent (5-25), +++=common (25-100) ++++=abundant (>100)

B = bone, BC = burnt clay, BF = burnt flint, CBM= ceramic building material, HS = hammerscale, P = pot, Fe = Iron

Notes: Some modern plant matter, insect remains, snail eggs. No grain or chaff

APPENDIX B

Windsor Round Table Chronicle Sources

LATIN AND FRENCH TEXTS WITH FACING TRANSLATION

I. Adam Murimuth, *Continuatio Chronicarum*, 155-6

IN THIS YEAR THE LORD KING ORDERED a most noble tournament or joust to be held in his birthplace, that is at Windsor Castle, on January 19, the 14th of the kalends of February, which he caused to be announced a suitable time in advance both abroad and in England. He sent invitations to all the ladies of the southern part of England and to the wives of the citizens of London. When the earls, barons, knights and a great number of ladies had gathered in that castle on the Sunday, January 19, the king gave a solemn feast, and the great hall of the castle was filled by the ladies, with just two knights among them, the only ones to have come from France to the occasion. At this gathering there were two queens, nine countesses, the wives of the barons, knights and citizens, whom they could not easily count, and to whom the king himself personally allocated their seats according to their rank. The prince of Wales, duke of Cornwall, earls, barons and knights ate with all the other people in tents and other places, where food and all other necessities had been prepared; everything was on a generous scale and served unstintingly. In the evening dancing and various entertainments were laid on in a magnificent fashion. For the three days following, the king with nineteen other knights held jousts against all comers; and the king himself, not because of his kingly rank but because of his great exertions and the good fortune that he had during the three days, was held to be the best of the defenders. Of the challengers, Sir Miles Stapleton on the first day, Sir Philip Despenser on the second, and Sir John Blount on the third, were awarded the prize. On the following Thursday, after the squires had jousted, the king gave a great feast at which he announced the foundation of his Round Table, and took the oaths of certain lords, barons and knights who wished to be members of the said Round Table. He fixed the day for the holding of the Round Table as the Whitsun following, and dismissed the company thanking them for all they had done. He afterwards commanded that a most noble building should be built, in which to hold the Round Table on the day assigned, and instructed masons, carpenters and other workmen to carry out the work, providing both wood and stone, and not sparing either labour or expense. This work was later stopped for various reasons.

I. Adam Murimuth, *Continuatio Chronicarum*, 155-6

Murimuth's title is 'Continuation of the Chronicles' and it was probably intended to supplement Nicholas Trivet's chronicle; he begins at 1303, but the valuable material is for the period 1325-47, when he was evidently keeping notes of current events. Most copies of his text give the following account of the Windsor festival.

HOC ANNO ORDINAVIT DOMINUS REX habere nobilissima hastiludia sive tirocinium in loco nativitatis suae, videlicet in castro de Wyndesore, die videlicet Januarii xix. et xiiij. kalendas Februarii, quae competenti tempore praecedenti fecit tam in partibus transmarinis quam in Anglia publice proclamari. Ad quae etiam fecit omnes dominas australium partium Angliae et uxores burgensium Londoniensium per suas literas invitari. Congregatis igitur comitibus, baronibus, militibus, et quam plurimis dominabus die Dominica, videlicet xiij. kalendas Februarii, in castro praedicto, fecit rex solempne convivium, ita quod magna aula ipsius castri plena exstitit dominabus, nec fuit aliquis masculus inter eas, preter duos milites qui soli de Francia ad solempnitatem hujusmodi accesserunt. In quo convivio fuerunt due regine, ix. comitissae, uxores baronum, militum, et burgensium, quae non potuerunt faciliter numerari, quas rex ipse personaliter in locis suis secundum ordinem collocavit. Princeps vero Wallie, dux Cornubiae, comites, barones, et milites, una cum toto populo in tentorio et locis aliis comederunt, ubi fuerunt cibaria et omnia alia necessaria praeparata et omnibus liberaliter et sine murmure liberata; et in sero choreae et tripudia diversa solempniter ordinata. Et tribus diebus sequentibus rex cum aliis decem et novem militibus tenuit hastiludia contra omnes ab extrinseco venientes ; et idem dominus, non propter favorem regium, sed propter magnum laborem quem sustinuit et propter fortunam quam dicto triduo habuit, inter intrinsecos gratias reportavit. Extrinsecus vero dominus miles de Stapeltona primo die, dominus Philippus Despenser secundo die, dominus Johannes Blount tertio die, gratias reportarunt. Die vero Jovis sequente post hastiludia domicellorum, dominus rex fecit coenam magnum in qua suam rotundam tabulam inchoavit, et juramenta quorundam comitum et baronum et militum quos voluit esse de dicta tabula rotunda recepit sub certa forma ad dictam rotundam tabulam pertinente; et prefixit diem rotundae tabulae tenendae ibidem in festo Pentecostes proxime tunc futuro, et omnibus praesentibus dedit licentiam cum gratiarum actionibus ad propria remeandi. Ordinavit etiam postea quod ibidem fieret una nobilissima domus, in qua posset dicta rotunda tabula teneri in termino assignato ; ad quam faciendam, cementarios et carpentarios ceterosque artifices deputavit, et tam ligna quam lapides provideri praecepit, non parcendo laboribus vel expensis. A quo opere fuit postea ex certis causis cessatum.

II. A. Adam Murimuth, *Continuatio Chronicarum*, 231-2

On the festival held at Windsor by the most illustrious king Edward, king of England and France, on the day of St George the Martyr[1]

IN THE YEAR OF OUR LORD 1343 [1344], but in the second year of the pontificate of pope Clement VI and in the seventeenth year of the reign of king Edward the Third from the Conquest, always beginning (and ending) at the feast of St Michael, from when until the feast of the Purification of the Blessed Mary nothing worthy of note happened. However, on the Sunday next after the feast of the Blessed Mary, at Windsor, the king kept a very great and solemn feast ; to which he invited his eldest son the prince of Wales, the earls, barons, and knights, and very many other nobles of his kingdom. There were also there queen Philippa, with her children, the king's mother queen Isabella, countesses, baronesses, as well as ladies and gentlewomen, with an indescribable host of people gathered to enjoy this great occasion. The feasts that followed were expensive and abundant, and the choicest drinks were served, until everyone had had as much as they wished. The lords and ladies danced together, exchanging embraces and kisses. The knights jousted continuously for three days: the minstrels played their best and most joyful melodies, and some were given clothes, some gifts of different kinds, and some gold and silver in plenty.

This feast lasted from Sunday to Wednesday. That night, after the end of the jousts, the king had it proclaimed that no lord or lady should presume to depart, but should stay until morning, to learn the king's pleasure. When the morning of Thursday came, at about nine o'clock the king caused himself to be solemnly arrayed in his most royal and festive attire; his outer mantle was of very precious velvet and the royal crown was placed upon his head. The queen was likewise dressed in most noble fashion. The earls and barons, and the rest of the lords and ladies, prepared themselves in appropriate fashion to go with the king to the chapel in the castle of Windsor and hear mass, as he commanded them to do. When mass had been celebrated, the king left the chapel; Henry earl of Derby, as steward of England, and William, earl of Salisbury, as marshal of England, went before him, each carrying the staff of his office in his hand, and the king himself holding the royal sceptre in his hand. There followed him the young queen,

---

[1] See notes 2 and 3 re dates.

II. A. Adam Murimuth, *Continuatio Chronicarum*, 231-2

Two copies of Murimuth's 'Continuation of the Chronicles' give a different account of the festival, which may or may not be by Murimuth himself. The second is slightly shorter, and is almost certainly the work of a different hand.

De solempnitate facta apud Wyndelsore per illustrissimum regem Edwardum, regem Angliae et Franciae, in die sancti Georgii martyris[2]

ANNO DOMINI MILLESIMO CCC^MO XLIII° pontificatus papae vero Clementis sexti anno secundo, et regni regis Edwardi tertii a conquestu xvij, incipiendo semper et finiendo ad festum sancti michaelis, a quo quidem festo usque ad festum Purificationis beatae Mariae non fuerunt aliqua facto, fama seu relatione multum digna, sed Dominica proxima post festum Purificationis beatae Mariae,[3] apud Wyndeshore, fecit dominus rex maximum solemnitatem et convivium grande; cui fecit convenire filium suum primogenitum, principem Walliae, comites, barones, et milites, et alios regni nobiles quam plures. Fuerunt etiam ibidem domina regina Philippa, cum liberis suis, domina regina mater, domina Isabella, comitissae, baronissae, necnon dominae et domicellae, cum cetero populo inenarrabili, super tanta solempnitate gavisuro. Sicque inter epulas pretiosas affuerunt et potus delicatissimi abundantes ad cujuscumque satietatem. Inter dominos et dominas non defuerunt tripudia, amplexus ad invicem commiscentes et oscula. Inter milites excerbantur hastiludia per triduum continuata; ab histrionibus summa fit melodia, laetaque diversa ; his dantur mutatoria; his abundabant donaria; hi auri et argenti ditabantur copia. Quae quidem solempnitas duravit diebus Dominica, Lunae, Martis, et Mercurii; quo die ad noctem, post finem hastiludorum, fecit dominus rex proclamari, ne aliquis dominus aut domina recedere praesumerent, sed per mane exspectarent, voluntatem domini regis scituri. Quo mane, hoc est, die Jovis, superveniente, circa horam primam fecit se dominus rex solempniter parari vestibus regalibus et solempnibus; sed superius habuit indutum unum mantellum de felveto preciosissimum, e coronam regiam in capite positam. Regina similiter nobilissime fuit adornata; comites, barones, ac ceteri domini et dominae, cum omni decentia qua potuerunt juxta preceptum domini regis, cum eodem apud capellam in castello de Wyndesore progressuri et missam audituri se paraverunt. Qua celebrata, exivit dominus rex a capella, quem praeibant dominus Henricus comes Derby, tanquam seneschallus Angliae, et dominus Willelmus comes Sarisburiae, tanquam mareschallus Angliae, utroque colore officii sui virgam in mane gestante; et ipso domino rege sceptrum regale in manu tenente. Sequebantur etiam domina regina juvenis,

---

[2]   This heading is due to a confusion with the later Garter feasts, and implies that the second version of the chronicle was written after 1348. As the third version (see below) evidently depends on the second, this too must be later than 1348.

[3]   This date is clearly wrong: the other version of Murimuth's chronicle is correct in saying that the festival began on 19 January.

and the queen-mother, the prince of Wales, the earls, barons, knights and nobles, with the ladies and all the people flocking to see such an extraordinary spectacle, to the place appointed for the assembly. There the king and all the others at the same time stood up. The king was presented with the Bible, and laying his hand on the Gospels, swore a solemn oath that he himself at a certain time, provided that he had the necessary means, would begin a Round Table, in the same manner and condition as Arthur, formerly king of England, established it, namely to the number of 300 knights, and would cherish it and maintain it according to his power, always adding to the number of knights. The earls of Derby, Salisbury, Warwick, Arundel, Pembroke, and Suffolk, the other barons and very many praiseworthy knights of probity and renown likewise made an oath to observe, sustain, and promote the Round Table with all its appendages. When this was done, trumpets and drums sounded together, and the guests hastened to a feast, where richness of fare, variety of dishes, and overflowing abundance of drinks were all to be found, to their unutterable delight and inestimable comfort. No murmurs spoilt their enjoyment and no cares troubled their cheerfulness. The occasion finished in the same manner that it had begun. When, on this fifth day, the royal feast was ended, everyone returned to their own affairs. A week afterwards, which was a cause for great grief, William de Montacute, earl of Salisbury, who had been wounded in the jousting, died of natural causes.

II. B. Continuation of Nicholas Trivet from BL MS Cotton Otho C II f.99

IN THE YEAR OF OUR LORD 1343 [1344], but in the second year of the pontificate of pope Clement VI and in the seventeenth year of the reign of king Edward the Third from the Conquest, beginning and ending at the feast of St Michael, on the Sunday next after the feast of the purification of the Blessed Mary, the king kept a very great and solemn feast at Windsor; to which he invited his eldest son the prince of Wales, the earls, barons, and very many other nobles of his kingdom. There were also there queen Philippa, with her children, the king's mother queen Isabella, countesses, baronesses, as well as ladies and gentlewomen, with an indescribable host of people gathered to enjoy this great occasion. The feasts were abundant,[4] and the choicest drinks were served. The lords and ladies danced together, exchanging embraces and kisses. The knights jousted continuously for three days.

This feast lasted[5] for the days of Sunday, Monday, Tuesday and Wednesday. That night, after the end of the jousts, the king had it proclaimed that no-one should presume to depart, but should stay until morning, to learn the king's pleasure. When the morning of Thursday came, at about nine o'clock the king caused himself to be solemnly arrayed in his most royal attire; his outer mantle was of very precious velvet and the royal crown was placed upon his head. The queen

---

[4] Margin: Great ceremony at Windsor.
[5] Margin: The king's triumph.

et domino regina mater, princeps Walliae, comites, barones, milites, et proceres, cum dominabus et omni populo, hujusmodi spectaculum visuri insolitum, usque ad locum stationi dispositum. in quo loco idem dominus rex et omnes alii insimul steterunt, et, oblato libro, dominus rex, tactis sacrosanctis, corporale dimisit dominuspraestitit juramentum quod ipse ad certum tempus ad hoc limitatum, dummodo sibi facultas arrideat, mensam rotundam inciperet, eodem modo et statu quo eam Arthurus quondam rex Angliae, scilicet ad numerum trecentorum militum, et eam foveret et manuteneret pro viribus, numerum semper inaugendo. Ad quod quidem observandum, sustinendum, promovendum in omnibus suis appendiciis, comites Derby, Sarisburiae, Warewykiae, Arundelliae, Pembrokiae, et Suffolkiae, ac alii barones et milites quam plures, quos probitas et fama promovit laude fore dignos, consimile fecerunt juramentum. Quo facto, sonantibus tubis et nachaiis universaliter, convivae properabant ad comestum ; qui quidem comestus fuit completus cum cibariorum opulentia, ferculorum varietate, potuum afflu- ente copiositate : gaudium fuit ineffabile, solatium inaestimabile, jocunditas sine murmuratione, hilaritas absque anxietate. Ultimis itaque primis respondentibus, terminatum est regale convivium, ut quinto die post prandium unusquisue ad propria remearet. Post hoc vero, in octavo die, unde dolendum est non minimum, dominus Willelmus de Monte acuto, Sarisburiae comes, in hastiludiis praedictis frustratus, mortem subiit naturalem.

II. B. Continuation of Nicholas Trivet from BL MS Cotton Otho C II f.99

ANNO DOMINI MILLESIMO CCC^MO XLIII° papae vero Clementis sexti anno iiio, et regis Edwardi tertii a conquestu xvij, incipiendo et finiendo ad festum sancti michaelis, Dominica proxima post festum Purificationis beatae Mariae, apud Wyndesore, fecit rex maximum solemnitatem; cui fecit convenire primogenitum suum, principem Walliae, comites, barones, et alios regni nobiles. Fuerunt etiam ibidem regina Philippa, cum liberis suis, regina Isabella regis mater, comitissae, baronissae, dominae et domicellae, cum cetero populo super tanta solempnitate gavisuro. Sicque inter epulas pretiosas[6] et potus delicatissimi affuerunt. Inter dominos et dominas non defuerunt tripudia, amplexus et oscula. Inter milites excerbantur hastiludia per triduum continuata . Quae quidem solempnitas duravit[7] diebus Dominica, Lunae, Martis, et Mercurii ; quo die post finem hastiludorum, fecit dominus rex proclamari, ne aliquis praesumerent recedere, sed per mane omnibus exspectarent, voluntatem domini regis audituri. Quo mane superveniente fecit se dominus rex vestis regalibus. Et superius habuit indutum unum mantellum de velveto preciosissimum, e coronam regiam in capite positam. Regina similiter

---

[6] margin: Maxima solempnitate apud Wyndesore.
[7] margin: Triumphus regis.

was likewise dressed in most noble fashion. The earls and barons, and the rest of the lords and ladies, prepared themselves in appropriate fashion to go with the king. When mass had been celebrated, Henry earl of Derby, as steward of England, and William, earl of Salisbury, as marshal of England, each carrying the staff of his office in his hand, went before the king who held the royal sceptre in his hand. There followed him the young queen, and the queen-mother, the prince of Wales, the earls, barons and nobles, with the ladies and all the people flocking to see such an extraordinary spectacle, to the place appointed for the assembly. There the king and all the others at the same time stood up. The king, having touched the holy books, swore a solemn oath that he himself at a certain time, provided that he had the necessary means, would begin a Round Table, in the same manner and condition as Arthur, formerly king of England, established it, namely to the number of 300 knights, and would cherish it and maintain it according to his power, always adding to the number of knights. The earls of Derby, Salisbury, Warwick, Arundel, Pembroke, and Suffolk, the other barons and very many praiseworthy knights of probity and renown likewise made an oath to observe, sustain, and promote the Round Table with all its appendages. When this was done, trumpets and drums sounded together, and the guests hastened to a feast, where richness of fare, variety of dishes, and overflowing abundance of drinks were all to be found, to their unutterable delight and inestimable comfort. No murmurs spoilt their enjoyment and no cares troubled their cheerfulness. The occasion finished in the same manner that it had begun. When, on this fifth day, the royal feast was ended, everyone returned to their own affairs. A week afterwards, William de Montacute, earl of Salisbury, who had been wounded in the jousting, died of natural causes.

Once the King of England had arrived in his country, as stated above, he proclaimed a very big joust at one of his castles called Windsor. Knights came there from all countries in order to gain renown. There he had planned to re-establish the Round Table and the adventures of chivalry, which had not been seen since the days of King Arthur. Yet in his heart he was thinking something quite different, which he did not show on the outside, for all this time he was readying a great fleet, and a establishing a large garrison in one of his ports, called Portsmouth. In the midst of these actions, news came to him that Charles, Duke of Brittany, had invaded the land of Brittany; and therefore the aforementioned feast was put off, and he once again sent the Earl of Northampton to Brittany to aid the countess of Montfort.

similiter nobilissime adornata fuit; comites, barones, ac ceteri omnes, cum omni in castello de Wyndesore progressuri et missam audituri se paraverunt. Qua celebrata dominus Henricus comes Derby, tanquam seneschallus Angliae, et dominus Willelmus comes Sarisburiae, tanquam mareschallus Angliae, utroque titulo officii sui virgam in mane gestantes ; et ipso rege sceptrum in manu teniente. Sequebantur et regina juvenis, et regis mater, princeps Wallie, comites et barones et proceres, cum dominabus et omni populo, hujus spectaculum visuri insolitum, usque ad locum stationi dispositum. in quo loco idem usque ad locum stationi dispositum. in quo loco idem dominus rex [tactis][8] sacrosanctis, corporale praestitit juramentum quod ipse ad certum tempus ad hoc limitatum, dummodo sibi facultas arrideat, mensam rotundam inciperet, eodem modo et statu quo eam dimisit dominus Arthurus quondam rex Angliae, scilicet ad numerum CCC^{orum} militum, et eam foveret et manuteneret pro viribus, numerum semper inaugendo. Ad quod quidem observandum, sustinendum, et promovendum in omnibus suis appendiciis, comites Derby, Sarisburiae, Warewykiae, Arundelliae, Pembrokiae, et Suffolkiae, ac alii barones et milites quam plures, quos probitas et fama promovit fore laude dignos,consimile fecerunt juramentum. Quo facto, sonantibus tubis et nacariis universitaliter, convivae properabant ad comestum ; qui quidem comestus fuit epulentissimus in cibrariorum et ferculorum varietate, potuum affluentem: gaudium fuit ineffabile, solatium inaestimabile, jocunditas sine murmuratione, hillaritas absque anxietate. Ultimis itaque primis respondentibus, terminatum est regale convivium, ut quinto die post prandium unusquisue ad propria remearet. Post hoc vero, in octo dies dominus Willelmus de [9]Monte acuto, Sarisburiae comes, in hastiludiis praedictis frustratus, mortem subiit naturalem.

III St Omer Chronicle

BN MS Fr. 693, f.254

Quant li rois d'Engleterre fu arives en son paiis, ainsi comme dessus est dit, si fist criier une tres grant jouste a .j. sien castel que on apelle Windesore. De toutes terres y vinrent chevalier pour pris acquerre. Illueques avoit ordene de relever le Taule Reonde et les aventures de chevalerie qui tres le tamps le roy Arthus estoient fallies. Tout autrement pensoit au cuer qu'il ne monstroit par dehors; car tout jours fist il grant navie apparillier et grant garnison mettre ens a .j. sien port que on apelle Portsemude. Entre ces entrefaites nouvellez li vinrent que Charlez dux de Bretaigne avoit envay le terre de Bretaigne, et pour chou fu la feste dessus dicte retardee. Et envoia derechief le comte de Norhantonne en Bretaigne pour aidier le comtesse de Montfort.[10]

---

[8] Supplied from BL MS Cotton Nero D X.
[9] margin: monte acuti Comes.
[10] I am grateful to Professor Clifford Rogers for providing both text and translation. He is preparing a full edition and translation of this text for publication.

IV. Thomas Walsingham, *Historia Anglicana*, I.263

A Round Table begun in both kingdoms
The Round Table in England   In the year of grace 1344, which is the eighteenth year of Edward's reign, king Edward summoned many workers to Windsor Castle and began to build a house which was called 'The Round Table'. Its size from the centre to the circumference, the radius, was 100 feet, and its diameter was therefore two hundred feet. The weekly expenses were at first a hundred pounds, but afterwards because of news which the king received from France, this was cut back to nine pounds because he needed a great deal of money for other business.
The Round Table in France   At the same time, Philip of Valois, king of France, spurred on by what the king of England had done, began to build a round table in his own country, in order to attract the knights of Germany and Italy, in case they set out for the table of the king of England.

V. Jean Froissart, *Chroniques*, II 304

At that time, king Edward of England wished and decided to restore and rebuild the great castle of Windsor, which king Arthur founded and built in times gone by, and where the Round Table was first begun and established. And the king made an order of knights consisting of himself and his children and the most valiant men of the land. They were to be forty in all and were called the *Knights of the Blue Garter*, and their feast each year was to be on St George's day. And to begin that festival, the English king assembled the earls, barons and knights from the whole country, and told them his intention and his great desire to establish the feast, to which they cheerfully agreed. And forty knights were elected there, known and reputed to be the most valiant of all. And they swore an oath of mutual allegiance with the king to hold the feast and to follow the ordinances that had been agreed. And the king founded the chapel of saint George in the castle of Windsor and established and put there canons to serve God, and gave them rents, and provided for them well. And so that the feast should be known in all parts, the English king sent his heralds to publish and announce it in France, Sicily, Burgundy, Flanders, Brabant, Germany and everywhere as far as Lombardy. And he gave fifteen days of safe conduct after the festival to all knights and squires who wished to come. And this festival was to be a joust of 40 knights as defenders with forty squires and it was to be on the next saint George's day, in the year 1344, in the castle of Windsor. And the queen of England was to be there accompanied by three hundred ladies and damsels as her attendants, all noble and gentle women and dressed in similar clothes.

IV. Thomas Walsingham, *Historia Anglicana*, I.263

Walsingham was writing in the 1380s and 1390s, but seems to have had access to the royal accounts; St Albans, where he was a monk, had strong links with the royal court

Rotunda Tabula incipitur in utroque regno.

ROTUNDA TABULA IN ANGLIA Anno gratiae millesimo trecentesimo quadragesimo quarto, qui est annus Edwardi octavus-decimus, Rex Edwardus fecit convocari plures artifices ad castrum de Wyndeshores, et coepit aedificare domum, quae 'Rotunda Tabula' vocaretur: habuit ejus autem area a centro ad cirumferentiam, per semidiametrum, centum pedes; et sic diametri ducentorum pedum erat. Expensae per hebdomadam erant primo centum librae; sed expost, propter nova quae Rex suscepit de Francia, resecabantur ad novem libras, eo quod censuit pro aliis negotiis thesaurum plurimum comportandum.

ROTUNDA TABULA IN FRANCIA Eodem tempore, Philippus de Valeys, Rex Franciae, hoc facto Regis Angliae provocatus, coepit et ipse Rotundam aedificare Tabulam in terra sua; ut sic sibi attraheret militiam Alemanniae et Italiae, ne ad Regis Angliae Tabulam properarent.

V. Jean Froissart, *Chroniques*, II 304

Froissart was writing in the 1380s and 1390s, but by this time he had fewer contacts in England, and he seems to have been relying on someone's recollections of the event rather than any written record

En ce tamps, vint em pourpos et en vollenté au roy Edouart d'Engleterre que il feroit refaire et redefiier le grant castiel de Windesore que li roys Artus fist jadis faire et fonder là où premierement fu conmenchie et estoree la noble Table Reonde dont tant de bons chevaliers yssirent par le monde. Et feroit li rois une ordonnance de chevaliers de lui et de ses enffans et des plus preus de sa terre et seroient en somme jusques a .XL. et lez nonmeroit on les *Chevaliers du Bleu Gertier* et le feste d'an en an le jour Saint Gorge. Et pour ceste feste conmenchier, li roys englés asambla de tout son pays comtes, barons, chevaliers et leur dist sen entention et le grant desir que il avoit de le feste emprendre, se li acorderent liement. Et la furent esleu .XL. chevalier par avis et par renommee lez plus preux de tous les autres. Et saielerent par foy et par sierement avoecq le roy a tenir et a pourssuiwir le feste et lez ordonnanches telles que elles en estoient accordees. Et fist le rois fonder et edeffiier une cappelle de saint Jorge où castiel de Windesore et y estabuli et mist chanonnes pour Dieu servir et les arenta et aprouvenda bien. Et pour ce que la feste fuist sceue et conneuwes par touttez marches, ly roys englés l'envoya publiier et denunchier par ses hirauls en Franche, en Escoce, en Bourgoingne, en Flandres, en Braibant, en Allemaingne et par tout jusqu'en Lombardie. Et donnoit à tous chevaliers et escuiers qui venir y volroient .XV jours de sauf conduit apriés le feste. Et devoit estre ceste feste une joustez de .XL. chevaliers dedens atendans et de .XL. escuiers et seoir, le jour Saint Jorge prochain venant que on compteroit l'an mil .CCC.XLIIII. ens où castiel de Windesore. Et devoit estre la roynne d'Engleterre acompaignie de.CCC. dammes et dammoiselles, tout pour son corps, touttes noblez et gentilz dammez et parees d'uns paremens sannables.

APPENDIX C

Windsor Building Accounts

RELATING TO WORK ON THE HOUSE OF THE ROUND TABLE

1. Works on Castle Bridges

1344, 25th-31st January.
To 2 carts with 2 men employed in carrying sand for covering the bridges of the Castle with the said sand lest they be broken with the heavy carriage of the Round Table, for 2 days 2s. 8d.
To 4 men scattering the said sand upon the said bridges for 2 days 16d.
For heather bought for covering and raising the said bridges with the said sand 12d.
For the carriage of the said heather 8d.

7th-13th March.
To the wages of Osbert le Taverner carrying in his cart sand to be scattered on the bridges for one day 8d. To the wages of Reginald le Kambere and Edmund le Palmer heling him for the same time 4d.

1344, 25th April-1st May.
To the wages of John of Rickmansworth, mason and his apprentice underpinning the bridge in the middle bailey and the bridge at the upper end of the chapel (3½ days) 21d.

6th-12th June.
To the wages of John of Rickmansworth and John Mason, masons, and their two apprentices strengthening the stonework under the bridge next to the chapel, etc.

11th-17th July.
To the wages of John de Brether scattering heather on the bridge leading into the upper bailey for 1½ days 3d.
To one cartload of heather bought to be scattered on the bridge 5d.

2. Finding carpenters, masons, carriage and boats for works

A: Choosing carpenters for the works at Windsor Castle

The king to the sheriffs, mayors, bailiffs, ministers and all his faithful subjects both within liberties and without, greetings. Know that we have assigned our beloved William Hurley, our carpenter, to choose by himself or his deputies, as many carpenters in the cities, towns, and other places of our kingdom of England, both within their liberties and without, wherever they can be found, as he may need for certain works which we have ordained to be done in our Castle of Windsor, and to bring them to the aforesaid Castle as quickly as he can, there to remain at our wages on the aforesaid works.
And therefore we command you and each of your men, firmly enjoining you, that you listen to, counsel and aid the same William and his deputies as often as you will be requested by

1. Works on Castle Bridges

Source: Particulars of Account for works at Windsor in the time of Thomas de
Foxle, Constable 1343-4, PRO E101/492/24

1344 25th-31st January.
In ij carettis cum ij hominibus conductis cariantibus arenam pro pontibus Castri cum dicta
arena cooperiendis ne frangerentur cum magno cariagio tabule rotunde per ij dies ij.s. viij.d.
In iiij hominibus spargentibus dictam arenam super dictos pontes per ij. dies xvj.d.
In bruera pro dictis pontibus onerandis et exaltandis cum dicta arena empta xij.d.
In cariagio dicte bruers [sic] viij.d.

1344 7th-13th March.
In stipendio Osberti le Taverner cum caretta sua cariantis arenam pro pontibus ponderandis
per j. diem viij.d. In stipendiis Reginald le Kembere et Edmundi le Palmere auxilantium
eidem per idem tempus iiij.d.

1344 25th April-1st May.
In stipendiis Johannis de Rikemeresworth cementarij et garcionis sui pinnancium subtus
pontem in media bailliva et subtus pontem ad caput capelle per iij dies et di. xxj.d.

1344 6th-12th June.
In stipendiis Johannis de Rikemeresworth et Johannis le Mason Cementariorum et ij
garcionum suorum pynnancium opus petrinum sub ponte juxta Capellam, etc.

1344 11th-17th July.
In stipendio Johannis de Brether ponderantis pontem versus superiorem ballivam per j
diem et di. iijd.
In una caretata bruere empta pro pontibus ponderandis, vd.

2. Finding carpenters, masons, carriage and boats for works
A-D   *Source:* Patent Roll 18 Edward III, part I, m.39d. [PRO C. 66/211]]
Printed: Rymer, *Fœdera* (new edn), iii. part i. 6; *Cal. Patent Rolls 1343-1345*, 279.

A. *De carpentariis eligendis pro operationibus in castro de Wyndesore.*

Rex Vicecomitibus Majoribus Ballivis Ministris et omnibus aliis fidelibus suis tam infra
libertates quam extra ad quos etc. salutem.   Sciatis quod assignavimus dilectum nobis
Willielmum de Horle carpentarium nostrum ad eligendum per se vel deputatos suos tot
carpentarios in civitatibus burgis et aliis locis regni nostri Angliæ tam infra libertates quam
extra ubicumque eos inveniri contigerit quot pro quibusdam operationibus quas in castro
nostro de Wyndesore fieri ordinavimus faciendis indigerit et eos ad castrum prædictum
cum ea celeritate qua poterit ducendos ibidem ad vadia nostra super operationibus prædictis
moraturos:
Et ideo vobis et cuilibet vestrum mandamus firmiter injungentes quod eidem Willielmo
et deputatis suis prædictis in præmissis faciendis et exequendis intendentes sitis consulentes et auxiliantes quociens et prout per ipsum Willielmum vel dictos deputatos suos seu

the same William or his said deputies, or any one of them, on our behalf. In [testimony of] this etc. Witnessed by the King at Westminster, 16 February. By the King himself.

B. *Choosing of masons*

The King etc. greetings. Know that we have assigned our beloved William Ramsey, our mason, to choose by himself or by his deputies as many masons [as he may need for the same works,] in the city of London and in the counties of Kent, Norfolk, Suffolk, Bedford, and Northampton. By the King himself.

Memorandum: It is to be remembered that these two abovesaid commissions have been duplicated/copied under the same date with this clause 'excepting those who work in churches and monasteries' after the word '*indignerit*' and then 'and them to the aforesaid castle' etc. as above. By the King himself.

C. *Works at Windsor*

The King etc. Know that we have appointed our beloved William of Langley to take as often as there may be need, by himself or his deputies, in the counties of Oxford, Berks, and Middlesex, sufficient carriage for stone and timber which we have ordered to be bought and provided in those counties for certain works in our Castle of Windsor, to be led and carried to the said Castle of Windsor for our moneys thereupon to be paid.

And we therefore command you listen to, counsel and aid the same William and his aforesaid deputies in taking those carriages and in the other foregoing matters as often as you or any one of your men will be caused to know on our behalf.

In [testimony of] this etc. Witnessed by the King at Westminster, 18 February. By the King himself. Stephen de Harpham has a similar commission to take this manner of carriages in the same counties. Witness as above.

D. *Taking of shouts (Thames boats) for the said works*

The King etc. Know that we have appointed our beloved John Knyght to arrest and take as often as there may be need, by himself or his deputies both in London and elsewhere by the water of Thames between London and Windsor, sufficient shouts [Thames boats] for bringing our different requisitions from various places, along the banks of the said river to our Castle of Windsor for our moneys thereupon reasonably to be paid.

And therefore we command you to listen to, counsel and aid the same John and his deputies in the arrest and taking of the aforesaid shouts/barges and in the other foregoing matters etc., as above. By the King himself.

E. *Purchase of stones*

The King etc. Know that we have appointed our beloved Master William Ramsey either himself or through his deputies to buy and purchase for the King all the stones wherever he can find whether within or without liberties to whatever quantity is needed for certain works which he has ordered to be done in the Castle of Windsor, excepting those reserved for work on churches and monasteries, and shall bring them as quickly as he can to the said

eorum aliquem super hoc ex parte nostra fueritis requisiti.   In cujus, etc.   Teste
Rege apud Westmonasterium xvi die Februarii.   Per ipsum Regem.

B. *De cementariis eligendis.*

Rex, etc. salutem. Sciatis quod assignavimus dilectum nobis Willelmum de Ramseye
cementarium nostrum ad eligendum per se vel deputatos suos tot cementarios in civitate
London. ac comitatibus Kanciæ, Norff' Suff' Bed' et Northt' tam infra libertates quam
extra, etc. *ut supra.*   [Same date.]   Per ipsum Regem.
Memorandum: Et memorandum quod ista duæ commissiones supradicta duplicatæ fuerunt
sub eadem data, cum ista clausula, *exceptis illis qui in ecclesiis et monasteriis operantur*, post
illud verbum *indignerit* et tunc sic *et eos ad castrum prædictum*, etc. ut supra.   Per
ipsum Regem.

C. *De operationibus apud Wyndesore.*

Rex, etc. Sciatis quod assignavimus dilectum nobis Willelmum de Langele ad capiendum
quociens opus fuerit per se vel suos deputatos in comitatibus Oxon' Berk' et Midd' sufficiencia cariagia pro petra et mæremio quæ in comitatibus illis pro quibusdam operationibus
in castro nostro de Wyndesore emi et provideri ordinavimus usque dictum castrum de
Wyndesore pro denariis nostris inde solvendis ducendis et cariandis
Et ideo vobis mandamus quod eidem Willielmo ac deputatis suis prædictis in captione
cariagiorum illorum et aliis præmissis intendentes sitis consulentes et auxiliantes quociens
vobis vel alicui vestrum scire fecerint ex parte nostra.
In cujus, etc.   Teste Rege apud Westmonasterium xviii. die Februarii.
Per ipsum Regem. Consimilem commissionem habet Stephanus de Harpham ad hujus-
modi cariagia in eisdem comitatibus capiendis.   Teste ut supra.

D. *De shutis capiendis pro operationibus prædictis.*

Rex, etc. Sciatis quod assignavimus dilectum nobis Johannem Knyght ad arestandum et
capiendum quociens opus fuerit per se vel suos deputatos tam in London' quam alibi per
aquam Thamisiæ inter London' et Wyndesore shutas competentes pro diversis estoveriis
nostris a locis variis per costeram dictæ aquæ usque ad castrum nostrum de Wyndesore pro
denariis nostris inde rationabiliter solvendis ducendis.
Et ideo vobis mandamus quod eidem Johanni ac deputatis suis prædictis in arestatione et
captione shutarum prædictarum et aliis præmissis intendentes sitis, etc. *ut supra.*   Per
ipsum Regem.

E-G   *Source:* Patent Roll 18 Edward III, part I, m.34d. [PRO C. 66/211]
Calendared: Cal. Patent Rolls 1343-1345, 283.

E. *De petris emendis*

Rex, etc. Sciatis quod assignavimus dilectum nobis magistrum Willelmum de Rameseye ad
emendum et providendum ad opus nostrum pro denariis nostris inde solvendis per se vel
deputatos suos totas petras ubicunque eas inveniri contigerit sive infra libertates sive extra
quot et quibusdam operacionibus quas in castro nostro de Wyndesore fieri ordinavimus
rationabiliter indignerit petras ad operacionibus ecclesiarum vel monasteriorum ordinatis

castle and organise the carriage of them. And we command you and firmly instruct you to listen, consult with and help the same William and his deputy in the carrying out and execution of the aforesaid as one or other of them shall make known to you on our behalf. Witnessed by the King at Westminster, 24 February. By the King himself.

F. *Taking of shouts (Thames boats)*

Know that we have assigned and chosen brother John Walerand to stop and take as many Thames boats as may be needed, either himself or through his deputies in diverse places on the Thames between Gravesend and Henley, for stone and other necessary materials which we have ordered to be supplied at various places along the banks of the said river for works at our castle of Windsor to carry these materials at our expense to that place.
Witnessed as above. By the King himself.

G. *Taking of means of carriage*

Know that we have assigned and chosen Hugo de Kymton to take such means of carriage as may be needed, either himself or through his deputies in the counties of Bedfordshire and Hertfordshire, both within and without liberties, for carrying stone from Eglemont in those counties which we have ordered to be provided and purchased for works at our castle of Windsor to carry these materials at our expense to that place.
Witnessed as above. By the King himself.

H. *Taking of carts on the king's behalf*

Know that we, trusting in his discretion, have assigned and chosen brother John Walerand, either himself or through his deputies in the counties of Kent, Surrey, Sussex, Hampshire, Middlesex, Berkshire and Buckinghamshire to obtain means of carriage by land and water for the stone for our works in our castle of Windsor at Worth, Reigate, Bletchingley, Ruislip, Holdshot and elsewhere in the said counties and take it to our castle at our expense. And we command you and firmly instruct you to listen, consult with and help the same John and his said deputies in the carrying out and execution of the aforesaid as one or other of them shall make known to you on our behalf. Witnessed by the King at Westminster 20th July. By a bill of the treasurer.

exceptis et eas usque castrum predictum cum omne celeritate qua poterit duci et cariand' faciend'. Et ideo vobis mandavimus firmiter injungentes quod eidem Willelmo ac deputatis suis prædictis in præmissis faciendis et exequendis intendentes sitis consulentes et auxiliantes quociens idem Willelmus vel dicti deputati unus seu eorum aliquis vobis vel alicui vestrum scire fecerint vel fecerit ex parte nostra. In cuius, etc. Teste Rege apud Westmon' xxiiij die Febr' Per ipsum Regem.

F. *Shutis capiendis*

Rex etc. Sciatis quod assignavimus dilectum nobis fratrum Johannem Waleraund' ad arestandum et capiendum quotiens opus fuerit per se vel deputatos suos in singulis locis in aquis Thamesie inter Graveshende et Henle shutas sufficientes pro petra et aliis necessariis que in diversis partibus per costeram aque predicte pro quibusdam operacionibus in castro nostro de Wyndesore emi et provideri ordinavimus usque castrum predictum pro denariis nostris inde solvendis ducendis et cariandis. Et ideo vobis mandavimus etc. Teste ut supra. Per ipsum Regem.

G. *Cariagiis capiendis*

Rex etc. Sciatis quod assignavimus dilectum nobis Hugonem de Kymton' ad capiendum quotiens opus fuerit per se vel deputatos suos in Comitatibus Bed' et Hert' tam infra libertates quam extra sufficiencia carriagia pro petra de Eglemound' quam in Comitatibus illis pro quibusdam operacionibus in Castro nostro de Wyndesore emi et provideri ordinavimus usque castrum predictum pro denariis nostris inde solvendis ducendis et cariandis. Et ideo etc. Teste ut supra. Per ipsum Regem.

H. *Source:* Patent Roll 18 Edward III, part II, m.39. [PRO C. 66/212]
Calendared: Cal. Patent Rolls 1343-1345, 319.

H. *Pro rege de cariagio capiendo*

Rex etc. Sciatis quod nos de circumspectione dilecti nobis fratris Johannis Walerand' confidentes assignavimus ipsum Johannem per se et deputandos ab ipso in Comitatibus Kanc', Surr', Sussex', Suth', Midd', Berk' et Buk' tam per terram quam per aquam in locis quibus expedire viderit extra feodum ecclesie cariagia pro maeremio pro operacionibus nostris in Castro nostro de Wyndesore apud Worthy, Reygate, Blechynleye, Risshlep', Holshute et alibi in Comitatibus predictis proviso usque Castrum nostrum ducendis pro denariis nostris inde solvendis. Et ideo vobis et cuilibet vestrum firmiter iniungendo mandamus quod eidem Johanni ec deputandis suis predictis in præmissis faciendis et exequendis in forma predicta intendentes sitis, consulentes et auxiliantes quociens et quando per ipsum Johannem et dictos deputandos suos fueritis ex parte nostra premuniti. In cuius, etc. Teste Rege apud Westm' xx die Julii. Per billam Thesaurarii.

3. Enrolled Accounts of Works

Account of Alan de Kilham clerk, assigned to carry out certain works within the king's castle of Windsor in the eighteenth year by the writ of the king under the privy seal dated 12 November of the same year addressed to the treasurer and barons, enrolled in the Memoranda (i.e. in the Memoranda roll) of Michaelmas term of the nineteenth year, by which the king ordered the same to account with the same Alan for the moneys received by him for carrying out the king's works at Windsor which the same Alan had engaged to undertake, allowing the abovesaid Alan a reasonable allocation by the testimony of brother John Walerand overseer and controller of the aforesaid works, that is, for his receipts, expenses and wages incurred and paid by the same Alan.

RECEIPTS

The same renders account for £13 6s 8d received from the treasurer and chamberlains at the Receipt of the Exchequer on 6 July of the same eighteenth year [1344] by the hand of Roger de Cotyngham in respect of certain new works at the said castle of Windsor, as is recorded in the memorandum roll of the same Receipt of the same year and in the roll of particulars which he delivered to the treasury. And for £10 received from the same there on 27 July of the same year by the hand of brother John Walerand for the same works as is contained in the same place. And for 102s. received from the same at the same place on 10 August by the hand of the same brother John for the aforesaid works as is contained in the same place. And for £8 received from the same at the same place on 9 September of the same year by the hand of the aforesaid brother John for the aforesaid works as is contained in the same place. And for £15 received from the same at the same place by the hand of the aforesaid brother John for the aforesaid works as is contained in the same place. And for £10 received from the same at the same place on 15 November of the nineteenth year [1345] by the hand of the aforesaid brother John for the aforesaid works as is contained in the [memoranda roll of the same nineteenth year and in the roll of particulars]. And for £400 received from John de Flete clerk of the king's exchange at the king's Tower of London by the hand of [Thomas] de Hattefeld, clerk of the king's chamber, paying the same moneys in four instalments in the said eighteenth year, as is contained in the said roll of particulars.

TOTAL OF RECEIPTS   £461 8s 8d

EXPENSES

The same accounts for divers stones both of Caen and Kentish rag and of Wheatley for the King's works aforesaid, for wood cut for fuel and faggots for lime at the lime pits, and timber for making a certain well within the aforesaid Castle, bought of divers persons and at divers times between the sixteenth day of February in the eighteenth year, on which day the said works were begun, and the 27th day of November next following, on which day those works came to an end, by view and testimony of the aforesaid brother John £108 17s. 0¼d. as is contained in a roll of particulars which he delivered into the treasury and also in the counter-roll of the aforesaid brother John delivered into the treasury.

And in tiles, laths, tile-pins and lath-nails bought for the said works in the same place, together with the carriage of the said tiles from Penn to the Castle £7 6s. 8d.

And in 77 barrows, of which 6 were of hurdles, 5 tubs, 12 troughs for putting mortar in, 10 bowls for sprinkling water upon the mortar, one pipe, 2 casks for carrying water in, 6 tubs

3. Enrolled Accounts of Works

Source: Pipe Roll 18 Edward III, m.45 [PRO E. 372/189][1]
Printed: Hope I, 124.

Compotus Alani de Killum clerici assignati ad quasdam operaciones infra Castrum Regis de Wyndesore faciendas anno xviij per breve Regis de privato sigillo datum xij die Novembris eodem anno directum Thesaurario et Baronibus irrotulatum in Memorandis de anno xix termino sancti Michaelis per quod Rex mandavit eisdem quod cum eodem Alano de denariis per ipsum receptis super factura operacionum Regis apud Wyndesore unde idem Alanus se vult onerare computent facientes prefato Alano racionabilem allocacionem per testimonium fratris Johannis Walerand supervisoris et Contrarotulatoris operacionum predictarum, videlicet de receptis suis et expensis et vadiis per ipsum Alanum factis et solutis.

Recepte

Idem reddit compotum de xiij li. vj s. viij d. receptis de Thesaurario et Camerariis ad Receptam scaccarij vj^to die Julii eodem anno xviij° [1344] per manus Rogeri de Cotyngham super quibusdam novis operacionibus apud dictum Castrum de Wyndesors sicut continetur in pelle memorandorum eiusdem recepte de eodem anno et in rotulo de particulis quem liberavit in thesauro. Et de x li. receptis de eisdem ibidem xxvij° die Julii eodem anno per manus Fratris Johannis Walleraund' super eisdem operacionibus sicut continetur ibidem. Et de Cij s. receptis de eisdem ibidem x° die Augusti per manus eiusdem fratris Johannis super operacionibus predictis sicut continetur ibidem. Et de viij li. receptis de eisdem ibidem ix° die Septembris eodem anno per manus eiusdem fratris Johannis super operacionibus predictis sicut continetur ibidem. Et de xv li. receptis de eisdem ibidem eodem die per manus predicti fratris Johannis super operacionibus predictis sicut continetur ibidem. Et de x li. receptis de eisdem ibidem xv^to die Novembris anno xix° [1345] per manus predicti fratris Johannis super operacionibus predictis sicut continetur [in pelle memorandorum de eodem anno xix° et in rotulo de particulis].[2] Et de CCCC li. receptis de Johanne de Flete clerico Escambii Regis apud Turrim ipsius Regis London' per manus […][3] de Hattefeld' clerici Camere Regis eosdem denarios solvent' per iiij^or vices dicto anno xviij° sicut continetur in dicto rotulo de particulis.

Summa Recepte: CCCClxj li. viij s. viij d.

Expense :

Idem computat in diversis petris tam de Cadamo et Raggis de Kancia quam de *Whetele* pro operacionibus Regis predictis Talwod et Fagotis pro calce apud lymeputtes et meremium pro quodam fonte infra Castrum predictum faciendo de diversis et per diversas vices emptis inter xvi diem Februarii anno xviij° quo die dicte operaciones incipiebantur et xxvij diem Novembris proximum sequentem quo die operaciones ille cessabant per visum et testimonium predicti fratris Johannis Cviij li. xvij s. q^a sicut continetur in Rotulo de particulis quem liberavit in thesauro et eciam in Contrarotulo predicti fratris Johannis similiter in thesauro liberato.

Et in tegulis lathis Tylepynnes lathenailes pro dictis operacionibus ibidem emptis una cum cariagia dictarum tegularum del penne usque castrum ibidem vij li. vj s. viij d. etc.

Et in lxxvij Barowes quorum vj de virgis v tinis xij alviolis pro morterio imponendo x bollis pro aqua super morterium spargenda j pipa ij doliis pro aqua infra cariandis vj cuvis pro

---

[1] A cancelled draft of the enrolment on the Pipe Roll appears to survive as a single sheet (E101/492/25).
[2] Text within square brackets interlined.
[3] Illegible.

for putting water in, a funnel and a scoop for pouring water in the same casks, 6 sieves and iron vessels for making mortar, 5 fir poles for measuring the said house, 4 grindstones for sharpening the masons' tools, 2 saws for sawing stone, 6 picks and 6 mattocks, 4 rakes of iron, 2 iron forks, 3 axes for chopping wood, 10 wedges for the quarry, 4 hammers, 4 trowels, 6 hurdles for the lime-pits, a sledge, an axe, 30 ladles for pouring cement, boards for squares, lath and lath-nail for chimney forges there, iron and steel for making and mending thence divers necessaries bought at divers times, together with the mending of the masons' tools and the cleaning of two wells within the Castle aforesaid for having water in the same place £9 1s. 5½d.

And in boatage and cartage of stones, timber, earth, lime and sand both by land and by water from divers places to the Castle aforesaid within the time aforesaid £82 1s. 6d.

And in wages of divers masons, carpenters, sawyers, smiths and divers other workmen working upon the King's works aforesaid during the whole time aforesaid £254 3s. 3½d

.

And in wages of the aforesaid Alan tarrying about the works aforesaid at the Castle aforesaid for 98 days within the aforesaid time, and of the aforesaid brother John Waleraund tarrying about the same works for 286 days, namely during the whole time aforesaid £46 8s., to each of them 2s. per day by the King's writ directed to the Treasurer and Barons, enrolled among the Memoranda of Michaelmas term of the nineteenth year, by which the King commanded the same that for the time during which the abovesaid Alan and John tarried upon the aforesaid king's works in the king's aforesaid castle 2s. were to be allowed to them, as is contained in the same place.

Sum of the expenses £507 17s. 11½d.

And he has a surplus £46 9s. 3½d.

Alan de Kilham, King's clerk, 67 barrows of which six are made of hurdles, 5 tubs, 12 troughs, 10 bowls, one pipe, 2 casks, 6 tubs, a funnel and a scoop, 6 sieves and iron vessels for making mortar, 5 fir poles, 4 grindstones, 2 saws, 7 picks, 5 mattocks, 4 rakes of iron, 2 iron forks, 3 axes, 10 wedges, 4 hammers, 4 trowels, 6 hurdles, a sledge, an axe, 30 ladles received in the abovesaid purchase as is contained abov*e*.

aqua imponenda .j. tunder et .j. skopa pro aqua in eisdem doliis infundenda .vj. cribris et culdors pro morterio faciendo .v. polis de firre pro dicta domo mensuranda iiij^{or} grynstones pro instrumentis Cementariorum acuendis .ij. sarris pro sarracione petre .vj. picoys et .vj. mattoks .iiij. Rastellis de ferro .ij. furcis ferreis .iij. securibus pro bosco coppandis .x. wegges pro quarrera .iiij. hamers .iiij. Trowellis .vj. hirdellis pro *lymepittes* .j. slegge .j. securi .xxx. ladlis pro cemento fundendo bordis pro squiris lath et lathenayl pro caminis forgis ibidem ferro et ascere pro diversis necessariis inde faciendis et reparandis per diversas vices emptis una cum emendacione instrumentorum Cementariorum et mundacione .ij. fontium infra castrum predictum pro aqua ibidem habenda .ix.li. xvij.d. ob.

Et in batillagio et cariagia petrarum meremii torre calcis et arene tam per terram quam per aquam de diversis locis usque predictum Castrum infra tempus predictum iiij^{xx}.ij.li. xviij.d.

Et in vadiis diversorum Cementariorum Carpentariorum Sarratorum fabrorum et aliorum diversorum operariorum operancium super operacionibus Regis predictis per totum tempus predictum .CCliiij.li. iij.s. iiij.d. ob.

Et in vadiis predicti Alani morancii super operacionibus predictis apud Castrum predictum per iiij^{xx} xviij dies infra tempus predictum et predicti fratris Johannis Walleraund' similiter morancii super eisdem operacionibus per CCiiij^{xx} vj dies, videlicet per totum tempus predictum – xlvj li. viij s. utrique eorum per diem ijs. per breve Regis direct' Thesaurario et Baronibus irrot' in memorand' de anno xix° termino Michaelis per quod Rex mandavit eisdem quod pro tempore quo prefati Alanus et Johannes super operacionibus Regis predictis in Castro Regis predicto morabantur utrique eorum ij s. per diem allocentur sicut continetur ibidem.

Summa expensarum .D.vij.li. xvij.s. xj.d. ob.

Et habet de superplusagio xlvj.li. ix.s. iiij.d. ob.

Alanus de Killum clericus Regis lxvij Barowes quorum vj de vergis, v tinis, xij alivolis, x bollis, j pipa, ij doliis, vj cunis, j tunder et j skopel, vj crebris et culdors, v polis de firre, iiij^{or} Grynstones, ij sarris, vij pycois, v mattocks, iiij^{or} Rastellis de ferr', ij furcis ferr', iij secur', x Wegges, iiij^{or} hamers, iiij^{or} Trowell', vj hirdell', j slegge, j secur', xxx ladlys receptis de supraempcione sicut supra continetur.

4. Counter-roll of Particulars of Accounts of Works

The counter-roll of Brother John Walerand, controller of Alan of Kilham the King's clerk, of divers expenses and wages incurred and paid by the same Alan about the foundation of a certain round house within the Castle of Windsor, from the sixteenth day of February in the 28th year of the reign of King Edward the Third after the Conquest to the 27th day of November next following.

4.1 [Monday 16 February – Saturday 21 February 1344]
First week:
Cutting Masons
To master William Ramsey for his wages at 7s. a week; of a mason-cutter for his wages at 4s.; of four, each 3s.; of two, each at 2s. 6d.; of three at 2s. 4d.; of two at 2s. 3d.; of one at 2s. 2d., and for ten, each at 2s. a week: between the sixteenth day of February and the 21st day of the same month, reckoned in the eighteenth year   61s. 8d.
Carpenters
To master William Hurley for his wages at 7s.; of three carpenters each at 4d. a day for 4 days within the said time 11s.
Workmen
And for wages of four, each at 4d. a day; and of thirteen, each at 2d. a day at the lime pits for 4 days within the said time 14s.
Sum £4 6s. 8d.

4.2 [Monday 23 February – Saturday 28 February 1344]
Second week:

Cutting Masons
To master William Ramsey for his wages at 7s.; of two at 4s. each: of four at 3s.; of eight at 2s. 6d.; of six at 2s. 4d. each; of six at 2s. 3d. each; of six at 2s. 2d. each ; of fifteen at 2s. each; of six at 21d. each, and of five at 12d. each per week from the 23rd day of February until the 28th day of the same month, each being reckoned for six days £6 13s.
Laying Masons
To William Bond, laying mason, for his wages at 2s. 2d.; of four at 2s. each; of three at 22d. each; of four at 20d. each; of three at 18d. each; and of three at 15d. each per week for the same time   30s. 7d.
Labourers at Bisham
 And for the wages of an overseer at the quarry of Bisham at 2s. 4d.; of five at 13d. each; of twenty-five at 11d. each ; of twenty-eight for 4½ days, of ten for 3½ days, and three for 2½ days at 2d. per day each, within the said time 58s. 9d.
Carpenters
 To master William Hurley for his wages at 7s.; of three carpenters at 2s. each; of one at 21d.; of two at 18d.; and of one at 15d. per week for the said time within the Castle   19s.

4. Counter-roll of Particulars of Accounts of Works
Source: Counter-roll [PRO E 101/492/26]
Part printed: Hope I, 124-7.

4.0
[rot. 1, m. 1.]
Contrarotulus Fratris Johannis de Walraund' contrarotularii Alani de Killum clerici Regis de diversis expensis ac vadiis per ipsum Alanum factis et solutis circa fundacionem cujusdam domus rotunde infra Castrum de Wyndesors a xvj^{to} die Februarii anno regni Regis Edwardi tercij post conquestum xviij° usque xxvij diem Novembris proximum sequentem.

4.1   [Monday 16 February – Saturday 21 February 1344]
i^a septimana

Cementarii Cissores
Magistro Willelmo de Rameseye pro vadiis suis ad .vij.s. per septimanam, unius Cementarii Cissoris pro vadiis suis ad iiij.s. iiij quolibet ad .iij.s. ij. utroque ad .ij.s. vj.d. iij. quolibet ad ij s. iiij.d.. ij. utroque ad ij.s. iij.d. unius ad. ij.s. ij.d. et x quolibet ad ij.s. per septimanam inter xvj. diem Februarij et xxj. diem ejusdem mensis comp. anno xviij lxj.s. viij.d.
Carpentarii
Magistro Willelmo de Hurle pro vadiis suis ad .vij.s.[4] ij. carpentariorum quolibet ad iiij.d. per diem per iiij dies infra dictum tempus xj.s.
Operarii
Et pro vadiis iiij quolibet ad .iiij.d. per diem: et xiij quolibet ad.ij.d. per diem apud Lympittes per iiij dies infra dictum tempus xiiij.s.
Summa. iiij.li : vj.s : viij.d.

4.2   [Monday 23 February – Saturday 28 February 1344]
ij^a Septimana]

Cementarii Cissores
Magistro Willelmo de Rameseye pro vadiis suis ad .vij.s. ij. utroque ad .iiij.s. iiij quolibet ad .iij.s. viij quolibet ad ij.s. vj.d. vj. quolibet ad ij.s. iiij.d. vj quolibet ad ij.s. iij.d. vj quolibet ad ij.s. ij.d. xv. quolibet ad .ij.s. vj quolibet ad xxj.d. et v. quolibet ad xij.d. per septimanam a xxiij die Februarii usque vicesimum octavum diem eiusdem mensis utroque comp'. per vj dies vj.li. xiij.s.
Cementarii Positores – Willelmo Bond' Cementario positori pro vadiis suis ad ij.s. ij.d. iiij quolibet ad ij.s. iij quolibet ad xxij.d. iiij quolibet ad xx.d. iij quolibet ad xviij.d. et ij quolibet ad xv.d. per septimanam per idem tempus xxx.s. vij.d.
Operarii apud Bristelsham – Et pro vadiis unius supervisoris apud Quarreram de Bristilsham ad ij.s. iiij.dv. quolibet ad xiiij.d. xxv quolibet ad xj.d. xxviij per iiij dies et dimidium.x per iij dies et dimidium et iij per ij dies et dimidium quolibet ad ij.d. per diem infra dictum tempus lviij.s. ix.d.
Carpentarij – Magistro Willelmo de Hurle pro vadiis suis ad vij.s. iij carpentariorum quolibet ad ij.s., unius ad xxj.d. ij ad xviij.d. et unius ad xv.d. per septimanam per dictum tempus infra Castrum xix.s.

---

4   An erasure above the line here appears to read *per idem tempus*.

Labourers

And for the wages of one smith at 2s.; of one at 12d.; and of one at 9d. per week for the same time 3s. 9d.

And for the wages of one hundred and ninety-one men working within the Castle at 12d per week   £10 11s

TOTAL: £22 16s. 1d.

4.3   [Sunday 29 February – Saturday 6 March 1344]

Third week

Cutting masons

To Master William Ramsey for his wages at 7s., 2 others at 4s., 7 at 3s. each, 9 at 2s. 6d. each, 8 at 2s. 4d. each, 12 at 2s. 3d. each, 11 at 2s. 2d. each, 33 at 2s., 12 at 21d. each, 6 at 18d. and 6 at 12d. each per week between the last day of February and the 6th day of March for one week [£11 10s.]

Laying masons

And for their wages 3 at 2s. 2d. each, 4 each at 2s. each, 16 at 22d. each, 19 at 20d. each, 14 at 18d. each, 4 at 15d. each, 2 others at 12d. each, one at 8d. and one at 6d. per week during the said period [104 s 8d.]

Stone dressers at Bisham

And for the wages of one at 2s.4d., 9 at 14d. each working at the quarry at Bisham per week [12s. 10d.]

Carpenters

To Master William Hurley for his wages at 7s., one at 3s., 3 at 2s. each, 4 at 21d. each, one at 3½d. per day for three days, 2 others at 18d. and 3 at 15d. each per week for the same period [30s. 7½d.]

Workmen both at the castle and elsewhere

And for the wages of one smith at 2s., one at 12d. and one at 9d. for this week [3s. 9d.]

And for the wages of 401 men working both at the castle and at the lime pits and the sand pits at 12d. each per week for this week [£20 12s.]

And for the wages of 122 men working at the quarry at Bisham at 12d. each for this week [£6. 2s.]

TOTAL: £45 4s. 10½d.

4.4   [Sunday 7 March – Saturday 13 March 1344]

Fourth week

Cutting masons

Master William Ramsey for his wages at 7s., 2 others at 4s. each, 7 at 3s. each, 9 at 2s. 6d. each, 11 at 2s. 4d. each, 13 at 2s. 3d. each, 13 at 2s. 2d. each, 36 at 2s. each, 16 at 21d. each, 9 at 18d. each, 4 at 15d. and 8 at 12d. each per week between the 7th day of March and the thirteenth day of the same month for one week [£13 8s. 1d.]

Operarij

Et pro vadiis unius fabri ad ij s. unius ad xij.d et unius . ad ix.d. per septimanam per idem tempus iij.s. ix.d.

Et pro vadiis Ciiij^{xx}. xj hominum operancium infra Castrum et xx apud Sandp' quolibet ad xij.d. per septimanam   x.li. xj.s.

Summa. xxij : li : xvj.: s : j : d.

4.3 [Sunday 29 February – Saturday 6 March 1344]

iij^a septimana
Cementarii Cissores

Magistro Willelmo de Ram' pro vadiis suis ad vij s., ij utroque ad iiij s., vij quolibet ad iij s., ix quolibet ad ij s. vj d., viiij quolibet ad ij s. iiij d., xij quolibet ad ij s. iij d., xj quolibet ad ij s. ij d., xxxiij quolibet ad ij s., xij quolibet ad xxj d., vj quolibet ad xviij d. et vj quolibet ad xij d. per septimanam inter ultimum diem Februarii et vj diem Marcij per unam septimanam .. .. xj li. x s.

Cementarii Positores

Et pro vadiis iij quolibet ad ij s. ij d., iiij quolibet ad ij s., xvj quolibet ad xxij d., xix quolibet ad xx d., xiiij quolibet ad xviij d., iiij quolibet ad xv d., ij utroque ad xij d., unius ad viij d. et unius ad vj d. per septimanam infra dictum tempus .. .. Ciiij s viij d.

Skapelers apud Bristilsham'

Et pro vadiis unius ad ij s. iiij d., ix quolibet ad xiiij d. operancium apud quarreram de Brist' per septimanam .. .. xij s. x d.

Carpentarii

Magistro Willelmo de Hurle pro vadiis suis ad vij s., unius ad iij s., iij quolibet ad ij s., iiij quolibet ad xxj d., unius ad iij d. ob. per diem per iij dies, ij utroque ad xviij d. et iij quolibet ad xv d. per septimanam per idem tempus .. .. xxx s. vij d. ob.

Operarii tam apud castrum quam alibi

Et pro vadiis unius fabri ad ij s., unius ad xij d. et unius ad ix d. pro ista septimana iij s. ix d.
Et pro vadiis CCCCj hominum operancium tam infra Castrum quam apud Lymp' et Sandp' quolibet ad xij d. per septimanam pro ista septimana .. .. xx li. xij s.
Et pro vadiis vj^{xx} ij hominum laborantium apud quarreram de Brist' quolibet ad xij d. pro ista septimana .. .. vj li. ij s.
SUMMA: xlv li. iiij s. x d. ob.

4.4 [Sunday 7 March – Saturday 13 March 1344]

iiij^a septimana
Cementarii Cissores

Magistro Willelmo de Rameseye pro vadiis suis ad vij s., ij utroque ad iiij s., vij quolibet ad iij s., ix quolibet ad ij s. vj d., xj quolibet ad ij s. iiij d., xiij quolibet ad ij s. iij d., xiij quolibet ad ij s. ij d., xxxvj quolibet ad ij s., xvj quolibet ad xxj d., ix quolibet ad xvij d., iiij quolibet ad xv d. et viiij quolibet ad xij d. per septimanam inter vij diem Marcij et xiij diem eiusdem mensis per unam septimanam .. .. xiij li. viij s. j d.

Laying masons

And for the wages of 4 at 2s. 2d. each, 4 at 2s. each, 16 at 22d. each, 20 at 20d. each, 20 at 18d. each, 5 at 15d. each, 2 others at 12d. each, one at 8d. and one at 6d. per week for the same period [118 s 9d.]

Workmen at Bisham

And for the wages of an overseer at Bisham at 2s. 4d. each, 11 at 14d. at Bisham for this week [15s. 2d.]

Carpenters

To Master William Hurley for his wages at 7s., one at 3s., 3 at 2s. each, 5 at 21d. each, 2 others at 18d. and 3 at 15d. each per week for the same period [31s. 6d.]

Smiths

And for the wages of 2 smiths at 2s. each, 2 others at 12d. and one at 9d. each per week for the same period [6s. 9d.]

Workmen

And for the wages of 193 men working both at the castle and at the lime pits and the sand pits at 12d. each per week for the same period [£9 13s.]

And for the wages of 130 workmen at Bisham at 11d. each per week for the same period [119s. 2d.]
TOTAL: £37 12s. 5d.

4.5   [Sunday 14 March – Saturday 20 March 1344]

Fifth week
Cutting masons

To Master William Ramsey for his wages at 7s., 2 others at 4s. each, 7 at 3s. each, 9 at 2s. 6d. each, 13 at 2s. 4d. each, 16 at 2s. 3d. each, 14 at 2s. 2d. each, 38 at 2s. each, 16 at 21d. each, 9 at 18d. each, 4 at 15d. each, and 8 at 12d. each per week between the fourteenth day of the said month of March and the 21st day of the same month accounting for one week [£14 5s. 8d.]

Laying masons

And for the wages of 4 at 2s. 2d. each, 4 at 2s. each, 16 at 22d. each, 20 at 20d. each, 20 at 18d. each, 5 at 15d. each, 2 others at 12d. each, one at 8d. and one at 6d. per week for the same period [118s 9d.]

Stone-dressers

And for the wages of one at 2s. 4d. each, 8 at 14d. each per week for the same period [12s. 10d.]

Carpenters

To Master William Hurley for his wages at 7s., one at 3s., 3 at 2s. each, 4 at 21d. each,

Cementarii Positores

Et pro vadiis iiij quolibet ad ij s. ij d., iiij quolibet ad ij s., xvj quolibet ad xxij d., xx quolibet ad xx d., xx quolibet ad xviij d., v quolibet ad xv d., ij utroque ad xij d., unius ad viij d. et unius ad vj d. per septimanam per idem tempus [Cxviij s ix d.]

Operarii de Bristilsham'

Et pro vadiis unius supervisoris apud Bristilsham ad ij s. iiij d., xj quolibet ad xiiij d. apud Brist' pro ista septimana .. .. xv s. ij d.

Carpentarii

Magistro Willelmo de Hurle pro vadiis suis ad vij s., unius ad iij s., ij quolibet ad ij s., v quolibet ad xxj d., ij utroque ad xviij d. et iiij quolibet ad xv d. per septimanam per idem tempus .. .. xxxj s. vj d.

Fabri

Et pro vadiis ij fabrorum utroque ad ij s., ij utroque ad xij d. et unius ad ix d. per septimanam per idem tempus .. .. vj s. ix d.

Operarii

Et pro vadiis Ciiij^xx xiij hominum laborantium tam infra Castrum quam apud Lymp' et Sandp' quolibet ad xij d. per septimanam per idem tempus .. .. ix li. xiij s.

Et pro vadiis Cxxx operancium apud Brist' quolibet ad xj d. per septimanam per idem tempus .. .. Cxix s. ij d.
SUMMA: xxxvij li. xij s. v d.

4.5 [Sunday 14 March – Saturday 20 March 1344]

v^a septimana
Cementarii Cissores

Magistro Willelmo de Ram' pro vadiis suis ad vij s., ij utroque ad iiij s., vij quolibet ad iij s., ix quolibet ad ij s. vj d., xiij quolibet ad ij s. iiij d., xvj quolibet ad ij s. iij d., xiiij quolibet ad ij s. ij d., xxxviij quolibet ad ij s., xvj quolibet ad xxj d., ix quolibet ad xviij d., iiij quolibet ad xv d., et viij quolibet ad xij d. per septimanam inter xiiij diem dicti mensis Marcij et xxj diem eiusdem mensis computando per unam septimanam .. .. xiiij li. v s. viij d.

Cementarii Positores

Et pro vadiis iiij quolibet ad ij s. ij d., iiij quolibet ad ij s., xvj quolibet ad xxij d., xx quolibet ad xx d., xx quolibet ad xviij d., v quolibet ad xv d., ij utroque ad xij d., unius ad viij d. et unius ad vj d. per septimanam per idem tempus .. .. Cxviij s ix d.

Skapelers

Et pro vadiis unius ad ij s. iiij d., viij quolibet ad xiiij d. per septimanam per idem tempus .. .. xij s. x d.

Carpentarii

Magistro Willelmo de Hurle pro vadiis suis ad vij s., unius ad iij s., ij quolibet ad ij s., iiij

2 others at 18d. and 3 at 15d. each per week for the same period [29s. 9d.]

Smiths

And for the wages of 2 smiths at 2s., 2 others at 12d. and one at 9d. per week [6s. 9d.]

Workmen

And for the wages of 180 men working both within the castle and at the lime pits and the sand pits at 12d. each per week for the same period [£9]

And for the wages of 2 men each at 12d., 69 at 11d. each per week working at Bisham for the same period [65s. 3d.]

TOTAL: £34 17s. 10d.

4.6 [Monday 22 March – Saturday 27 March 1344]

Sixth week

Cutting masons

To Master William Ramsey for his wages at 7s., 2 others at 4s., 6 at 3s. each, 8 at 2s. 1d. each, 13 at 23½d. each, 12 at 22½d. each, 11 at 22d. each, one at 4d. for one day each, 39 at 20d. each, 14 at 17½d. each, 9 at 15d. each, 4 at 12½d. each, 7 at 10d. between the 22nd day of March and the 28th day of the same month for six days [£11 4s. 9½d.]

Laying masons

And for the wages of 2 each at 22d. each, 3 at 20d. each,, 5 at 18½d each, 9 at 17d. and one at 3½d. for 2 days each, 15 at 15d. each, 5 at 12½d. each, and one at 10d. for the same period [53 s 8d.]

And for the wages of 9 at 11d. at Bisham [8s. 3d.]

Carpenters

To Master William Hurley for his wages at 7s., one at 3s., 3 at 2s. each, 4 at 21d. each, 2 others at 18d. and 3 at 15d. per week for the same period [29s. 9d.]

Smiths

And for the wages of 2 smiths at 2s., 2 others at 12d. and one at 9d. per week [6s. 9d.]

Workmen

And for the wages of 180 men working both within the castle and at the lime pits and the sand pits at 10d. for the same period.

And for the wages of 63 men working at Bisham for 5 days each at 10d. [£10 2s. 6d.]

TOTAL: £26 5s. 8½d.

quolibet ad xxj d., ij utroque ad xviij d. et iiij quolibet ad xv d. per septimanam per idem tempus .. .. xxix s. ix d.

Fabri

Et pro vadiis ij fabrorum utroque ad ij s., ij utroque ad xij d. et unius ad ix d. per septimanam .. .. vj s. ix d.

Operarii

Et pro vadiis Ciiij^{xx} hominum laborancium tam infra Castrum quam apud Lymp' et Sandpitt' quolibet ad xij d. per septimanam per idem tempus .. .. ix li.

Et pro vadiis ij hominum utroque ad xij d., lxix quolibet ad xj d. per septimanam, laborantium apud Bristilsham per idem tempus .. .. lxv s. iij d.

SUMMA: xxxiiij li. xvij s. x d.

4.6   [Monday 22 March – Saturday 27 March 1344]

vj^a septimana

Cementarii Cissores

Magistro Willelmo de Ram' pro vadiis suis ad vij s., ij utroque ad iiij s., vj quolibet ad iij s., viij quolibet ad ij s. j d., xiij quolibet ad xxiij d. ob., xij quolibet ad xxij d. ob., xj quolibet ad xxij d., unius ad iiij d. per unum diem, xxxix quolibet ad xx d., xiiij quolibet ad xvij d. ob., ix quolibet ad xv d., iiij quolibet ad xij d. ob., vij quolibet ad x d. inter xxij diem Marcij et xxviij diem eiusdem mensis per vj dies .. .. xj li. iiij s. ix d. ob.

Cementarii Positores

Et pro vadiis ij utroque ad xxij d., iij quolibet ad xx d., v quolibet ad xviij d. ob., ix quolibet ad xvij d. et unius ad iij d. ob. per ij dies, xv quolibet ad xv d., v quolibet ad xij d. ob., et unius ad x d. per idem tempus .. .. liij s viij d.

Et pro vadiis ix quolibet ad xj d. apud Bristilsham .. .. viij s. iij d.

Carpentarii

Magistro Willelmo de Hurle pro vadiis suis ad vij s., unius ad iij s., iiij quolibet ad ij s., iiij quolibet ad xxj d., ij utroque ad xviij d. et iij ad xv d. per septimanam per idem tempus .. .. xxix s. ix d.

Fabri

Et pro vadiis ij fabrorum utroque ad ij s., ij utroque ad xij d. et unius ad ix d. per septimanam .. .. vj s. ix d.

Operarii

Et pro vadiis Ciiij^{xx} hominum laborancium tam infra Castrum quam apud Lymp' et Sanp' quolibet ad x d. per idem tempus.

Et pro vadiis lxiij hominum operancium apud Brist' per v dies quolibet ad x d. x li. ij s. vj d.

SUMMA: xxvj li. v s. viij d. ob.

[rot. 1, m. 2.]

4.7 [Monday 29 March – Saturday 3 April 1344]

Seventh week
Masons
And for the wages of Master William Ramsey and Master William Hurley, each at 7s., between the 29th day of March and the 4th day of April accounting for 7 days [14s.]
And for the wages of an overseer to arrange the accumulation of graded stones, lest they be broken, for his wages at 6d. per day for four days, of one at 4d. per day and 15 at 2d. per day each
Workmen
And for the wages of 4 each at 3d. and 8 at 2d. per day dwelling at the lime pits for 4 days for the same period. [13s. 4d.]
TOTAL: 36s. 8d.

4.8 [Monday 5 April – Saturday 10 April 1344; Easter Week]

Eighth week
Masons
And for the wages of Master William Ramsey and Master William Hurley each at 7s. between the 5th day of April and the tenth day of the same month accounting for one week [14s.]

Workmen and cartage
And for the wages of 10 workers at 2d. per day within the said period for 2 days. [3s. 4d.]
And for carting chalk (lime) by two carts for two days within the said period [3s. 4d.]
TOTAL: 20s. 8d.

Easter April 4
4.9 [Monday 12 April – Saturday 17 April 1344]

Ninth week
And for the wages of Master William Ramsey at 7s., one at 4s., 2 others at 3s., 4 at 2s. 4d. each, 2 others at 2s. 3d., 2 others at 2s., 17 at 12d. per day between the 10th day of April and the seventeenth day of the same month accounting for one week [51s. 10d.]

And for carting chalk (lime?) and sand by 3 carts for 6 days [15s.]
TOTAL: 66s. 10d.

4.10 [Sunday 18 April – Saturday 24 April 1344]

Tenth week
And for their wages of Master William Ramsey at 7s., 2 others at 3s., 4 at 2s. 4d. each, 2 others at 2s. 3d., 2 others at 2s. and 17 at 12d. each per week between the eighteenth day of April and the 24th day of the same month for 6 days [47s. 10d.]

[rot. 1, m. 2.]

4.7   [Monday 29 March – Saturday 3 April 1344]

vij^a septimana
Cementarii
Et pro vadiis Magistri Willelmi de Ram' et Magistri Willelmi de Hurle utroque ad vij s.
inter xxix diem Marcij et iiij diem Aprilis computando per vij dies .. .. xiiij s.
Et pro vadiis unius supervisoris ad ordinandum accumulationis lapidorum gradatum ne
frangerentur, pro vadiis suis ad vj d. per diem per iiij dies, unius ad iiij d. per diem et xv
quolibet ad ij d. per diem ad idem opus faciendum in Castro .. .. xiij s. iiij d.
Operarii
Et pro vadiis iiij quolibet ad iij d. et viij quolibet ad ij d. per diem existent' apud Lymp' per
iiij dies per idem tempus. .. .. xiij s. iiij d.
SUMMA: xxxvj s. viij d.

4.8   [Monday 5 April – Saturday 10 April 1344; Easter Week]

viij^a septimana
Cementarii
Et pro vadiis Magistri Willelmi de Ram' et Magistri Willelmi de Hurle utroque ad vij s.
inter v diem Aprilis et x diem eiusdem mensis computando per unam septimanam ..xiiij s.

Operarii et cariagium
Et pro vadiis x laboratorum quolibet ad ij d. per diem infra dictum tempus per ij dies. .. ..
iij s. iiij d.
Et pro cariagio calcis per ij carettas per ij dies infra dictum tempus .. .. iij s. iiij d.
SUMMA: xx s. viij d.

Pascha iiij die Aprilis
4.9   [Monday 12 April – Saturday 17 April 1344]

ix^a septimana
Et pro vadiis Magistri Willelmi de Ram' ad vij s., unius ad iiij s., ij utroque ad iij s., iiij
quolibet ad ij s. iiij d., ij utroque ad ij s. iij d., ij utroque ad ij s., xvij quolibet ad xij d. per
diem inter x diem Aprilis et xvij diem eiusdem mensis computando per unam septimanam
.. .. lj s. x d.
Et pro cariagio calcis et arene per iij carettas per vj dies .. .. xv s.
SUMMA: lxvj s. x d.

4.10   [Sunday 18 April – Saturday 24 April 1344]

x^a septimana
Et pro vadiis Magistri Willelmi de Ram' ad vij s., ij utroque ad iij s., iiij quolibet ad ij s. iiij
d., ij utroque ad ij s. iij d., ij utroque ad ij s. et xvij quolibet ad xij d. per septimanam inter
xviij diem Aprilis et xxiiij diem eiusdem mensis per vj dies .. .. xlvij s. x d.

And for their wages of one at 3½d. for 3 days and one at 3½d. for 2 days within the said period [17½d.]
And for carting with one cart for 6 days and for one cart for 2 days [6s. 8d.]
TOTAL: 55s. 11½d.

4.11   [Sunday 25 April – Saturday 1 May 1344]

Eleventh week
And for the wages of Master William Ramsey at 7s., one at 3s., 4 at 2s. 4d. each, 2 others at 2s. 3d. and 2 others at 2s. and 15 at 10d. each per week between the 25th day of April and the first day of May accounting for 6 days. And for their wages 2 laying masons at 12d. for the same period [43s. 10d.]
And for carting with two carts for the same time 10s
TOTAL; 53s.10d

4.12   [Sunday 2 May – Saturday 8 May 1344]

Twelfth week
[And for their wages brother John at 14s., of A. de Kilham for 3 days at 2s.], of Master William Ramsey at 7s., one at 3s., 4 at 2s. 4d. each, 2 others at 2s. 3d., 2 others at 2s., 2 others at 12d., 15 at 10d. each per week between the second day of May and the seventh day of the same month accounting for 6 days [43s. 10d.]
And for carriage with two carts for 5 days, each at 10d. per day [8s. 4d.]
TOTAL: 52s. 4d.

4.13   [Sunday 9 May – Saturday 15 May 1344]

Thirteenth week
To [Brother John Walerand for his wages at 2s. per day from February sixteenth aforesaid until the 8th day of May next following, accounting for 83 days]
And for the wages of brother John at 14s., of Master William Ramsey at 7s., one at 3s., 4 at 2s. 4d. each, 2 others at 2s. 3d., 2 others at 2s., 2 others at 21d. and 14 at 11d. each per week between the ninth day of May and the fifteenth day of the same month accounting for 6 days [58s. 2d.]
And for four trowels bought for the laying masons at 3d each and for 4 iron hammers for breaking stones for 2d. each [20d.]
And for the carriage of sand by two carts for 6 days for the same period, each at 10d. per day [10s.]
TOTAL: 55s. 10d.

4.14   [Sunday 16 May – Saturday 22 May 1344]

Fourteenth week

Et pro vadiis unius ad iij d. ob. per iiij dies et unius ad iiij d. ob. per ij dies infra dictum tempus .. .. xvij d. ob.
Et pro cariagio per unam carettam per vj dies et per unam carettam per ij dies ..vj s. viij d.
SUMMA: lv s. xj d. ob.

4.11 [Sunday 25 April – Saturday 1 May 1344]

xjᵃ septimana
Et pro vadiis Magistri Willelmi de Ram' ad vij s., unius ad iij s., iiij quolibet ad ij s. iiij d., ij utroque ad ij s. iij d. et ij utroque ad ij s. et xv quolibet ad x d. per septimanam inter xxv diem Aprilis et primum diem Maij computando per vj dies. Et pro vadiis ij Cementariorum positorum utroque ad xxj d. per idem tempus .. .. xliij s. x d.
Et pro cariagio per ij carettas per idem tempus .. .. x s.
SUMMA: liij s. x d.

4.12 [Sunday 2 May – Saturday 8 May 1344]

xijᵃ septimana
[Et pro vadiis fratris Johannis ad xiiij s., A. de Killum per iij dies ad ij s.]⁵, Magistri Willelmi de Ram' ad vij s., unius ad iij s., iiij quolibet ad ij s. iiij d., ij utroque ad ij s. iij d., ij utroque ad ij s., ij utroque ad xxj d., xv quolibet ad x d. per septimanam inter ij diem Maij et vjj diem eiusdem mensis computando per vj dies .. .. xliij s. x d.
Et pro cariagio per ij carettas per v dies utroque ad x d. per diem .. .. viij s. iiij d.
SUMMA: lij s. iiij d.

4.13 [Sunday 9 May – Saturday 15 May 1344]

xiijᵃ septimana
[Fratri Johanni Walrand' pro vadiis suis ad ij s. per diem a xvj die Februarii predicto usque viij diem Maij computando proximum sequentem per iiij*** iij dies.]
Et pro vadiis fratris Johannis ad xiiij s., Magistri Willelmi de Ram' ad vij s., unius ad iij s., iiij quolibet ad ij s. iiij d., ij utroque ad ij s. iij d., ij utroque ad ij s., ij utroque ad xxj d. et xiiij quolibet ad xj d. per septimanam inter ix diem Maij et xv diem eiusdem mensis computando per vj dies .. .. lviij s. ij d.
Et pro iiij Trowels emptis pro cementariis positoribus pro quolibet iij d. et pro iiij hamers ferreis pro petris frangendis pro quolibet ij d. .. .. xx d.
Et pro cariagio sabulonum per ij carettas per vj dies per idem tempus quolibet ad x d. per diem .. .. x s.
SUMMA: lv s. x d.⁶

4.14 [Sunday 9 May – Saturday 15 May 1344]

xiiijᵃ septimana

---

⁵ Cancelled.
⁶ Corrected from lxix s. x d.

And for the wages of brother John at 14s., of Master William Ramsey at 7s., one at 3s., 4 at 2s. 4d. each, 2 others at 2s. 3d., 2 others at 2s., 2 others at 21d. and 17 at 11d. each per week between the sixteenth day of May and the 22nd day of the same month accounting for 6 days [60s. 11d.]

And for carriage for 5 days by one cart within the said period taking 10d. per day [4s. 2d.] TOTAL: 51s. 1d.

4.15 [Whitsunday, 23 May – Saturday 29 May 1344]

Pentecost
[And for the wages of brother John at 14s.], of Master William Ramsey at 7s. per week between the 23rd day of May and the 29th day of the same month accounting for 6 days TOTAL: 21s. 7s. (sic.)

4.16 [Sunday 30 May – Saturday 5 June 1344]

Sixteenth week
[And for the wages of brother John at 14s.], of Master William Ramsey at 7s., one at 3s., 3 at 2s. 4d. each, 2 others at 2s. 3d., 2 others at 2s., 2 others at 21d. and 17 at 11d. each per week between the 30th day of May and the 5th day of June accounting for 6 days [44s. 7d.]

And for bringing stones by boat from Bisham to Windsor on four occasions, each trip (?) costing 6s. 8d. [26s. 8d.]
And for the carriage of stones, by three carts, from the bridge to the castle, one for 5½ days, one for four days and one for one day within the said period each receiving 10d. per day [8s. 9d.]
TOTAL: £4.

4.17 [Sunday 6 June – Saturday 12 June 1344]

Seventeenth week
[And for the wages of brother John at 14s.], of Master William Ramsey at 7s., one at 3s., 4 at 2s. 4d. each, 2 others at 2s. 3d., 2 others at 2s., 2 others at 21d. and 17 at 11d. each per week between the 6th day of June and the twelfth day of the said month accounting for 6 days [45s. 6d.]

Et pro vadiis fratris Johannis ad xiiij s., Magistri Willelmi de Ram' ad vij s., unius ad iij s., iiij quolibet ad ij s. iiij d., ij utroque ad ij s. iiij d., ij utroque ad ij s., ij utroque ad xxj d. et xvij quolibet ad xj d. per septimanam inter xvj diem Maij et xxij diem eiusdem mensis computando per vj dies .. .. lx s. xj d.
Et pro cariagio per v dies per unam carettam infra dictum tempus capiendo per diem x d. .. .. iiij s. ij d.
SUMMA: lj s. j d.[7]

4.15   [Whitsunday, 23 May – Saturday 29 May 1344]

Pentecost
[Et pro vadiis fratris Johannis ad xiiij s.][8], Magistri Willelmi de Ram' ad vij s. per septi-manam inter xxiij diem Maij et xxix diem eiusdem mensis computando per vj dies.
SUMMA: xxj s. vij s. (sic.)

4.16   [Sunday 30 May – Saturday 5 June 1344]

xvj^a septimana
[Et pro vadiis fratris Johannis ad xiiij s.][9], Magistri Willelmi de Ram' ad vij s., unius ad iij s., iij quolibet ad ij s. iiij d., ij utroque ad ij s. iiij d., ij utroque ad ij s., ij utroque ad xxj d. et xvij quolibet ad xj d. per septimanam inter xxx diem Maij et v diem Junii computando per vj dies .. .. xliiij s. vij d.[10]
Et pro Batillagio petrarum de Bristilsham usque Wynd' per iiij vices pro qualibet vice vj s. viij d. .. .. xxvj s. viij d.
Et pro cariagio pertrarum a ponte usque Castrum per iij carettas, unius per v dies et dimidium, unius per iiij dies et unius per unum diem infra dictum tempus qualibet capi-endo x d. per diem .. .. viij s. ix d.
SUMMA: iiij li.[11]

4.17   [Sunday 6 June – Saturday 12 June 1344]

xvij^a septimana
[Et pro vadiis fratris Johannis ad xiiij s.][12], Magistri Willelmi de Ram' ad vij s., unius ad iij s., iiij quolibet ad ij s. iiij d., ij utroque ad ij s. iiij d., ij utroque ad ij s., ij utroque ad xxj d. et xvij quolibet ad xj d. per septimanam inter vj diem Junii et xij diem mensis computando per vj dies .. .. xlv s. vj d.[13]

---

7   Corrected from lxv s. j d.
8   Cancelled.
9   Cancelled.
10   Corrected from lviij s. vij d.
11   xiiij s. crossed through.
12   Cancelled.
13   Corrected from lix s. vj d.

4.18   [Sunday 13 June – Saturday 19 June 1344]

Eighteenth week
[And for the wages of brother John at 14s.], of Master William Ramsey at 7s., one at 3s., 4 at 2s. 4d. each, 2 others at 2s. 3d., 2 others at 2s., 2 others at 21d. and 17 at 11d. each per week between the thirteenth day of June and the 29th (sic.) day of the said month accounting for 6 days [46s. 11d.]
And for carriage by one cart for 9 days over the previous three weeks, taking 10d. per day [7s. 6d.]
TOTAL: 49s. 9d.

4.19   [Sunday 20 June – Saturday 26 June 1344]

Nineteenth week
[And for the wages of brother John at 14s.], of Master William Ramsey at 7s., one at 3s., 2 at 2s. 4d. each, 2 others at 2s. 3d., 2 others at 2s., 2 others at 21d. and 17 at 11d. each per week between the 20th day of June and the 26th day of the said month accounting for 6 days [42s. 3d.]
 And for carriage by one cart for 9 days in the previous three weeks, taking 10d. per day [7s. 6d.]
TOTAL: 49s. 9d.

4.20   [Sunday 27 June – Friday 2 July 1344]

Twentieth week
For the wages of [brother John Walerand] and William Ramsey as above, one at 3s., 3 at 2s. 4d. each, 2 others at 2s., 2 others at 15d., 4 at 12d. each per week between 27th day of June and 2nd day of July next following, accounting for 6 days [27s. 6d.]

4.21   [Saturday 3 July – Saturday 10 July 1344]

Twenty-first week
To [Brother John] and William for their wages as above, one at 3s., 3 at 2s. 4d. each, 2 others at 2s., 2 others at 15d., 4 at 21d. each per week between the third day of July and the tenth day of the same month accounting for one week [27s. 6d.]

4.18 [Sunday 13 June – Saturday 19 June 1344]

xviij^a septimana

[Et pro vadiis fratris Johannis ad xiiij s.][14], Magistri Willelmi de Ram' ad vij s., unius ad iij s., iiij quolibet ad ij s. iiij d., ij utroque ad ij s. iij d., ij utroque ad ij s., ij utroque ad xxj d. et xvij quolibet ad xj d. per septimanam inter xiij diem Junii et xxix (sic.) diem eiusdem mensis computando per vj dies .. .. xlvj s. xj d.[15]

4.19 [Sunday 20 June – Saturday 26 June 1344]

xix^a septimana

[Et pro vadiis fratris Johannis ad xiiij s.][16], Magistri Willelmi de Ram' ad vij s., unius ad iij s., ij utroque ad ij s. iiij d., ij utroque ad ij s. iij d., ij utroque ad ij s., ij utroque ad xxj d. et xvij quolibet ad xj d. per septimanam inter xx diem Junii et xxvj diem eiusdem mensis computando per vj dies .. .. xlij s. iij d.[17]
Et pro cariagio per unam carettam per ix dies in iij septimanis preteritis capient' x d. per diem .. .. vij s. vj d.
SUMMA: xlix s. ix d.[18]

4.20 [Sunday 27 June – Friday 2 July 1344]

xx septimana

Pro vadiis [fratris Johannis Walrand'][19] et Willelmi de Rames' ut supra, j^us ad ij s., iiij quolibet ad ij s. iiij d., ij utroque ad ij s., ij utroque ad xv d., iiij quolibet ad xij d. per septimanam inter xxvij diem Junij et ij diem Julij proximum sequentem compotando per vj dies .. .. xxvij s. vj d.[20]

4.21 [Saturday 3 July – Saturday 10 July 1344]

xxj septimana

[Fratri Johanni et][21] Willelmo pro vadiis suis ut supra, j ad iij s., iiij quolibet ad ij s. iiij d., ij utroque ad ij s., ij utroque ad xv d., iiij quolibet ad xij d. per septimanam inter iij diem Julij et x diem eiusdem mensis computando per septimanam[22] .. .. xxvij s. vj d.[23]

---

[14] Cancelled.
[15] Corrected from lx s. xj d.
[16] Cancelled.
[17] Corrected from lvj s. iij d.
[18] Corrected from lxiij s. ix d.
[19] Cancelled.
[20] Corrected from xlj s. vj d.
[21] Cancelled.
[22] Corrected from *vij dies*.
[23] Corrected from xlj s. vj d.

4.22   [Sunday 11 July – Saturday 17 July 1344]

Twenty-second week

To [Brother John Walerand and] William Ramsey for their wages as above, one at 3s., 3 at 2s. 4d. each, 2 others at 2s., 2 others at 15d., 4 at 11d. each per week between the eleventh day of July and the seventeenth day of the same month accounting for one week [27s. 6d.]

4.23   [Sunday 18 July – Saturday 24 July 1344]

Twenty-third week

To [Brother John Walerand and] William Ramsey for their wages as above, one at 3s., 3 at 2s. 4d. each, 2 others at 2s., 2 others at 15d., 4 at 11d. each per week between the eighteenth day of July and the 24th day of the same month for seven days and with the mending of tools for 11d. in this week [28s. 1d.]

4.24   [Sunday 25 July – Saturday 31 July 1344]

Twenty-fourth week

To [the aforesaid brother John and] William for their same wages, William Hurley, carpenter receiving 7s. per week, 2 others at 3s., 3 at 2s. 4d., 2 others at 2s., 2 others at 15d., 4 at 11d. each between the 25th day of July and the 31st day of the same month accounting namely up to the last day [37s. 2d.]

4.25   [Sunday 1 August – Saturday 7 August 1344]

Twenty-fifth week

To [Brother John] William Ramsey and William Hurley for their same wages, 2 others at 3s., 3 at 2s. 4d. each, 2 others at 2s., 2 others at 15d., 4 at 11d. each per week between the first day of August and the 7th day of the same month accounting for 7 days with the mending of tools [given] to the brother (sic) by the masons in this week. Total 12d. [38s. 2d.]

4.22   [Sunday 11 July – Saturday 17 July 1344]

xxij septimana

[Fratri Johanni Walrand' et][24] Willelmo de Rames' pro vadiis suis ut supra, j^us ad iij s.,
iij quolibet ad ij s. iiij d., ij utroque ad ij s., ij utroque ad xv d., iiij quolibet ad xj d. per
septimanam inter xj diem Julij et xvij diem eiusdem mensis compotando per septimanam[25]
.. .. xxvij s. vj d.[26]

4.23   [Sunday 18 July – Saturday 24 July 1344]

xxiij septimana

[Fratri Johanni Walerand' et][27] Willelmo de Rames' pro vadiis suis ut supra, j^us ad iij s.,
iij quolibet ad ij s. iiij d., ij utroque ad ij s., ij utroque ad xv d., iiij quolibet ad xj d. per
septimanam inter xviij diem Julij et xxiiij diem eiusdem mensis per vij dies cum emedatione
(sic.) instrumentorum pro xj d. in ista septimana .. .. xxviij s. j d.[28]

4.24   [Sunday 25 July – Saturday 31 July 1344]

xxiiij septimana

[Predictis fratri Johanni et][29] Willelmo pro consimilibus vadiis suis, Willelmo de Hurle
carpentario rec' ad vij s. per septimanam, ij utroque ad iij s., iij quolibet ad ij s. iiij d., ij
utroque ad ij s., ij utroque ad xv d., iiij quolibet ad xj d. inter xxv diem Julij et xxxj diem
eiusdem mensis computando videlicet ultimum diem .. .. xxxvij s. ij d.[30]

4.25   [Sunday 1 August – Saturday 7 August 1344]

xxv septimana

[Fratri Johanni][31] Willelmo de Rames' et Willelmo de Hurle pro consimilibus vadiis suis, ij
utroque ad iij s., iij quolibet ad ij s. iiij d., ij utroque ad ij s., ij utroque ad xv d., iiij quolibet
ad xj d. per septimanam inter j diem Augusti et vij diem eiusdem mensis computando per
vij dies cum emendatione diversorum instrumentorum fratri per cementarios in ista septimana. Summa xij d. .. .. .. xxxviij s. ij d.[32]

---

[24] Cancelled.
[25] Corrected from *vij dies*.
[26] Corrected from xlj s. vj d.
[27] Cancelled.
[28] Corrected from xlij s. j d.
[29] Cancelled.
[30] Corrected from lj s. ij d.
[31] Cancelled.
[32] Corrected from lij s. ij d.

4.26 [Sunday 8 August – Saturday 14 August 1344]

Twenty-sixth week

To [Brother John] William and William aforesaid for their same wages, 2 others at 3s., 3 at 2s. 4d. each, 2 others at 2s., 2 others at 15d., 4 at 11d. each per week between the 8th day of August and the fourteenth day of the same month [37s. 2d.]

[rot. 1, m. 3.]

4.27 [Sunday 15 August – Saturday 21 August 1344]

Twenty-seventh week

To [Brother John] William and William for their wages as above, 2 others at 3s., 3 at 2s. 4d. each, 2 others at 2s., 2 others at 15d., 4 at 11d. each per week between the fifteenth day of the month of August and the twelfth day of the same month accounting for 7 days, and also for the wages of 2 carpenters working [on] a well in the castle to supply water for 6 days, each at 4d. for the same period [41s. 2d.]

4.28 [Sunday 22 August – Saturday 28 August 1344]

Twenty-eighth week

To [Brother John] William and William for their same wages as above, 2 others at 3s., 3 at 2s. 4d. each, 2 others at 2s., 2 others at 15d., 4 at 11d. each per week between the 22nd day of August and the 28th day of the same month accounting for one week [37s. 2d.]

4.29 [Sunday 29 August – Saturday 4 September 1344]

Twenty-ninth week

To [Brother John] William and William for their same wages as above, 2 others at 3s., 3 at 2s. 4d. each, 2 others at 2s., 2 others at 15d., 4 at 11d. each per week between the 29th day of August and the 4th day of the month of September next following for one week [37s. 2d.]

4.26 [Sunday 8 August – Saturday 14 August 1344]

xxvj septimana
[Fratri Johanni][33] Willelmo et Willelmo predictis pro consimilibus vadiis suis, ij utroque ad iij s., iiij quolibet ad ij s. iiij d., ij utroque ad ij s., ij utroque ad xv d., iiij quolibet ad xj d. per septimanam inter viij diem Augusti et xiiij diem eiusdem mensis .. .. xxxvij s. ij d.[34]

[rot. 1., m. 3.]
4.27 [Sunday 15 August – Saturday 21 August 1344]

xxvij septimana
[Fratri Johanni][35] Willelmo et Willelmo pro vadiis suis ut supra, ij utroque ad iij s., iiij quolibet ad ij s. iiij d., ij utroque ad ij s., ij utroque ad xv d., iiij quolibet ad xj d. per septimanam inter xv diem mensis Augusti et xxj diem eiusdem mensis computando per vij dies ac etiam pro vadiis ij carpentariorum operancium [circa?] fontem in castro pro aqua habenda per vj dies utroque ad iiij d. per idem tempus .. .. xlj s. ij d.[36]

4.28 [Sunday 22 August – Saturday 28 August 1344]

xxviij septimana
[Fratri Johanni][37] Willelmo et Willelmo pro consimilibus vadiis suis ut supra, ij utroque ad iij s., iiij quolibet ad ij s. iiij d., ij utroque ad ij s., ij utroque ad xv d., iiij quolibet ad xj d. per septimanam inter xxij diem Augusti et xxviij diem eiusdem mensis computando per j septimanam .. .. xxxvij s. ij d.[38]

4.29 [Sunday 29 August – Saturday 4 September 1344]

xxix septimana
[Fratri Johanni][39] Willelmo et Willelmo pro consimilibus vadiis suis ut supra, ij utroque ad iij s., iiij quolibet ad ij s. iiij d., ij utroque ad ij s., ij utroque ad xv d., iiij quolibet ad xj d. per septimanam inter xxix diem Augusti et iiij diem mensis Septembris proximum sequentem per j septimanam .. .. xxxvij s. ij d.[40]

[33] Cancelled.
[34] Corrected from lj s. ij d.
[35] Cancelled.
[36] Corrected from lv s. ij d.
[37] Cancelled.
[38] Corrected from lj s. ij d.
[39] Cancelled.
[40] Corrected from lj s. ij d.

4.30   [Sunday 5 September – Saturday 11 September 1344]

Thirtieth week
To [Brother John] William and William aforesaid for their same wages as above, 2 others at 3s., 3 at 2s. 4d. each, 2 others at 2s., 2 others at 15d., 4 at 11d. each per week between the 5th day of the month of September and the eleventh day of the same month accounting for one week [37s. 2d.]

4.31   [Sunday 12 September – Saturday 18 September 1344]
T
hirty-first week
To [Brother John] William and William for their same wages as above, 2 others at 3s., 3 at 2s. 4d. each, 2 others at 2s., 2 others at 15d., 4 at 11d. each per week between the twelfth day of the month of September and the eighteenth day of the same month accounting for one week [37s. 2d.]

4.32   [Sunday 19 September – Saturday 25 September 1344]

Thirty-second week
To [Brother John] William and William for their same wages as above, 2 others at 3s., 3 at 2s. 4d., 2 others at 2s., 2 others also 15[d.], 4 at 11d. each per week between the nineteenth day of the month of September and the 25th day of the same month accounting for one week and for mending tools 18d. [38s. 8d.]

4.33   [Sunday 26 September – Saturday 2 October 1344]

Thirty-third week
To [Brother John] William and William aforesaid for their same wages as above, 2 others at 3s., 3 at 2s. 4d. each, 2 others at 2s., 2 others at 15d., 4 at 9d. each per week between the 26th day of the month of September and the 2nd day of the month of October accounting for one week [36s. 6d.]

4.34   [Sunday 3 October – Saturday 9 October 1344]

Thirty-fourth week
To [Brother John] William and William for their same wages as above, 2 others at 3s., 3 at

4.30   [Sunday 5 September – Saturday 11 September 1344]

xxx septimana

[Fratri Johanni][41] Willelmo et Willelmo predictis pro consimilibus vadiis suis ut supra, ij utroque ad iij s., iij quolibet ad ij s. iiij d., ij utroque ad ij s., ij utroque ad xv d., iiij quolibet ad xj d. per septimanam inter v diem mensis Septembris et xj diem mensis eiusdem computando per j septimanam .. .. xxxvij s. ij d.[42]

4.31   [Sunday 12 September – Saturday 18 September 1344]

xxxj septimana

[Fratri Johanni][43] Willelmo et Willelmo pro consimilibus vadiis suis ut supra, ij utroque ad iij s., iij quolibet ad ij s. iiij d., ij utroque ad ij s., ij utroque ad xv d., iiij quolibet ad xj d. per septimanam inter xij diem mensis Septembris et xviij eiusdem mensis computando per j septimanam .. .. xxxvij s. ij d.[44]

4.32   [Sunday 19 September – Saturday 25 September 1344]

xxxij septimana

[Fratri Johanni][45] Willelmo et Willelmo pro consimilibus vadiis suis ut supra, ij utroque ad iij s., iij quolibet ad ij s. iiij d., ij utroque ad ij s., ij utroque xv (sic.), iiij quolibet ad xj d. per septimanam inter xix diem mensis Septembris et xxv diem eiusdem mensis computando per j septimanam et pro emendatione instrumentorum xviij d. .. .. xxxviij s. viij d.[46]

4.33   [Sunday 26 September – Saturday 2 October 1344]

xxxiij septimana

[Fratri Johanni][47] Willelmo et Willelmo predictis pro consimilibus vadiis suis ut supra, ij utroque ad iij s., iij quolibet ad ij s. iiij d., ij utroque ad ij s., ij utrique (sic.) ad xv d., iiij quolibet ad ix d. per septimanam inter xxvj diem mensis Septembris et ij diem mensis Octobris computando per j septimanam .. .. xxxvj s. vj d.[48]

4.34   [Sunday 3 October – Saturday 9 October 1344]

xxxiiij septimana

[Fratri Johanni][49] Willelmo et Willelmo pro consimilibus vadiis suis ut supra, ij utroque

---

[41] Cancelled.
[42] Corrected from lj s. ij d.
[43] Cancelled.
[44] Corrected from lj s. ij d.
[45] Cancelled.
[46] Corrected from lij s. viij d.
[47] Cancelled.
[48] Corrected from l s. vj d.
[49] Cancelled.

2s. 4d. each, 2 others at 2s., 2 others at 15d., 4 at 11d. each per week. Item, for the wages of one carpenter mending the wheel of the well for 3 days each day at 4d. as well as the cost of mending iron tools for the workmen, that is 12d., between the 3rd day of the month of October and the 9th day of the same month accounting for one week [39s. 11d.]

4.35 [Sunday 10 October – Saturday 16 October 1344]

Thirty-fifth week
To [Brother John] William and William aforesaid for their wages as above, 2 others at 3s., 3 at 2s. 4d. each, 2 others at 2s., 2 others at 15d., 4 at 11d. each, and also the wages of 3 carpenters covering the wall of the round table, that is at 2s. each per week between the tenth day of the month of October and the sixteenth day of the same month accounting for one week [43s. 2d.]

4.36 [Sunday 17 October – Saturday 23 October 1344]

Thirty-sixth week
To [Brother John] William and William aforesaid for their wages as above, 2 others at 3s., 3 at 2s. 4d. each, 2 others at 2s., 2 others at 15d., 4 at 11d. and also 3 carpenters each at 2s. each per week between the seventeenth day of the month of October and the 23rd day of the same month accounting for one week [43s. 2d.]

4.37 [Sunday 24 October – Saturday 30 October 1344]

Thirty-seventh week[
To [Brother John] William and William aforesaid for their wages as above, one man bringing the king's commission for impounding carts 3s., 3 carpenters at 2s. each, one man working on the covering with two helping him at 8d. per day, 2 sawyers at 7d. per day. Item, 2 others at 15d., 4 at 11d. each per week between the 24th day of the month of October and 30th day of the same month accounting for one week, with the driving of one cart for fetching the tiles at 5s. per week for the next week [41s. 8d.]

ad iij s., iij quolibet ad ij s. iiij d., ij utroque ad ij s., ij utroque ad xv d., iiij quolibet ad xj d. per septimanam. Item pro vadiis j carpentarii ad rotam fontis emendandam per iij dies quolibet die ad iiij d. cum emendatione instrumentorum ferrorum pro operariis, videlicet xxj d., inter iij diem mensis Octobris et ix diem eiusdem mensis computando per j septimanam .. .. xxxix s. xj d.[50]

4.35   [Sunday 10 October – Saturday 16 October 1344]

xxxv septimana

[Fratri Johanni][51] Willelmo et Willelmo predictis pro vadiis suis ut supra, ij utroque ad iij s., iij quolibet ad ij s. iiij d., ij utroque ad ij s., ij utrique (sic.) ad xv d., iiij quolibet ad xj d. cum vadiis iiij carpentariorum circa muros cooperandos tabule rotunde, videlicet quolibet ad ij s. per septimanam inter x diem mensis Octobris et xvj diem eiusdem mensis computando per j septimanam .. .. xliij s. ij d.[52]

4.36   [Sunday 17 October – Saturday 23 October 1344]

xxxvj septimana

[Fratri Johanni][53] Willelmo et Willelmo predictis pro vadiis suis ut supra, ij utroque ad iij s., iij quolibet ad ij s. iiij d., ij utroque ad ij s., ij utroque ad xv d., iiij quolibet ad xj d. et eciam iiij carpentariis quolibet ad ij s. per septimanam inter xvij diem mensis Octobris et xxiij diem eiusdem mensis computando per j septimanam .. .. xliij s. ij d.[54]

4.37   [Sunday 24 October – Saturday 30 October 1344]

xxxvij septimana

[Fratri Johanni][55] Willelmo et Willelmo predictis pro vadiis suis ut supra, j portant' commissionem domini nostri Regis pro cariagio capiendo iij s., iij carpentiis quolibet ad ij s., j coopertoro cum ij sibi servientibus ad viij d. per diem, ij sarratoribus ad vij d. per diem. Item, ij utrique ad xv d., iiij quolibet ad xj d. per septimanam inter xxiiij diem mensis Octobris et xxx diem eiusdem mensis computando per j septimanam cum conductu j carette pro tegulis querendis ad v s. per septimanam pro ista septimana proxima .. .. xlj s. viij d.[56]

---

[50] Corrected from liij s. xj d.
[51] Cancelled.
[52] Corrected from lvijs. ij d.
[53] Cancelled.
[54] Corrected from lvijs. ij d.
[55] Cancelled.
[56] Corrected from lvs. viij d.

4.38   [Sunday 31 October – Saturday 6 November 1344]

Thirty-eighth week
To [Brother John] William and William for their same wages as above, one man bringing the king's commission at 3s., to three carpenters each at 4d. per day for five days, one man working on the covering with two helping him at 8d. per day per five days, 2 sawyers at 7d. per day for the same period, two others at 12d., 4 at 9d. each with the use of one cart for 4 days during this week at 10d. per day between the last day of the month of October and the 6th day of the month of November next following [36s. 7d.]

4.39   [Sunday 7 November – Saturday 13 November 1344]

Thirty-ninth week
To [Brother John] William and William for their wages as above, one at 3s., 3 at 20d. each, one working on the covering with two helping him at 3s. 11d., 2 sawyers at 3s. 6d. each, 2 others at 12d., 4 at 11d. each with the use of one cart for 3 days taking 8d. per day between the 7th day of the said month of November and the [1]3th day of the same month accounting for one week [37s. 1d.]

4.40   [Sunday 14 November – Saturday 20 November 1344]

Fortieth week
To [Brother John] William and William for their wages as above, one at 3s., 3 at 20d. each, one working on the covering with two servants at 3s. 11d., 2 sawyers at 3s. 6d., 2 others at 12d., 4 at 11d. each per week with the use of one cart for 3 days at 8d. per day during this week between the fourteenth day of the month of November and the 20th day of the same month accounting for one week [37s. 1d.]

4.41   [Sunday 21 November – Saturday 27 November 1344]

Forty-first week
To [Brother John] William and William for their wages as above, one at 3s., one working on the covering with two servants at 3s. 11d., 2 others at 12d., 4 at 11d. each per week with the use of one cart for 5 days taking 8d. per day during this week between the 21st day of the month of November and the 27th day of the same month accounting for one week [29s. 11d.]

4.38   [Sunday 31 October – Saturday 6 November 1344]

xxxviij septimana

[Fratri Johanni][57] Willelmo et Willelmo pro consimilibus vadiis suis ut supra, j portant' commissionem domini Regis ad iij s., iij carpentariis quolibet ad iiij d. per diem per v dies, j coopertoro et ij sibi servientibus ad viij d. per diem per v dies, ij sarratoribus ad vij d. per diem per idem tempus, ij utroque ad xij d., iiij quolibet ad ix d. cum allocacione j carette per iiij dies infra ista septimana ad x d. per diem inter ultimum diem mensis Octobris et vj diem mensis Novembris proximum sequentem .. .. xxxvj s. vij d.[58]

4.39   [Sunday 7 November – Saturday 13 November 1344]

xxxix septimana

[Fratri Johanni][59] Willelmo et Willelmo pro vadiis suis ut supra, j ad iij s., iiij quolibet ad xx d., j coopertoro et ij sibi servientibus ad iij s. xj d., ij sarratoribus similiter ad iij s. vj d., ij utroque ad xij d., iiij quolibet ad xj d. in allocacione j carette per iij dies capiendo viij d. per diem inter vij diem mensis Novembris et iij (sic.) diem eiusdem mensis computando per j septimanam .. .. xxxvij s. j d.[60]

4.40   [Sunday 14 November – Saturday 20 November 1344]

xl septimana

[Fratri Johanni][61] Willelmo et Willelmo pro vadiis suis ut supra, j ad iij s., iiij quolibet ad xx d., j coopertoro cum ij servitoribus ad iij s. xj d., ij sarratoribus similiter ad iij s. vj d., ij utroque ad xij d., iiij quolibet ad xj d. per septimanam cum allocacione j carette per iij dies capiendo viij d. per diem infra ista septimana inter xiiij diem mensis Novembris et xx diem eiusdem mensis computando per j septimanam .. .. xxxvij s. j d.[62]

4.41   [Sunday 21 November – Saturday 27 November 1344]

[*xlj septimana*]

[Fratri Johanni][63] Willelmo et Willelmo pro vadiis suis ut supra, j ad iij s., j coopertoro et ij sibi servientibus ad iij s. xj d., ij utroque ad xij d., iiij quolibet ad xj d. per septimanam cum allocacione j carette per v dies capiendo viij d. per diem infra ista septimana inter xxj diem mensis Novembris et xxvij diem eiusdem mensis computando per j septimanam .. .. xxix s. xi d.[64]

[57] Cancelled.
[58] Corrected from ls. vij d.
[59] Cancelled.
[60] Corrected from ljs. j d.
[61] Cancelled.
[62] Corrected from ljs. j d.
[63] Cancelled.
[64] Corrected from xliijs. xj d.

[rot. 2, m. 1.]

4.42

Commissioners

For the wages of Richard Neweman / Martin de Wodhirst / Thomas Coursy and John Erle sent to the parts of Norfolk, Suffolk, Kent, Surrey, Northampton, Bedfordshire, London and Middlesex with commissions and letters under the privy seal for attaching workmen and bringing them to Windsor to carry out certain of the king's works there, for their wages each at 6d., and for the wages of Thomas Forester, John Wodward, John Tournour, and Richard Durham sent similarly to the aforesaid parts for the aforesaid reason, for their wages, each at 4d. per day, between the sixteenth day of February and the 21st day of March for 28 days, deducting the wages of four of the aforesaid for one day at 4d per day

£4 12.s

4.43

Blechingley

And for the wages of one carpenter supervisor at 6 d. from the twentieth day of February and the sixteenth day of March for 14 days 7s. and one at Blechingley and Reigate at 4d. for day for 28 days 9s. 4d. And for the wages of 16 carpenters at Blechingley each at 3d. a day for 14 days and one for one day 56s 3d.   Total 72s. 7d.

Reigate

And for the wages of 2 carpenters each at 4d. for day at Reigate for 4 days one for 3 days one for 2 days 2 others at 2d for 2 days and 2 other sawyers at 4d. for one day   6 s.

Holdshot

And for the wages of one carpenter at 6d. at Holdshot from the ninth day of March and the first day of April next following for 18 days 9s. And for the wages of 2 others at 4d. for 14½ days 3 for 11 days, one for 12 days and one for 5½ days each receiving the same as above for the said period 26 s. 6 d.. And for the wages of 5 each for 14½ days, one for 13 days, 2 for 11 days and one for 10 days each of the aforesaid receiving 3d. per day during the said time 29s. 1d. And for the wages of 4 woodcutters for one day, 2 for 3½ days each of the aforesaid receiving 4d. per day and for 5 at 3d. per day for 3½ days during the said time 8s per day. and for 5 at 3d. for day for 3½ days during the said time 53s. – 72s. 11.d.   Total 78s. 11d.

Worth

And for cutting twelve trees in the forest of Worth as per contract   2s.

Ruislip

And for cutting twelve trees at Ruislip as per contract 2s. And for the wages of two carpenters both at 4d. per day two both at 3¼d. per day and one at 3d. working in the park at Ruislip from the twentieth day of March to the first day of April for five and a half days 8s. 3d. – 10s. 3d.

And for the wages of one at 6d. per day for twenty days two both at 4d. for sixteen days

[rot. 2, m. 1.]

4.42

Commissionarii

Pro vadiis Ricardi Neweman / Martini de Wodhirst / Thome Coursy et Johannis Erle missorum usque partes Norff' Suff' Kanc' Surr' Norht' Bed' London' et Midd' cum commissionibus et literis sub privato sigillo pro operariis attachiandis et adducendis usque Wyndesors pro quibusdam operibus Regis ibidem faciendis pro vadiis suis quolibet ad .vj.d., et pro vadiis Thome Forester, Johannis Wodward', Johannis Tournour, et Ricardi Durham similiter missorum usque partes predictas ex causa predicta pro vadiis suis quolibet ad .iiij.d. per diem inter xvj. diem Februarij et xxj. diem Marcij per xxviij. dies deductis vadiis iiij. de predictis ad iiij.d. per unum diem . . iiij.li. xij.s.

4.43

Bletchyngle

Et pro vadiis unius Carpentarii supervisoris ad vj.d. inter xx. diem Februarij et xvj. diem Marcij per xiiij dies .vij.s. Et unius apud Blechyngle et Raigate ad .iiij.d. per diem per xxviij dies .ix.s. iiij.d. Et pro vadiis xvj. carpentariorum apud Blechyngle quolibet ad .iij.d. per diem per xiiij. dies et unius per unum diem .lvj.s. iij.d. Summa lxxij.s. vij.d.

Raigat

Et pro vadiis ij carpentariorum quolibet ad iiij.d. per diem apud Raigat per iiij dies unius per iij dies unius per ij dies .ij. utroque ad iij.d. per ij dies et ij sarratorum utroque ad .iiij.d. per unum diem vj.s.

Holshet

Et pro vadiis unius Carpentarii ad vj.d. apud Holshet inter ix diem Marcij et primum diem Aprilis proximum sequens per xviij dies .ix.s. Et pro vadiis .ij. utroque ad iiij.d. per xiiij. dies et dimidium iij. per xj dies unius per xij dies et unius per v. dies et dimidium quolibet capiente ut supra infra dictum tempus xxvj.s. vj.d.. Et pro vadiis v quolibet per xiiij dies et dimidium unius per xiij. dies ij per xj dies et unius per x dies quolibet predictorum capiente iij.d. per diem infra dictum tempus xxix.s. j.d. Et pro vadiis iiij copatorum per unum diem ij per iij. dies et dimidium quolibet predictorum capiente iiij.d. per diem. Et pro v. ad iij.d. per diem per iij. dies et dimidium infra dictum tempus viij.s. – lxxij.s. xj.d.

Summa. lxxviij.s. xj.d.

Worth

Et pro Copagio xij. arborum apud Forestham de Worth ex certa convencione ij.s.

Ryslep

Et pro Copagio xij. arborum apud Ryslep ex certa convencione .ij.s. et pro vadiis ii. carpentariorum utroque ad iiij.d. per diem ij. utroque ad iij.d.ob. per diem et unius ad iij.d. laborantibus in parco de Ryslep inter xx diem Marcii et primum diem Aprilis per v. dies et dimidium viij.s. iij.d –x.s. iij.d.

Et pro vadiis unius ad vj.d. per diem per xx dies ij. utroque ad iiij.d. per xvj dies ij utroque

two both at 3¼d. for 16 days and one at 3d. for sixteen days from the twenty-ninth day of March to the last day of April makes 33s   Total 46 s. 3d.

4.44

Sawyers
And for the wages of two sawyers at the castle for ten days utroque at 3¼d. per day from the first day of March to the fourteenth day of the same month 5s. 10d.
And for the wages of four workmen cutting firewood and faggots for the limepits for eleven days at 3d. per day each for the said period 11s. And for the wages of one man working elsewhere cutting bushes and carting them outside for 12 days – 2s.   Total 18s. 10.d.

Plumber
And for the wages of one plumber at 6d. and his assistant at 2d. for the same from the last day of February and the fourteenth day of March following for nine days   Total 6s.

Also at Reigate – William of Winchelsea carpenter assigned to supervise the workmen in the park at Reigate and elsewhere for his wages at 6 d for day for twenty-one days six carpenters at Reigate for four days each at 4d for day seven others at the same place at 4d for 3 days three at 4d each for 2 days 12 carpenters at 4d each for one and a half days and one at 4d. for one day between the first day of May and the seventeenth day of July at different times   33s. 10.d.

4.45

Purchase of stone

To the Dean of St Paul's London for Caen stone bought from him...	40	0	0
To Richard of Colchester for stones bought of him in the same place...	4	10	0
To William of Abbotsbury for stones bought of him...	8	5	0
For carriage of the same stones from [omitted] to the Thames...	2	0	0
To Walter Harrard for 106 gobets of Caen stone bought in the same place...	3	3	0
To the same for 450 stones called 'Cune Marchant' ...	1	16	0
John Blom for 180 gobbets, 100 quoins by measure, and 50 'Cune marchant'...	6	8	8
To John Mulard for 101 quarter-gobbets, and 401 quarter 'Cune marchant' ...	5	9	0
For pilotage of 3 ships bringing the said stones from the parts of Caen...		1	6
To John Marberer for 150 feet of quoins from the parts of Kent...	1	0	0
To the same for 27 corbels at 4d. each...		9	0
To the same for 1800 feet of rag from the parts of Kent, for each hundred 8s...	7	4	0
To John Peg' for 63 feet of Wheatley skews...		9	3¼
To the same and his fellows for 1000 feet of Wheatley stone, for each foot 1¼d...	5	4	2
To William Abbot for 98 Reigate stones...	1	10	0
To William of Wighthill for 67 pieces from the parts of Stapleton coming to London in a ship, weighing 20 loads, for each by weight 5s...	7	10	0
To John Maill of London for 100 gobbets of Caen (stone)...	3	0	0
To Robert le Hore for 233 feet of Bentley stone, for each hundred 4s. 6d.		10	6

Total   ..   £98   10   1½

ad iij.d.ob. per xvj. dies et unius ad iij.d. per xvj dies inter xxix diem Marcij et ultimum diem Aprilis Computat. – xxxiij.s

Summa xlvj.s. iij.d.

4·44

Sarratores

Et pro vadiis ij sarratorum infra Castrum per x dies utroque ad iij.d. ob. per diem inter primum diem Marcij et xiiij diem ejusdem mensis v.s. x.d.

Et pro vadiis iiij operariorum facientium Talwod et Fagot pro Lympittes per xj. dies quolibet ad iij.d. per diem per dictum tempus .xj.s.   Et pro vadiis unius hominis existentis ultra copagium bosci et ultra cartacionem ejusdem per xij. dies – ij.s.   Summa xviij.s. x.d.

Plumbarius

Et pro vadiis unius plumbarii ad vj d. et unius garcionis sui ad ij.d. per idem inter ultimum diem Februarii et xiiii diem Marcii proximum sequens per ix dies Summa vj.s. adhuc Raygate – Willelmo de Wynchelse carpentario assignato ad supervidendos laborarios in parco de Raygate et alibi pro vadiis suis ad vj.d per diem per xxj dies vj carpentariis apud Raygate per .iiij. dies quolibet ad iiij.d per diem vij. aliis ibidem ad iiij.d per iij. dies iiij quolibet ad iiij.d per ii dies xij carpentariis quolibet ad iiij.d per j. diem dimidium et unius ad iiijd. per j diem inter primum diem Maij. et xvij diem Julij per vices   xxxiij.s. x.d.

4·45

Empcio Petrarum

De Decano Sancti Pauli London pro petris de Caine ab eo emptis	xl.li.
Ricardo de Colecestre pro petris ab eo emptis ibidem	iiij.li. x.s
Willelmo de Abbotesbiry pro petris ab eo emptis	viij.li. v.s.
Pro cariagio dictarum petrarum apud (sic) usque Tamisiam	xl.s.
Waltero Harrard pro Cvj. gobet de Caine emptis ibidem	lxiij.s.
Eidem pro iiij^c dimid. petris vocatis Cune Marchaunt	xxxvj.s.
Johanni Blom pro C.xx/iiii gobetis .C. Cunes de mesura et l. Cure Marchant	vj.li.viij.s.viij.d.
Johanni Mulard pro Cj quart. gobetis iiij^c j. quart. Cune Marchant	C.ix.s.
Pro Lodmenagio .iij. Navium ducentium dictas petras de partibus de Caine	xviij.d.
Johanni Marberer pro C. dimid. pedibus de Cune de partibus Kancie	xx.s.
Eidem pro xxvij. Corbels pro quolibet iiij.d.	ix.s.
Eidem pro M^l viij^c pedibus de Rag' de partibus. Kancie pro quolibet C.viij.s.	vij.li. iiij.s.
Johanni Peg' pro lxiij pedibus de skues de Whatele	ix.s. iij.d. qr.
Eidem et sociis suis pro M^l pedibus petrarum de Whatele pro quolibet pede j.d. qr.	C.iiij.s. ij.d.
Willelmo Abbot pro xviij petris de Raygate	xxx.s.
Waltero de Wighthill pro lxvij peciis de partibus de Stapelton venientibus Londoniam in una Navi ponderantibus xxx dolia pro quolibet pondere v.s.	vij.li. x.s.
Johanni Maill de London pro C. gobetis de Caine	lx.s.
Roberti le Hore pro ij^c xxviij pedibus petrarum de Bentele pro quolibet C.iiij.s. vj.d.	x.s. vj.d.
Summa	iiij^{xx} xviij.ri. x.s. j.d. qr.

4.46

Purchase of wood

To William Heryng for 1000 [bundles of] wood for fuel spent at the lime-pits ..	1	15	0
To John Bonat by Walter Bonat for 1403 [bundles of] wood for fuel ..	2	19	0
To John de Cranstokes for 1000 faggots bought from him ..	1	7	6
To Thomas atte Lefe for 900 [bundles of] wood for fuel bought from him	1	13	3
To John atte Loke for 1000 [bundles of] wood for fuel bought from him	2	2	0
To John Godfray for lime bought from him		10	2
Total ..	£10	6	11

4.47

Equipment

For narrow vessels for the masons 22 d.and for mending the round well 18 d [ijs.v.d.]			
For 54 board barrows	1	8	7
For 6 hurdle barrows			9
For 5 tubs		2	11
For 12 troughs bought for putting in mortar..		2	2
For 10 bowls for sprinkling water upon mortar..			11
For a pipe and 2 barrels for carrying water and three barrels for making casks from...		8	0
For 14 hoops for casks and tubs			7
For the mending and sawing of the casks			3
For a funnel and a scoop for pouring water into barrels			5
For 13 great boards and 12 boards of Norwegian timber for squares for the masons		7	9
For lines for the same masons and carriage of the aforesaid squares and other tools		2	2
For one great ladle for the masons and grease for the cistern			8
For sieves and iron vessels bought for making mortar			9
For 350 laths for making thence the chimney of the forge..	1	5½	
For poles of fir bought for measuring the hall....		2	4½
For 4 grindstones for sharpening the masons' tools		15	4½
For 2 saws for sawing stones		4	6
For 29 lbs of bronze for turning the gudgeons of the well wheel.....		6	2
For 4500 iron nails for the wheel and other necessaries and for 1000 lath-nails		5	0
For 27 pieces of iron bought for making and mending divers necessaries.. ..		6	0
For 6 bundles of steel		3	6
For a barrel of pitch, 12 lbs of rosyn, and 10¼ lbs of wax for making cement:		7	6
For 7 pickaxes and 6 iron mattocks bought...		11	0
For the repair of the same and 14 others at the limepits by turns ..		1	6
For 4 iron rakes bought for the limepits		2	0
For 2 iron forks bought for the same...		2	6
For 3 axes for chopping wood there		2	0
For 10 wedges of iron bought for the quarry at Windsor...		3	4
For hooks and hasps for the storehouse at the limepits			4
For 4 pairs of iron hinges for 4 carts newly made for carrying lime		1	6
For a counting cloth		2	0

4.46

Empcio bosci

Willelmo Heryng pro M^l Talwod expens. apud lympittes	# xxxv.s.
Johanni. Bonat ex Waltero Bonat pro M^l iiij^c. iiij4^q Talwod	lix.s.
Johanni de Cranstokes pro M^l Fagot ab eo empt.	xxvij.s. vj.d.
Thome atte Lefe pro ix^c di. Talwod eo empt.	xxxiij.s. iijd.
Johanni atte Loke pro M^l Talwood ab eo empt.	xlij.s.
Johanni Godfray pro maeremio ab eo empto	x.s. ij.d.
Summa	x:li:vj:s:xj:d

4.47

Necessaria

Pro acutis vesselis cementariorum, xxiijd., pro emendacione rotunde fontis	xviijd. [ijs.v.d.]
Pro .liiij. Barowes de Bord.	xxviij.s. vij.d.
Pro .vj. Barowes de virgis	ix. d.
Pro v. Tynes	ij.s. xj.d.
Pro xi alviolis emptis pro morterio imponendo	ij.s. ij.d.
Pro x. Bollis pro aqua aspergenda super morterium	x d.
Pro una pipa et ij doliis pro aqua carianda et iij doliis pro.Cuvis inde faciendis	viiij.s.
Pro xiiii Circulis pro Cuvis et Tynis	vij.d.
Pro emendacione et sarracione Cuvarum	iij.d.
Pro uno Tundor et uno skopo pro aqua infundenda in dolio	v.d.
Pro xiij. bordis grossis et xij. estrich. bordis. pro squiris pro Cementariis	vij.s. ix.d.
Pro Lynes pro eisdem Cementariis et cariagio squirarum predictarum et aliorum instrumentorum	ij.s. ij.d.
Pro uno grosso Ladles. pro Cementariis et.uncto pro Cisterna	viij.d.
Pro Cribris et culdors emptis pro morterio faciendo	ix.d.
Pro iij^c et dimidio Lathis pro camino forg.. inde faciendo	xvij.d. ob.
Pro v. polis de Firre emptis pro admensuracione aule	ij.s. iiij.d. ob.
Pro iiij Gryndstons pro instrumentis Cementariorum acuendis	xv.s. iiij.d. ob.
Pro ij sarris pro sarracione petrarum	iiij.s. vj.d.
Pro xxix libris eris pro gogons rote fontis involvendis	vj.s. ij.d.
Pro iiij M^l D. Clavis ferreis pro rota et aliis necessariis et pro M^l Lathnailes	v.s.
Pro xxvij peciis ferri emptis pro diversis necessariis faciendis et reparandis	vj.s. ix.d.
Pro vj. garbis asseris	iij.s. vj.d.
Pro uno Barello picis xij lb. rosyn x. lb. et uno.quarterio Cere. pro Cimento faciendo	vij.s. vj.d.
Pro .vij. Picois et vj Mattoks ferri emptis	xj.s.
Pro reparacione eorundem et xiiij aliorum apud Lympittes per vices	xviij.d. ob.
Pro iiij rastellis ferri emptis pro Lympittes	xij.d.
Pro .ij. furcis ferri emptis pro eisdem	xviij.d.
Pro .iij. securis pro bosco coppando ibidem	ij.s.
Pro .x. Weggis ferri emptis pro quarrera apud Wyndesore	iij.s. iiij.d.
Pro hokes et haspes pro storhous apud Lympittes	iiij.d.
Pro iiij paribus gemellorum ferri pro iiij carectis de novo factis pro calce cariando	xviij.d.
Pro uno Countyngcloth	ij.s.

For 4 great hurdles bought for the limepits...	1	4
For the night watch at the limekiln for 12 men for 5 weeks ..	8	6
For 18 barrows, a sledge, and an axe, with the mending of tools by turns at Bisham	12	6½
For the making of hurdles for the limepits	1	0
For cleaning the well on two occasions	1	0

For mending the masons' vessels, 23d. ; mending the well wheel, 18d. ; for 4 hooks for the doors of the Round Table, 10s. ; for grease, 2d. ; for 2 bands of iron for the wheel, 18d. ; for a hasp for the well wheel, 2s. 5d... .. [17 6]

Total .. £8.14s.7½d

4.48

Cartage

For cartage at Windsor from 23rd February until 28th of the same month for 26 carts for 6 days, each at 8d. a day... .. .. .. 5 4 0

For like cartage in the same place from 1st March until 6th of same month for 6 days for 30 carts, viz. 20 at 10d. a day and 10 at 8d. a day within the said time

7 0 0

For like cartage in the same place from 7th March until fourteenth day of the same month for 18 carts, each at 10d. a day, and of one at 8d. a day, for 6 days and of one for half a day... .. .. 4 14 4

For cartage of stones, sand, lime, and water at Windsor between 14th March and 21st of same month reckoning for 6 days viz. 18 carts each at 10d. for 6 days, 3 at 10d. for 5 days, 3 at 10d. for 4 days, 2 each at 8d. for 2 days, 2 each at 8d. for one day, and 4 each at 6d... .. .. 5 18 6

For cartage of 71 carts carrying as above at Windsor between 22nd and 28th March viz. 23 at 10d. for 4 days, 15 at 8d. for 3 days, 13 at 10d. for 2 days, 20 at 10d. for one day 7 5 0

For cartage between Bentley and Windsor for 16 carts	18	8
For cartage between Wheatley and Windsor for 116 carts on 30 turns	8	0 6
For cartage of timber from Easthampstead...	2	5

For cartage of 1250 [bundles of] wood for fuel between Hartley Park and Windsor at 8d per hundred 8 4

For cartage of 41 stones bought at London to the Thames by a certain contract

8

Total £39 12 5

For cartage of stone from the bridge to the Castle by 4 carts for 4 days, for each cart 10d.
Total 10 0

4.49

Boatage

For boatage of stone from London on 24 turns by divers shouts, for each turn 13s. 4d., less 4s. from 3 of the aforesaid turns, viz. from each turn 16d. 15 16 0

Pro .iiij. Hirdls grossis emptis pro Lympittes   xvj.d.

Pro vigiliis apud Lymkiln nocturnis per xij homines per v. septimanas   viij.s.vj.d.

Pro xviij Barowes. uno sleg. uno securi cum emendacione instrumentorum per vices apud Bristilsham   xij.s. vj.d. ob.

Pro factura hirdlis pro Lympittes   xij.d.

Pro mundacione fontis per ij. vices   xij.d.

Pro emendacione vessellorum Cementariorum xxiij.d. emendacione rote fontis .xviij.d. pro .iiij. hokis pro hostio domus tabule rotunde x^s pro uncto .ij.d. pro .ij. ligatis ferri pro rota .xviij.d. pro j. hap. pro rota fontis   .ij.s. v.d.

Summa   .viij.li. xiiij.s. vj.d. ob.

4.48

Cariagium

Pro cariagio apud Wyndesore a xxiij die Februarij usque xxviij diem ejusdem mensis pro xxvj carectis per vj. dies quolibet ad viij.d. per diem   Ciiij.s.

Pro consimili cariagio ibidem a primo die Marcij usque vj diem ejusdem Mensis per vj. dies pro xxx. carectis viz. xx ad .x.d. per diem et x. ad viiij.d. per diem infra dictum tempus   vij.li.

Pro consimili cariagio ibidem a .vij. die Marcij usque xiiij. diem ejusdem Mensis pro xviij carectis quolibet ad x.d per diem et unius ad viij.d. per diem per vj. dies et unius per dimidium diem   iiij.li. xiiij.s. iiij.d.

Pro cariagio petre. arene. Calcis. et aque apud. Wyndesore inter xiiij diem Marcij et xxj. diem ejusdem mensis computante per vj. dies viz. xviij carectis quolibet ad x.d. per vj. dies iij. ad .x.d per v dies .iiij. ad x.d. per iiij dies ij. utroque ad viij.d. per ij. dies ij. utroque ad .viij.d. per unum diem et quatuor quolibet ad .vj.d.   C.xviij.s. vj.d.

Et pro cariagio lxxj. carectarum cariand. ut supra apud Wyndesore inter xxij diem ejusdem mensis Marcij et xxviij. diem ejusdem Mensis viz. xxiij. ad .x.d. per .iiij. dies xv. ad viij.d. per .iiij. dies xiij ad x.d. per ij dies .xx ad x.d. per unum diem   vij.li. v.s.

Pro cariagio inter Bentele et Wyndesore per xvj. carectas   xviij.s. viij.d.

Pro cariagio inter Whetele et Wyndesore per cxvj carectas per .xxx. luc.   viij.li. vj.d.

Pro cariagio maeremii de Yeshampsted   ij.s. v.d.

Pro cariagio M^l ij^c di Talwod inter parcum de Hertle et Wyndesore pro quolibet C. viij.d.   viij.s. iiij.d.

Pro cariagio xlj petrarum emptarum apud London usque ad.Tamisiam per.certam convencionem   viij.d.

Summa   xxxix.li. xij.s. v.d.

Pro cariagio petrarum de ponte usque Castrum per iiij carectas per iiij dies pro qualibet carecta x.d.

Summa   x.s.

4.49

Batillagium

Pro batillagio petrarum de London per xxviij vices per diversas shutas pro qualibet vicexiij. s. iiij.d. deduct. iiij.s de ij de predictis vicibus viz. de qualibet vice xvj.d.   xv.li. xvj.s.

For boatage of stone from Bisham on 51 turns for each turn 6s. 8d., and 7 turns for each 6s...   19   1   0

Total...   £34   18   0

For boatage of stone from Bisham to Windsor in August and September by 4 shouts, for each 6s. 8d., 26s. 8d. ; and for boatage of timber from Kingston to Windsor by 2 shouts bringing 17 pieces of timber in the month of August, 14s.

Total..   £2 0 8

4.50

For forty thousand tiles bought for the covering of the walls of the house of the Round
  Table, and for the covering of stones in the same place; price per thousand 2s.   4   0   0

For carriage of the same from Penn to Windsor   10   0

For six thousand laths, 20s. ; for forty thousand pegs for tiles, 3s. 4d.; for thirty-two
  thousand lath-nails, price per thousand 7½d., 20s.; for four thousand board nails, 13s. 4d.
.. ..   [2   16   8½]

Total.....   £7   6   8

5. Removal of tiles

To the wages of Robert Petipas, Osbert le Taverner, and John Herand carting with their carts the tiles which were left over from the covering of the walls of the Round Table at 9d per day. And for the wages of Richard Mundy and his assistant collecting and packing the said tiles at 3d per day.

6. The Prior of Merton's oaks, 1356

Prior of Merton
Money paid to the prior of Merton by the hand of Geoffrey de Chaddesley, a canon of that place, in full settlement of the money owed to the same prior for 52 oaks taken from the same prior's woods near Reading for the round table at Windsor, which oaks were carried to Westminster for the king's works by letter under the privy seal   £26 13s. 4d

Pro batillagio petrarum de Bristilsham per Lj vices pro qualibet vice vj.s. viij.d. et vij vicibus proqualibet vj.s.   xix.li. xij.d.
Summa   xxxiiij.li. xviij.s.
Pro batillagio petrarum de Bristilsham usque Wyndesore mense Augusti et Septembris per .iiij. shoutas pro qualibet vj.s. viij.d. xxvj.s. viij.d et pro batillagio maeremii de Kyng' usque Wyndesore per ij. shoutas ducentes xvij.pecias maeremii mense Augusti xiiij.s.
Summa   xl.s. viij.d.
[*A long erased entry.*]
Summa [*total erased*]

4.50
Pro .xl. m^l Tegulis emptis pro coopertura murorum domus Tabule Rotunde et pro coopertura petrarum ibidem precij Milleni .ij.s. iiij.li.   Pro cariagio eorundem del Penne usque Wyndesore x.s.   Pro vj. M^l lathis xx.s. Pro xl. m^l pynnes pro tegulis iij s. iiij.d. Pro xxxij. Mill. lathnayl precii Milleni vijd. ob. xx.s. pro iiij M^l Bordnail xiij.s. iiij.d.
Summa   vij.li. vj.s. viij.d.

5. Removal of tiles
Source: Particulars of Account for works at Windsor in the time of Thomas de Foxle, Constable 1343-4, PRO E101/492/24 (m.3)

In stipendiis Roberti Petipas Osberti le Taverner et Johis Herand' cum carectis suis cariancium tegulas que remanserunt de coopertura murorum tabule rotunde per di diem ix.d. Et in stipendiis Ricardi Mundy et garcionis sui compictancium et cubancium dictas tegulas per di' diem iij.d

6. The Prior of Merton's oaks, 1356
Source: Issue Roll, Michaelmas 30 Edward III, m.23 , PRO E403/378
Printed: Hope, I, 127.

Prior de Mertoñ.
Priori de Mertoñ in denariis sibi liberatis per manus Galfridi de Chaddesleye unius canonicorum ejusdem loci in plenam satisfaccionem denariorum eidem Priori debitorum pro lij. quercubus captis in bosco ejusdem Prioris juxta Redyng pro tabula rotunda apud Wyndesore que quidem quercus cariate erant usque Westmonasterium pro operibus Regis ibidem per breve de privato sigillo int' mand' hoc termino   xxvj.li. xiij.s. iiij.d.

7. Kitchen accounts

PRO E36/204
Account Book of Richard de Eccleshale, lieutenant of Robert de Kyldesby, controller of the king's wardrobe, from 25 November 1341 – 21 July 1342, and lieutenant of Walter de Wetwang, his successor as controller, from 21 July 1342 – 1 April 1344.

Daily expenses of the king's household, January 1344:

- Sunday, 4 January[1] [£31 12s. 1½d.]
- Monday, 5 January [£25 11s. 1½d.]
- Tuesday, 6 January [£26 15s. 10¼d.]
- Wednesday, 7 January [£26 17s. 2¾d.]
- Thursday, 8 January [£26 4s. 8¼d.]
- Friday, 9 January [£23 4s. 8d.]
- Saturday, 10 January: pantry [47s. 3¾d.]; buttery [52s. 3½d.]; wardrobe [40s. 7¼d.]; kitchen [£11 13s. 11½d.]; scullery [23s. 1¾d.]; saucery [3s. 1¾d.]; hall [9s. 3½d.]; chamber [22d.]; stable [79s. 11½d.]; wages [£4 13s. 4d.]; alms [nil]; TOTAL [£29 4s. 9½d.]

[f. 65v.]

- Sunday, 11 January: pantry [38s. 10d.]; buttery [50s. 6¼d.]; wardrobe [15s. 8¼d.]; kitchen [£9 19½d.]; scullery [15s. 6d.]; saucery [3s. 2d.]; hall [9s. 4½d.]; chamber [22d.]; stable [77s. 5¾d.]; wages [£4 13s. 4d.]; alms [nil]; TOTAL [£24 7s. 3¼d.]
- Monday, 12 January: pantry [47s. 2d.]; buttery [44s. 1¾d.]; wardrobe [15s. 0½d.]; kitchen [105s. 11¼d.]; scullery [15s. 8d.]; saucery [3s. 11d.]; hall [9s. 10½d.]; chamber [22d.]; stable [£4 3s. 9¼d.]; wages [£4 16s. 4½d.]; alms [nil]; TOTAL [£21 13s. 8¾d.]
- Tuesday, 13 January: pantry [32s. 8½d.]; buttery [48s. 9d.]; wardrobe [13s. 9½d.]; kitchen [£10 14½d.]; scullery [17s. 3½d.]; saucery [3s. 0¾d.]; hall [15s. 7d.]; chamber [nil]; stable [71s. 3d.]; wages [£4 17s. 7½d.]; alms [nil]; TOTAL [£25 15¼d.]
- Wednesday, 14 January: pantry [32s. 6d.]; buttery [55s. 1¼d.]; wardrobe [15s. 10½d.]; kitchen [11 7s. 8d.]; scullery [30s. 7¼d.]; saucery [2s. 6¾d.]; hall [8s. 6¼d.]; chamber [nil]; stable [72s. 1d.]; wages [101s. 1½d]; alms [nil]; TOTAL [£27 5s. 11½d.]
- Thursday, 15 January: pantry [43s. 11½d.]; buttery [£4 18s. 5¼d.]; wardrobe [43s. 9¼d.]; kitchen [£17 9s. 7¾d.]; scullery [20s. 3½d.]; saucery [6s. 8½d.]; hall [8s. 9¼d.]; chamber [nil]; stable [72s. 10¾d.]; wages [101s. 1½d.]; alms [nil]; TOTAL [£37 5s. 7¼d.]
- Friday, 16 January: pantry [48s. 1½d.]; buttery [£4 10s. 10½d.]; wardrobe [£6 5s. 2¾d.]; kitchen [**£15 19s. 2d.**]; scullery [20s. 9½d.]; saucery [12s. 10½d.]; hall [11s. 0½d.]; chamber [nil]; stable [78s. 3¾d.]; wages [104s.]; alms [nil]; TOTAL [£40 10s. 5d.]
- Saturday, 17 January: pantry [64s. 3½d.]; buttery [£7 6s. 4d.]; wardrobe [£12 6s. 9d.]; kitchen [**£55 12s. 6¾d.**]; scullery [77s. 0½d.]; saucery [13s. 0½d.]; hall [49s. 4½d.]; chamber [9s.]; stable [79s. 5½d.]; wages [£6 5s. 9d.]; alms [nil]; TOTAL [£86 3s. 7¼d.]

---

1   The day of the week is given wrongly in the original; for Sunday January 4 read Sunday January 5. All following days are similarly out by one day.

[f. 66r.]

- **Sunday, 18 January**: pantry [£14 19s. 1½d.]; buttery [£65 18s. 2¾d.]; wardrobe [£103 15d.]; kitchen [**£115 11s. 6d.**]; scullery [£6 7s. 0½d.]; saucery [£4 9½d.]; hall [50s. 5d.]; chamber [£25 14s. 5d.]; stable [79s. 9¾d.]; wages [£6 5s. 9d]; alms [nil]; TOTAL [**£348 8s. 4d.**]

- **Monday, 19 January**: pantry [£15 5d.]; buttery [£67 10s. 2¾d.]; wardrobe [£44 1d.]; kitchen [**£125 12s. 9½d.**]; scullery [£74 3s. 6d.]; saucery [100s. 6d.]; hall [51s.]; chamber [£22 9s. 5d.]; stable [£4 19½d.]; wages [£6 5s. 9d.]; alms [nil]; TOTAL [**£366 15s. 3¾d.**]

- **Tuesday, 20 January**: pantry [£15 5d.]; buttery [£67 10s. 2¾d.]; wardrobe [£53 7s. 6d.]; kitchen [**£140 5s. 5½d.**]; scullery [£12 8s. 2d.]; saucery [100s. 6d.]; hall [54s.]; chamber [£21 16s. 7d.]; stable [73s. 3½d.]; wages [£6 5s. 9d.]; alms [nil]; TOTAL [**£328 22¾d.**]

- **Wednesday, 21 January**: pantry [£15 12d.]; buttery [£67 10s. 2¾d.]; wardrobe [£39 19s. 8d.]; kitchen [**£129 4s. 3½d.**]; scullery [117s. 4d.]; saucery [54s.]; hall [50s.]; chamber [£21 19s.]; stable [66s. 0½d.]; wages [£6 5s. 9d.]; alms [nil]; TOTAL [**£293 9s. 10¾d.**]

- **Thursday, 22 January**: pantry [£15 12d.]; buttery [£67 10s. 2¾d.]; wardrobe [£51 15s. 7d.]; kitchen [**£161 16s. 11½d.**]; scullery [£15 4s.]; saucery [101s.]; hall [50s.]; chamber [£20 19s. 7d.]; stable [67s. 0½d.]; wages [£6 5s. 9d.]; alms [nil]; TOTAL [**£349 11s. 1¾d.**]

- Friday, 23 January: pantry [£7 19s 7¾d.]; buttery [£33 12s. 1¾d.]; wardrobe [£12 19s. 8d.]; kitchen [£99 7s. 5½d.]; scullery [23s. 9d.]; saucery [21s.]; hall [2s. 2½d.]; chamber [£15 19s. 11½d.]; stable [76s. 6d.]; wages [£6 5s. 9d.]; alms [nil]; TOTAL [£182 8s. 1d.]

- Saturday, 24 January: pantry [37s. 9½d.]; buttery [64s. 4¾d.]; wardrobe [43s. 4d.]; kitchen [£17 12s. 6½d.]; scullery [8s. 3½d.]; saucery [3s. 9¼d.]; hall [5s. 6d.]; chamber [nil]; stable [74s. 11½d.]; wages [112s. 1½d.]; alms [nil]; TOTAL [£35 2s. 9½d.]

These larger sums are some of the biggest recorded from this period (1342-5). Those comparable are: £317 4s. 5½d. spent at Dunstable on 12 February 1342 on the occasion of a tournament there (f. 23v.); the feast of the Assumption (15 August) 1342 [£231 14s. 8d.] (f. 28v.); at les Donnes on 13 October 1342 prior to passage to Brittany [£481 8s. 6¼d.] (f. 33r.); 12 May 1343 on the day Edward of Woodstock was made Prince of Wales, when the Prince ate with the king, the archbishops, bishops and other magnates [£118 15s. 8¾d.] (f. 48r.); Christmas Day 1343 [£117 12s.] (f. 64r.); 10 April 1344 at Alyndon' [£281 10s. 15½d.] (f. 71v.)

Generally speaking daily household expenditure fluctuates between £15 and £30 per day and rarely gets above £40 in the period covered by the account. January 1344 appears to be a time of significantly increased spending; the daily average in the fortnight after this week of excess is around £35-£45 and this persists until the first week of March.

APPENDIX D

Arthurian re-enactments

LE TOURNOI DE CHAUVENCY

Lodewijk van Velthem, VOORTZETTING VAN DEN SPIEGEL HISTORIAEL

The Entry of the Knight of the Lion

(*Reprinted from Nancy Freeman Regalado, 'Performing Romance: Arthurian Interludes in Sarrasin's* Le Roman du Hem, *(1278)' in* Performing Medieval Romance, *ed. Evelyn Birge Vitz, Nancy Freeman Regalado and Marilyn Lawrence, Woodbridge & Rochester, NY, 2005, 117-19*)

WHILE THE QUEEN was in the grandstand and watching the good, strong jousters, she saw coming from outside four maidens all alike. Their palfreys were trotting and they were so shapely I dare say that no man ever saw prettier. They were all dressed identically in summer clothing. They wore white chemises, finely pleated, which suited them well. They preceded the knight who delivered them from the castle and he gave each of them four great brooches and large clasps. The knight who brings them pauses outside the lists. He calls Miss Long-Suffering ('madamoiselle Sueffre-Paine') and she comes forward wearing (if I remember aright) a cape; her head was wrapped in a huge kerchief; she wore yellow and black and was very tall. My Lord gives her a letter sealed with a mirror, saying: 'You are to go without delay to the Queen, who is seated up there in the grandstand; you'll recognise her among her maidens. As soon as you get through the crowd, if Sir Kay catches sight of you, he'll escort you to the queen in order to make fun of you; but I warn you not to answer him back.' Long-Suffering sets off and comes straight to the Queen. And meanwhile, Sir Kay came up to the knight seated on his warhorse as he disarmed (for he had sustained great blows). Kay was the first to spot Long-Suffering. He went to meet her, saying: 'Welcome, maiden. Now tell me, are you she for whom so many knights have died? I swear that you'll not leave here without a lover, if you'll just listen to me, for your great beauty takes me by surprise.' The damsel sees that Kay is mocking her; and says nothing. She goes to the Queen and greets her courteously. The Queen arises, for she is good and full of honour. [Kay says] 'Lady, here is the good Orable[2] come to bring you a letter. Since she came to the gate, thrice someone has snatched her from me because of her beauty.' 'Be quiet, sir Kay', said the Queen, 'Everyone is concerned because you're so ill-mannered. But thorns must prick and sharp tongues speak. No-one can change your ways which are so long-standing. No one can teach an old dog new tricks.' The damsel immediately begs to deliver her message, saying 'Queen, have this letter read out, which I bring, for I must leave soon.' The Queen takes the letter in her hand and calls a chaplain who reads out every word for her. And as soon as the Queen hears that the Knight of the Lion begs as his reward to join her court, the Queen is so happy she is beside herself. 'Damsel, have your lord, whom God honours, come forward!' 'Lady , it is right that my lord remain in your court.' 'God be praised,' says the Queen, 'and may He keep him.' At this point, the maiden leaves, comes to her lord and tells him all. 'Sire, there are dukes and counts

---

[2] A Saracen married to a Christian hero in the epic poem *The Taking of Orange*, the city in southern France.

over there where you sent me; I was escorted by a knight to my lady the Queen; I don't know if he spoke out of hate, but he begged me for my love. The Queen, in all honour, stood up as soon as she saw me. When she heard the letter, Sire, which I brought to her, I was gratified to see how she rejoiced over your arrival. You and your company are to join her court, even if you were four thousand strong. I saw knights in four jousts, fierce and mighty, horses and broken shoulders, and gear lying about within the lists. The Queen has no desire greater than to see you.' The knight orders his lion to move forward, and his maidens go two by two, singing more beautifully than sirens. After the lion, who leads them, the maidens come to the court. Everyone rushes forward to greet them; there are trumpets and tabors; they pass through the entry of the lists in such fine order that nothing is lacking. The ladies in the grandstand see the Vassal with the Lion. They look only at him and at his lion and his maidens; the knight was armed with armor like wings. He enters the lists ready to joust; he lacks nothing. 'By the head of St John of Amiens', says Fortrece,[3] what a warrior! And, God save me, I never saw with my own eyes any man who looked more like my lord, the Count of Artois.'

---

[3] One of the queen's attendants.

Lodewijk van Velthem
Voortzetting van den Spiegel Historiael

translated by David Johnson and Geert Claassens

HOW KING EDWARD TOOK A WIFE, AND CONCERNING THE CELEBRATIONS THAT WERE HELD AT THAT TIME.

In the time that these things happened,
of which I now tell,
an extraordinary thing transpired
in the realm of marital affairs.   1075
For previous to this
Edward had sent messengers into Spain
to the king there, (asking)
whether he would give to him
his daughter in marriage.   1080
These men arrived, I tell you,
just after they had
captured the city, and brought news
that the King of Spain would gladly
give his daughter in marriage, as he wished.   1085
For this reason the question
of the prisoners was postponed,
such that it would not be deliberated upon,
but the king commanded at once
that they be securely guarded: 1090
"And if it should happen by anyone's fault
that any of them should escape,
I will mete out such immediate justice,
that those who witness it
would never again let a prisoner escape."   1095
And he also kept the city
and immediately established
by his own hand all the laws
that would govern that city
and preserve it from misfortune.   1100
Thus the king set out at once
to meet his bride, God knows,
who was being brought to him with haste.
Thus this wedding came to pass
about which many were pleased and happy.   1105
There were festivities of every kind.
Into London she was brought
where she was safest, by his thinking,
for he had been welcomed there first
before he had control   1110

Lodewijk van Velthem
Voortzetting van den Spiegel Historiael

edited by David Johnson and Geert Claassens

HOE DIE CONINC EDEWARD EEN WIJF NAM, ENDE VANDER FEESTE DIE MEN DAER DREEF.

In desen tide dat dit gesciede
Daer ic nu af hier bediede,
So was i. sake sonderlinge
Alse van huwelike dinge.   1075
Want hier vore had gesant
Edeward in Spaengenlant
Ane den coninc deser gelike:
Of hi hem in huwelike
Siere dochter geven wille nu.   1080
Dese liede quamen, seegic u,
Recht doemen dese stat
Gewonnen hadden, ende brachten, dat
Die coninc van Spaengen gerne soude
Siere dochter geven, op dat hi woude.   1085
Om dit so was geverst al daer
Van dien gevangenen over waer,
Datmer niet en over rechte,
Mar die coninc beval bedichte
Datmense vaste hoeden soude: 1090
"Ende ward oec dat bi yemens scoude
Enich van hem ontginge daer,
Ic soude den genen rechten so naer,
Dat diet sagen meer vord an
Hem lieten ontgaen gevangen man."   1095
Die stat heeft hi oec beward,
Ende daer in geset mede ter vard
Met siere hant alle gerechte
Die die stat selen berechten,
Ende hueden vort van mesvalle.   1100
Dus trac die coninc vandaer met alle
Jegen sine bruut, godweet,
Diemen hem brinct jegen gereet.
Dus quam dese huwelijc toe,
Daer menich om blide was ende vroe.   1105
Feeste was daer in allen sinne.
Te Lonnen was si vort binnen
Daer was si sekerst, na sijn verstaen,
Want hi was daer eerst ontfaen,
Doen hi ongeweldich was   1110

of his lands, as I have recounted earlier.
Dancing, roundels, singing, leaping –
there is no one who could describe
the celebrations of the citizenry.
The man who wrote of this in Latin   1115
described so many of these things,
that it is unbelievable to recount;
for so great was the merriment
that was enjoyed by those citizens.
If I were to tell you about it,   1120
you would not believe it, without a doubt.
All day long, for eight days,
one might hear the greatest din
of trompets, fiddles and drums,
zithers, harps; in every household   1125
in the city there was extraordinary music.
How could anyone do justice
to describing all of this,
the celebrations those citizens held,
amongst themselves? Not easily.   1130
I shall leave off telling of this
and write now about the king,
about matters that were fitting to be done.
The Kings feast was organised thus:
There anyone who wished might   1135
go in and out, without being invited;
and games, dancing, drinking, eating –
none of these were denied anyone there.
In the course of the feast there was prepared
a Round Table of knights and squires,   1140
such that whoever wished might there take
up weapons and joust with them.
According to custom there was enacted
a play of Arthur the King,
and things were arranged accordingly,   1145
and the best (men) chosen without delay
and there named (without doubt)
after the lords who, in the olden days,
had once belonged to the Round Table.
The king had also previously ordered that   1150
squires were to announce
the news from every land
concerning battles and wars of all kinds;
and how they were to urge each one
of these knights, who were all   1155
outstanding according to their own valour,

Dansen, reyen, singen, springen,
Sijns lants, alsict hier voren las.
Hets niemen diet mochte vort bringen,
Die feeste die de stede dreef.
Die gene diet dlatijn bescreef,   1115
Seide so vele van deser saken,
Dat ongelovelijc waer in spraken;
Want so grote behagelhede
Alse men daer dede in die stede,
Dadict u also verstaen,   1120
Gine gelovets niet, sonder waen.
Alle dage, al .viij. dage uut,
Was in die stat dmeeste geluut
Van trompen, vedelen ende tambusen,
Sitolen, harpen; in allen husen   1125
Van der stat was sonderlinge spel.
Hoe soudemen dit toe bringen wel
Datment al mocht gescriven,
Die feeste die si onderlinc driven,
Die vanderstat? Ens lichtelijc niet.   1130
Ic late bliven alsoet gesciet,
Ende scrive vanden coninc vord
Van dingen die te hem behord.
Des coninc feeste was dus gedaen:
Daer mochte uut ende in gaen   1135
Wie dat wille, ende ongeheten;
Ende spelen, dansen, drinken, eten,
Dit was niemen daer wederseit.
Binnen der feeste ward daer geleit
Ene tafelronde van ridderen ende cnapen,   1140
Dat wie so wille, mochter wapen
Dragen ende joesteren mede.
Daer was gemaect na den sede
Een spel van Artur den coninc,
Ende geordineert also die dinc,   1145
Ende ut gescoren die beste saen,
Ende genoemt daer sonder waen
Na die heren van ouden stonden
Diemen hiet vander tavelronden.
Oec had die coninc geheten te voren   1150
Cnapen, die daer souden doen heren
Neuwe boetscape ute alle lande
Van stride, van orloge alte hande;
Ende hoemen vermane van desen
Elken ridder, die ut gelesen   1155
Ware na siere werdichede,

that he set out to protect this city,
that castle, or that land,
of which the page delivered his message.
The king had deliberately   1160
decreed, firmly and resolutely,
that each man would play his part,
after having been assigned his role;
and swear then and there
to follow King Arthur's example   1165
in that game and Table Round.
But they did not know at that time,
nor did they suspect,
that the king had commanded his squires
to bring into the game   1170
the opposition from all the cities   [lit. 'strife']
that would hinder or hurt them,
and that they, because of this opposition,
that they must swear thus,   1175
or they would with great shame
be utterly condemned there
by their companions. Thus
was it decreed, in all truth.

How the Round Table began, and concerning the lords of the Round Table.
XVI.

The king led the way,   1180
and those who belonged to the Round Table
set out in force,
and all of these lords came into the field.
When that play began
as described here above   1185
each man chose his part:
their virtue shall now become apparent.
There was Lancelot and Gawain
and Perceval and Agravain,
and Bors and Gareth,   1190
and Lionel and Mordred,
and a Kay, too, was created there.
These and more (why deny it?)
who had been chosen for it,
were the highest born   1195
and the greatest in the realm.
It was on an early morning
When it was set in motion,
just as the day dawned

Dat hi bescudden vare die stede,
Oft dien casteel, ofte dat lant,
Daer hem die bode af dade becant.
Dit hadde die coninc met vorrade 1160
Gemaect, so vast ende so gestade,
Dat elc sijn recht houden sal
Na datmen daer ordinieren sal;
Ende swoerent daer, opter stede,
Te houden na coninc Artur sede 1165
Dat spel ende die tavelronde.
Mar sine wisten niet ter stonde,
Noch en hoeden hem oec niet
Van dat die coninc sinen cnapen hiet,
Datmen int spel soude vortbringen 1170
Van allen steden die werringen
Die hem letten ende die hem deren;
Ende dat si om dit verweren
Selen sijn gemaent daer toe
Dat sijt daer moeten geloven alsoe, 1175
Oft si selen met scanden groet
Ontwijst sijn daer albloet
Van haren gesellen. Dus waest daer
Geordineert daer al vor waer.

HOE DIE TAVELRONDE BEGAN, ENDE VANDEN HEREN VANDER TAVELRONDE. XVI.

Die coninc es ut vercoren voren, 1180
Ende die ter tavelronde behoren
Trocken uut al met gewelde,
Ende alle dese heren quamen te velde.
Doe daer dat spel was op geleit,
Alse hier vore es af geseit, 1185
So vercoes daer elc den sinen:
Haer vromicheit sal daer nu scinen.
Daer was Lanceloet ende Walewein,
Ende Perchevael ende Eggrawein,
Ende Bohort ende Gariet, 1190
Ende Lyoneel ende Mordret,
Ende .i. Keye was daer gemaect.
Dese ende andere (wat holpt ontsaect ?)
Die hier toe waren gecoren,
Waren verre best geboren 1195
Ende die meeste vanden rike.
Dit was .i. margens tidelike
Dat dit was begonnen;
Recht int opgaen vander sonnen

the Round Table began there. 1200
The weather was fair and bright,
and there were ladies and damsels in attendance
who would witness the play.
It had also been proclaimed throughout all of England
that whosoever wished to come to that plain 1205
to the wedding and to the play,
might truly do so,
without wrath or resentment.
No matter what had transpired
before, that would be set aside 1210
until the feast was over.
On account of this, many a man
traveled there to witness the great play;
it is a marvel to realize how many
and which people made the journey there. 1215
Now, then, it has come to pass
that every man there has taken
spear in hand and ridden there,
bravely to joust for all to see.
The lords of the Table Round 1220
stood up for each other,
if misfortune should befall one of them,
of this you may be sure;
the others would avenge him immediately.
In this way they defeated there 1225
many a man in a short time.
Key was slightly wounded there,
and that was done on purpose;
for no fewer than twenty
young turks had decided amongst themselves 1230
that they would harm Keye
and shame him, and all in jest,
so that many would say
as of old and mockingly:
'Herein lies proof of Keye's fame!' 1235
This plan was taken so far
that it nearly cost Keye dearly:
for before he let himself be taken,
because as Keye he had been commanded to do so,
he was beaten so severely it was a wonder to behold; 1240
and moreover his saddle-girths
had been sliced through, and cut loose from his saddle.
Thereupon he was without delay
thrust from his saddle (with such force)
that he thought his neck was broken. 1245
This caused a great outcry

Began die tavelronde aldaer.   1200
Het was scone weder ende claer,
Ende daer waren vrouwen ende joncfrouwen
Die dat spel souden ane scouwen.
Daer was oec geboden in al Ingelant :
Die daer comen wilde opt sant   1205
Te brulocht ende tesen spele,
Dat hire comen mochte wele,
Sonder toren ende verdriet.
Al ware enige dinc gesciet
Hier vormaels, dat soudemen laten staen   1210
Tote dat die feeste waer gedaen.
Om dit so quam daer menich man
Dat grote spel te siene an;
Hets .i. wonder te verstane
Wat daer volcs was comen ane.   1215
Nu sijn die dinge toe comen
So, dat elc daer heeft genomen
Spere in hant, ende reden daer
Starke joeste openbaer.
Die heren vander tavelronden   1220
Hilden hem te dien stonden
Te gader, dat verstaet nu wel;
Al waest dat den enen mesvel,
Die andre wraect daer optie stat.
Om dit maecten si daer mat   1225
Menigen man in corter stont.
Key ward daer .i. luttel gewont,
Ende dat ward daer al willens gedaen;
Want wel si xx. sonder waen
Jonger liede hadden hem beraden,   1230
Dat si Keyen souden scaden
Ende scande doen, ende al te spele,
Om datmer secgen soude vele
Van outs ende borde maken:
'Hier scinen noch wel Keys saken!'   1235
Dit ward ginder soe toe brocht
Dat Keye wel na had becocht:
Want eer hi hem verwinnen liet
Om datmer Keye daer hiet,
Ward hem geslegen .i. wondekijn;   1240
Ende hem waren oec die daremgarden sijn
Ontwee gesneden, ende van sinen gereiden.
Doen ward hi daer al sonder beiden
Van sinen orsse so gesteken,
Dat hem dochte die hals breken.   1245
Om dit ward ginder gerochte groet

and the call went up: 'Sir Keye is in dire straits,
He lies and tumbles in the sand!
It seems to me that the great deeds
he performs are here demonstrated for all to see.'   1250
This was oft repeated there;
this caused a great deal of merriment,
and all the great lords laughed the most,
once they realised that
he had not been severely wounded.   1255
The king and the queen
were very pleased
that it had turned out thus.
The king sent word to them all
that enough was enough. 'Let us ride   1260
to court and eat. This splendid play
has turned out in true Arthurian fashion,
now let us continue in the
same way as he (= Arthur) was wont to do.
Let each man play his part as he is able!'   1265
Thus all present vowed publicly
that they would do so.

CONCERNING THE FOOD, AND ABOUT THOSE WHO BROUGHT MESSAGES THERE.

And so those lords rode to court,
where no expense would be spared
for the food and drink.   1270
The king sat down to a table,
and at the same time he had
the lords of the round table
seated with him in chairs
just as King Arthur had done   1275
when he held a feast, as we
have often read. In similar fashion,
then, Edward now ordered
these knights to take their seats.
Many were those who followed them there   1280
in order to behold the festivities,
and all who wished were allowed
to eat and drink their fill then and there;
But there were many who did not eat a thing
in order to better take in the festivities.   1285
And so, once the knights had been seated
and the food had been brought in
and the first course finished,
the king ordered one of the squires to
rap on a window with a rod   1290

Met roepen daer: 'her Keye heeft noet,
Hi leit ende tumelt op dat sant!
Mi donct, hier ward wel becant
Van sinen daden die hi pleget.'   1250
Dit ward ginder dicke geseget;
Daer was om gedreven feeste,
Daer logen omme al die meeste:
Doen si geware worden das
Dat hi niet sere gequets en was.   1255
Die coninc ende die coningine
Warens blide in haren sinne
Dat dit also was gevallen.
Die coninc geboet doer hem allen,
Dat genoech waer. 'Laet ons eten   1260
Varen te hove. Dit spel vermeten
Es recht na Arturs wise comen,
Nu laet ons dit vort begomen
Dies gelike dat hi plach.
Ele doet tsine oft hi mach!'   1265
Dus geloefdense noch alle daer
Dit te volbringen openbaer.

VAN DEN ETENE, ENDE VANDEN GENEN DIE DAER BOETSCAP BRINGEN.

Dus sijn die heren te hove gevaren,
Daer men genen cost sal sparen
Van datmen drinken mach ende eten.   1270
Die coninc es tere tafel geseten,
Entie heren vander tavelronden
Dede die coninc ter selver stonden
In sittene sitten oec daer mede,
Gelijc dat coninc Artur dede   1275
Alse hi feeste hilt, dat wi gelesen
Dicke hebben. Gelijc oec desen,
So dede Edeward nu, godweet.
Die ridders sitten daer gereet.
Menich minsce volgede daer naer   1280
Om die feeste te siene daer,
Ende al die wilden, mochten mede
Eten ende drinken daer ter stede;
Mar daer was menich die niet en at,
Om die feeste te siene bat.   1285
Dus als die ridder waren geseten
Ende men vort brachte teten,
Ende teerste gerechte was gedaen,
Dede die coninc ane enen venster slaen
Met ere roede i. der cnapen,   1290

in order to call for silence.
All those present fell still.
Thereupon the king spoke:
'By my crown I swear this pledge
that before another course is served here   1295
I must hear some tidings!'
 'May God grant us that pleasure!'
said the lords who were seated there.
Not long thereafter an extraordinary squire
entered at great speed,   1300
and he was spattered in fresh blood,
and he rode right up to the table
and first addressed the king directly:
'Craven and cowardly king,
and those who sit here with you, how   1305
reluctantly would they ride where men engage in battle!
I see clearly, oh king, at this time
that they sit there like craven cowards.
Behold how this one sits here and tarries
hesitantly with his hat!   1310
I daresay he would be reluctant
to fight a battle against two others.
Lord king, all of you are gathered here
at your feast, and your lands
are better known to the Welsh   1315
than you realize. To what good end
do you deserve the name of king?
I must tell you now at once:
Behold, how I am wounded
and bleed for your sake.   1320
And if you do not avenge this,
I tell you that you are no king.
And those who now sit here
and eat and drink by your side ,
may God ruin them all   1325
if they do not help me take revenge
upon the Welsh!' In answer to this speech
the king replied, 'Messenger, God knows,
you have been wronged, and that pains me,
and by my crown I swear to you   1330
that I shall avenge that in such a way
that no man will dare do so again,
or I myself will die in the attempt!'
Thereupon the others at the Round Table
spoke up together, in one voice: 1335
'Lord king, we will ride with you
with all our power, and help you;

Om .i. gestille daer doen maken.
Doe sweech al dat ginder was.
Die coninc sprac doen na das:
'Bi mire cronen sweric dit word
Eer hier heden gerecht comt vord,   1295
So moetic niemare hebben vernomen!'
–'God geve datse ons moete vromen!'
Spraken die heren die daer saten.
Niet lange daer na quam utermaten
Sere gereden .i. wonderlijc cnecht,   1300
Ende met bloede bespringet echt
Al versch, ende reet, ter taflen alsoe,
Ende sprac den coninc irstwerf toe:
'Versaect coninc ende oec blode,
Ende die hier sitten bi u, hoe node   1305
Souden si comen daer men soude striden!
Ic sie wel, coninc, nu ten tiden
Dat si sitten al versaect.
Siet, hoe die gene sit ende traect
Onverwect met sinen hode!   1310
Ic wane hi vechten soude wel node
Enen camp teghen hem tween.
Her coninc, gi sijt hier al in een
Met uwer feest, ende u lant
Es den Waloysen bat becant   1315
Dant u es cont. Waer toe eest goet
Dat gi coninc heten doet ?
Ic moet u secgen nu ter stont:
Siet, hoe ic ben gewont
Ende bebloet om uwe sake.   1320
En doedi hier af gene wrake,
Ic secge, dat gi geen coninc sijt.
Ende die hier saten nu ter tijt
Bi uwer siden eten ende drinken,
God hi moetse alle scrinken,   1325
Of si mi niet helpen wreken
Over die Waloyse!' Na dit spreken
Antworde die coninc : 'bode, godweet,
Datti mesdaen es, dats mi leet,
Ende bi mire crone besweric di toe,   1330
Dat ic dat sal wreken soe,
Dat mens nemmermere sal gewagen,
Oft ic bliver selve verslagen!'
Doen spraken die vander tavelronden
Alle gader ute enen monde: 1335
'Her coninc, wi willen mede varen
Met al onser macht, ende hulpent waren;

And anyone here who fails in this,
we would want to have his eyes put out.'
Thus did the king receive there a pledge   1340
from those who had frequently
abandoned him before;
The king has now caught them in a trap,
and he will tighten the noose
before the meal is done.   1345

CONCERNING MORE OF THE SAME. XVIIJ.

When these words had been spoken,
the next courses were were brought in
with great joy, for in truth
few there paid much heed to that
message; rather service was rendered there   1350
such as one gives to a friend.
When the third course had been served,
the king once again rapped
on the wall with a rod,
and spoke immediately thereafter,   1355
'I should eagerly wish to hear some news,
if anyone would offer some
before we continue with our meal.'
The knights who sat there
all expressed their praise fo him on the spot.   1360
Not long thereafter a squire all of a sudden
came riding in on a sumpter,
and his hands and feet were bound,
the bridle wrapped around his arm.
The man lamented loudly   1365
and entered thus the hall
and stood before the table, where all
the lords of the round table are seated.
'Deus! How eagerly would I learn,'
said the squire, 'what barons these are   1370
who sit here in this crowd
and deliberate on such things ...'
He addressed the king first
and then continued his harangue at Lancelot,
'Yes!' said he, 'since these companions ...   1375
Thus I wish to protest my suffering
to Lancelot, and else to no man.
He will avenge me, I am sure of it!

Ende die u hier toe oec gebrect,
Wi willen, datmen hem dogen uut stect.'
Dus had die coninc daer .i. belof   1340
Vanden genen, die hem of
Daer vore dicke waren gegaen;
Die coninc heefse nu bevaen
Ende noch sal bestricken meer.
Eer die maeltijt doet sinen keer.   1345

VANDEN SELVEN MEER. XVIIJ.

Doen gesproken waren dese word.
Brachtmen dander gerechte vord
Met groter feeste, want over waer
Om dese boetscap was lettel daer
Gesorget ; mar daer was gedient   1350
Gelijc dat .i. man doet sinen vrient.
Doen terde rechte ward gedregen,
Heeft die coninc echt geslegen
Met ere roede an die want,
Ende sprac daer na alte hant   1355
'Noch soude gerne niemare horen,
Wilse ons yeman bringen voren
Eer wi mer vorward aten.'
Gene ridders, die ginder saten,
Loefdent alle daer ter steden.   1360
Niet lange daer na so quam gereden
Enen knape op enen somer ter stonden,
Dien hande ende voete waren gebonden,
Ende den breidel in sinen arm.
Dese maecte groet gecarm   1365
Ende quam aldus in dien zale
Vore die tafle, daer altemale
Die vander tavelronden sijn geseten.
'Deus ! hoe gerne soudic weten,'
Sprac die gene, 'wat heren dit waren.   1370
Die hier sitten in deser scaren
Ende berechten een der dinc ...'[4]
Ende beg011an daer opten coninc
Ende seide vort tote Lancelote
'Ja!' seit hi, 'sint dat dese genote ...'[3]   1375
So willic Lancelote clagen dan
Mijn verdriet, ende els geen man.
Hi sal mi wreken, wetic wale!

---

[4] The manuscript is here presumably corrupt; there is a clear gap in the text, rendering a break in the translation unavoidable.

I would never bring my complaint to the king,
for he is incapable of seeking justice for himself.   1380
Why would he fight on my behalf?'
Then that man addressed Lanceloet:
'Lanceloet du Lac, noble man!
I greet you as one of the best (knights)
the sun has ever shone upon;   1385
and also before all of those present here
my heart of hearts greets you.
Lanceloet, milord, understand these words,
you must step forward yourself
and free me from my bonds.   1390
Of all my lord king's companions,
no one has the power
to do this except you alone;
in your hands rests my salvation!'
Lanceloet stood up at once,   1395
and released him from his bonds.
When he had been freed, he next
gave Lanceloet in all haste
a letter, in which was written:
'He who has freed this squire   1400
is summoned at once by
the king of Ireland, and accused
of being a false knight, of that you may be sure,
and a traitor, and an evil (knight).
And if he dares avenge the offense   1405
that was done to the one he has freed,
and should he journey to the border of England,
where it meets the border of Wales,
he will then find there the undaunted
king of Ireland, with his companions on the plain,   1410
waiting for the one who freed this man.
Whoever he might be under the sun,
no matter his lineage, no matter his kin,
however wise, however strong, however powerful he be,
he will find me there, of this you may be sure.'   1415
When this letter had been read,
it made Lanceloet fearful
and weak. Then spoke Walewein:
'Lanceloet, we will ride onto the field
with you to oppose the enemies.   1420
And the king will help us with
his army, on this expedition.'
The king spoke: 'Do not fear,
there is no one here who will fail you!
I shall help avenge   1425

Nu maecs den coninc nember tale,
Want hine can hem selven berechten.   1380
Wat soudi dan over mi vechten?'
Doen sprac die gene Lanceloet an:
'Lanceloet van Lac, edel man!
Ic groete u vorden besten een
Die sonne nie besceen;   1385
Ende oec vor alle die hier sijn
So groet u die herte mijn.
Lanceloet, here, verstaet dit word,
Ghi moet hier selve comen vord
Ende mi van dere noet ontbinden.   1390
Van al mijns heren coninc gesinden
Sone heeft niement macht gemene
Dit te doene, dan gi allene;
An u staet mijn toeverlaet!'
Mettien Lanceloet op staet,   1395
Ende ontbant den genen daer.
Als hi ontbonden was, daer naer
Gaf hi Lanceloet metter spoet
Ene lettere, daer in gescreven stoet:
'Die desen cnape heeft ontbonden,   1400
Hem ontbiet ten selven stonden
Die coninc van Irlant, dat hi es
Een valsch ridder, des sijt gewes,
Ende .i. verrader, ende een quaet.
Ende dar hi oec wreken dese daet   1405
Die dien gedaen es, dien hi ontbant;
Ende comme optie zide van Ingelant,
Optie side te Gales ward,
Daer vint hi den coninc onvervard
Van Irlant, met sinen lieden opt lant,   1410
Tontbeidene tgeens diene ontbant.
Wie hi oec es onder die sonne,
Van wat geslachte, van wat connen,
Hoe vrome, hoe starc, hoe rike hi es,
Hi vint mi daer, sijt seker es.'   1415
Doen dese letter was gelesen,
Ward Lanceloet hier af in vresen
Ende versaect. Doe sprac Walewein:
'Lanceloet, wi selen comen int plein
Met u, te wederstane dese dinc.   1420
Ons sel oec helpen die coninc
Met siere macht, te deser vard.'
Die coninc sprac: 'Sijt onvervard,
Dat ic hier yemen sal gebreken!
Ic sal elken hulpen wreken   1425

every man's woe and misfortune.
Just as Arthur himself rode through every land
on behalf of the knights of the round table,
in the same way I shall now
set out with every knight.   1430
Of all the feats of arms they will perform
fearlessly in this play,
I wish to be a witness.
I also desire that you pledge the same
to me, and do so as noble knights.'   1435
All those present there pledged to do so.
Then the king spoke to the messenger at once,
'Friend, whensoever Lanceloet learns
that the king of Ireland has arrived
in that place of which you have spoken,   1440
Lanceloet will come to avenge you.'
The messenger thanked him sincerely for this.
We leave this for what it is,
and turn instead to describe the feast
about which you have not heard enough.   1445

CONCERNING THE THIRD MESSENGER, WHO WAS EQUIPPED WONDROUSLY. XIX.

Now there was great joy
amongst the entire company.
All courses were served
as is fitting at a feast.
Two courses had been served there: 1450
One before, and one after.
When the king wished to speak,
He called out loudly, 'Quiet, everyone!
I wish to hear some tidings
before another course is served.'   1455
All who sat there praised him for this.
Not long after this was said, there
entered an ugly creature.
She did not have the appearance of a
woman, for the nose on her   1460
was a foot long, if an inch,
and more than a hand's width wide;
The ears on her were, God knows,
like the ears of an ass;
she wore her hair in braids both in front and behind,   1465
such that they hung to her waist;
they were so coarse, as they hung there,
like horsehair, or even rougher;
she had a goiter under her chin

Sinen ween ende sinen scande.
Gelijc dat Artur in allen lande
Voer om die vander tavelronde,
Al dier gelijc willic ter stonde
Met elken ridder oec nu varen.   1430
Van allen sticken die si selen baren
In dit spel, al sonder vresen,
Daer willic een geselle af wesen.
Oec willic dat gi dat oec mi
Geloeft, ende doet alse ridderen vri.'   1435
Dit geloefdense alle daer.
Doe sprac die coninc ten bode daer naer
'Vrient, welc tijt dat Lanceloet heeft vernomen
Dat die coninc van Irlant es comen
Ter stat, daer du af seges teken,   1440
Lanceloet sal di comen wreken.'
Die bode bedanctem sere van desen.
Dit late wi nu aldus wesen,
Ende scriven vander feesten vord
Die gi genoech niet hebt gehord.   1445

Vanden derden bode, die wonderlije gemaect was. xix.

Nu was ginder bliscap groet
Onder alle die genoet.
Men brachte die gerechten vord
Also alse ter feesten hord.
Twee gerechten brachtmen daer.   1450
Dene vore ende dander naer.
Eer die coninc spreken wille.
Doe riep hi sere: 'Hout al stille!
Ic wil eer niemare hebben gehort
Eermen enich gerechte brinct vort.'   1455
Si loefdent alle die saten daer.
Niet lanc was dit geseit, daer naer
En quam ene lelike creature.
Die nie was na wives figure
Gemaect, want die nese van hare   1460
Was eens voets lanc openbare
Ende meer dan ere palme breet;
Die horen waren haer, godweet,
Gelijc vanden esel die oren;
Vlechten hadsi achter ende voren.   1465
So datsi toten gordele gingen;
Si scenen so grof, daer si hingen,
Als peerts vlechten of grover vele;
Enen crop hadse onder die kele,

as big as a goose's egg;   1470
her neck was long and bright red;
her mouth was wide, and misformed:
on one side her jaw
stretched to her ears,
 it went up, I do not know how,   1475
and stood awry, opening wide and upwards.
Some of the teeth one saw there
were black, and others white,
and long as a finger, and crooked, to boot,
two large teeth jutted out on front.   1480
She came riding on a small
red horse, that was thin
and severely limping, too, of this you may be sure,
both in front and from behind.
This damsel quickly rode   1485
right up to the table,
where she was stared at in wonder;
for not one of them had ever
seen a stranger creature.
The damsel did not at all resemble   1490
the one we read about in Perchevael,
so strangely was she shaped.
Now hear what she undertook
to say to that company.
'Do you know,' she said, 'whom I greet   1495
before all those who are in this hall?
Sir Perceval it is.
I greet him before all of you!'
I know all things that have transpired,
and all of your thoughts, without a doubt,   1500
I could here and now reveal to you;
and the name of each of you
according to the prideful Table Round:
Lanceloet, Perchevael, Walewein,
Mordret, Keye and Ecgrawein,   1505
and Gariet, and all the rest
who sit here in this place;
all of this is known to me at this time.
Hear now my adventure,
that I bring to all of you   1510
who belong to the Round Table.
I address Perchevael first and foremost,
and make known to him now
that he must quickly ride to Licester.
There may he receive honour and glory   1515
before the castle, I shall tell you why;

Alse een gansey es groet;   1470
Den hals lanc, ende harde roet;
Den mont wijt, ende ongescepen
In dene side haddi begrepen
Die kinnebacken toten oren toe;
Hi ginc op, in weet hoe,   1475
Ende stont slem, opward wide ontdaen.
Die tande diemen daer in sach staen,
Waren som sward ende som wit,
Ende vinger lanc, dat qualijc sit
Rageden haer uut ij. tande groet.   1480
Op .i. pardekijn dat was roet
Quam si gereden, dat mager was,
Ende dat house oec, sijt seker das,
Achter ende vore harde sere.
Dese joncfrouwe met enen corten kere   1485
Es comen vordie tafel gereden,
Daer mense an sach te selsenheden;
Want wonderliker vorme vort an
Sone hadde gesien geen man.
Die joncfrouwe diemen in Perchevael vint   1490
En geleec derre niet .i. twint,
Soe selsen so was dese gescepen.
Nu hort watse heeft begrepen
Te secgene onder die genote.
'Wetti,' seitsi, 'wien ic groette   1495
Vor alle die sijn in dien zale?
Dat es den here Perchevale.
Hem so groetic vor u allen!
lc weet alle dinge die gevallen,
Ende alle u meninge, sonder waen,   1500
Soudic u hier wel doen verstaen;
Ende wie dat elc es geheten
Nader tavelronde vermeten:
Lanceloet, Perchevael, Walewein,
Mordret, Keye ende Ecgrawein,   1505
Ende Gariet, ende dander mede
Die hier sitten in die stede;
Dits mi al cont op dese ure.
Nu hort hier vort mine aventure,
Die ic u allen bringe te voren   1510
Die ter tavelronde behoren.
Perchevale sprekic irst ane,
Ende doe hem hier nu te verstane,
Dat hi te Licester vare saen.
Daer mach hi prijs ende lof ontfaen   1515
Vor den casteel, ic secge twi;

for its lord wishes to attack
his neighbors, and assault them.
If there is any way for you to
win honour, it is there.   1520
And if you should hesitate in this,
I will disgrace you in every court
that I visit, and deprive you of honour.
Walewein, I greet you as well,
and say to you that there is strife   1525
in Cornuaelge, which you must quell,
between the commons and the barons,
on account of the men imprisoned there
who have committed crimes against the king.
For the barons are intent upon freeing them,   1530
but the commons resist;
and you should know that King Richard
has sent for the prisoners.
Sir Walewein, set out now at once,
and help the commons defend themselves!   1535
If you do not do this, I say to you in truth
that you will not dare show yourself
for your cowardice, know this well.'
Walewein then stood up,
and said, 'By my faith, this I shall do,   1540
or may my shield fail me
and my good sword, God knows!'
Perchevael also stood up at once
and said that he would win Licestre
from those inside the city   1545
or he would die trying.
Then all those seated in that hall
heard a great noise and a great din;
they all rose to their feet
on account of the marvel they saw there.   1550
The damsel then made her way out of
the hall, this you should know,
under cover of this noise,
and thus slipped away from there
without anyone noticing, in truth.   1555

CONCERNING THE DAMSEL, AND HOW THE COURT ADJOURNED. XX.

Once the damsel had left the hall,
she knew the way very well.
She soon slipped away,
And removed her garments
with which she was disguised.   1560

Want hi wilt dingen die hem bi
Sijn geseten, ende asselgieren.
Seldi in eniger manieren
Prijs bejagen, dat sal daer wesen. 1520
Ende trecti achter oec van desen,
Ic sal u lachteren, in allen hove
Waric comen, van uwen love.
Walewein, ic groete u mede,
Ende seg u, dat te Cornuaelge in die stede 1525
Ompays es, dat moetti keren,
Tusscen die gemeente entie heren,
Om die liede dier liggen gevaen
Die den coninc hebben mesdaen.
Want uut dadense die heren gerne, 1530
Entie gemeente staet te werne;
Ende Ridsard die coninc heeft daer gesint
Om die gevangen, si u bekint.
Her Walewein nu vart daer saen,
Ende helpt der gemeente dit wederstaen! 1535
En doedijs niet, so secgic twaren
Dat gire niet en dorret voren
Van bloetheiden, dat si u cont.'
Walewein die doe op stont,
Ende seide: 'Bi trouwen, dit salic wreken, 1540
Oft mi sal mijn scilt gebreken
Ende mijn goede sward, godweet!'
Perchevael stont op oec gereet
Ende seide, Licestre soudi winnen
Optie gene vandaer binnen, 1545
Oft hi souder sterven voren.
Doe mochtmen in dien sale horen
Groet geruchte ende groet geclanc;
Het stont al op eer yet lanc
Om dit wonder dat daer was. 1550
Die joncfrouwe maecte haer na das
Uter zale, datsi u cont,
Diewile dat geruecht stont,
Ende es hem dus van daer ontgaen,
Dat niemen en weet, sonder waen. 1555

VANDER JONCFROUWE NOCH, ENDE HOE DAT HOF SCIET. XX.

Alse dese joncfrouwe was uter zale,
Const si daer die pade wale.
Si was ontslopen saen,
Ende heeft die paruren af gedaen
Daer si mede ontlicsent was. 1560

This damsel was, as I read it,
one of the king's squires:
for the king had had this livery
and this mask and wig
secretly made, you may be sure,   1565
so he looked like a damsel.
And all these words together
that these messengers delivered,
they had heard from the king
and memorised very carefully.   1570
When the commotion in the hall
had died down, people began to wonder
where the loathly damsel had gone.
Many rushed about in search of her,
but she had escaped them all.   1575
This caused quite a stir;
and frankly there were some who claimed this:
that she had been an evil spirit.
The king, who knew better,
disabused them all of this, and said: 1580
'I tell you this, lords, in all truth:
this adventure that you saw transpire here
was a part of our celebration.
This I know for sure, and am well informed:
if we wished to be deserving of the glory   1585
of the Knights of the Round Table,
sufficient messages, as of yet undelivered,
would reach us in due time.
If we wished to avenge every wrong
and this would be known throughout the land,   1590
more than enough wonderous
marvels would come of it, '
All present then said, 'Hear, hear!'
Thus the king persuaded them
then and there, without their realizing it,   1595
to help him in all matters
that plagued him in his realm,
and some against their own kinsmen.
The king was not at all slow to
confirm this advantage, believe me.   1600
'You lords,' he said, 'give me counsel.'
'You know full well that I have promised
to march quickly against Wales;
assist me now in this endeavor,
if you wish me to help you in turn.   1605
If you help me well, I tell you,
I will never abandon you under any circumstances!

Dese joncfrouwe, daer ic af las,
Was .i. van des coninc cnapen
Entie coninc had dese wapen,
Ende dit ansicht, ende dit hoeft
Heymelike doen maken, des geloeft,   1565
So dat na een joncfrouwe sceen.
Ende alle dese worde overeen
Die dese boden brochten vort,
Haddensi vanden coninc gehort,
Ende gevest oec harde wale.   1570
Doent geruechte inden zale
Leden was, vraechdemen daer nare
Waer die lelike joncfrouwe ware.
Daer liep so menich soeken gaen,
Mar si was hem allen ontgaen.   1575
Om dit ward noch geruchte groet;
Men wilde daer seggen nu albloet:
Dattie quade geest had gewesen.
Die coninc, die wel wiste van desen,
Ontgaeft hem allen, ende seide daer: 1580
'Ic secgu, heren, dit over waer:
Dese aventure, die gi saecht hier,
Die quam bi onser feesten fier.
Dat wetic wel, ende bens wijs:
Wilde wi noch staen inden prijs   1585
Der heren vander tavelronden,
Ons soude comen te enigen stonden
Boetscap die nu blivet achter.
Wilde wi wreken elkes lachter,
Ende men dat gevreist int lant,   1590
Ons soude comen genoech te hant
Selsenheide van dien, van desen.'
Doe seidense alle 'Het mach wel wesen!'
Dus brachtem daer die coninc toe
Datsi moesten, sine weten hoe,   1595
Hem hulpe doen van allen saken
Die hem in sijn lant gebraken,
Ende som oec jegen haers selfs mage.
Die coninc ne was hier toe niet trage
Dit te vervorderne, dat verstaet.   1600
 'Gi heren,' seiti, 'geeft mi raet.'
'Gi wet wel, ic heb geloeft diere
Jegen Gales te vechten sciere;
Help mi dier gelike hier nu,
Alse gi wilt dat ic helpe u.   1605
Hulpti mi wel, ic segt u bloet,
In ga u of in gere noet !

As surety for all you have pledged,
I will offer my head,
if you will be loyal to me.'   1610
They answered him, 'Set a time limit
for us for all these things to which
you and we have pledged.
We will be ready at that time
to fulfill with you our vows   1615
with all our might, know this well;
and whoever amongst us reneges on this pledge
shall be regarded by all as our enemy.'
To this they made their vow at once,
and they gave their pledge   1620
according to their Christian law.
That they would all be his companions
from that hour hence,
they once again gave their word.
Thereupon the appointed day was set   1625
at a fortnight hence
to be at Cornuaelge, at the gates of the city,
and from there onward to Wales,
and next to campaign against Ireland:
And that they would come equiped,   1630
and, if they were able, prepared well,
before they returned.
To this all those barons gave their word.
Thus this court was adjourned.
Each of them set out homeward, (in order) to provide himself   1635
with everything that he was lacking.
Now listen for a while to something else …

Van al dat gi hebt geloeft,
Daer willic vore setten mijn hoeft,
In dien dat gi getrouwe wilt wesen.'   1610
Si antworden hem : 'Van alle desen,
Daer gi ende wi heroepen af sijn,
Set ons daer af een termijn.
Wi wilden dan sijn gereet
Met u te volbringen onsen eet   1615
Met al onser macht, dat verstaet;
Ende die ons hier toe af gaet,
Dien sel wi houden over viant.'
Des gaven si haer trouwe te hant,
Ende hi geloefdem daer met   1620
Bi siere kerstenliker wet.
Dat hise van der uren sal
Houden over sine gesellen al
Dit geloefdense weder daer.
Doen ward die dach geset daer naer   1625
Binnen xiiij. nachten in termine
Te Cornuaelge vor die stat te sine
Ende vandaer te Gales ward
Ende Irlant mede in die vard:
Ende dat si warneert comen,   1630
Ende, datsi mogen, begomen,
Eer si weder omme keren.
Dit geloefden daer alle die heren.
Dus es dit hof gesceden.
Ende elc voer thuus ward, hem gereden   1635
Dat hem gebrac daer sonderlingen.
Nu hort een lettel van andren dingen …

ABBREVIATIONS

BAR	British Archaeological Reports
BL	British Library
CCR	*Calendar of Close Rolls*
CPR	*Calendar of Patent Rolls*
EETS	Early English Text Society
ES	Extra Series
History of the King's Works	R.A. Brown, H.M. Colvin, and A.J. Taylor, *The History of the King's Works: The Middle Ages* (3 vols., London 1963)
Lancelot-Grail	*Lancelot-Grail: The Old French Arthurian Vulgate and Post-Vulgate in Translation,* ed. Norris J. Lacy, New York and London 1993-6
NS	New Series
OS	Original Series
RS	Rolls Series
Saul, *St George's Chapel*	N. Saul (ed.) *St George's Chapel, Windsor in the Fourteenth Century* (Woodbridge and Rochester, NY, 2005)
St John Hope, *Windsor Castle*	W.H. St John Hope, *Windsor Castle: An Architectural History* (2 vols. and portfolio, London 1913)
Vale, *Edward III and Chivalry*	J. Vale, *Edward III and Chivalry*, Woodbridge 1972
VCH	*Victoria County History*

Primary sources

Adam of Murimuth, *Continuatio Chronicarum* ed. E. M. Thompson, RS 93, London 1889

Alberic des Trois Fontaines, *Chronica* in Monumenta Germaniae Historica: Scriptores XXIII, Hamburg 1872

Annales de Wigornia in *Annales Monastici* IV, ed. H.R. Luard, RS 36, London 1869

'Benedict of Peterborough', *Gesta Regis Henrici Secundi Benedicti Abbas,* ed. William Stubbs, RS 49, 2 vols, London 1867

BL Additional MS. 60584

[The] Brut ed. F. W. D. Brie, EETS OS 131, London 1906

Calendar of Close Rolls, Henry III, 1251-3, London 1928

Calendar of Miscellaneous Inquisitions II, Edward II – 22 Edward III, London 1916,

Calendar of Patent Rolls, Henry III, 1247-1258, London 1908

Calendar of Patent Rolls, Edward III, X, 1354-58, London 1910

Domesday Book, Berkshire

Dugdale, W. *Monasticon Anglicanum*, ed. J. Caley, H. Ellis and B. Bandinel, London 1830

Ebulo, Petrus de *Liber ad honorem Augusti sive de Rebus Siculis*, ed. Theo Kölzer and Marlis Stähli, Sigmaringen 1994

Flores historiarum, ed. H. R. Luard, RS 95, London 1890

Froissart, Jean *Chroniques. Livre I: Le Manuscrit d'Amiens* ed. G.T. Diller, Textes littéraires français, Geneva 1992

Garmonsway, G.N. (trans.) *The Anglo-Saxon Chronicle*, 2nd edn, London 1954

Gerald of Wales, *Speculum Ecclesie*, ed. J.S. Brewer, Rolls Series 21, London 1873

[Les] Gestes des Chiprois, ed. G. Raynaud, Société de l'Orient Latin, V, Paris 1887; continuation, *Les Gestes des Chiprois,* in *Recueil des historiens des croisades, Documents latins et francais relatifs à l'Arménie, Documents arméniens* II, Paris 1906

Gray, Sir Thomas *Scalacronica*, ed. & tr. Andy King, Publications of the Surtees Society 209, Woodbridge & Rochester NY, 2005

Hamaker H. G., ed., *De rekeningen der grafelijkheid van Holland onder het Henegouwsche Huis*, Werken uitgegeven door het Historisch Genootschap gevestigd te Utrecht, NS 24, 1876

Henry, Archdeacon of Huntingdon, *Historia Anglorum*, ed. and trans. D. Greenway, Oxford 1996

Jean le Bel, *Chronique,* ed. Jules Viard and Eugène Déprez, Société de l'Histoire de France, Paris 1914

[Die] Königssaaler Geschichtsquellen, ed. Johann Loserth, in *Fontes rerum Austriacarum, Scriptores* VIII, Vienna 1875

Laʒamon: Brut, ed. G.L. Brook and R.F. Leslie, EETS OS 277, Oxford 1978

Liechtenstein, Ulrich von, *Frauendienst*, tr. (into modern German) V. Spechtler, Klagenfurt 2000

Livy, *History of Rome*, I, ed. & tr. B. O. Foster, London 1919

Lodewijk van Velthem, *Voortzetting van den Spiegel Historiael (1248-1316)*, I, ed. H. Vander Linden, W. de Vreese and P. de Keyser, Commission royale d'histoire 38, Brussels 1906

Lydgate, John *The Fall of Princes,* ed. Henry Bergen, EETS ES 123, Oxford 1924

[The] Mabinogion, translated by Gwyn Jones and Thomas Jones, London & New York 1974

Malory, Sir Thomas *Works,* ed. Eugène Vinaver, rev. P. J. C. Field, Oxford 1990

Matthew Paris, *Chronica Majora*, V, ed. H. R. Luard, RS 57, London 1880

Merlin and the Grail: the trilogy of Arthurian Romances attributed to Robert de Boron, tr. Nigel Bryant, Arthurian Studies XLVIII, Woodbridge & Rochester, NY, 2001

Muntaner, Ramon de *The Chronicle of Muntaner,* tr. Lady Goodenough, Hakluyt Society Second Series XLVII

[L']ordene de chevalerie in Raoul de Houdenc, *Le roman des eles*, ed. Keith Busby, Amsterdam and Philadelphia 1983.

Pauli, Sebastiano *Codice diplomatico del sacro militare ordine gerosolimitano oggi di Malta*, Lucca 1738, II 80

Perceforest: quatrième partie ed. Gilles Roussineau, Geneva 1987, i. ix-xiv

Reports from the Lords Committees touching the Dignity of a Peer of the Realm, London 1819

Rossell, Cayetano (ed.), *Cronicas de los Reyes de Castilla*, Biblioteca de autores españoles 66, Madrid 1953

Rymer, Thomas *Foedera*, London 1816

Sarrasin, *Le roman du Hem,* ed. Albert Henry, Travaux de la faculté de philosophie et lettres de l'Université de Bruxelles IX, Paris 1938

Sawyer, P.H. *Anglo-Saxon Charters*, London 1968

Scharfenberg, Albrecht von *Jüngerer Titurel*, ed. Werner Wolf, Deutsche Texte des Mittelalters XLV, Berlin 1955; translation by Cyril Edwards, *Arthurian Literature* XX, 2003, 95-96

[Las] Siete Partidas, tr. Samuel Parsons Scott, ed. Robert I. Burns, SJ, Philadelphia 2001

Smit H. J., ed., *De rekeningen der graven en gravinnen uit het Henegouwsche Huis*, Werken uitgegeven door het Historisch Genootschap gevestigd te Utrecht, third series, 69, 1939

St Omer continuation of the *Grandes Chroniques*, BN MS Fr. 693

[La] tavola ritonda, ed. Marie-José Heijkant, Milan 1997; tr. Anne Shaver, *Tristan and the Round Table, A Translation of La Tavola Ritonda*, Binghamton, NY, 1983

Thomas Walsingham, *Historia Anglicana*, I, ed. H. T. Riley, RS 28, London 1863

Thomas Walsingham, *Gesta Abbatum Sancti Albani*, II, ed. H. T. Riley, RS 28, London 1868

William of Malmesbury, *Gesta Regum*, ed. W. Stubbs, RS 90, London 1887-9

Secondary Sources

[Ajuntament de Palma], *Bellver 1300-2000 700 anys del castell*, Palma 2001

Archaeologia Cantiana, 2, 1859, 111-132

Ashmole, E. *The Institution, Laws and Ceremonies of the Most Noble Order of the Garter*, London 1672

Astill, G.G. *Historic Towns in Berkshire: an archaeological appraisal*, Reading 1978

Ayton, A. 'Edward III and the English Aristocracy at the beginning of the Hundred Years' War' in M. Strickland, ed., *Armies, Chivalry and Warfare in Medieval Britain and France*, Harlaxton Medieval Studies VII, Stamford 1998

Barber, R. and J. Barker, *Tournaments. Jousts, Chivalry and Pageants in the Middle Ages*, Woodbridge and New York 1989

Barber, R., ed. and tr., *Life and Campaigns of the Black Prince*, Woodbridge & Rochester, NY, 1986

Bellet, M. *The City of Aigues-Mortes*, Paris 2001

Biddle, M. 'Seasonal festivals and residence: Winchester, Westminster, and Gloucester in the tenth to twelfth centuries,' *Anglo-Norman Studies*, 8, 1985, 64-7.

Biddle, M. *King Arthur's Round Table,* Woodbridge & Rochester, NY, 2000

Biddle, M. *The Tomb of Christ*, Stroud 1999

Blair, John 'Purbeck Marble', in J. Blair and N. Ramsay, *English Medieval Industries,* London 1991, 41-56

Bock, F. *Das deutsch-englische Bündnis von 1335-1342 i. Quellen,* Quellen und Erörterungen zur bayerischen Geschichte, NS XII, Munich 1956

Boessneck, J. H-H. Müller, and M. Teichert, 'Osteologische Unterscheidungsmerkmale zwischen Schaf (Ovis aries Linné) und Ziege (Capra hircus Linné)', *Kühn-Archiv*, 78, 1964

Bond, M. *The Story of Windsor*, Newbury 1984

Boulton, D'A. J. D. *The Knights of the Crown: The Monarchical Orders of Knighthood in Later Medieval Europe 1325-1520,* rev. ed., Woodbridge & Rochester, NY, 2000

Bradley, R., S. Lobb, R. Richards, and M. Robinson, 'Two late Bronze Age settlements on the Kennet gravels: excavations at Aldermaston Wharf and Knight's Farm, Burghfield, Berkshire', *Proceedings of the Prehistoric Society* 46, 1980, 217-95

Brault, G. J. *Early Blazon*, 2nd edn, Woodbridge & Rochester, NY, 1997

Brindle, S. and B. Kerr, *Windsor Revealed: new light on the history of the castle,* London 1997

Brindle, S. 'Windsor Castle: the 1992 Fire, the Restoration, Archaeology and History', in L. Keen and E. Scarff (eds.), *Windsor, Medieval Archaeology, Art and Architecture of the Thames Valley*, British Archaeological Association Conference Transactions XXV, 2002, 110-124.

British Archaeology 89, 2006

Brown, R. A. 'King Edward's clocks', *Antiquaries Journal*, 39, 1959, 283-6

Brown, R.A. *English Castles*, 2nd edn, London 1976

Camden, W. *Britannia*, London 1586

Cathcart-King, D.J. *The Castle in England and Wales, an interpretative history*, London 1988

Chaucer, Geoffrey *The Canterbury Tales*, tr. Neville Coghill, London 1977

Creswell, K. A. C. *The origin of the plan of the Dome of the Rock*, British School of Archaeology in Jerusalem, Supplementary papers 2 , 1924

Crook J.M. and M.H. Port, *History of the King's Works VI 1752-1951*, London 1973

Cunliffe, Barry and Julian Munby, *Excavations at Portchester Castle IV: Medieval, the Inner Bailey*, Society of Antiquaries. Research Report xliii, London 1985

Curnow, P.E. 'Royal lodgings of the thirteenth century in the lower ward of Windsor Castle: some recent archaeological discoveries,' *Friends of St George's Chapel Annual Report*, (1965), 218-220

Daumet, Georges 'L'ordre castillan de l'écharpe', *Bulletin hispanique*, xxv, 1923

Delcorno Branca, Daniela *Boccaccio e le storie di re Artù*, Bologna 1991

De Vic, C and J. Vaissete, *Histoire générale de Languedoc*, 2nd edn., Toulouse 1885

Dixon-Smith, S. 'The image and reality of alms-giving in the great halls of Henry III', *Journal of the British Archaeological Association*, 142 , 1999, 79-96

Driesch, A. von den *A guide to the measurement of animal bones from archaeological sites*, Harvard 1976

Durliat, Marcel 'Le Château de Bellver à Majorque', *Etudes Roussillonnaises* V, 1956

Durliat, Marcel *L'Art dans le Royaume de Majorque. Les débuts de l'art Gothique en Roussillon, en Cerdagne at aux Baleares*, Toulouse 1962

Eames, E.S. *Catalogue of Medieval Lead-glazed Earthenware Tiles in the Department of Medieval and Later Antiquities British Museum*, London 1980

Ekwall, E. *English Place-names*, 4th edition, Oxford 1960

Fox, J.H. *Robert de Blois: son oeuvre didactique et narrative*, Paris 1950

Galloway, J.A. D. Keene and M. Murphy, 'Fuelling the City: Production and Distribution of Firewood and Fuel in London's Region, 1290-1400', *Economic History Review*, NS 49.3, 1996, 447-472

Gee, E. 'Stone from the medieval limestone quarries of South Yorkshire', in *Collectanea Historica, Essays in memory of Stuart Rigold*, Maidstone 1981, 247-255.

Gelling, M. *Place Names of Berkshire*, Cambridge 1973-76

Goodall, J.A.A. 'The Aerary Porch and its influence and its influence on Late Medieval English vaulting' in Saul, *St George's Chapel*, 165-202

Gorman, Michael 'Adomnán's De Locis Sanctis: The Diagrams and the Sources', *Revue Bénédictine* 116.i, 2006, 1-41

Götze, H. *Castel del Monte*, Munich and New York 1998

Green, Richard F. 'King Richard's Books revisited', *The Library*, 5th Series, 31, 1976, 235-39

Grose, F., ed., *Antiquarian Repertory*, London 1807

Habermehl, K-H. *Die Altersbestimmung bei Haus- und Labortieren.* 2nd edn. Berlin, Hamburg, 1975

Hall, M. 'The prehistoric pottery', in J. Moore and D. Jennings, *Reading Business Park: a Bronze Age landscape,* Thames Valley landscapes: the Kennet Valley, I, Oxford 1982, 63-82

Harvey, B. *Westminster Abbey and its estates in the Middle Ages,* Oxford 1977

Harvey, J. *English Mediaeval Architects. A Biographical Dictionary Down to 1550,* rev. edn, Gloucester 1984

Harvey, Ruth 'Occitan Extravagance and the Court Assembly at Beaucaire in 1174', *Cultura Neolatina,* LXI, 2001

Henig, M. and J. McNeill, *The Medieval Cloister in England and Wales, Journal of the British Archaeological Association.* 159, 2006

Hewett, C. *English Cathedral and Monastic Carpentry*, Chichester 1985

Hope-Taylor, B. 'Excavations at Kingsbury, Old Windsor, *Berkshire Archaeological Journal,* 54, 1954-5, 147, and *Medieval Archaeology* II, 1958, 183-5

Hubbard, E *Buildings of Wales: Clwyd ,* Harmondsworth 1986

Huet, G. 'Les traditions arturiennes chez le Chroniqueur Louis de Velthem', *Le Moyen Age,* XXVI, 1913, 173-197

Janse, Antheun, 'Tourneyers and Spectators' in *The Court as Stage,* ed. Steven Gunn and Antheun Janse, Woodbridge and Rochester, NY 2006

Janse, Antheun *Ridderschap in Holland,* Hilversum 2001

Jefferson, Lisa 'MS Arundel 48 and the earliest statutes of the Order of the Garter', *EHR,* CIX, 1994

Johnstone, Hilda *Edward of Caernarvon,* Manchester 1946

Jope, E. M. 'The archaeology of Wheatley stone' in W.O. Hassall (ed.). *Wheatley Records, 956-1956,* Oxon Record Society, 37 1956, 17-26

Jovellanos, G.M. de *Memorias historicas sobre el Castillo de Bellver en la isla de Mallorca, etc,* Palma 1813

Jovellanos, G.M. de *Obras en Prosa,* ed. J. Case Gonzales, Madrid 1970

Kealey, E.J. *Roger of Salisbury, viceroy of England,* Berkeley, Los Angeles & London 1972

Keen, Maurice *Chivalry,* New Haven and London 1984

Kelly, Robert L. 'Royal Policy and Malory's Round Table', *Arthuriana,* 14, 2004, 43-71

Knoop, D. and G.P. Jones, 'The Building of Eton College 1442-1460', *Transactions of the Quattuor Coronati Lodge,* XLVI, 1933, 70-114

Longley, D. *Runneymede Bridge 1976: excavation in the site of a late Bronze Age settlement,* Surrey Archaeol Res 6, Guildford 1980

Loomis, Laura Hibbard 'Secular Dramatics in the Royal Palace, Paris, 1378, 1389, and Chaucer's "Tregetoures"', *Speculum,* 33, 1958, 242-255

Loomis, Roger Sherman 'Chivalric and Dramatic Imitations of Arthurian Romance' in *Medieval Studies in memory of A. Kingsley Porter,* ed. William R. W. Koehler, Cambridge, Mass, 1939, rp New York 1969, 81-97

Löseth, Eilert *Le Roman en prose de Tristan*, Bibliothèque de l'École pratique des Hautes Études 82, Paris 1890 (rp Geneva 1974)

Lyman, R.L. *Vertebrate taphonomy*, Cambridge 1996

McFarlane, K. B., *The Nobility of Later Medieval England*, Oxford 1973

Meale, Carol 'Manuscripts, readers and patrons in fifteenth century England: Sir Thomas Malory and Arthurian romance', *Arthurian Literature* IV, 1985

Meehan, Denis (ed.) Adamnan's *De Locis Sanctis*, Scriptores Latini Hiberniae III, Dublin 1958

Morris, E. 'Later prehistoric pottery', in A. Brossler, R. Early and C. Allen, *Green Park (Reading Business Park). Phase 2 Excavations 1995 – Neolithic and Bronze Age sites,* Thames Valley landscapes monograph 19, Oxford 2004, 61-2

Mortimer, I. *The Perfect King, the life of Edward III, father of the English Nation* London 2006, 19-20

Mut Calafell, A. 'Inventarios de los castillos de Alaró, Bellver ...', *Bolletí de la Societat Arquelogica Lul-liana* XLI, 839, 1985, 57-78

Newman, John *Buildings of England: North East and East Kent* Harmondsworth 1969

Newton Stella, *Fashion in the Age of the Black Prince*, Woodbridge and Totowa, NJ, 1980

O'Connell, M. 1986 *Petters Sports Field, Egham. Excavation of a late Bronze Age/ early Iron Age site,* Surrey Archaeol Res 10, Guildford 1986

O'Loughlin, T. 'The Diffusion of Adomnán's *De Locis Sanctis* in the Medieval Period', *Eriu,* LI, 2000, 93-106

Ormrod, W. M. *The Reign of Edward III*, Stroud and Charleston, SC, 2000

Oxford Archaeology 2006, *Archaeological Investigations – Upper Ward, Windsor Castle, Post-Excavation Assessment and Publication Proposal V.1.1*, unpublished client document

Oxford Archaeology/Cambrian Archaeology 2006, *Windsor Castle – Upper Ward and College of St George, Project Design for an Archaeological Investigation V.1-3.0(1)* unpublished client document

Oxford Archaeology/Cambrian Archaeology 2006, *Windsor Castle – Upper Ward and College of St George, Updated Project Design for an Archaeological Investigation V.4-5.0(1)* unpublished client document

Paravicini, Werner *Die Preussenreisen des Europäischen Adels,* Sigmaringen 1989

Pevsner, N. *The Buildings of England:Berkshire*, Harmondsworth 1966

Poole, A.L. *From Domesday Book to Magna Carta, 1087-1216*, 2nd edn, Oxford 1955

Proceedings of the Society of Antiquaries XXIV, 1912, 52-65

Prummel, W. and H-J. Frisch, 'A guide for the distinction of species, sex and body side in bones of sheep and goat,' *Journal of Archaeological Science*, 13, 1986, 567-577

Rackham, O. Ancient Woodland, London 1980

Ralegh Radford, C.A. *Restormel Castle,* London 1980

Regalado, Nancy Freeman 'Performing Romance: Arthurian Interludes in Sarrasin's *Le roman du Hem* (1278)', in *Performing Medieval Romance*, ed. Evelyn

Birge Vitz, Nancy Freeman Regalado and Marilyn Lawrence, Woodbridge and Rochester, NY, 2005, 103-119

Renn, D.F. *Norman Castles in Britain*, 2nd edn, London 1973

Renn, Derek *Three Shell Keeps*, London 1969

Richmond C. and E. Scarff (eds.) *St George's Chapel, Windsor in the late Middle Ages*, Windsor 2001

Roberts, E. 'Totternhoe stone and flint in Hertfordshire churches', *Medieval Archaeology*, 18, 1974, 66-89

Roberts, J. *Royal Landscape, the gardens and parks of Windsor*, New Haven & London 1997

Roberts, J. *Views of Windsor, watercolours by Thomas and Paul Sandby*, London & New York 1995

Rocque, Jean *Actual Survey of Berkshire*, London 1752

Rogers, Clifford *The Wars of Edward III*, Woodbridge & Rochester, NY, 1999

Salvador, L. *Die Stadt Palma*, Leipzig 1882

Salzman, L. F. *Building in England, down to 1540,* Oxford 1952

Schmid, E. *Atlas of animal bones. For prehistorians, archaeologists and quaternary geologists.* Amsterdam, London, New York 1972

Schmolke-Hasselmann, Beate 'The Round Table: Ideal, Fiction, Reality', *Arthurian Literature* II, 1982

Sir Gawain and the Green Knight, tr. Brian Stone, Harmondsworth 1974

Strong, Roy *Art and Power*, Woodbridge & Rochester, NY, 1984

Sumbler, M.G., *British Regional Geology: London and the Thames Valley*, 4th ed., Norwich 1996

Sumption, Jonathan *The Hundred Years War: Trial by Battle*, London 1990

Tadeo Villanueva, Lorenzo 'Memorial sobre la orden de Caballeria de la Banda de Castilla', *Boletin de la real academia de la historia*, lxxii, 1918, 436-65, 552-74

Tatton-Brown, T. 'Building stone in Canterbury, c.1070-1525' in D. Parsons (ed.) *Stone, quarrying and building in England AD43-1525*, Chichester 1990, 70-82

Tatton-Brown, T. 'La Pierre de Caen en Angleterre' in M. Baylé (ed.) *L'Architecture Normande au Moyen Age*, Caen 1997, 305-14

Tatton-Brown, T. 'The Deanery, Windsor Castle', *Antiquaries Journal.* 78 (1998), 345-390

Tatton-Brown, T. 'The Medieval building stones of St Alban's Abbey: a provisional note', in M. Henig and P. Lindley (eds.), *Alban and St Albans, Roman and Medieval Architecture, Art and Archaeology,* Leeds 2002, 118-123

Tatton-Brown, T. 'The quarrying and distribution of Reigate stone in the Middle Ages', *Medieval Archaeology* 45, 2001, 189-201

Tatton-Brown, T. 'The Rebuilding of the nave and western transepts, 1377-1503' in K. Blockley, M. Sparks and T. Tatton-Brown, *Canterbury Cathedral Nave , Archaeology History and Architecture* , Canterbury 1997, 128-146

Tous Meliá, Juan *Palma a Través de la Cartografia (1596-1902)*, Palma 2002

Tout, T.F. *Chapters in the Administrative History of Mediaeval England*, Manchester 1920-33

Tucoo-Chala, Pierre avec Roger Barbe et Philippe Araguas, *Le Château de Montaner*, Supplement to *Revue de Pau et Bearn* (1984)

VCH Beds i (1904), iii (1912)

VCH Berks iii (1925)

VCH Bucks iii (1925)

VCH Hants iv (1911)

VCH Middlesex, iv (1971)

VCH Surrey, iii (1911)

VCH Surrey, iv (1912)

Vitz, Evelyn Birge *Orality and Performance in Early French Romance,* Woodbridge & Rochester, NY, 1999

Vretemark, M. *Från ben till boskap. Kosthåll och djurhållning med utgångspunkt i medeltida benmaterial från Skara*, Skrifter från Länsmuseet Skara, Nr 25, 1997

Ward-Perkins, J.B., *Roman Imperial Architecture,* London 1992

Warren, W.L. *King John*, 2nd edn, Harmondsworth 1978

Wheatley, Abigail *The Idea of the Castle*, Woodbridge & Rochester, NY, 2004

Willis, Robert *The Architectural History of the Church of the Holy Sepulchre at Jerusalem*, London 1849

Wilson, B., C. Grigson and S. Payne, eds., *Ageing and sexing animal bones from archaeological sites,* BAR British Series 109, Oxford 1982

Wilson, C. 'The Royal Lodgings of Edward III at Windsor Castle: form, function, representation' in Keen, L. and E. Scarff, *Windsor*, 15-94

Worssam, B. C. and T. Tatton-Brown, 'Kentish Rag and other Kent building stones', *Archaeologia Cantiana* 112 (1993), 93-125

English Heritage 'monument description': http://www.eng-h.gov.uk/mpp/mcd/sub/shell12.htm

'History of Tents' website of Stephen Francis Wyley: http://www.geocities.com/historyoftents/.

INDEX

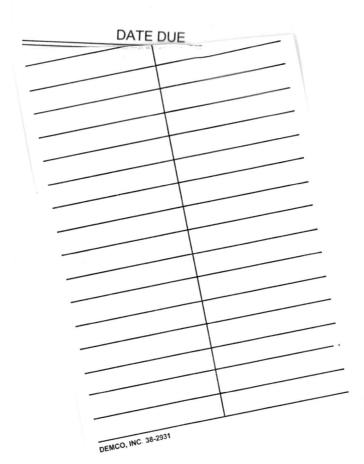

DATE DUE

DEMCO, INC. 38-2931